U.S. State Names

The Stories of How Our States Were Named

Kathy Guyton

MOUNTAIN STORM PRESS

NEDERLAND, COLORADO

Mountain Storm Press
Copyright 2009 by Kathy Guyton
All Rights Reserved. Published in the United States.

Printed at Automated Graphic Systems
Baltimore, Maryland

Contributing Editor: Tess Thomas

Cover Art by Susan Davis Churches and Andy Guyton

ISBN 978-0-9825239-0-2

Printed in the United States of America

For Jim

Table of Contents

Introduction: 1

Chapter 1: *Alabama* 5

Chapter 2: *Alaska* 17

Chapter 3: *Arizona* 31

Chapter 4: *Arkansas* 43

Chapter 5: *California* 53

Chapter 6: *Colorado* 63

Chapter 7: *Connecticut* 75

Chapter 8: *Delaware* 85

Chapter 9: *Florida* 97

Chapter 10: *Georgia* 107

Chapter 11: *Hawai'i* 115

Chapter 12: *Idaho* 127

Chapter 13: *Illinois* 137

Chapter 14: *Indiana* 147

Chapter 15: *Iowa* 155

Chapter 16: *Kansas* 163

Chapter 17: *Kentucky* 173

Chapter 18: *Louisiana* 183

Chapter 19: *Maine* 193

Chapter 20: *Maryland* 203

Chapter 21: *Massachusetts* 213

Chapter 22: *Michigan* 223

Chapter 23: *Minnesota* 233

Chapter 24: *Mississippi* 241

Chapter 25: *Missouri* 253

Chapter 26: *Montana* 263

Chapter 27: *Nebraska* 271

Chapter 28: *Nevada* 279

Chapter 29: *New Hampshire* 289

Chapter 30: *New Jersey* 301

Chapter 31: *New Mexico* 309

Chapter 32: *New York* 317

Chapter 33: *North Carolina* 325

Chapter 34: *North Dakota* 333

Chapter 35: *Ohio* 343

Chapter 36: *Oklahoma* 351

Chapter 37: *Oregon* 361

Chapter 38: *Pennsylvania* 373

Chapter 39: *Rhode Island and Providence Plantations* 385

Chapter 40: *South Carolina* 395

Chapter 41: *South Dakota* 403

Chapter 42: *Tennessee* 413

Chapter 43: *Texas* 423

Chapter 44: *Utah* 435

Chapter 45: *Vermont* 447

Chapter 46: *Virginia* 455

Chapter 47: *Washington* 463

Chapter 48: *West Virginia* 473

Chapter 49: *Wisconsin* 481

Chapter 50: *Wyoming* 489

Books of Interest 501

Acknowledgements 503

Index 505

Introduction:

Websites, websites, everywhere, but...

Google "state names," and you will be rewarded with almost fifty-million websites that teach you some or all of the name derivations for each of the fifty United States. Many sites provide the "dictionary definition" for all of the names: "*Colorado* is named after the Colorado River," for instance, or "Colorado means 'ruddy' or 'red' in Spanish." Some sites assert confidently one particular definition, while another site will assert with just as much certainty a completely different meaning. Many of these Internet sites copy each other (literally, copy and paste), so that after reading a few of them you will have difficulty finding any *new* information. And few websites go into any real detail of the word or history of how that word came to name one of our states.

You might think that finding a *book* on the derivation of the states' names would be met with more success, but you would be wrong. Surprisingly few attempts (until now, of course) have been made to catalog even the sparsest of information about the derivation of all fifty of the names. It was that absence of a central reference for the topic that was the motivation for this book. It was, in fact, a desire to *read* such a collection — and being unable to find one — that prompted the writing of *U.S. State Names*.

Names on the Land

George Rippey Stewart was a giant — perhaps *the* giant — among name derivation scholars called onomaticians[*]. A founding member of the *American Name Society*, his timeless <u>Names on the Land: A Historical Account of Place-Naming in the United States</u> (1945) was the first serious attempt at a thorough toponymy for the entire country. New editions of it were published several times before Stewart's death in 1980, and it was re-printed with a new introduction in 2008 by *The New York Review of Books*.

---

[*] *The study of name derivation is "onomastics." While some scholars of onomastics choose to call themselves* onomatologists, *Stewart himself preferred the more modest* onomatician.

Stewart was the first to describe the difference between what he termed the "American" and "European" styles of onomastics. The "European" style, he posited, was to focus on the etymology of the word—its origin and definition—while the "American" method dealt much more with intentions or, in Stewart's own words, "the motivation of the namer." This "American" study of toponymy—the study of *place* names—was an almost wholly new concept in 1945 when George Stewart first codified it, which might explain the dearth of books today about how our states came to be named.

The study of place names is something of an orphan field, a fact that becomes exquisitely apparent when one chooses to partake in it. It is almost impossible to tell the entire story of a place name like "California" without delving into such broader subjects as U.S. and World History, Spanish Literature, Linguistics, World Religions, Cartography, and even French Chivalry. And even then, one might not expect to read about such far-flung topics as the Gettysburg Address, Amazonian women, and "The Rocky and Bullwinkle" cartoon, all within the investigation of how this one word came to be applied to this one well-defined set of borders on the North American continent.

This book was intended to give not only the "dictionary definition" of each state name, but to tell its story. It is impossible to convey the symbolism, sentiment, and history embodied within the name "Mississippi" by writing simply, "named for the river." Such brevity begs for clarity and detail: Okay, then, how did the *river* get its name? It's an Indian word—what tribe? Where did they live? What did the word mean to them? How did the Americans learn it? Why did they use that word for *this* state instead of one of the others along the river? And who got to decide?

These are all questions that come up when persuing what George Stewart declared the "American" method of onomastics. And while this book attempts to also include some etymology, it is this American method we have chosen to try to convey. Besides being simply more informative, this method includes the *human* element in naming, which allows us to convey the bravery, desperation, humor, or any other human trait that may be included in the story.

It also allows the story to be updated. You see, the word "California" means something entirely different to us today than it did when the name was conceived in the fifteenth century, which means something still different than when it was applied to the land.

Today?

Think of the word "Texas" and certain images come to mind. They might be stereotypical—cowboys, thick accents, big hair; or they might be personal—your funny Aunt Karen, the time you got a speeding ticket in Amarillo, or the color *blue* (because that was the color of the "Texas" piece in the U.S. puzzle you had as a child); or, if it is a state where you live or grew up, your images might be more specific and accurate—former Governor Ann Richards, the Cowboys beating the Cardinals in overtime last Sunday, or massive fields of bluebonnets and Indian paintbrush in the springtime. Now, what about the words "Montana," "North Carolina," "Connecticut," or "New Mexico?" Our images might be vivid or vague, immediate or delayed, happy, sad or ambivalent. But we do have images. The words mean something to us.

Our instant impression, of course, is that they are the names of our states. They name a specific geographic region on planet Earth. But they also name a set of images that can't be conveyed by any other word or words, images that are probably somewhat different among individuals, but which include some common themes, be they stereotypical or even somewhat prejudiced. We may think of rude people when we hear "New York," African-Americans at the mention of "Georgia," or long-haired pot-smokers when the word "California" is uttered.

Having become part of the story, these modern images and impressions cannot honestly be omitted from the stories of our state names. And so each of the following chapters will begin with an attempt to convey the intersection of our collective stereotypes: what the word means today.

Chapter 1: Alabama

*I have a dream that one day the state of Alabama, whose governor's lips
are presently dripping with the words of interposition and nullification,
will be transformed into a situation where little black boys and black girls
will be able to join hands with little white boys and white girls and walk
together as sisters and brothers.*

— *Martin Luther King, Jr.*

Big wheels keep on turnin'
Carry me home to see my kin
Singin' songs about the southland
I miss ole' Bamy once again, and I think it's a sin…

— *"Sweet Home Alabama"*
Lynyrd Skynyrd

Southern Comfort

The word *Alabama* is gentle and lyrical, like a sweet, southern belle.
It's a word that lends itself easily to the notions of southern hospitality and
down-home southern comfort that characterize the southeastern states.
Collectively, they call themselves "Dixie*," and Alabama is their self-pro-
claimed heart.

Alabama is a symbol of "the South," with all its various images, those
of comfort as well as those of rebellion, and the state has found a nitch in
popular music culture. A country music group of the 1980s named themselves for Alabama and recorded a hit song that professed their loyalty to
it: "My home's in Alabama / No matter where I lay my head / My home's
in Alabama / Southern born, and Southern bred." Perhaps more popular, if

---

*   *The most commonly referenced origin of the word "Dixie" is from
the word "dix," French for ten. The word appeared on a ten dollar note
circulated in New Orleans.*

Edmund Pettus Bridge in Selma, Alabama on "Bloody Sunday," March 7, 1965 when police attacked peaceful civil rights marchers

a little less gentle, was Lynyrd Skynyrd's "Sweet Home Alabama," a song that has survived the decades and has been recorded by the likes of Mötley Crüe and Peter Gabriel.

In actuality Alabama's heritage is anything but gentle and comfortable. If the character of a place is defined by the important events of its past, then Alabama owes its character to a legacy of racial turbulence and cultural conflict. The state could be called the nation's conscience, serving as it has as the stage for the Civil Rights movement, that enormous struggle to wash away the stain of slavery and the years of oppression suffered by African-Americans. The 1955 Montgomery bus boycott, the 1963 murder of four young girls at the Sixteenth Street Baptist Church in Birmingham, and the 1965 march from Selma to Montgomery are icons of the Civil Rights movement, and icons of Alabama.

There are, of course, other images strongly associated with Alabama, some flattering, others painful. The "Crimson Tide" of the state's University of Alabama, and the powerful football legacy of U of A's Paul "Bear" Bryant and his trademark hounds-tooth hat, might top the list. Non-sports fans might remember the creative genius of childhood-friends-cum-novelists Truman Capote and Harper Lee, growing up together in Monroeville in the 1930's. Some may go further back into history and call to mind massive cotton plantations worked by armies of black slaves and lorded over by genteel white families. Those who have visited Alabama might at once envision the tiny, but accessible coastline with sugar-white beaches and bird sanctuaries, or the historical covered bridges, lush state parks, and winding rivers.

Alabama struggles not to escape but to live with its past; indeed, the sites of conflict are now tourist attractions. Not only are many of the Civil

War battlefields open to tourists but so are the Sixteenth Street Baptist Church and the Edmund Pettus Bridge—scene of Bloody Sunday, where the 1965 Civil Rights march to Montgomery was twice turned back.

Among the states that condoned, even embraced slavery, Alabama was one of the youngest, having inherited the practice from her parent territory Mississippi. Alabama did not invent slavery, but Alabama, with the nation looking uncomfortably on, seems to have done the most penance for it.

Hernando de Soto

Culture Clashing

In 1540 Spanish conquistador Hernando de Soto led an expedition to explore La Florida. Members of his party were the first to record in writing the word "Alibamu," "Alibamo," or "Limamu," among other spellings of the name they learned for the locl tribe. One of these conquistadors, known to history only as the Gentleman from Elvas, wrote of their first meeting with this native tribe:

"A few days afterward they came with him (a chief of a local tribe) accompanied by their Indians, one being named Limamu..."

Ironically de Soto, the Gentleman from Elvas, and all of the other conquistadors would later be instrumental in the decimation of that same tribe.

The Spanish conquistadors, not generally known for their ethnic sensitivity, must have startled the Native Americans. Historian Marquis Childs describes the impression that the Spaniards must have made:

"For all their fearful suffering, one cannot help but be a little amused at the spectacle they made. They were like angry children in a rage at the sun or the moon, these gentlemen adventurers stumbling through swamp and forest with their futile armies... They were beset by fever, hunger, and the constant hostility of the Indians, whom they slaughtered and enslaved with casual cruelty."[1]

By the time Hernando de Soto arrived, the natives of what are now the southeast United States knew of the cruelty that had been ministered by his predecessor, Panfilo de Narváez. Narváez proved a particularly brutal conquistador, "incompetent to the point of stupidity,"[2] who ravaged tribes of the southeast coast in his brief expedition of 1528. Narváez' expedition never traveled beyond what is now Florida, but word of his cruelty spread among the tribes of modern Georgia and Alabama. As de Soto penetrated into northern Alabama, it became apparent that the natives of the region were braced for Narvaez-type cruelty.

A year and a half into his exploration of "La Florida" de Soto encountered the Indian chief Tuscaluza at his home village in modern northern Georgia or northern Alabama. Tuscaluza's domain was large and dominated the region. His people were the Alabama Indians, a division of the Creeks who spoke a Muskhogean dialect. De Soto greeted Tuscaluza with a demand for natives to be used as slaves and concubines. Tuscaluza replied that he was unaccustomed to serving others and was in fact accustomed to being served *by* others; however, the chief told de Soto that a village under his domain was available with the items de Soto was requesting. It was called "Mabila", and it was located at the southern edge of his kingdom, a few days march south along the Coosa and Alabama Rivers.

De Soto took Tuscaluza with him—part guide and part prisoner—and marched his army of 600 men to Mabila. The village was well-fortified and, forewarned of the approaching Spaniards, occupied by thousands of Tuscaluza's warriors who were bracing for a fight. When de Soto's army arrived Tuscaluza slipped into a dwelling where he was sheltered by his people. Realizing the defiance of the natives, de Soto and his men became enraged and perhaps a bit nervous.

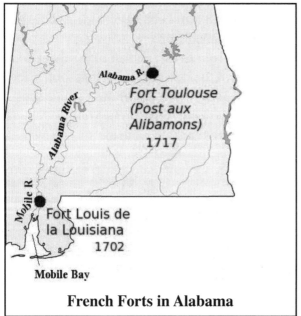

French Forts in Alabama

One of the Indians was attacked with a sword, his arm severed. At that point the warriors emerged from homes with bows and arrows and began attacking the Spaniards. De Soto called for a retreat, and it appeared that Tuscaluza had turned back the powerful Spaniards, but only briefly.

De Soto would not be humiliated in this way and quickly returned to Mabila ready to defend his Christian honor against the heathens. Spanish soldiers attacked the village with an intense fury, killing every Indian they encountered and burning every structure to the ground. The battle lasted nine hours and resulted in the near complete decimation of the tribe. A first-hand report of the battle by one of de Soto's men declared that 11,000 natives had been killed, but modern estimates put the number nearer to 2,500. Casualties on the Spanish side were fewer: only about 20 men killed, but over two hundred injured including de Soto himself.

The victory at Mabila was a hollow one for the Spaniards. The Europeans were forced to recognize that the natives of this land would not always acquiesce to their demands, no matter how much brute force was shown them—a precursor, perhaps, for the coming centuries of ethnic struggle in the region.

The Indians did not recover from their first encounter with Europeans. But while the battle with de Soto was brutal, and casualties heavy, the continued demise of the tribe, just like the destruction of tribes all over the Americas, resulted more from the diseases that Europeans brought with them. Epidemic after epidemic of smallpox, measles, and other scourges

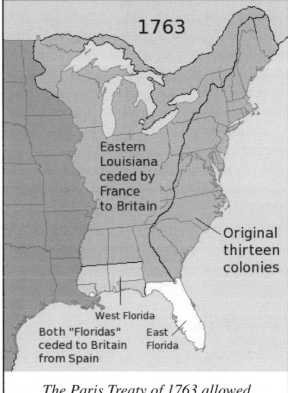

The Paris Treaty of 1763 allowed Great Britain to gain control of all of North America east of the Mississippi River.

destroyed the civilization at Mabila as well as countless others. The battle, however, stood out prominently in chronicles of de Soto's travels, and the name of the village would long be remembered. Today the exact location of Mabila is not known, but the name lives on in one of the largest and oldest port cities on the Gulf. "Mabila," or "Mobile" as the French had it, came to refer to the place where the remnants of the tribe settled almost two centuries later.

The French

When the French explored Mobile Bay in 1702 with the hope of establishing a fort and a new French stronghold in what they now called "Louisiana," they encountered the remaining Mobile Indians about five miles upriver from the Bay. The natives befriended them and invited them to settle in their region, hoping to gain protection from the more powerful tribes to the north. In return the natives taught the French how to farm the land, and survive in the wilderness and introduced them to tribes of the interior with whom the French wished to trade. The French called their new palisade "Fort Louis de la Louisiana" or simply "Fort St. Louis" but continued to refer to the river and the bay it empties into as "Mobile."

Fifteen years later the natives of the interior invited the French to build another fort further north on a different river. When it was finished it was called *Post aux Alibamons*, or sometimes *Fort des Alibamons*, although on official occasions it was referred to as *Fort Toulouse*. The river upon which this fort was built was, naturally enough, named for the tribe who had invited the French to build it—"Alabama". When the English in South Carolina learned of the new construction they called it that "mischievous French garrison *Alebamah*.[3]"

The British

In southeastern North America the first half of the eighteenth century was marked by the struggles of the Spanish, French, and British over control of the region. Playing one against the other, the tribes of "Alabama Country" made alliances with whomever offered the most favorable trading possibilities, and they enjoyed the position of being courted for their friendship. Increasingly it was the British who won the Indians' favor, and ultimately also won the war with France that produced the Paris Treaty of 1763. In return for peace, this treaty allowed Great Britain to receive La Florida from Spain, France's ally, and eastern Louisiana—all the land south of the Great Lakes and east of the Mississippi river—from France.

With the British now claiming all of North America east of the Mississippi as their own, the Indians no longer enjoyed the luxury of having two nations competing for their favor. No longer could they rely on help against enemy tribes, and no longer could they demand better trade goods from the British by comparing them with those of the French. More importantly, they began to see the prospect of their land being encroached upon and taken from them.

The native's fears were allayed somewhat by King George III. Almost immediately after the Paris Treaty was signed, the King forbade his subjects from moving west of the crest of the Appalachian mountain range, partly to reduce the risk of Indian wars. The colonists, who had just fought along side the British army to wrest control of that same land from the French, despised this proclamation. As colonial grumblings increased, King George's proclamation proved to be a launching pad for revolution.

At Mobile the French handed over Fort St. Louis, and the English promptly renamed it "Fort Charlotte" in honor of the Queen, wife of George III. Fort Toulouse was handed over as well, and many of the French traders moved west to New Orleans rather than pledge their allegiance to Great Britain. Gradually, their Indian friends followed them and eventually settled in what is now East Texas. By 1780 virtually the entire tribe of Alabama Indians had migrated west. And so it was that by the time the United States came into existence, the region that would become Alabama was no longer home to the Alabama Indians.

Queen Charlotte, wife of King George III

The Americans

During the American Revolution in 1780, the Spanish, who fought on the side of the colonists, took the opportunity to regain their earlier loss. They laid siege to Mobile and won Fort Charlotte back from the British. When the 1783 Paris Treaty was signed signaling the end of the American Revolution, Spain was allowed to keep Mobile and the rest of Florida (all of present-day Florida and a thin strip of coastline to its west, all the way to and including New Orleans).

In 1803 the U.S. claimed that the Mobile District of what was then called West Florida was included in the Louisiana Purchase and in 1812 officially annexed it. Spain, however, had occupied the district for years and protested the annexation diplomatically. When the War of 1812 broke out between the U.S. and Britain, the U.S. accused the Spanish—somewhat speciously—of aiding the British, and in 1813 General James Wilkinson marched 600 troops into Mobile and demanded the surrender of the city from the Spanish Commandant Cayetano Perez. Because no declaration of war between the two countries was in place, Perez was surprised by the attack and had no choice but to hand over the district to Wilkinson. While the surrender of Mobile was a mere footnote to the War of 1812—a war fought primarily between the U.S. and Great Britain over trade practices and maritime policies—it represented the only land acquired by the U.S., indeed the only land that changed hands at all, as a result of the conflict.

The U.S. had now succeeded in organizing Mississippi Territory—the modern states of Mississippi and Alabama—on maps and finally removed any Spanish or British claim on the land. Now the Americans had only to wrest control from the region's inhabitants, the Creek Indians. This was accomplished primarily by Andrew Jackson in the Creek War of 1814. The decisive Battle of Horseshoe Bend saw the annihilation of hundreds of Creek braves. The Creeks' devastating loss to Jackson forced the surrender of their homeland to the U.S. government.

The way now paved, "Alabama Fever" gripped many easterners who flooded into what was commonly called "Alabama Country" but was still technically part of Mississippi Territory. Upon arrival, these new settlers began farming in the lush river valleys. From 1810 to 1820 the white population of Alabama Country, and eventually the state of Alabama, increased ten-fold to over 127,000 people, and that population would double in the decade to follow.[4]

A Mystery

On December 23, 1816, a bill was introduced in the U.S. House of Representatives to establish a separate territorial government for the eastern half of Mississippi Territory. After defining a set of borders roughly identical to those of modern-day Alabama, the bill proposed that the region "constitute a separate territory, and be called 'Mobile.'" The next month, on January 17th, 1817, a similar bill was introduced in the Senate again suggesting the name "Mobile" for the proposed territory. The person who proposed the latter bill was Charles Tait, a senator from Georgia who had family in the potential new state and who had plans to move there himself.

Charles Tait

Tait's bill was referred to committee, amended, read again on January 20th, and a third time on January 30th. It passed the Senate and by all rights should then have been sent to the House of Representatives. Instead, for reasons that have never been made clear, Tait requested that the bill be sent back to a select committee on which he served. On February 4th Tait's committee introduced a new bill in place of the one that had already passed, this one proposing a territory with the same borders but with the name "Alabama."

In the Territorial Papers for Alabama, editor Clarence Edwin Carter provides a footnote to these proceedings:

"There are certain aspects in the evolution of this legislation which cannot now be resolved. We do not know, for example, what amendments were proposed or adopted, nor why the substitute bill was introduced. Whatever debate the various bills may have evoked has not been reported, and no relevant papers in the form of amendments and reports have been discovered. For the same reason we do not know why the House of Representatives shelved its own bill of Dec. 23, 1816."[5]

Indeed, one of the "aspects" which could not be "resolved" in 1952 when the territorial papers were assembled was why the name was changed from "Mobile" to "Alabama." Both names had been used to describe the eastern portion of Mississippi Territory for many years, and either would have been appropriate. But the name change is completely ignored in history books, and so the change must remain a mystery. "Alabama" became the name of the new territory. Less than three years later, on December 14, 1819, President James Monroe signed the legislation admitting Alabama as the 22nd state of the Union.

The Alabamas

For a time it was generally (and erroneously) believed that the word Alabama meant "Here we rest." According to the Alabama Department of History and Archives this translation was put forth in an unsigned newspaper article in 1842. A poet and Alabama statesman named Alexander Beauford Meek took that definition and proliferated it in his writings in the mid 1800s. Meek was popular within the state and traveled it extensively as a judge and state congressman, much of that travel by steamboat along Alabama's meandering rivers. One of Meek's most important works was a book entitled *Romantic Passages in South Western History*, published in 1857, which ends with the climactic words, "From such rude and troublous beginnings, the present prosperous population of Alabama, acquired the right to say, 'Here we rest!'" Alabama historians have spent decades attempting to correct Meek's mistake.

The word *Alabama* is actually derived from the Choctaw language, specifically the words *alba*—for "plants" or "weeds,"—and *amo*—for "to cut," "to trim," or "to gather." Combined, the words translate to "those who clear the land," or "thicket clearers."[6] The word *Alibamons* appeared on early French maps and labeled the river along which this tribe befriended the French in the early 1700's. The word remained on maps as the official appellation for the river, even after the tribe departed to Texas.

The Alabama Indians were known by neighboring tribes as those who cleared the dense thickets to establish their villages and farm the land.[6] In an interesting linguistic turn of events, when the Alabama Indians moved into eastern Texas, joined by their close allies the Koasati or Coushatta Indians, they settled in a region that is now commonly called the "Big Thicket." This area near Nacogdoches, Texas on the Angelina and Neches rivers was perceived by the Spanish in the early 1800's as too densely wooded to attempt to settle, or even to build a road through, and so they skirted its edges to the north and south. The Alabamas and Coushattas were accustomed to such dense woodlands, however, and were perfectly suited to build their new homes in it. There they settled, and there they have remained. Today the combined Alabama-Coushattas own 2,800 acres of land in the Big Thicket, which supports about half of their 1,100 tribe members.

While the Alabama Indians strive to maintain their cultural identity, their name lives on in a place where the clash and mixing of cultures is a defining theme.

1.   Childs, Marquis, <u>Mighty Mississippi: Biography of a River</u> (New York, 1982), pp. 3-4.

2.   Severin, Timothy, <u>Explorers of the Mississippi</u> (New York, 1968), p. 12.

3.   Jackson, Harvey H. III, <u>Rivers of History: Life on the Coosa, Tallapoosa, Cahaba and Alabama</u> (Tuscaloosa, 1995), p. 15.

4.   Rogers, William Warren, et al, <u>Alabama: The History of a Deep South State</u> (Tuscaloosa, 1994), p. 54.

5.   Carter, Clarence Edwin, ed., *The Territorial Papers of the United States, Vol. XVIII, The Territory of Alabama 1817-1819* (Washington, 1952), p. 18*t*

6.   William A. Read, <u>Indian Place-Names in Alabama</u>, (Baton Rouge, 1937), p. 4.

Chapter 2: Alaska

Baked Alaska

1 8-inch round cake
1/2 gallon of ice cream
5 egg whites
1/2 tsp. cream of tartar
2/3 cup of sugar

Place cake on cookie sheet. Form softened ice cream into an igloo shape on top of cake. Trim cake to within 3/4" of the ice cream. Refreeze cake and ice cream. Preheat oven to 450°. Whip egg whites until they form stiff peaks. Gradually add cream of tartar and sugar. Spread meringue over "igloo" till ice cream is completely covered. Bake for 3 minutes. Serve immediately.

North to Alaska! Go North, the rush is on…

> — *"North to Alaska"*
> *Johnny Horton*

Frozen but Fascinating

Alaska is the only U.S. state with which words like "Arctic" and "frozen tundra" can be readily associated. And since the 2008 presidential election, some new words are now associated with Alaska—words like "Sarah," "Palin," "Wasila," and the crowd favorite, "I can see Russia from my house." The name Alaska conveys images not only of ice and snow but of a wild frontier, unspoiled by humans, the last of its kind in the nation.

More and more, Americans have learned to embrace the diversity, not to mention the shear breadth, of our largest state. Its hundreds of islands stretch into the eastern hemisphere and southward to the same latitude as London, and its northern boundary reaches deep into the Arctic Circle. Alaska contains twice the landmass of the state of Texas. On a map of the

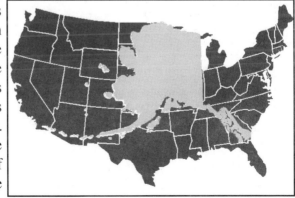

lower forty-eight states overlaid with a map of Alaska, the edges of the state reach from Atlanta to San Francisco, from Green Bay to Tucson. It's big.

Controversy over drilling for oil in the Arctic National Wildlife Refuge has introduced many Americans to this pristine land. The debate, which has raged for decades, has polarized the nation over concern for a land that the vast majority have never seen, never been anywhere near, nor are likely to be. Indeed, the closest many of us have gotten to the Arctic National Wildlife Refuge is watching "Ice Road Truckers" on the History Channel. But then, that is the point. To many Americans, Alaska is our last chance to leave nature alone on a scale that is no longer possible in the lower forty-eight.

But that doesn't stop us from fantasizing about, even glamorizing, an existence in the United States' own chunk of the Great White North. Movies like John Wayne's *North to Alaska* and the wildly successful TV show *Northern Exposure* exposed (pardon the pun) the love affair Americans have with Alaska, while at the same time demystifying what, to most people, is a rather mysterious place. Intellectually we know that in Alaska the sun hardly sets in the middle of summer, and barely rises in the dead of winter. We know that Alaska is the coldest place (and, incidentally, the least warm place, which is to say its average high temperature is lower than that of any other state) in the nation. We understand that it is separated from the rest of the country by a boat ride, a plane ride, or a very long road trip through Canada. Still we ask ourselves…wouldn't it be cool to live in Alaska?

Bering vs. Columbus

A comparison of the North American explorers Christopher Columbus and Vitus Bering is striking not only for the similarities it reveals but also for the extreme differences. Columbus was not a Spaniard but an Italian sailing for the Spanish monarchs in 1492. Vitus Bering was not a Russian but a Dane in the employ of Czar Peter I of Russia. In 1725 Peter instructed Bering to go to Kamchatka, a peninsula in eastern Siberia and from there to sail "along the land which goes to the north, and according to expectations (because its end is not known) that land, it appears, is part of America." He further ordered Bering…

Semen Dezhnev

"to search for that [place] where it is joined with America, and to go to any city of European possession, or if you see any European vessel, to find out from it what the coast is called and to write it down, and to go ashore yourself and obtain first-hand information, and, placing it on a map, to return here[2]."

Clearly the *name* of the land, according to those who inhabited it, was of great importance to Czar Peter. Columbus had no such instructions from his benefactors and, just as clearly, cared not at all how the natives referred to their own land.

Unlike Christopher Columbus, who was looking for—and expected to find—a water passage to the Orient but found instead land in his path, Bering expected to see land always to the north, but instead found the strait that now bears his name. But like Columbus' accomplishment it turns out that Bering's discovery had already been made. Few doubt Lief Ericson's journey to North America five hundred years before Columbus; likewise, it is now commonly held that a Cossack sailor named Semen

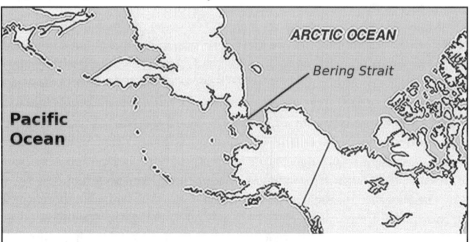

It is widely believed that Semen Dezhnev discovered the Bering Strait almost eighty years before Vitus Bering.

Dezhnev sailed through the Bering Strait in 1648, almost eighty years before Bering. By the time of the Czar's order to Bering, however, Dezhnev's report had either not been received in St. Petersburg or had been altered dramatically so as not to be believed. A port city along the strait now bears Dezhnev's name, at least in a small way acknowledging his feat.

Like those of Columbus, Bering's "discoveries," while not considered entirely successful in their day (neither, for example, has the honor of having a U.S. state named for them), were important because of the new exploration they spawned. Among their contemporaries they had indeed made great discoveries. Columbus returned to Portugal with gold for his benefactors; Bering returned to St. Petersburg with furs for his. Columbus and his successors brutally enslaved the natives of the Caribbean Islands in their unquenchable search for treasure; Bering's successors—mostly Siberian hunters called *promyshleniki*—brutally enslaved the Aleutian natives in their quest for furs, almost totally destroying the population of sea otters, not to mention Aleutian natives, in the process.

The Islands

The promyshleniki were not settlers. They sailed their primitive boats to the Aleutian Islands during hunting season, lived among the natives whom they forced to do the hunting, and returned to Siberia to sell their pelts. This cycle continued for decades.

Many Alaskan history books make no mention of Stephan Glotov, one of the promyshleniki, but he is widely credited among those that do include him with determining the name by which the Aleutians referred to the mainland. Venturing further than his colleagues in the mid 1700's, Glotov explored several of the larger Aleutian Islands, including Kodiak and Unimak. While on Unimak Island in 1759, Glotov heard the natives use a specific word to describe the mainland. That word is today often written "alaxsxaq," or something similar, but its contemporary pronunciation is subject to debate. The Russians pronounced it something like "alyashka."

The Russians, in the person of Mikhail Gvozdev, had actually reached the mainland fifteen years earlier than Glotov, but since their focus was on the fur trade, and the fur trade existed in the islands, the "discovery" of the Alaska mainland was considered a relatively minor accomplishment. The word *Alaska* (which the spelling eventually evolved to) would later

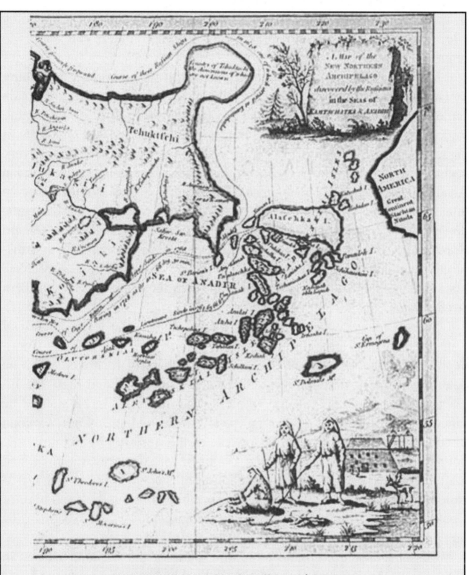

Stählin's map of Russian discoveries, 1774
In *An Account of the New Northern Archipelago* (London, 1774), by Jacob von Stählin

The Stählin map used by Captain James Cook on his third voyage. Cook initially praised the map as "a very accurate little map" but railed against it when he learned the true nature of the Alaskan peninsula. Note that "Alaska" (with a quasi-Cyrillic spelling) labels a large island, while the peninsula to the east is labelled three different ways: "North America," "Great Continent," and "Stachtan Nitada."

be translated as "object toward which the sea flows," and once reported by Glotov, would be used continually by the Russian hunters and traders to refer to the mainland.

Maps of the region were typically inaccurate, drawn in St. Petersburg by cartographers using second- or third-hand information. When Captain James Cook made his third and final voyage beginning in 1776, attempting to determine once and for all the existence—or absence—of a northwest passage, he used as one of his most trusted guides what he called a "very accurate little map," drawn by Jacob von Stählin, secretary of the Russian Academy of Sciences. The map, as Cook would learn, was not so accurate after all. As one historian asserts, it "looks as if some large fist has come down on the fragile surface of [former Russian historiographer Gerhard Friedrich] Müller's north-west American peninsula, shattered it into displaced fragments and sent some of it into thin air." Stählin drew "Alaschka" not as the mainland but as the largest island in what is labeled the "Northern Archipelago."

The mainland, which appears as a mere nub on the western coast of Canada, is labeled three different ways: "North America," "Great Continent," and "Stachtan Nitada." Cook was immensely frustrated when he determined that "Alaschka" was, in fact, the mainland and that "the Indians and the Russians call the whole by that name..." In his journal he railed against Stählin for publishing "so erroneous a Map[2]." Cook's second in command, Captain Clerke, also wrote of the mistakes by Stählin: "... both Russians and Indians call the Continent of America, Alaschka, and are altogether Strangers to the Appellation of Stachtan Nitada which it is called by Mr. Stählin.[3]" J.C. Beaglehole, editor of a 1967 compilation of Cook's journals, concludes that the phrase *Stachtan Nitada* "seems to be quite meaningless[4]."

Russia finally got around to settling parts of the Aleutian Islands in 1784, when a businessman named Gregor Shelikov started a colony at Three Saints Bay on Kodiak Island. Despite Spain's half-hearted challenges to the Russian claim for what *they* called "Florida Blanca," or "Land of White Blossoms," the world soon, and peacefully, began to acknowledge the land as Russian, and Alaska started appearing on maps as "Russian America."

The name "Alaska" was used to refer to the region also, but it usually appeared in the form "Alaskan peninsula" to describe the land that juts out from the continent without any distinct borders or any political connotations. The Russians called it "the colonies" or "our holdings in America," and managed it poorly. The natives continued to be brutalized, and the wildlife continued to be hunted and fished to near-extinction.

Seward and Sumner

In 1867 Abraham Lincoln and his vice president and successor, Andrew Johnson, along with their Secretary of State William Seward, finalized a deal with Baron de Stoeckl of Russia for the purchase of Russian America for $7,200,000. Although the region came to be known by such comical epithets as "Seward's Folly," "Seward's Icebox," "Icebergia," and "Walrussia" in newspapers of the day, the purchase of Russian America was not as unpopular as some history books maintain. Even while some newspapers were lampooning the purchase

William Seward

on their cartoon page, they were applauding it in their editorials. Still, while Americans were not acrimonious concerning the purchase of a northern wilderness, they had little notion of why it was acquired or what to do with it.

Charles Sumner, Senator from Massachusetts, proposed the purchase in Congress. His speech to the Senate lasted three hours and takes up eighty dense pages in the Congressional Record. He described in detail Alaska's history, natives, natural resources, geography, and any other information he had gleaned on the territory. Near the end of the speech, Sumner had this to say about what to call the new acquisition:

"As these extensive possessions, constituting a corner of the continent, pass from the imperial government of Russia they will naturally receive a new name. They will be no longer Russian

America. How shall they be called? Clearly any name borrowed from classical history or from individual invention will be little better than a misnomer or a nickname unworthy of such an occasion. Even if taken from our own history it will be of doubtful taste. The name should come from the country itself. It should be indigenous, aboriginal, one of the autochthons [earliest known inhabitants] of the soil..."

Sumner did not think of this notion on his own. The 1850's and 60's were big decades for territory- and state-making, and the use of aboriginal names was quite in fashion. Sumner would have known of the recent proposals of names such as Kansas, Nebraska, Dakota, Wyoming, and Utah. He continued...

Charles Sumner

"...Happily such a name exists, which is as proper in sound as in origin. It appears from the report of Cook, the illustrious navigator, to whom I have so often referred, that the euphonious name now applied to the peninsula which is the continental link of the Aleutian chain was the sole word used originally by the native islanders, 'when speaking of the American continent in general, which they knew perfectly well to be a great land.' It only remains that, following these natives, whose places are now ours, we, too, should call this 'great land' Alaska[5]."

Eloquent as Sumner's speech was, it perpetuated a myth that had developed surrounding the name "Alaska." The meaning of the word had been widely reported as "great land" which was, in fact, a phrase lifted directly from Cook's journal. But the evolution of the definition of "Alaska" probably skewed this translation to some extent. "Great" had most likely meant "big" or "large" when originally translated but took on the connotations of "wonderful" and "magnificent" for those English speakers who found it convenient or useful. Nevertheless Sumner's speech achieved its objective, and the treaty breezed through the Senate easily. The House of Representatives, which was charged with appropriating the money for the purchase, took a little more convincing but finally gave its approval, and the deal was done.

The *Country* of Alaska?

"Alaska's boundary seems to defy geography and common sense," writes one historian. "The clean slash that marks the 141st meridian moves unerring from north to south across the ridges but stops just short of the Pacific. From St. Elias it straggles to the southeast across the mountains, enclosing a long appendage that reaches as far south as Dixon Entrance and bars access to the interior[6]." He goes on to describe the complicated negotiations of the Alaska Boundary Tribunal in 1824 and 1825 involving Russia, the U.S. and Great Britain, which produced the convoluted line. The talks were often heated and sometimes

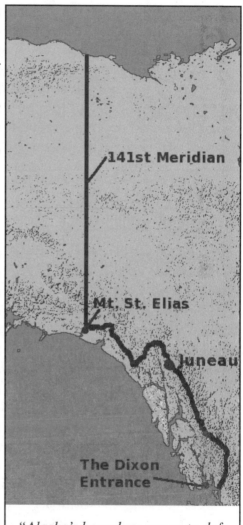

"Alaska's boundary seems to defy geography and common sense."

clandestine but eventually produced the official border of Russian America, which would become the district of Alaska created by the United States from the lands purchased from Russia in 1867.

The U.S. established a military government in Alaska for the first seventeen years following the purchase, during which time the U.S. Navy was in charge. Finally, in 1884, the Organic Act of Alaska organized the region as a District and provided for the installation of government agencies including courts and schools. Unfortunately many of the first government appointees in Alaska were incompetent and/or unethical, and the situation of most residents was made worse instead of better. Alaskans, becoming increasingly frustrated, actually offered in 1890 to repurchase their homeland for twice the sum that the U.S. had paid to Russia[7]. The proposition, while rejected, got the attention of the U.S. government who now knew that Alaskans were serious about official organization. Congress began, albeit slowly, to pay more attention to the process of bringing Alaska into the statehood fold.

A National Treasure

Even before it became a territory, the valuable natural resources of Alaska caused endless political disputes, both domestic and international. The discovery of gold near Fairbanks in 1902 touched off one of many boundary disputes, this one between the U.S. and Canada. A compromise between the two countries determined the current position of the line that meanders from the 141st parallel at Mount St. Elias (named by Vitus Bering for the holy day on which he first saw the peak) to the Dixon Entrance, or southeastern tip of the state.

The investments in mining also increased the opportunities for other industries in Alaska, such as railroads and the timber and fishing industries, many of them controlled by an "Alaskan Syndicate" which included the Guggenheim family and J. P. Morgan. The rapid development of all of these industries increased the possibilities for fraud and corruption.

A famous dispute was touched off in the Taft administration in 1909 involving Secretary of the Interior Richard A. Ballinger and Gifford Pinchot, who served in the Department of Agriculture as head of the Forestry Service. Pinchot had been appointed by Taft's predecessor, Teddy Roosevelt, and agreed strongly with Roosevelt's policy of land conservation and wilderness preservation. Ballinger was more sympathetic to the mining and business interests in Alaska and used his power to return to the public domain (i.e. make available for sale) several million acres of Alaskan land that Pinchot had previously set aside as ranger stations. Perhaps in retaliation, Pinchot strongly supported a colleague who publicly accused Ballinger of improperly issuing some Alaska coal mining claims. Ballinger was cleared of any wrongdoing in a congressional investigation, but the

Warren G. Harding

public debate had far-reaching effects. Taft and Roosevelt, formerly allies, became political rivals and split the Republican Party, allowing democrat Woodrow Wilson to win the next presidential election.

In 1912, after several Supreme Court decisions and constitutional challenges, and with the passage of the Second Organic Act, Alaska was transformed from a District to a Territory with a guarantee of eventual statehood, and yet that status was still more than half a century away. The Depression and World War II delayed many domestic matters, including the statehood issue for Alaska and Hawaii.

While Alaska waited for statehood to be conferred, there existed separatist movements in the Alaska Territory, some of which would have divided the state into as many as five separate states. Among these was a strong push by the population of the panhandle region—the finger of coastline that runs from the 141st meridian to the Dixon Entrance—to separate from the rest of the territory. Their plan was to break off this most populated portion, that which included the largest city, Juneau (also to have been the name for the new territory/state) and try to achieve statehood sooner for that section. This proposal was given favorable attention by then President Warren G. Harding in 1923 when he visited Alaska for a gold spike ceremony to celebrate the opening of the Alaska Railroad. Had he not died in San Francisco on his way home from the territory*, the shape of Alaska could look very different today.

---

* *The death of Warren G. Harding is even today subject to suspicion and controversy. It is known that while away from office Harding's administration was revealed to be deeply corrupt, and that on his return, Harding was facing imminent impeachment. For this reason many have suspected that he was murdered in San Francisco. The official cause of death was "apoplexy", a term that refers to the loss of consciousness before death but gives little real information as to why he died. He had, days earlier, suffered from what was diagnosed as severe food poisoning and had shortly after that developed pneumonia. Some believe he was poisoned, and that his wife, Florence Harding, may have been involved given that she would not consent*

On January 3, 1959, President Dwight Eisenhower finally signed the proclamation admitting Alaska to the Union as the 49th state. The fight for statehood involved many political issues, but chief among them was the concept of self-determination, or the desire by the people of Alaska to determine the fate of their state's resources as well as their own political destiny. But even that goal would prove to be elusive. To this day, the national image of Alaska is that of a mysterious gem being fought over by millions of people who...don't live there.

---

to an autopsy. There is no doubt that because of the corruption in his White House, many people would have benefited from Harding's death. Even so, any real evidence of murder has never been satisfactorily proven.

1.   Fisher, Raymond H., <u>Bering's Voyages: Whither and Why</u> (Seattle, 1977), p. 23.

2.   Beaglehole, J.C. ed., <u>The Journals of Captain James Cook on his Voyages of Discovery</u> (Cambridge, 1967), p. 456.

3.   Beaglehole, ed., p. 1337.

4.   Beaglehole, ed., p. lxiv.

5.   "Speech of Hon. Charles Sumner, of Massachusetts, on the Cession of Russian America to the United States," in *U.S., Congress, House, House Executive Document No. 177, 40 Congress, 2 Session*, p. 188.

6.   Tompkins, Stuart R., *"Drawing the Alaska Boundary,"* Sherwood, Morgan B. (ed) <u>Alaska and its History</u>, (Seattle: University of Washington Press, 1967), p. 83.

7.   Frederick, Robert A., <u>Alaska's Quest for Statehood 1867-1959</u>, (Municipality of Anchorage, 1985), p. 7.

Chapter 3: Arizona

Arizona take off your rainbow shades
Arizona have another look at the world
...
Arizona cut off your Indian braids
Arizona hey won'tcha go my way

> — "Arizona"
> Mark Lindsay

"If you can find lower prices anywhere, my name ain't Nathan Arizona."

> —from the film "Raising Arizona"

Deserts

A desert, any dictionary worth its weight in sand will tell you, is a barren ecosystem that receives less than 250 millimeters of rainfall annually. The label is bestowed upon many places in the U.S., some more deserving than others. The central plains states, currently productive farmland, were referred to as "The Great American Desert" for much of the 1800's because of the lack of trees and hills. The appellation is still used today, albeit nostalgically. Perhaps the most famous deserts in the nation are the Mojave in southern California and the Great Basin of Utah and Nevada, both deserving of the designation, as they receive less than the defining amount of rainfall per year. Some deserts are not as widely known, like the Red Desert of southwestern Wyoming and the Great Sandy Desert in southeastern Oregon. These smaller regions are often designated "deserts" to suit local purposes such as tourismor agricultural grants, but are actually parts of larger deserts.

The state name with which we tend to associate the word "desert" more than any other must be "Arizona." In this diverse land we see petrified rocks, the Grand Canyon, Navajo and Apache Indians, towering saguaro cacti, and lots of heat and sun. We find the appropriately named city of Phoenix, rising from the sweltering ruins of the mysterious Hohokam Indians. We think of Wyatt Earp and his brothers dueling it out with the Clanton gang in another colorfully named town, Tombstone. We remember Holly Hunter and Nicholas Cage fumbling their way through crimes and misdemeanors in Tempe to care for a stolen child named Nathan Arizona. The Arizona deserts seem to be the number one choice for Hollywood's desert-based film locales.

Yet deserts aren't the only natural wonders of The Grand Canyon State. For starters, you can find, well, the Grand Canyon there, one of the world's top tourist attractions and grandest natural marvels. The Kartchner Caverns were discovered in 1974 and developed into an Arizona state park in 1988—the birthing site for hundreds of myotis bats each year. And even with the minimal precipitation measurements found throughout most of the state, cities like Flagstaff boast winter attractions with an annual snowfall of 100 inches and terrain ideal for alpine and Nordic skiing. Despite the blistering arid summer temperatures contradicted by the thundering torrential downpours of the monsoon season, Arizona just might have something for everyone.

Arid Zone?

There are various strange theories about the origin of the word "Arizona," and one of the strangest is found in Henry Gannett's <u>State Names, Seals, Flags, and Symbols</u>, which claims that the word is Spanish for "arid zone." The phrase "árida zona" is often used as a quaint, comical reference to the state, and at least one author in the early 1900's fiercely defended it as the correct origin for the name: "...others reject the obvious árida zona of the Spanish in favor of some strained etymologies from the Indian dialects, about which no two of them agree. Why should the name not have come from the Spanish, and why should it not mean just simply arid zone or belt[1]?" Even though the correct Spanish would be "zona árida," this fanciful theory of etymology hangs around to this day.

Another oft-quoted theory about the name Arizona is that it comes from an Aztec word, *Arizuma*, meaning "silver-bearing." Writing in 1889 pre-eminent American historian Hubert Howe Bancroft dismissed this theory as "extant, founded on the native tongues, offer[ing] only the barest possibility of partial and accidental accuracy[2]."

Bancroft rejects other possible derivations for the same reason:

ari, 'maiden,' and *zon*, 'valley,' from the Pima; *ara* and *sunea*, or *urnia*, 'the sun's beloved,' from the Mojave; *ari*, 'few,' and *zoni* 'fountains;' *ari*, 'beautiful,' and the Spanish *zona*; ... *Arezuma*, an Aztec queen; *Arizunna*, 'the beautiful;' *Arizonia*, the maiden queen or goddess who by immaculate conception gave being to the Zuñi Indians[3]

Indeed the story of the naming of Arizona must reach back into the history of what is now the region of the international border between Arizona and Mexico's state of Sonora.

The Real de Arizonac (or just *Arizonac*) was a ranchería (village) in the area south of modern Tucson, and is the undisputed source of the name *Arizona*. But how did a tiny mining village that existed for less than two decades, and was then cleanly wiped from the map, come to be elevated to the rank of U.S. state name? The events were indeed circuitous, winding through San Francisco and Washington D.C., and the outcome was never certain.

The Silver of Arizonac

It is believed that Arizonac was founded in 1730 by a Spanish Captain named Gabriel de Prudhon who served as *Alcalde Mayor* of Sonora from 1727 until 1733. In 1733 he published a map of northern Sonora which included "Arizonac", one of several mining towns in the area.

In 1736 a Yaqui Indian named Antonio Sirumea discovered some large chunks of silver in a small arroyo just north of Real de Arizonac. Word of the find spread, and prospectors flocked to the region. While mineral strikes in Sonora were not uncommon, this one became legendary, in part because of the nature of the ore. The silver appeared very pure, almost refined, and was found in large nuggets that averaged twenty-five to fifty pounds. Also found were slabs, or *planchas,* of silver, some weighing hundreds and even thousands of pounds, which could only be moved with great difficulty, usually by breaking them into smaller pieces. Some of the miners dug the ground in search of a vein, but in every case the silver went no further than about sixteen inches under the surface.

Historians speculate that what these miners found was horn silver (cerargyrite, or chloride of silver) which can form when hot water containing a type of silver in solution meets a shallow pool of salt water. When subjected to volcanic heat, it can harden into slabs or plates.

When Spanish officials learned of the find, they sent Juan Bautista de Anza, commander of the presidio at nearby Santa Rosa de Corodéguachi (Fronteras), to investigate. The contentious issue was whether the remarkably pure silver nuggets constituted natural ore that had been "mined," in which case the king would receive twenty percent—a *quinto*—or whether it was buried treasure which had been "found," which would allot the king half. The finder would keep the other half, minus a *quinto* for weighing, assaying, and stamping.

When de Anza arrived at Arizonac and was shown the site of the silver find, no more ore was left, nor were any of the prospectors. The region was Apache territory, and once the silver was exhausted and the Indians began to gather, the miners fled with their riches into the nearby towns. De Anza ordered a thorough investigation and demanded that all of the silver be confiscated. Angry residents and merchants of the region began to petition for the return of their silver, but the legal battle would drag on for years. Finally, in 1741, King Philip V of Spain declared the silver his own and levied judgments against some of the Sonoran merchants for defrauding him of duties on his treasure.

The value of the silver found at Arizonac in 1736 was not historically significant. But the litigation and controversy surrounding it made it famous, and accounts of the events written in the decades following the king's decree declared the silver "fabulous," "incredible," "a sight never before seen." In at least two of these accounts, the name of the mining village is written "Real de Arizona," dropping the final "c."

Mining resumed in the region of Real de Arizonac in 1754 but only briefly. The remoteness of the region, the expense of bringing in equipment and provisions, as well as shipping the ore out, and the hostility of the Apaches proved the effort too expensive, and for the next century the region was virtually deserted.

Papago or Basque?

In the 1960 edition of Will C. Barnes' *Arizona Place Names*, it is claimed that the word "Arizonac" derives from the Papago Indian words *ali* ("small") and *shonak* ("place of the spring"). Barnes goes on to quote

James H. McClintock, another state historian, who claims that the Spanish dropped the final "c" to adapt the word to Spanish phonetics. This "Papago theory" of derivation has been widely accepted as correct, but there is another possible etymology for the word.

In 1979 William A. Douglass published a paper in the periodical *Names*, which sets forth convincing evidence that the word *Arizona* is actually derived from the Basque dialect of Northern Spain. Douglass asserts that the aforementioned McClintock cut short the research on the history of the state's name by declaring the Papago theory to be correct in 1916 and discouraging further research. Douglass' own research does not discount the Papago theory but offers thorough arguments that suggest the word originated in the Basque (a region in northern Spain) language as either *arritza-ona*, "the good (or valuable) rocky place," or *aritza ona*, "the good (or valuable) oak."

He cites the map created in 1733 by Gabriel de Prudhon—who was of Basque descent—in which Prudhon labels "Real de Arizonac" and names himself founder of the tiny mining village. Douglass accounts for the final "c" by noting that it is a Basque pluralizer. Finally, Douglass justifies his proposed definitions by explaining the importance of oak in the Basque culture—and the prominence of oak trees in northern Sonora—as well as the prevalence of the Basque ethnicity among Spanish explorers of the region where the silver was found.[4]

The name "Arizona" was applied to the nearby mountains and to a small arroyo near the ranchería and would continue to appear on maps as such, even after the mines were abandoned. But the actual location of the ranchería once called "Real de Arizonac," or of the site where the silver was found, is not known today. Researchers point to the fact that the operation was so brief, and the mines so shallow, that any infrastructure could easily have degraded to almost nothing over the decades of abandonment. Also, again because of the brevity of the town's existence, no formal government was ever established, no surveying accomplished, and no detailed maps generated.

Gadsden and Santa Anna

From about 1750 until 1848, Nuevo Mexico (modern New Mexico and Arizona, as well as much of northern Mexico) reverted to a sparsely populated region of small pueblos, poor missions, and belligerent Indians generally ignored by the rest of the world, even by its own Spanish, and later Mexican, government. According to Arizona historian Rufus K. Wyllys,

> "The reasons for this obscurity of Pimería Alta…largely centered around the Apache Indians, but the breakdown of the efforts to bind California to Sonora and New Mexico caused the viceroys to neglect the Pima country and leave it to look out for itself."[5]

During this period "Arizona," "Real de Arizona," and "District of Arizona," described a vague area of New Mexico surrounding the old ranchería in the vicinity of what would more famously become the territory of the Gadsden Purchase.

Then, in 1848 distinct borders for Arizona began to take shape with the signing of the Treaty of Guadalupe Hidalgo that ended the Mexican-American War. The terms of Mexico's surrender involved ceding to the U.S. any claims on Texas as well as the New Mexico Territory north of the Gila River and all of Alta California. The war and the treaty were controversial in Mexico and the U.S., Mexicans angered at the loss of so much territory, and some Americans feeling that the U.S. had taken unfair advantage of their southern neighbor at a time when Mexico was struggling to maintain its independence from Spain. Nevertheless, the deal was done, and many Mexicans—once Spaniards—now found themselves American citizens.

Shortly after the war, a group of railroad men, including one James Gadsden, determined that the most direct route for a southern railroad line to connect the southeastern U.S. to the Pacific Coast lay just south of the new border with Mexico. Conveniently, a survey of the area had been riddled with mistakes, and the actual border was still under dispute. In 1852 and 1853 Gadsden negotiated the Treaty of Mesilla with Mexican President Antonio Lopez de Santa Anna and

obtained almost thirty thousand acres for ten million dollars in order to obtain the needed land for the train route. Historically better known as the Gadsden Purchase, it too was unpopular in both countries and contributed to the downfall of Santa Anna's dictatorship of Mexico. The region purchased was south of the Gila River and contained the fertile Mesilla valley and the city of Tucson but did not contain the region of the ranchería of Arizona, which still lay just south of the border. While today the specific location of the small village that lent its name to our 48th state is not known, it is generally agreed that "Arizona" is not in Arizona, but in Mexico.

The Father of Arizona

Enter Charles D. Poston, widely referred to as the "Father of Arizona," though it is probable that he applied the nickname himself. Poston was a native of Kentucky who was working as a customs clerk in San Francisco during the gold rush of the early 1850's. He lived at the "government boarding house," so called because of the large number of state and federal officials who also resided there, where he and his friends would sit and talk nightly over bottles of brandy of the possibilities for exploration in the newly acquired territory of New Mexico.

Poston and his fellow boarders were intrigued by the appearance in San Francisco of an attorney representing the family of the former Mexican emperor Don Augustin de Iturbide. Iturbide was declared "Emperor" of Mexico in 1822 after that nation had won its independence from Spain. His reign, however, lasted only eight months until he was overthrown and executed by revolutionaries led by Santa Anna. The attorney who arrived in San Francisco had with him a legal land grant from the Mexican government

Charles D. Poston

37

for millions of acres of land in northern Sonora which had been given to the Iturbide family as an indemnity after the emperor's death. As the heirs' representative, he was offering incentives for land speculators to go and find the grant in Sonora and begin colonization.

According to Poston, "Old Spanish history was ransacked for information, from the voyages of Cortés in the Gulf of California to the latest dates, and maps of the country were in great demand." One book that was probably consulted was *Noticias Estadisticas del Estado de Sonora, etc.,* by José Francisco Velasco. Published a few years earlier (1850) in Mexico, it contained exciting reports of the mineral wealth to be had with ease in the northern Sonora region, and it refers specifically to "Arizona," describing the pure silver found there a century earlier and the controversy that it sparked.

From Velasco as well as other sources, the prospectors in San Francisco learned that

" ...the State of Sonora was one of the richest of Mexico in silver, copper, gold, coal, and other minerals, with highly productive agricultural valleys in the temperate zone. That the country north of Sonora, called in the Spanish history "Arizunea," (rocky country) was full of minerals, with fertile valleys washed by numerous rivers, and covered by forests primeval."[6]

Poston quoted these sources in this excerpt from a magazine article in 1894, well after his years in Arizona and after its formation into a territory, but no explanation is given for the unique spelling of the name, "Arizunea" or of his brief definition, "rocky country."

What is clear is that Poston's life would be forever changed by the information he gleaned while in San Francisco. In 1854 he made his first reconnaissance mission to the area and founded the township of Colorado City which would later become "Arizona City" and still later "Yuma."[7] During this first trip Poston became enchanted with the region, writing later "The country...is the most marvelous in the United States." He was also impressed with the Pima Indians who lived there, gushing that they had "... many features worthy of imitation by more civilized people."

The following year he went to New York and gathered support and funding for a new company which he called the "Sonora Exploring and Mining Company," of which he was manager and commandant. In 1856 he returned to New Mexico and set up his mining operations at the old Spanish presidio of Tubac, just a few miles south of the relatively large village of Tucson.

For the next four years, Poston oversaw the operations of the silver mines in Arizona and acted as a de facto governor for the region, referring to himself as *Alcalde* (Spanish for "mayor") of Tubac. Under his stewardship, this community of mostly Mexicans and Pima and Papago Indians enjoyed relative peace with the Apaches. They formed their own currency and saw the beginning of the first local newspaper, the *Arizonian*. It was common knowledge that the actual territorial government located in Santa Fe was too remote and too disinterested in the affairs of Arizona to be of any consequence to its inhabitants, and Poston's mines were easily the largest legitimate employer for miles. So while he enjoyed some power, he seems to have ruled with a judicious hand. He even performed marriage ceremonies and wrote with pride of his many godchildren named "Carlos" or "Carlotta."[8]

Virtually everyone involved in New Mexico, which at that time consisted roughly of the current states of New Mexico and Arizona, wished to amputate the western section of the territory. As early as 1854 authorities in Santa Fe who were reluctant to take on the problem of the Apaches in the far west, petitioned Congress to create a separate territory out of the western half of New Mexico. They even proposed names: Pimeria, one of the region's historic names, Gadsonia, derived from Gadsden of purchase fame, and Arizona, which was becoming widely used to refer not only to the southern part of the region, but the entire western half of New Mexico. The bill was defeated in 1854, and would be resubmitted several times, always unsuccessfully.

The Confederate Arizona

The Civil War forced further change in Arizona, albeit temporarily. In June of 1861 the U.S. Army abandoned the area completely, and Poston was forced to flee as well. Without the presence of any military, it was clear that the Apaches would soon attack the mining camp, and in fact before Poston

John R. Baylor

could leave, Apache marauders stole all of the company's horses, making his departure not only necessary but difficult.

On July 23, 1861, Confederate troops led by Lieutenant Colonel John R. Baylor seized Fort Fillmore in the southern Mesilla Valley of New Mexico. This area was populated mostly by farmers who had moved there from Texas and therefore tended to ally themselves with the southern cause. On August 1, Baylor declared the southern half of New Mexico, all that land below the 34th parallel to the Mexican border and stretching all the way to California, to be the new Confederate Territory of Arizona with himself as governor.

After the Union victory at Glorieta near Santa Fe—a grisly two-day battle that has been given the poetic label "Gettysburg of the West"—the Confederate troops retreated to Texas, and the borders of New Mexico territory reverted to their original positions. The short-lived Confederate Territory of Arizona was of little consequence, except to point out to Congress that the region, far from being a barren wasteland, contained vast mineral wealth that could help the Union cause.

But the area needed some attention. Charles Poston had gone to Washington and was engaged in an effort to divide the territory. It was during his talks with Senator Ben Wade of Ohio, Chairman of the Committee on Territories, that Wade expressed his oft-repeated description of Arizona, "O, yes, I have heard of that country,—it is just like hell—all it lacks is water and good society." Finally, Congress passed the bill creating Arizona out of the region of New Mexico west of the 111th degree of longitude west

and in February, 1863, President Abraham Lincoln signed it. Poston was named Superintendent of Indian Affairs for the new territory and later would be its first elected delegate to Congress.

Like New Mexico, with which its fortunes were perpetually linked, statehood was elusive for Arizona. Congress was rife with prejudice against the Mexican and Indian populations of the area and rejected proposals for statehood for almost fifty years. In 1902, the Chairman of the Senate Committee on Territories, Albert Beveridge of Indiana, a particularly outspoken bigot toward the indigenous populations of the southwest, proposed recombining the two territories with the name "Arizona the Great." His motive was to dilute the Indian and Mexican populations of New Mexico with the now Anglo majority in Arizona[9]. (Arizona's Anglo population had grown substantially during the half-century of territorial status. White prospectors came to mine, and white railroad men and ranchers flocked to the area, once the Apache threat was mitigated by the presence of new federal forts and troops.) The jointure project was defeated, and the struggle for statehood continued.

Finally on February 14, 1912, only weeks after New Mexico achieved statehood, Arizona was proclaimed the 48th state of the U.S., completing the puzzle of the continental United States of America. One Arizona historian notes, "There was rejoicing by flagmakers."[10]

1.   Van Dyke , John C., <u>The Desert: Further Studies in Natural Appearances</u> (New York, 1903), p. 208n.

2.   Bancroft , Hubert Howe, <u>The Works of Hubert Howe Bancroft. Vol. 17: History of Arizona and New Mexico, 1530-1888</u> (San Francisco, 1889), pp. 520-521.

3.   Ibid., p. 521[fn].

4.   Douglass, William A., "On the Naming of Arizona," *Names*, December, 1979, pp. 217-234.

5.   Wyllys, Rufus Kay, <u>Arizona: The History of a Frontier State</u> (Phoenix, 1950), p. 60.

6.   Poston, Charles D., "Building a State in Apache Land", *Overland Monthly*, July, 1894, p. 88.

7.   Gressinger, A.W., <u>Charles D. Poston: Sunland Seer</u>, (Globe, Arizona, 1961), p. 18.

8.   *Overland Monthly*, Aug., 1994, p. 208.

9.   Powell, Lawrence Clark, <u>Arizona: A Bicentennial History</u> (New York, 1976), pp. 60-61.

10.   Powell, p. 62.

Chapter 4: Arkansas

An old man sat in his little cabin door,
And fiddled at a tune that he liked to hear,
A jolly old tune that he played by ear...

> — "Arkansas Traveler," *folksong that has*
> *inspired plays, paintings, and musical ren-*
> *ditions performed by, among others, Jerry*
> *Garcia*

You can tell your Ma
I moved to Arkansas
You can tell your dog to bite my leg
Or tell your brother Cliff
whose fist can tell my lip
He never really liked me anyway

> — "Achy Breaky Heart"
> *Billy Ray Cyrus*

The other man was a stalwart ruffian called "Arkansas," who carried two
revolvers in his belt and a bowie knife projecting from his boot, and who
was always drunk and always suffering for a fight.

> —*Mark Twain, in* "Roughing It"

Stack of States

Several mid-continent states are neatly stacked on top of each other and, with heavy shoulders Arkansas sits near the bottom. Its two most famous cities, Hot Springs and Little Rock are memorable for the imagery they convey. Names like this tend to imply the culture of Native Americans, and indeed this state's history is rich with that of many tribes of Indians. But

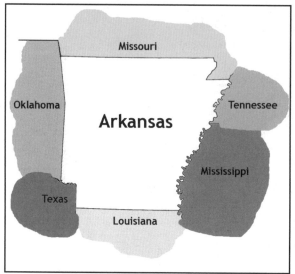

the name "Little Rock" was actually applied by French explorers to designate a landmark ("*la petit roche*") along the Arkansas River. And the thermal waters at Hot Springs, while no secret to native Americans, came to be known by the English description of them, a name which came also to be used for the city that was built up around them.

On a map, it appears as if Arkansas may have been embroiled in a few border wars—and lost them all. Sandwiched in between Missouri and Louisiana, the northern border of Arkansas is shoved down a bit as compared to that of Oklahoma, disrupting the straight line that otherwise runs almost undisturbed from the Atlantic Ocean to Utah, until it dead-ends into southern Nevada. This line also gives way to the Jackson Purchase region of Kentucky, and then to a rather illogical looking appendage to Missouri (the "bootheel"—see "Missouri") that takes a notch out of Arkansas's northeast corner. In the southwest corner of Arkansas there is a notch matching the one in the northeast, this one cut by an imposing corner of East Texas. All of these border intrusions make for a rather small, squarish state that historically has been pushed along with the tides of nation building, mostly being managed, formed, and molded by outsiders while its residents struggled to create for themselves an identity.

In the past, the reputation of Arkansas has been mingled with that of its neighbors to create the image of a "southern state," albeit one on the fringes of the western frontier. It isn't Creole, but the French influence is apparent (even in the name). It isn't the deep south of Alabama, but it has a sort of homey, southern flavor. And it doesn't have the clan-warfare of Tennessee and Kentucky, but its history is spiced up with some mountain-boys nuances (bootlegging, bar-fights, etc.) built up within its own Ozark Mountains. The result has historically been a somewhat derogatory reputation as backward and hillbillyish. James R. Masterson, in his 1943 compilation

Tall Tales of Arkansaw (sic), opens the book with the chapter "A Dog with a Bad Name," and describes the state's reputation this way: "From Territorial times to the present the reputation of Arkansas has been notorious. Her ill fame has marked her, more than any other State of the Union, as a target for reproach and ridicule. Even today the legend of her absurdity continues to flourish, and she remains a favorite victim of humorists[1]."

Another dubious distinction is Arkansas' notable leadership in the swine industry. The state, which since the 20th century has also had thriving poultry and beef industries, may actually have been no more prolific at pork production than, say, North Carolina. But Arkansas embraced hogs when, in 1909, its largest university, The University of Arkansas, took as its mascot the Razorback hog (or "hawg," as any good Arkansan will tell you), forever linking the state with swine.

In the twenty-first century, though, mention of the word Arkansas conjures up some notable political memories. Love him or hate him, Arkansas claims as a native son Bill Clinton. The "hate him" may stem more from the scandals surrounding his tabloidesque personal life, than from his policies or administration. The memories will no doubt fade in time, but one must wonder if people in Arkansas long for the good old days when their state's name was more commonly connected with hogs than with Monica Lewinsky.

Down-Stream People

The first written record of anything approaching the word "Arkansas" was in a journal by Jacques Marquette and Louis Jolliet in 1673. These two Frenchmen traveled down the Mississippi River farther than any European had yet gone. When they reached the mouth of the Arkan-

Jacques Marquette, addressing the Quapaw Indians in Arkansas in June 1673, while fellow explorer Louis Joliet looks on

sas River, they encountered natives who possessed Spanish trade goods and decided to go no further for fear of a confrontation with their Spanish enemies. These natives were Quapaw, a name morphed by French and English speakers from the tribe's own word "Ugakhpa," meaning "down stream people." The Quapaw are one of the five Dhegiha Sioux people (the others are the Poncas, Kansas, Omahas, and Osages) who once inhabited the Ohio Valley. Some time before European contact these tribes split and moved apart. The Quapaw moved south along the Mississippi River, settling near the mouth of the Arkansas.

Marquette wrote of a village that his Illini guides called "Arkancea," which, in their own language, meant roughly "land of the down-stream people." In later years the word would be used by the French to describe the people as well as the region. But even though the French would maintain a friendly alliance with this tribe, the name they would continue to use in describing them was the Illini word "Arkansas" and not their own word for themselves, "Quapaw." The French spoke of the "Arkansas Indians" as handsome and generous, and indeed the French continued to have a peaceful relationship with the tribe.

In time the southern section of the Mississippi River was referred to as "Arkansas Country," which was just south of "Illinois Country." These were vague regions, named for the friendly natives living in them, where the French would sometimes set up missions or trading posts, but "settlement," per se, was not a priority.

Like many aboriginal names, "Arkansas" was spelled and pronounced many different ways for at least two centuries, mostly by the French who controlled the Mississippi River until 1803. They wrote "Arkansoa," "Akamsea," "Arkancas," and "Akanscas," among others. Many of these forms lead people to infer a connection between the words "Arkansas" and "Kansas," sometimes even claiming that the two tribes are the same and that the words are interchangeable. The fact that both tribes descended from the Dhegiha Sioux makes it even more tempting to simply declare them identical. But most researchers argue against this connection, noting that the word "Arkansas" in all of its early forms already contained the "ark-" prefix, and that early explorers, including Marquette himself, distinguished between the Kansa or Kansas Indians and the Arkansas or Quapaw Indians[2]. They also point out that "Arkansas" is the Algonquian word for a Sioux tribe who called themselves "Ugakhpa," while "Kansas" was a Siouxan word for a tribe who called themselves by the name "Kansas."

De Tonti

The person probably most responsible for making the name "Arkansas" stick is the one-handed explorer, Henri de Tonti, a good friend of the explorer Rene-Robert Cavelier, Sieur de La Salle (see Louisiana). De Tonti was born to Sicilian parents (his father invented the form of life insurance known as the "tontine") but spent most of his life in France and joined the French army as a young man. He wore a hook on one arm after having lost his hand in battle and eventually, after transferring to the French Navy, he became a close colleague of La Salle. In 1682, when La Salle became the first European to navigate the Mississippi to its mouth in the Gulf of Mexico, de Tonti was by his side.

Henri de Tonti

When in 1685, La Salle attempted to plant a settlement at the mouth of the Mississippi River, de Tonti was stationed at Fort St. Louis on the Illinois River. He left that post and sailed south in an attempt to meet up with his old friend. On the way he left a small group of men at the mouth of the Arkansas River to build a trading house which he called Arkansas Post, and to cultivate a relationship with the Quapaw Indians. After establishing the post, de Tonti learned that La Salle's attempt at colonization had been a disastrous failure, and that his old friend was murdered by others in his party. De Tonti went on to search for survivors, and continue his military career. He would never return to the trading post he founded.

The Tenacious Arkansas Post

This tiny outpost, built in a flood plain near the Quapaw village of Oso-tuoy, seemed doomed to failure. The fur trade proved weak, and the post was abandoned by the soldiers around the beginning of the 18th century. It was rebuilt, however, twenty years later by a group of settlers organized by John Law, a Scottish financier who had, for a brief time, a French monopoly on colonizing the Louisiana Territory. Still, though, the colony did not thrive.

The settlers had difficulty clearing the rocky soil for farming, and in 1749, Arkansas Post was attacked by a band of Chickasaw Indians who killed six men and kidnapped eight women and children. To avoid vulnerability to this kind of attack and to the constant flooding, the post was moved to a place called "Ecores Rouges" (Red Bluffs) a few miles upstream. But when the new site proved too inconvenient to river traffic on the Mississippi, it was moved again, this time closer to the confluence of the Arkansas and Mississippi Rivers.

Always tenacious, Arkansas Post survived as a small but strategic French outpost. It served as a military station as well as a hunting village but was still vulnerable to flooding. And so, after the Spanish took control of Louisiana in 1763 with the end of the French and Indian War, they moved it back to Ecores Rouges, thirty-six miles from the mouth of the Arkansas[3]. After the American Revolution, settlers began to slowly cross the Mississippi into French Louisiana. Arkansas Post saw very few of these Americans, but it was still the only settled village in the region. Even the Indian population had been drastically reduced due mainly to disease, alcoholism, and tribal warfare. So by the time of the Louisiana Purchase in 1803, this tiny colony—now numbering about 150 people—was the only one available as a foothold—and a name—for the land between "Illinois Country" and "New Orleans."

Post-Purchase

After the United States paid France for their claim to a vast and mostly borderless region in the middle of the continent, the areas west of and adjacent to the Mississippi River were the first to be settled, organized and named. In 1804 the vast region was divided at the 33rd parallel, creating what would become Arkansas' southern border. South of the line was the Territory of Orleans; north was the District of Louisiana. The following year, the District became the Territory of Louisiana, and *its* southernmost district was named New Madrid and included the settlement of Arkansas Post.

All this time settlers were beginning to file in to northern Arkansas, migrating south from St. Louis, the capital of Louisiana Territory. In 1806 a "District of Arkansas" was created; then in 1807 it was eliminated, and in 1808, *re*-created[4] in order to govern the growing population. In 1812 the Territory of Louisiana became Missouri Territory, and Arkansas was quickly made a southern county.

In February of 1819 it was proposed in Congress that "the Arkansas country" be officially divided from Missouri and made a separate territory. The ensuing debate was a continuation of the heated arguments surrounding

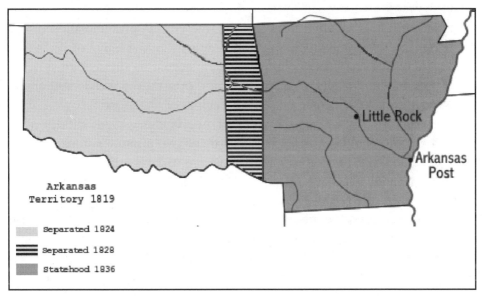

Arkansas
Territory 1819

Separated 1824

Separated 1828

Statehood 1836

slavery and its future in any new territories, and so almost no attention was paid to the name proposed. In fact, during the arguments "Arkansas" was referred to (with its modern spelling) as if it already existed as a territory in order to further the conversation regarding slavery. The following month, without yet acting on the Missouri statehood question, Arkansas was indeed separated and made a U.S. Territory, albeit with wider boundaries than it has today.

Statehood and the Name

The first newspaper of the region was the *Arkansas Gazette,* which did much to standardize the spelling of the state's name, both by adopting it as its title and by appealing fervently for statehood between 1819 and 1836. Statehood was granted to Arkansas on June 15th of 1836, with the signature of President Andrew Jackson, but the most famous deliberation concerning the name of the 25th state was yet to come.

No doubt, the spelling and pronunciation of "Arkansas" are firmly embedded in the linguistic history of the region, with its Indian and French origins. One Arkansas historian, Judge U. M. Rose, noted that the final "s" was added in the earliest French writings to make plural the name of the river and the natives—in order to create such phrases as "les pays des Arkansas" and "la riviere des Arkansas." He claims that even in 1803, when the region was ceded to the U.S., the issue of the final "s" was still unsettled.[5] Rose's research indicates that the current pronunciation of the word, as if it were spelled "Arkansaw," is consistent with that of its Indian heritage and that any pronunciation with the accent on the second syllable (as if pronouncing "Kansas" with an "Ark-" prefix) was considered an innovation around 1836 when the territory achieved statehood.

Legendary, however, is the story of two Congressmen, shortly after statehood, who could not agree between these two pronunciations, one insisting on being introduced as a representative of "AR-kan-SAW," and the other just as adamant that he was from "Ar-KAN-sas." Legendary too, and just as difficult to trace historically, is the account of Cassius M. Johnson, a fictitious Arkansas congressman who was said to have delivered a fiery, and according to most versions, vulgar speech entitled "Change the Name of Arkansas?! Hell No!" The Johnson story is said to have been related orally as early as the 1880's but has been published with varying degrees of profanity several times since. Here's an excerpt from one of the more sanitized versions:

> And now comes this pusillanimous, blue-bellied Yankee who wants to change the name of Arkansas. Why, Mr. Speaker, he compares the great state of Arkansas to KANSAS! You might as well liken the noonday sun in all its glory to the feeble glow of a lightning-bug's ass, or the fragrance of an American Beauty rose to the foul quintessence of a Mexican burro's fart![6]

This version of the speech has been reproduced several times on the Internet, once with an excellent history of the legend written by Michael Simmons, who asserts that the original was likely written by Mark Twain.

What is verifiable is that in 1881 the Arkansas State General Assembly passed a resolution determining the official pronunciation of the state's name, as well as its correct spelling. Though there are those who claim whimsically that this law made it illegal to mispronounce "Arkansas," the resolution was not exactly binding. As state-name historian George Shankle describes, the law rather "specifies that the first and last syllables of the word shall carry the accents, and that the pronunciation with the accent on the second syllable with the *a* in this syllable sounding short as it does in the word *man*, and sounding the final *s*, is to be discouraged."

Clear enough? Well, consider this. The law does not specify what people from Arkansas are to be called. Those who resent any connection to Kansas refer to themselves as "Arkansawyers." Others prefer "Arkansans," which is more commonly used, but is difficult to pronounce in accordance with the aforementioned law.

1.   Masterson, James R., Tall Tales of Arkansaw, (Boston, 1943), p. 1.

2.   Shankle, George E., State Names, Flags, Seals, Songs, Birds, Flowers, and Other Symbols, Rev. Ed. (Westport, Connecticut: Greenwood Press, Publishers, 1970), p. 59.

3.   Bolton, Charles S., Territorial Ambition: Land and Society in Arkansas 1800-1840 (Fayetteville, 1993), p. 15.

4.   Bolton, p. 23.

5.   Shankle, p. 60.

6.   Simmons, Michael, "Change the Sacred Name of Arkansas?!," 8/6/09, <http://members.cox.net/pdzjlvksnkcw/pub/arkansaw-history.html>.

Chapter 5: California

I wish they all could be California girls...

> — *"Wish They All Could Be California Girls"*
> *The Beach Boys*

And California dreamin' is becomin' a reality.

> — *"California Dreamin'"*
> *The Mamas and the Papas*

Yeah, and now I'm runnin' down California Five
With your laughter in my head

> — *"I'm Alive"*
> *Jackson Browne*

Drama Queen of the Nation

From the desolate Mojave Desert to the lush vineyards of Napa Valley, to the sprawling metropolis that is Los Angeles, to the spectacular Golden Gate Bridge, California seems to want to fulfill people's life-long dreams. It is a place people go to seek out their fortunes—from the budding young actors and screenwriters of small-town, USA, to the immigrants risking everything to cross the international border and begin a new life. It is appropriate that the state was named for a fabled land of riches, complete with Amazonian women and exotic animals. Today the word "California" often conveys that very image.

For some, though, "California" is the land of the self-involved, the cradle of psychoanalysis, a place full of weirdoes and wannabes. What people who live outside of California may know about the state is that Arnold Schwarzenegger is governor, that there are lots of earthquakes and fires, and that the newest teen idol will make the "news" virtually every day. And then those people may smile, shake their head, and tsk-tsk it away, congratulating themselves for not living in such a place. But then they perhaps remember their childhood dreams of appearing on the "Tonight Show" with Johnny Carson (okay, Conan, for those of more tender years), pressing their hands into the cement at Grauman's Chinese Theatre, riding a horse along a beautiful beach at sunset...; and they might once again feel the temptation to live in a land where, alas, those things really do happen.

Despite its reputation as "laid back," California seems in reality to be quite a stressful place to live. Its population is greater than that of any other state, and its economy larger than that of France. The fortunes of the state swing to wild extremes—earthquakes here, energy shortages there, economic booms and busts that, like a Hollywood movie, keep the rest of the nation riveted to the goings-on within her borders. As one modern columnist puts it, "California is not the entertainment capital of the world for nothing."

Even her history is the stuff of movies, full of drama, romance, comedy, and action: Spanish missions, the "Gold Rush", Hollywood of the 1930's, Berkley during the Vietnam War, and the AIDS crisis that hit San Francisco in the 1980's. California has its own flare for the dramatic and a name that, to its bestowers, and to the Quixotic dreamers of today signifies an earthly paradise.

Edward Everett Hale

The key to unlocking the history of how California was so named begins with Edward Everett Hale, a late 19th century author and clergyman. Hale is most famous for his short story "The Man Without a Country," published in the Atlantic Monthly in December of 1863. The fictional story, a first person account of the court martial and punishment of Philip Nolan for his part in the

Edward Everett Hale

54

Aaron Burr conspiracy to invade Texas and Louisiana, was written so realistically that people mistakenly believed Hale was reporting a true story.

Edward Everett Hale is also famous for his lineage. He was the nephew and namesake of Edward Everett, a famous orator and politician who served his country as Ambassador to Britain, Secretary of State, and Senator from Massachusetts. As one of the most famous orators of the time, Everett was the main speaker at the dedication of the Gettysburg National Cemetery. He delivered a speech that lasted two hours and was followed by Abraham Lincoln's brief, but brilliant, Gettysburg Address. Hale was also related to Nathan Hale, his great uncle, after whom Edward Everett Hale's father, Nathan, was named. His great uncle Nathan Hale, the famous Revolutionary War captain, was hanged by the British as a spy and is famous for the words he supposedly delivered on his way to the gallows moments before his death: "I only regret that I have but one life to lose for my country." And last, but not least, there is Edward Everett Horton, Hale's grandson, to whom he lent *his* name. Horton was a prolific comedic actor in Hollywood in the 1930's but may be best known as the narrator of "Fractured Fairy Tales" in the Rocky and Bullwinkle Show.

As American history goes, it is fascinating to find a family with such notable and diverse accomplishments. But what does all this have to do with the name *California*?

The origin of the name "California" has, like that of many states, generated debate through the years. Theories included derivation from the Latin *calida fornax* meaning "hot oven"; from an Indian word meaning "high hill"; and, among the most ridiculous, from the name of a Spanish priest, Padre "Cal y Fornia." But on April 30, 1862, Edward Everett Hale presented a paper to the American Antiquarian Society in Boston which cleared up some of the confusion and set forth what he determined—and has proven to be—the most plausible of the theories. Hale's study of the subject is still generally regarded as authoritative and proposes quite believably that the name "California" originated in a romance novel published in 16th century Spain.

Las Sergas de Esplandian

For centuries humans have sought a paradise on earth. From the Garden of Eden to the Seven Cities of Cibola, from Atlantis to Norumbega, these mythical places were first described by imaginative authors and then searched for by persistent explorers.

After Christopher Columbus stumbled onto the West Indies in 1492, providing—it was soon learned—vast new acreage in which to search for this elusive paradise, new interest in its discovery and conquest energized the Spanish conquistadors. Soon the popular culture of 16th century Spain contributed elaborate new descriptions of the fabled lands for which the explorers and conquistadors were actively searching.

One of these descriptions, published in 1510 by Garci Ordóñez de Montalvo, was entitled *Las Sergas de Esplandian* (*The Labors of [the Very Brave Knight] Esplandian*). It was written as a continuation of the romance novel *Amadis of Gaul*, a series of tales of chivalry that had been translated into Spanish by Montalvo several years earlier. The original story, which was almost certainly never printed, is often attributed to a Portuguese troubador named João Lobeira and was probably inspired by French folklore, in particular the epic poem *La Chanson de Roland* (*The Song of Roland*). *Las Sergas de Esplandian*, which was immensely popular in Spain, chronicled the life of Esplandian, son of Amadis, and contained a chapter that describes a mythical island called "California," spelled precisely as we now spell the name of the state, "which was very close to the region of the Earthly Paradise."

The island's name is generally believed to have been fabricated by Montalvo but possibly based on the Arabic root "khalifa" or "caliph," which is a title for the leader of an Islamic group or state that literally means "successor to Mohammed." Indeed *La Chanson de Roland* contains a reference to a place called "Califerne," a probable reference to the Muslim world which may have been the direct inspiration for Montalvo.

The fictional island of California is a strange paradise inhabited by one-breasted Amazonian women who wear "golden armor studded all over with very precious stones, which were found on California Island as abundantly as rocks in a field." These women had domesticated a mythical creature called a "griffin" which had the head and wings of an eagle and the body of a lion. The griffins were used to attack and kill any male invaders and male offspring except those men used by the Amazons for purposes of procreation. In the story, the queen of California, Queen Califia "who was bigger and more beautiful than the other women on the island," assembles many of her warriors and leaves the island to achieve fortune and glory in distant wars.

The popularity of the novel probably thrust the word "California" into the general vernacular of the mid-1500's, especially among conquistadors, who were engaged in finding it. But it was several decades before the word began to appear on maps.

Image of a Griffin from Lewis Caroll's
Alice and Wonderland

Baja y Alta

The question of who first applied the name "California," and when they applied it, to any part of western North America has long been the subject of controversy and study[1]. What is clear is that the name first designated the southern tip of the Baja peninsula, which was thought to be an island (as was Montalvo's California), and only gradually began to describe points further north.

The name probably appeared first on navigational maps around the mid 1560's as "Golfo de California" and "C[abo] California." Antonio de Herrera, a primary Spanish historian, claimed that it was Hernán Cortes himself "who placed this name upon it" ("que le puso este nombre")[3], though it is possible that the name was applied two years earlier when Cortes sent an expedition to explore the Baja peninsula (still believed to be an island) in 1533. That expedition, commanded by Diego de Becerra, was soon overtaken by a mutinous crew led by Fortun Ximenez. After murdering Becerra, Ximenez took the ship and the mutineers to points north where natives allegedly killed Ximenez and some of the others. A few of the survivors returned to Cortes with tales of having visited a strange land abundant in pearls. It is possible that these mutineers applied the name "California" to their discoveries and that it stuck—if not immediately with Cortes, then with the other sailors and conquerors who heard their tales. Cortes himself set out for this "island" in 1535, reaching what is now the Bay of La Paz on May 3 of that year. He named Puerto de Santa Cruz after the feast day on which his expedition had set sail and named the land surrounding it La Tierra de Santa Cruz.

But even while Cortes was applying his "official" name, chroniclers of his expeditions as well as those of other explor-

1639 Dutch map showing Baja California as an island

ers began to use the more popular label "California," first to the sea and the "island," and later to the peninsula and the coast as far north as the 42nd parallel. "There were, of course, exceptions," points out a 1993 article in *Californians* magazine, "...some early maps also applied the name Islas Carolinas (in honor of Charles V of Spain) to those Gulf islands, and some sources say that while Sir Francis Drake camped on the California coast near Point Reyes at what is now known as Drake's Bay, in 1579 he allegedly took possession of the land in the name of the Queen and called it New Albion, which appellation also shows up on several early maps."[2]

Meanwhile, in 1542, Juan Rodriquez Cabrillo sailed north along the west coast of the continent and laid official claim to the land for Spain. Cabrillo, like many later Spaniards, was searching for the fabled Strait of Anian, the Spanish version of the Northwest Passage, that non-existent waterway connecting the North Atlantic to the North Pacific. The futile search for this strait would spur exploration of the west coast for centuries.

During this time, the area consisting of the southern part of the current state of California was often drawn as "Quivera," yet another "earthly paradise" sought by explorers, and the area north of San Francisco was, as mentioned earlier, named New Albion by Sir Francis Drake in 1579 after the Celtic name for Great Britain. Early in the 1700's the southern peninsula of California became established on European maps. For purposes of prior claim, the British continued to refer to the northern Pacific Coast as New Albion, and the Spanish as California.

But until the late 1700's, neither of these "Californias" was settled by Europeans. Baja California was too barren and unforgiving a land, the Spaniards learned, and Alta ("upper" or northern) California, while its coastline was certainly explored by those searching for the Strait of Anian, was too remote from Mexico with no immediate prospects for wealth to expend serious resources in colonization. Ironically it was the promise of gold that would, one hundred years later, prompt the feverish rush to California by Americans.

European Settlement

The dearth of settlers changed, however, with the end of the Seven Years War—a global conflict fought between 1756 and 1763 that included the North American "French and Indian War." Once peace was established between England and France, both of these countries had people and money to spend on new exploration and colonization, and settlement of California was a coveted goal for both. Also poised to encroach upon Alta California were the Russians who had established a lucrative fur trade in Alaska and were attempting to push south.

In 1769 a Franciscan priest named Padre Junipero Serra began establishing missions in conjunction with the Spanish military's efforts to build presidios along the coast of Alta California. Beginning with the mission of San Diego, Serra established nine missions along the western shores. More would be constructed after his death, but his efforts had the desired effect for the Spanish authorities. Though not heavily populated, the missions and their Indian citizenry gave Spain the control, albeit tenuous, they needed in the region to maintain their claim to the land.

Life changed very little for the Californios with the Mexican revolution and the establishment of Mexico as a sovereign nation in 1822, but change would come rapidly for the next three decades. In 1836 a revolution led by Juan Bautista Alvarado, a savvy and pragmatic Mexican diplomat, established California as a sovereign state. When, however, Alvarado was offered the official governorship of the province by Mexican government officials, he accepted and brought California back into the Mexican fold. He was deposed in 1842, by which time American settlers were beginning

Photograph of the original Bear Flag used during the revolt of 1846. It was destroyed in the fires following the 1906 earthquake.

to dot the California landscape.

Four years later, on June 14, 1846, a group of thirty-three Americans led by William Ide and supported by the famous "Pathfinder" John C. Fremont, took control of the town of Sonoma, raising their hastily constructed Grizzly bear flag in what would later be called the "Bear Flag Revolt." The Bear Flaggers declared California an independent republic and named Ide their commander-in-chief, but he would hold that office for less than a month. On July 9 the U.S. officially declared war with Mexico, and the clear objects of the confrontation were Texas and California.

Before the end of the Mexican-American War, the U.S. won California with the surrender of Mexican forces to Fremont in January of 1847. The war's official end would not come for another year with the Treaty of Guadalupe Hidalgo in February of 1848.

And Not a Moment Too Soon

Days before the official end of the war, on January 24, 1848, gold was discovered near Sutter's Mill in Coloma, about fifty miles northeast of Sacramento, on the banks of the American Fork River. Within two years, more than half a million people from all over the world descended upon the region to claim their share of the gold. Unlike previously acquired territory where the tiniest of populations would request territorial status with ambitions of statehood, California's population grew rapidly with no government in place to manage it. The result was chaos in many areas, and vigilantism was codified as the only law in some mining communities. The U.S. Congress, mired in the politics of slavery and the Missouri Compromise, had difficulty agreeing on the future of the region, but something clearly had to be done.

A contingent of powerful Californians drafted their own constitution in September of 1849 and determined they would request admission to the U.S. as a state, bypassing the territory phase. They also proactively decided the pressing question of slavery, voting unanimously to ban the institution.

Sutter's Mill in 1850

The federal government acted relatively quickly, as such things usually went, and passed the Compromise of 1850, which inducted California as a free state. It would be one of only two states since Ohio (the 17th) that would come into the union bypassing the normal territorial process.[*]

Perhaps because of the need for quick action, the overwhelming issue of slavery, and the centuries-old name that had already been established on the land, the subject of a new name for the region was never seriously debated, and the statehood bill was signed by President Millard Fillmore on September 9, 1850. California became the 31st state in the union, and one of only three (Texas and Vermont are the others) that had known life as an independent republic, albeit for only a few short weeks.

It is fitting that California, a state with one of the most dramatic and unique paths to statehood, be our nation's ground-zero for film and television entertainment. Her legacy as a drama queen was well established by the time she entered the union, and no other state seems imminently able or willing to wrest that title from her.

---

[*] *The other was Texas.*

---

1.   André R. Willieme, "Stalking the Origins of a Singular Name," *Californians*, 11(3).

2.   Willieme, p. 18.

3.   Davidson, George, "The Origin and Meaning of the Name California: Califia the Queen of the Island of California," *Transactions and Proceedings of the Geographical Society of the Pacific,* Volume VI, Part I; Series II, 1910.

Chapter 6: Colorado

But the Colorado Rocky Mountain high
I've seen it rainin' fire in the sky
The shadow from the starlight is softer than a lullaby
Rocky Mountain high

> — "Rocky Mountain High"
> *John Denver*

I guess he'd rather be in Colorado...

> — "I Guess He'd Rather Be in Colorado"
> *John Denver*

Mountains

Colorado invites us into the rugged Rocky Mountains of the American West. It calls us to climb its snow-capped peaks, its forbidding ridges, its engaging summits, and then encourages us to career down them at unnatural speeds with only a couple of waxed boards strapped to our feet for some perceived measure of control. Aspen, Vail, Telluride—the ski resorts of the mountains are just as easily associated with Colorado as the big cities of the eastern slope—Denver, Boulder, and Colorado Springs. Colorado's four ninety-degree angles and two pairs of parallel sides contradict its name and its reputation. Not only does the boxy shape of the state defy the curves, crags, and crests of the mountains for which it is so famous, it also ignores the winding river from which it took its name.

Colorado, like many states, has its own Hollywood stereotype. Unlike her northern neighbors with whom the state shares the largest mountain range in North America, Colorado's mountains seem less conducive to solemnity and peace than to recreation and challenge. Hollywood uses these mountains as a backdrop for films about human endurance and adventure—

films like *Butch Cassidy and the Sundance Kid*, *City Slickers*, *How the West Was Won*, and *True Grit*.

Colorado's mountains are its very essence, even though fully a third of the state is comprised of flat plains and farmland that looks more like its next-door neighbor, Kansas. The state cultivates an image of rugged western culture—Denver hosts a major stock-show and rodeo each year, and Colorado Springs is home to the Rodeo Hall-of-Fame. But it was the miners of the mountains, not the ranchers of the plains, who truly created Colorado.

Finding the River

Colorado takes its name from the most dominant river in the American Southwest. One source of the Colorado River is in the state of Colorado, but the river is fed by a system of tributaries that reach northward into Wyoming and westward to California. The bulk of the river's basin is the eastern half of Utah and virtually all of Arizona, while the lowest section divides the Mexican states of Baja California and Sonora, then the river empties into the Sea of Cortés. Providing water to what is otherwise a massive desert, the river boasts some of the most wondrous landmarks in America.

Glen Canyon Dam was completed in 1959 creating Lake Powell, a prime vacation spot for house boaters, along the Arizona-Utah border. Lake Powell was named for John Wesley Powell, the first white man known to have navigated the Colorado River through the Grand Canyon. This he did in 1869 with a small crew after having lost his right arm in the Civil War. Further

John Wesley Powell

The Colorado River Watershed

down the river sits another impressive dam. Sometimes called "Boulder Dam" after the name of the canyon in which it was built, Hoover Dam was officially named for the 31st president, Herbert Hoover, who presided over its early development in the 1920's.

Hoover Dam forms Lake Mead, named for a Commissioner of Reclamation Dr. Elwood Mead, who designed much of the Boulder Canyon Project. After Hoover Dam, what's left of the water in the Colorado River makes its way to perhaps the most famous natural landmark in the country, possibly in the world—the Grand Canyon. One of the seven natural wonders of the world, the Grand Canyon, rises along the banks of the Colorado River for 277 miles. From there the river winds south to form the border between California and Arizona, and then continues into Mexico where it empties into the Sea of Cortéz.

Naming the River

Native tribes of the Southwest had their own names for the Colorado River, but they all meant "red river." The A'a'tam a'kimult, or Pima Indians, called it "Buqui Aquimuri." The Kwitcyana, or Yuma, Indians who lived along its banks near its mouth called the river "Haweal." The redness of the water is, and was, caused by iron in the abundant silt washed along the river through the southwestern desert.

While vital to the arid Southwest for the water it supplies, the Colorado River was considered useless to Europeans when they found it in the 1500's because it was impossible to navigate. Its quick current and many rapids forbade even the smaller vessels of the world's sailors from traveling very far. Perhaps for this reason, credit for "discovering" the river usually goes to "the Spaniards" and not to one Spaniard in particular, as if the accomplishment of finding it was simply too unimportant for anyone to claim for himself. When a name is mentioned in connection with the feat, it is generally one of three.

The first of these is Francisco de Ulloa who sailed to the north end of the Gulf of California in 1539 hoping to explore the Pacific Coast, the Spaniards still believing the Baja peninsula to be an island. Ulloa, it is said, did not so much find the Colorado River as "sense" it, which is to say he noted the current flowing from the north, and the silt being deposited by it. At any rate, he turned south to head back to New Spain and died shortly thereafter, either lost at sea or stabbed by a fellow sailor, according to conflicting reports.

The next Spaniard to discover the Colorado was Hernando de Alarcón whose small fleet sailed north from Mexico to support the massive overland expedition of Coronado in 1540. Alarcón would be the first European to sail into the Colorado River, though the current against him was so strong that he needed one of his smaller ships to do so, and even then he was unable to get very far. It is unclear how far north Alarcón traveled, but some researchers maintain he got no further than the current international border. Oddly, he named the river *Rio de Buena Guia* or "River of Good Guidance."

The third Spaniard to occasionally get credit for the discovery is Juan de Oñate who explored the American Southwest in 1605 looking for a water route to the South Sea (Pacific Ocean). By the time of Oñate, the Spaniards had given the river other names including *Rio de Cosninas* (a Spanish version of the name of a local Indian tribe), *Rio de San Rafael*, and *Rio de Tizon* ("Firebrand River"). Oñate's contribution to the discovery is that he added the name *Rio Colorado* to the list. Technically speaking, it was a padre/historian named Zarate Salmeron who studied the records of Oñate's 1605 voyage in 1626 and wrote "Rio Colorado" as the river's name, noting Oñate's description of the nearly red water.

Around the beginning of the 18th century, the name *Rio Colorado* began to appear on maps, though it would be almost two more centuries before the name would apply to a section of river in the state that bears its name. Not until 1921, at the request of the state of Colorado, was the section of the

The Spanish Peaks in southern Colorado

river then known as the "Grand River" renamed "Colorado River." Now, at long last, there was a *Colorado River* in Colorado.

There was, however, and still is a *Colorado River* in Texas, and a *Red River* to boot (not to be confused with the *Red River* of the northern plains that forms the border between North Dakota and Minnesota). None of these is at all connected to the Colorado River that gave the state its name, except that all are, or were—one must assume—red. And to seriously belabor the subject of color, while there is no *Red River* in Colorado, there is a *White River*, which winds down from the Rocky Mountains and into the *Green River*, which delivers water to...the *Colorado*.

Barrier Land

The European powers of the 16th and 17th centuries recognized Spain's claim to the American Southwest as far north as New Albion, or what is currently Oregon and Idaho. But when Rene Robert Cavelier, Sieur de la Salle claimed Louisiana for France in 1682, a boundary seemed in order to separate the claims of the two countries. That boundary was determined to be the Continental Divide, though where that line lay was more theoretical than physical. In fact, the region that is now the state of Colorado is referred to in history books as a "buffer land," "barrier land," and "no man's land" because of its sparse settlement until the 1800's and because it contained the boundary line between Spanish California and French Louisiana.

The Spanish did not settle the region, but a few Spanish explorers wandered through what they named the *Sangre De Cristo* (Blood of Christ) mountains in the southern part of the state. The first of these was explorer Juan de Uribarri who in 1706 left Santa Fe and explored the region of what are now called the "Spanish Peaks" just west of Walsenburg, Colorado. The native Indians called these twin mountains "Wahatoya" or "Breasts of the Earth" for what must be obvious reasons. Uribarri declared the region

Zebulon Pike

to be the province of "San Luis", but then went back to New Mexico never to return, allowing his appellation to fade. Today "San Luis" refers to the highest desert in the United States, the San Luis Valley of south central Colorado.

International politics concerning the parallelogram we call Colorado changed slightly when France transferred the western half of Louisiana to Spain in 1762, making a boundary no longer necessary. But a border became critical around 1803 when, through the machinations of Napoleon Bonaparte, Louisiana passed back from Spain to France (see Louisiana) and then quickly to the United States. Once the Americans began aggressively settling and exploring their new western frontier, the limits of that frontier needed firm definition.

In 1806, Zebulon Pike made his famous journey westward under the authority of General James Wilkinson. Ostensibly looking for the headwaters of the Arkansas and Red Rivers, what Pike discovered was the mountain that now bears his name. He made a now famous, yet unsuccessful attempt to climb to the summit of what he called "Grand Peak," then continued his explorations until he was arrested by the Spanish for trespassing. Pike and his men were released a few months later, but his journals and maps were confiscated by the Spanish, and not returned to the United States for over a hundred years. Even so, Pike published an account of his journey that quickly became a bestseller and influenced all future exploration of the Southwest.

Pike also influenced the names of scores of places in the United States. Ten states (though not Colorado) contain a "Pike County," and several towns, an island, a national forest, and even a Navy ship were named for him. And while he gave the name "Grand Peak" to the mountain he attempted to climb,

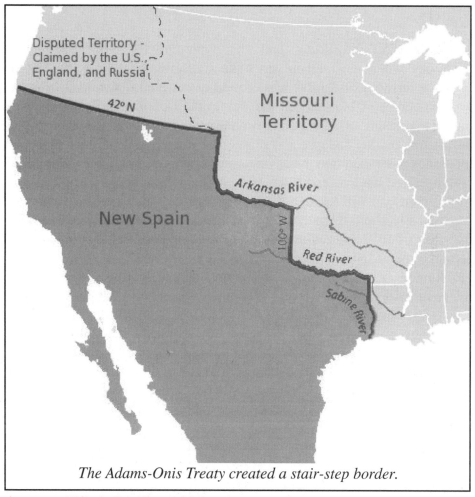

The Adams-Onis Treaty created a stair-step border.

the name "Pike's Peak" would become popular fifty years later through the writings of another famous American explorer, John C. Fremont.

In 1819 the U.S. and Spain agreed on a border with the Adams-Onis Treaty. The boundary stair-stepped up over Texas and divided what is now Colorado between the two countries. Thirty years later, with the end of the Mexican-American War in 1848, that border was erased by the Treaty of Guadelupe Hidalgo. Now the American frontier was unobstructed all the way to the Pacific Ocean, and the almost instantaneous discovery of gold in California gave rise to the migration of a new breed of Americans.

Miners

In the 1850's prospectors and other opportunists filed over and around the Rocky Mountains on their way to the California gold fields. In May of 1854 the territory of Kansas was created out of land that spread from the western border of Missouri all the way to the Continental Divide, including a large chunk of what is now southeastern Colorado. Then in 1857 a devastating market collapse and subsequent economic depression launched thousands more men into the adventurous trade of mining. Men who could no longer find work as carpenters, storekeepers, even doctors, and who had lost fortunes yet still had families to support, decided to follow rumors of gold and silver into the mountains of the west. Some historians assert that the panic of 1857 spurred the onset of the Civil War. What is much more certain is that it spurred the creation of Colorado.

Rumors of gold in the Rocky Mountains had been swirling for years by the time some small deposits of gold were found in streams near what is now Denver in 1858. News of the find along Cherry Creek, so named for the chokecherries that grow along its banks, spread quickly, and miners from the Midwest and points further east began to move into the inhospitable plains and foothills just east of the mountains in what was then western Kansas Territory. Then in 1859, George Jackson found a small deposit of placer gold near what would become Idaho Springs, and a few months later, and not far away, John Gregory found an even larger vein of gold in Clear Creek. While not exceedingly large finds, "Jackson's Diggings" and "Gregory's Diggings" meant the hope of wealth to the economically depressed communities in the East and Midwest. Storekeepers closed their shops, farmers left their fields, and whole families moved to western Kansas, eastern Utah, and northern New Mexico Territories to try their luck at mining.

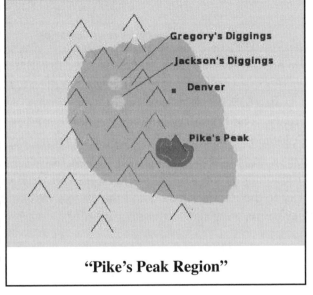

"Pike's Peak Region"

While these gold finds were situated about eighty-five miles north of Pike's Peak, the whole region, including Denver City, became known informally as the Pike's Peak region, as that mountain was the most famous landmark anywhere near the mines. The historical exclamation "Pike's Peak or Bust!" scrawled on the side of covered wagons, referred not to what we now know as Pike's Peak, but to land slightly north of the I-70 corridor that winds through the Rocky Mountains. So many miners, tens of thousands, had flooded into these mining communities in 1858 that the clamor for local government, which is to say statehood, came before the year's end.

Jefferson

The first attempt to organize a new territory out of the Pike's Peak region was instigated in the U.S. House of Representatives early in January of 1859. The name proposed was "Colona," but the measure failed quickly. The feeling was that just because a bunch of men had moved into the area to dig for gold didn't oblige the U.S. Congress to grant them statehood.

Meanwhile, the miners in the camps needed and wanted local government. They took matters into their own hands and created the "Territory of Jefferson," then began electing officials and passing laws. The miners also sent a delegation to Washington to press for territory status. When they began levying taxes, however, the rogue government fell apart, and the miners waited for Congress to act on their request. When the petition was brought before the House of Representatives on January 31, 1859, it was quickly referred to committee but not before one amendment could be proposed. Galusha Grow, a powerful senator from Pennsylvania who had recently switched political parties from Democrat to Republican, objected to the name "Jefferson" (Thomas Jefferson being historically associated with the Democratic Party) and suggested the substitution of "Osage," a regional native tribe. He was told the matter would be discussed in committee and he relented, but it was clear that the name of the state was a politically sensitive matter.

Back home, the miners, much more interested in gaining territory status than in retaining the name "Jefferson" tried out several other potential names:

Yampa, Idahoe, Nemara, San Juan, Lula, Weapollao, Arapahoe, Colorado, Tahosa, Lafayette, Columbus, Franklin—so many in fact, that as late as February 1861, a miner informed his correspondent to direct his letters "to Denver City with the name of this Territory, whatever Congress is pleased to call it."[1]

Gradually "Colorado" won acceptance, and the efforts to create a new territory now assumed its new name.

The creation of new territories in Congress was stalled, however, because of the sectional slavery issues that were dividing the country in half. When Abraham Lincoln was elected in 1860, and the southern states seceded, the way was cleared for what was left of Congress to begin creating new territories again. In January of 1861 a previously tabled bill to create Colorado Territory was dusted off and voted on. After some machinations that almost renamed the territory "Idaho" (see Idaho), it passed, and Colorado Territory came into existence on February 28, 1861. "Jefferson," having lost out as the Territorial name, became the name of the most populated county in the new territory, the county which contained the city of Golden, the first capital of the new territory.

For the next fifteen years the miners and other settlers would make several attempts at statehood. The Civil War, political contention, and resentment by easterners of so laudable a status to be granted to "a few handfuls of miners and reckless bushwhackers"[2] delayed the process. But finally, with no further attempts to change the name, a constitution was passed, officials were elected, and President Ulysses S. Grant signed the declaration conferring statehood on August 1, 1876. Colorado became the 38th state in the Union in the year of the nation's 100th birthday, conferring upon the state its nickname, the Centennial State.

---

1.   Carl Ubbelohde, Maxine Benson, Duane A. Smith, *A Colorado History* (Boulder, 1995) p. 95

2.   Ubbelohde, et al., *A Colorado History*, p. 149

Chapter 7: Connecticut

I am an American. I was born and reared in Hartford, in the State of Connecticut—anyway, just over the river, in the country. So I am a Yankee of the Yankees—and practical; yes, and nearly barren of sentiment, I suppose—or poetry, in other words.

— "A Connecticut Yankee in King
Arthur's Court" *by Mark Twain*

Kim Eberhart: *Daddy, I just saw a man carrying a naked lady.*
Walter Eberhart: *Well, that's why we're moving to Stepford.*

— "The Stepford Wives" *1975*

Insurance and Basketball

It is a word that can make one think of something as quaint as a New England style town square, or something as modern as college basketball, or something as mundane as the insurance industry. "Connecticut," the name of the third smallest state in the U.S., seems packed with images. A perfect rectangle with imperfect borders, Connecticut is one hundred miles from east to west and 50 miles from north to south; even the slowest driver could tour the state in less than a day. It's where affluent New Yorkers live; it's Yale; and it is the place from whence appeared Mark Twain's Yankee in King Arthur's court.

Connecticut is proudly known as the "Constitution State." This title refers to The Fundamental Orders which were established in the colony in the late 1630's, ostensibly the first constitutional document in America.

Basketball fans add "The University of" to "Connecticut" to name arguably the best women's basketball program in history and a pretty decent men's hoops program to boot. But they like to shorten it. Rather than the eleven-syllable mouthful that officially names the institution, they speak of "UConn", and pronounce it "Yukon". To the uninitiated, this of course may produce images of Eskimos wearing fur parkas throwing a frozen basketball into a hoop as baby seals look on.

Interestingly, many places in Connecticut are well known as Connecticut places, even to complete outsiders. Names like New Haven, Hartford, Stamford, and Greenwich are instantly recognizable as Connecticut towns, even though none of them have populations greater than such lesser known places as Garland, Texas or Naperville, Illinois. It is no doubt their history, and the history of their state, that makes them famous. Connecticut seems the epitome of rural New England, of quaint farmhouses, rolling green meadows, and puritan values spiced with a touch of revolutionary spirit.

Could you spell that, please?

It has been called the "place with the unpronounceable name". Unspellable name is more like it. Seventeenth century Europeans, just like schoolchildren today, struggled mightily with how to represent in writing the word they heard uttered by the natives that described the Connecticut River Valley. But spell it they did, in lots of different ways—Connittetuck, Counitegou, Kwenihtekot, Quanehta-cut, Quenticutt, Quienetucquet, Quinatucquet, Quinnehtukguet, Quinnehtukqut, and Quonehtacut, just to name a few.

In 1665 the Duke and Duchess of Hamilton in England attempted to claim a land grant that had been conferred upon an ancestor of the duke. In the petition, however, the name of the valley—which everyone involved knew to be the Connecticut River valley—was spelled "Converticu." The appeal was denied when the Connecticut Assembly rather cheekily "protested [their] ignorance of any 'Converticu' River."[1]

But thirty years earlier the English were just learning of this river from the natives they traded with. The Puritans wrote and spoke of Connecticut with a covetous—if cautious—tone, for once Plymouth and the Massachusetts Bay Colony (MBC) were established and settled, the great Puritan Migration of the 1630's began to pour into new towns and villages of New England, and more space was quickly needed.

However you spell it, *Connecticut* means "on the long tidal river" or "place of the long estuary." It is Algonquian, and was used by several different tribes in the area south of Massachusetts—Narragansett and Nipmuck among others—all of whom spoke dialects of Algonquian. The Indians told the colonists about the Connecticut valley, about its rich, fertile land and bountiful river, which was used as a trade route into prime beaver hunting grounds. They also talked of the Dutch who were pushing into the area from New Amsterdam.

The Dutch, incidentally, solved the problem of the unspellable name by providing their own. In 1614 Adriaen Block (after whom Block Island would be named) sailed up the Connecticut River, the first European explorer to do so, and found its water to be clear and sweet, as opposed to the brackish water of the rivers to the south. He named it "Varshe" or "Fresh" River, and his countrymen quickly began to trade regularly with the Indians who lived on and near its banks.

The Puritans in Massachusetts were told of these Indians, which ac-

Thomas Hooker's company reaches the Connecticut river

counted for much of their caution in attempting to settle in the area. The neighboring tribes called them "Pequot," which means "destroyers," and they dominated the Connecticut River valley through force and intimidation. The Pequot were, by most accounts, contentious and belligerent and made enemies of nearly every other tribe in the region in their efforts to maintain a monopoly on trade with the Dutch. The Dutch initially invited the English to join them in settling the valley in order to strengthen the position of the "civilized" Europeans against the "savages." Even some Indian tribes asked the English to move into the Connecticut region, hoping for a buffer between themselves and the hostile Pequot. But the English balked. They distrusted the Dutch and preferred not to act as "muscle" for one group of natives against another.

The Connecticut Towns

After a few years, however, the situation changed. The Puritans' need for more space, and the philosophical divisions arising in the Massachusetts colonies, made them more willing to take on the risks of settling among the Pequot and the now openly hostile Dutch. By 1633 two Englishmen had led separate reconnaissance missions into Connecticut territory. The first was Edward Winslow, governor of the Plymouth colony and genuine Mayflower passenger, who rather quaintly proclaimed himself "discoverer" of the river and valley and who began to make arrangements for colonization. The other was John Oldham, a Puritan from Watertown, and an enthusiastic merchant and trader. He and three colleagues ventured to Connecticut by land along the Indian paths. Their report was glowing, even speaking kindly of the natives with whom they had lodged on their journey, and confirming the natives' descriptions of lush farmland and plentiful fish and game.

These expeditions would spawn three townships in as many years. In September of 1633 Winslow sent William Holmes to set up a trading post on the Connecticut River. A few settlers followed and endured a brutal winter, calling their small village Dorchester after the English town in which many of them had lived before their pilgrimage to the New World. The town would later be named Windsor. In the spring of 1635 John Oldham and a group of settlers from Watertown, Massachusetts established a township at a place the natives called Piquag; the English named it Wethersfield. And finally, in the spring of 1636 Hartford was founded by a group of Puritans from Newtown (Cambridge). They were led by Thomas Hooker, a fiery and energetic preacher who is commonly referred to as the "Father of Connecticut" because of his wide travels in the region and his efforts in helping to settle disputes among colonists and colonies, and because he was instrumental in the creation of the "Fundamental Orders of Connecticut," which will be discussed later.

These three towns would gain legal status from the Massachusetts Bay Colony, and while technically still under the jurisdiction of the ever-expanding MBC, they began to be referred to collectively as "the River Colony" or simply "Connecticut" with one of its various spellings.

The Warwick Patent

The legality of their towns and settlements under English law was of great importance to most of the English in the New World. With respect to the Indians, they generally satisfied their legal consciences by "buying" the land from them. A tribe would take payment, agreeing to allow the Europeans to settle land that that tribe controlled either by conquest or simple proximity to their own villages. In return, those natives would promise not to harass or hinder the Europeans. These transactions were often fraught with deceit, fraud, and sheer ignorance, but many, especially in the early days of the MBC, were made in good faith with relatively informed consent on both sides.

The procedures for obtaining legal rights to the land from their own government (i.e. the king) were better established, but the results often just as confused. Generally, once a map of territory was charted, and claim was made to it — as John Smith had done in New England (see Massachusetts) — it was up to the king to decide which of his subjects would be allowed to colonize, improve, and collect rent for the said land. In 1622, The Council of Plymouth, the king's agent in such matters, according to its own records granted, or at least intended to grant, to its president, the Earl of Warwick,

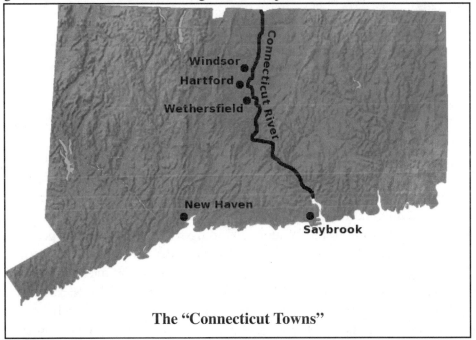

The "Connecticut Towns"

a charter for some land in southern New England. Unfortunately Warwick never produced the charter, and it has never been found.

Nevertheless in 1632 Warwick drew up a patent authorizing a group of men led by Lord Say and Seale (one person, Lord of both Say and Seale) and Lord Brooke to colonize for profit a section of land described in the patent as "...All that part of New England in Americah (sic)...from a river there called Narrogancett River, the space of Forty leagues...neere the Sea Shore towards the Sowth west..." The Connecticut River Valley was the obvious object of this patent, and two of the patentees quickly tried to claim land in Windsor, land being technically squatted on by other Englishmen. Their attempts failed miserably, the squatters claiming right to the land by possession (nine-tenths of the law and all that), and the agents of the patent holders went home empty-handed.

Another set of patent holders, however, successfully established a new colony at the mouth of the Connecticut River in 1636, naming it Saybrook after the two primary benefactors. Saybrook became the fourth major township in Connecticut and was governed initially by John Winthrop, Jr. (son of John Winthrop of the MBC, who is often referred to as the "Father of New England"). Winthrop, a restless soul in his youth, left Saybrook abruptly at the outbreak of hostilities with the Pequot but would return to a different Connecticut town a few years later and have an enormous impact on the colony's future, in fact eventually saving it from being absorbed by New York. Saybrook muddled along without him and was eventually absorbed into the River Colony, maintaining control over the lower portion of the river.

War and Orders

The Pequot War, one of the first conflicts between Indians and English settlers, began to brew in earnest with the establishment of the River Colony. The Pequots still dominated the region with respect to other Indian tribes, but the encroachment of the English brought complications, most notably the division of the Pequots regarding which group of Europeans to trade with—Dutch or English. The flashpoint for the war was the Pequot involvement in the murder of John Oldham, aforementioned founder of Wethersfield, on July 20, 1636. While Oldham was killed by Narragansett Indians, a band of Pequot harbored the murderers, and their already hostile relationship with the English intensified to all-out brutal warfare. Almost a year later, at the height of hostilities, a brutal massacre was perpetrated by a group of colonists led by Captain John Mason.* This proved the beginning of the end for the Pequot, and within a few months the whole tribe was virtually annihilated.

Partly because of the Pequot hostilities, the River Colony in 1637 set up a cursory legislature, which would provide for the defense of the three original communities. But for Thomas Hooker the need for a more formal government was of primary importance. On May 31, 1638 he delivered a famous sermon which outlined a civil government to complement the laws of the church. Later that year the River Colony adopted the Fundamental Orders of Connecticut, incorporating much of Hooker's sermon into what would now be civil law. This document is often referred to as a precursor to the U.S. Constitution, thus conferring the nickname, "Constitution State" on what was now still a loyal English colony.

New Haven

While New Haven is now indelibly associated with Connecticut, it began as a completely seperate colony. New Haven was founded in April of 1638 by a group of Puritans from Massachusetts led by John Davenport. Situated at the Indian village of Quinnipiack, New Haven from its founding maintained a separateness from the River Colony. Indeed as New Haven thrived and prospered, it added new towns—Milford, Stamford, Guilford, Branford, and Southold on Long Island—to what in 1643 was officially consolidated into New Haven Colony.

For almost two decades the Connecticut River Colony and New Haven Colony functioned independently, each a member of the short-lived New England Confederacy. The River Colony was governed by John Winthrop, Jr. who only a few years earlier had founded and then abandoned Saybrook, while New Haven thrived under the leadership of John Davenport.

The fortunes of these colonies changed with the restoration of Charles II to the English throne in 1660. Once again concerned about the legality of their colony Connecticut sent Winthrop to England to attempt to negotiate

---

*   *It is not clear if this John Mason is related to the Captain John Mason who founded New Hampshire. Some sources call him a "descendant".*

a new royal charter. Even though he was forced to admit the non-existence of the Warwick Patent, Winthrop was able to convince the King and his court of the value of Connecticut as a separate colony, especially as a foil to that thorn in the Royal side, Massachusetts, and Winthrop was granted all he asked for and more.

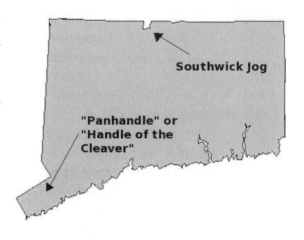

The "more" was a set of boundaries so generous and so non-specific that it created border disputes on virtually every edge of the colony. It also created a major disturbance in New Haven, because the charter empowered Connecticut to absorb New Haven completely. New Haven, especially the aging Davenport, fought bitterly to maintain its independence, but Connecticut made generous offers and slowly enticed most of the towns in New Haven into annexation. New Haven itself held out for several years, but in 1664 found itself faced with the choice of rule by Connecticut or rule by the Duke of York (James Stuart II, brother of Charles II and heir to the English throne). The duke had just been granted the territory south of Connecticut, land which the Dutch had called New Amsterdam but which had been seized by the English and renamed New York. New Haven chose Connecticut on January 5, 1665, the day the Colony of New Haven ceased to exist.

Except for the two notable exceptions below, Connecticut would do very little morphing of shape from this point on. On January 9, 1788 Connecticut, the "Constitution State," ratified the fledgling U.S. Constitution. In doing so, it became the fifth colony to join the United States.

Connecticut's Boundaries

Connecticut's borders contain two interesting anomalies. One is known as the Southwick Jog. It is a tiny notch of land which is set into the otherwise straight line that marks the border between Massachusetts and Connecticut. The jog (near Southwick, Massachusetts) has its origins in a survey performed in 1642 by Nathaniel Woodward and Solomon Saffery which was supposed to determine the border between the two colonies. The story goes that the two men surveyed about half the line, but then turned back to Boston for fear of a confrontation with Indians. They took a boat from Boston around Cape Cod and up the Connecticut River to complete their survey. When it was completed, the eastern half of the line was eight miles south of the western half, and the location of the "correct" border was now even more in dispute. The disagreement raged on for a hundred and fifty years until finally, in 1804, Connecticut agreed to a compromise that gave a tiny portion of the Congomond Lakes area to Massachusetts.

The other anomaly in Connecticut's borders is sometimes called "the handle of the cleaver," or more commonly "the panhandle." It is the result of conflicting Royal charters (go figure) for Connecticut and New York. This conflict was resolved relatively quickly in 1683, with New York conceding the panhandle to Connecticut and taking for itself a strip of land to the north, which is sometimes called "The Oblong."

---

1.   Robert C. Black III, *The Younger John Winthrop* (New York, 1966) p. 288.

Chapter 8: Delaware

Q: What did Dela Wear?
A: Her New Jersey.

> *—old riddle*

And I will see you again,
I will see you again,
a long time from now

> *— "Hello, I'm in Delaware"*
> *Dallas Green*

Obscurity

If any state suffers from obscurity, it must be Delaware. It is probably the least likely to be found on a map of the U.S. by all but the most geographically inclined Americans. Many of us, frankly, would be hard pressed to name a single city within the state, even the capital. (Dover is the capital. Wilmington is the largest.) While tiny, Delaware does not have the distinction of being the smallest state (Rhode Island), nor even the least populated (Wyoming). Delaware hosts no major sports teams and except for Delaware Bay—which it shares with New Jersey—has few recognizable landmarks to distinguish it.

If Delaware has a reputation at all it seems to have to do with the tax advantages of incorporating a business and of spending your shopping money within the state. While Delaware boasts a beautiful bay with beaches and islands, one of its most famous tourist attractions is the lack of state or local sales taxes. And for reasons that will make any non-MBA's eyes glaze over, more than half of the publicly traded companies in the U.S. have chosen Delaware as the state in which their business is incorporated.

Delaware also has the reputation of being "owned" by the Dupont family. The name appears on countless buildings, roads, and even a state park.

Kathy Guyton

Eleuthere Irenee DuPont settled near Wilmington in 1800, having emigrated from France to escape that country's revolution. Soon he became the leading supplier of gunpowder in the new United States, and over two centuries, the Dupont company has prided itself on the research and manufacturing of scientifically innovative products. It's not difficult to guess where the company is incorporated.

There is one other thing may seep into one's consciousness when thinking of Delaware—Dover, Delaware, in particular. The U.S. Air Force base there is the entry point and mortuary for all U.S. servicemen/women and some U.S. government civilians who die overseas. During the Vietnam War, television footage from Dover of flag-draped coffins being offloaded from airplanes was an almost nightly occurance and contributed to the welling dissatisfaction with the war. Because of that history, one of the many controversial issues of the Iraq War was the initial ban on any images coming out of Dover Air Force Base involving said coffins. The state may suffer from inconspicuousness but it sure knows how to involve itself in a political brouhaha.

For all of its obscurity as an American state, Delaware does boast perhaps the most eyebrow-raising superlative of them all. It was the first.

Discovering the Bay

The story of Delaware begins in the spring of 1609, when two ships went to sea. One, the *Half Moon (Halve Maan)*, sailed out of Amsterdam under the auspices of the Dutch East India Company. The other, the *Sea Venture*, was at the head of a nine-ship fleet sailing to bring badly needed provisions to the occupants of Jamestown, a struggling colony in "Virginia" (as the east coast of North America was then called on British maps).

In command of the Dutch ship was Captain Henry Hudson, an Englishman, whose instructions were to try to find a north-east passage to the "spice islands," or Southeast Asia. The *Half Moon* was commissioned specifically for this type of exploration, and this was her maiden voyage. Hudson got as far as Novaya Zemlya, a large archipelago that separates the Barents Sea from the Kara Sea inside the Arctic Circle north of Asia. Then he turned around, deciding either on his own or at the insistence of a mutinous crew, to search for a passage to the north*west* instead. By July, Hudson's ship was sailing the open waters of the Atlantic Ocean.

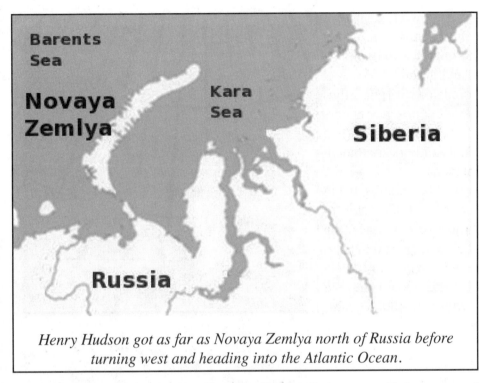

Henry Hudson got as far as Novaya Zemlya north of Russia before turning west and heading into the Atlantic Ocean.

The *Sea Venture* was captained by George Somers, a widely respected English seaman in the employ of the Virginia Company. Somers was in charge of the entire nine-ship fleet, historically called the "Third Supply," as it was intended to re-supply Jamestown with both provisions and people. Passengers on the *Sea Venture* included the new Lieutenant Governor of Jamestown, Sir Thomas Gates, as well as Pocahontas' future husband, John Rolfe.

It turns out that the summer of 1609 was a bad time to be sailing the Atlantic Ocean anywhere near North America. Fierce storms and hurricanes battered ships from Maine to Florida. Hudson's crew made multiple repairs to the *Half Moon*, including, at one point, replacing the mast. But the most famous storm was a hurricane that hit off the coast of North Carolina in late July that tossed and jostled the Third Supply fleet. One of its ships was lost, with all souls perishing. Seven others limped into the Jamestown colony with 600 or so passengers but without the necessary provisions to support them—those supplies having been lost overboard during the storm. The *Sea Venture* itself and her passengers miraculously crashed ashore on the island of Bermuda without losing a single life.

Bermuda, named for a Spanish sailor Juan Bermudez who found the island around 1503, was populated with pigs*, thus the crew and passengers of the *Sea Venture* had plenty of pork to nourish them as they spent the next nine months using scraps from their ship to build two new ones, the *Deliverance*, and the *Patience*. The adventures of those aboard the *Sea Venture* would eventually make for fascinating news back in England and would inspire William Shakespeare to pen *The Tempest*. For a few years during the 17th century, the English referred to Bermuda as "Somers' Island."

Sir George Somers.

A portrait believed to be of Admiral Sir George Somers

Meanwhile in Jamestown Colony, life was harsh. The winter of 1609 and spring of 1610 saw the deaths of nearly all of the colonists due mainly to starvation. People resorted to eating snakes and horseflesh and even to cannibalism. Historically known as "the Starving Time," as many as 600 colonists perished during these months, leaving only about 60 desperate and destitute souls.

---

* *The story of Bermuda's pigs is one in itself. When Bermudez found it, there were no humans living on the island. The Spaniards, very shortly thereafter, left twenty or so pigs on the island, though it is not clear whether that was accidental or intentional. The pigs thrived and for decades the island was used as a stop-over point for Spanish sailors to resupply their ships with pork.*

It was August 28, 1609, during the time that Somers and his passengers and crew were shipbuilding on Bermuda and Jamestown was just beginning to experience hard times, when Henry Hudson sailed into Delaware Bay, noting it on maps for future European navigation. Hudson, however, did not name the bay. One of his men described it in a journal, along with the land and the natives, as he viewed them from the *Half Moon*. But the name that we use today for the bay, the river, and the state would come from someone else entirely. Hudson continued north along the coast and eventually reached the river that now bears *his* name.

Naming the Bay

In May of 1610, Somers and his crew sailed their two rebuilt pinnaces from Bermuda on to Jamestown and found the 60 survivors of the Starving Time. After about two weeks—and still without necessary provisions—the colony's new Lieutenant Governor, Sir Thomas Gates, made the executive decision to abandon the colony. Several ships were loaded up and started down the river to Chesapeake Bay but less than twenty-four hours later, they were met by another English convoy.

Captain Samuel Argall, an experienced seaman at the helm of one of the arriving ships, instructed Somers to turn around and go back to Jamestown. A few days later Sir Thomas West, Lord de la Warr, arrived at Jamestown with a commission from the Virginia Company to take over as Governor of the colony. West and Argall began immediately creating new rules and new organization for Jamestown.

Within weeks of their arrival, Argall and Somers left Jamestown for Bermuda in order to "fetch six months' provision of flesh and fish, and some live hogs to store our colony again."[1]

Unlike Argall, Somers had recently spent the better part of a year on the island and presumably knew how to find it. But when they began to run out of food, water, and nautical "guidelines,"[2] they sailed instead for Cape Cod, where they fished and restored their provisions. The two ships headed back to Jamestown, but fog and other bad weather separated them.

Somers sailed for Bermuda, this time successfully, but before he could load up with hogs and return to Jamestown, he died of food poisoning. Many historians assert that his illness was the result of eating too much pork. This assumption comes from the journals and contemporary reports that attribute his death to a "surfeit of pork." More likely, however, is that he ate pork that had been undercooked and contracted a food-borne illness such as salmonella or trichinosis.

Meanwhile, Argall sailed south toward Jamestown. On August 27th he "came to an anchor in nine fathoms in a very great Bay," where he found a "great store of people which were very kind."[3] Argall bestowed upon the bay and river the name "Delaware" after Sir Thomas West, Lord De La Warr.

Who?

Lord De La Warr was an early investor in the Virginia Company, which provided the initial investment for the establishment of an English colony in the Americas. In 1609, when the reports reached England of dismal, anarchic conditions in the Jamestown colony, the Company outfitted the ill-fated *Sea Venture* armada and sent the aforementioned George Somers and Third Supply to restore the colony. The Company also sought and was granted by King James I a new charter, replacing the governing council of the colony (of which John Smith had, until recently, been president), with a governor-general who would have much more control. Lord De La Warr was the first to receive the title "Governor-General of Jamestown."

Though Lord De La Warr had been appointed governor for life of Virginia, he fell ill less than a year into his appointment and left the colony to return to England in March 1611. Not until 1618 did he

Sir Thomas West, 3rd (or 12th) Lord de la Warr

sail again for Virginia, and on that trip he is said to have sailed into Delaware Bay, though other reports have him going no closer to Delaware than Bermuda. It was during this voyage that Thomas West, Lord De La Warr, died of an unidentified illness.

While the "De La Warr" name lived on in England as well as in America, it is clearly associated more with Virginia than Delaware. In 1870 Delaware historian Francis Vincent wrote "Earl Delaware, who lived in England a few years ago (and probably may be yet living) is a descendant of his. All, however, that he had to do with our State, was the honor of giving us a name."[4]

And What a Name

The Surname "De La Warr" is not Spanish, as the two determiners "de" and "la" might indicate. Nor is it Latin, Anglo-Saxon, German, nor even French. Strictly speaking, it is a Viking name that can be traced back to the days before William the Conqueror invaded England in 1066. In those days northern France was inhabited by Viking descendants who had pillaged and plundered the region in the 900's and then decided to stay. These North Men, or Normans (thus, the name Normandy), were among the followers of William the Conqueror when he gained control of England, and they were rewarded with land grants and seats in parliament.

The name De La Warr (also spelled Warre, Ware, Weare, Werre, and War and often without the "De") begins to appear on census reports and land registries as early as the late 11th century. In 1125 a solid record of the lineage begins with Jordan de la Warre whose son was granted Wicken Manor in Gloucestershire by King Richard the Lionheart, and whose lordship was granted by Richard's brother, King John.

One of King John's childhood friends, it turns out, was a man named Fulk Fitzwarin. An old story goes that one day John and Fulk were playing a game of chess, and Fulk won. John angrily broke the chessboard over Fulk's head, and in retaliation Fulk punched the Prince in the stomach. When John ran crying to his father, King Henry II, about the scuffle, Henry punished *John* for being a sore loser. Years later, when John became king, he retaliated against Fulk by stripping him of his ancestral lands, and awarding them to an enemy of Fulk's. The feud between the two men lasted years, and some historians believe that Fulk Fitzwarin is the man upon whom the legend of Robin Hood is based.

Fitzwarin, it so happens, was the great-grandfather of Clarice de Tregoz who married Roger de la Warre; their descendent, Joan de la Warr was the mother of Sir Thomas West. While connecting the dots can make your head spin, and some suspension of disbelief is certainly required, the implication is that our Sir Thomas West is a direct descendant of Robin Hood.

The name *De La Warr* can be translated as "of the war" or "warrior." The removal of the spaces in the name appears to be a true Americanism. In an article for a translators' newsletter, Charles M. Stacy points out that other non-English words, when translated in America, were combined to form one word from two, three or more[5]. Besides Delaware, he cites the conversion of "Van der Straaten" to "Vanderstraaten." Another example is of course, "Dupont."

Zwaanendael, New Sweden, and Beyond

In 1631 the first attempt at colonization along the Delaware River was made by a group of Dutch settlers. They called their small village *Zwaanendael*, or "Valley of Swans," but in a dispute with local Indians that was touched off by the meaningless destruction of a coat of arms by a local native, the entire Dutch settlement was massacred. Then in 1638, a group of Swedish settlers under the leadership of Peter Minuit, a Dutchman who previously had governed New Amsterdam (see New York), established Fort Christina near present-day Wilmington. As the colony grew, it became known as New Sweden and survived until the Dutch captured it and took control in 1655. Now the settlements along the Delaware River were part of New Amsterdam, which stretched all the way up to Manhattan and was captured by the English in 1664.

In 1681 King Charles II granted William Penn his colony of Pennsylvania, and later that same year, Penn obtained from the Duke of York (Charles' brother) the counties on the south side of the Delaware River so that Pennsylvania would have a seaport. This touched off a dispute between Penn and Cecil Calvert, the 2nd Lord Baltimore, who had inherited his father's royal charter for the province of Maryland. The dispute lasted almost one hundred years, with generations of the Penn and Calvert families taking up the cause through the decades. Finally, from 1763 until 1767, the border between Pennsylvania and Maryland was surveyed by Charles Mason and Jeremiah Dixon. Now firmly under the control of Pennsylvania, the eastern portion of what today is called the "DelMarVa Peninsula" was referred to as the "Three Lower Counties."

Delaware may have been the first state, but it was the last of the thirteen colonies to be formed. Technically speaking, it wasn't even a colony. The word "colony" implies a "mother" country, or some other state supplying the colony with people and provisions. Delaware was never a recognized English colony—always a part of Pennsylvania—but in 1702, after years of discontent with their parent government, the Lower Counties were allowed by Penn to govern themselves separately from Pennsylvania, though they still acknowledged that colony's Royal governor as their own. They were called officially "The Counties of New Castle, Kent, and Sussex upon Delaware"—just "Delaware" for short—and they had their own legislative assembly.

Revolutionary rumblings were heard early in Delaware. In 1767, the same year that the Mason-Dixon survey was completed, John Dickinson wrote his famous "Letters from a Farmer in Pennsylvania," which roused anti-British sentiments and called on colonists to rebel against the Stamp Act. Dickinson's farm, as he states in the opening line of the first letter, was actually situated on the banks of the Delaware River in what is now Delaware just south of Dover.

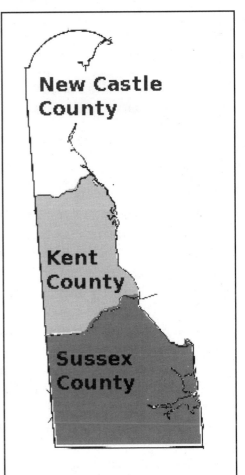

The "three lower counties" of Pennsylvania became the state of Delaware. The county names have remained the same.

On June 15th, 1776, with just one document, the Delaware Assembly declared itself separate—not only from England, but from Pennsylvania and the Penn family. "Separation Day" is still celebrated in New Castle, Delaware, every year in early June. In August of 1776 the legislature adopted a constitution that proclaimed in Article I, "The government of the counties of New-Castle, Kent and Sussex, upon Delaware, shall hereafter in all public and other writings be called The Delaware State." Eleven years later, on December 7, 1787, Delaware became the first state to ratify the U.S. Constitution, giving it its very genuine source of pride as the "First State." Five years after that, in 1792, the state would be renamed one final time in the second of Delaware's constitutions. The change from "The Delaware State" to "The State of Delaware" took the emphasis, once and for all, off of the river and gave it firmly to the people on the east side of the Mason-Dixon line.

The Delaware Indians

The name "Delaware" applies not only to the state, the river, and the bay, but to the Native Americans whose ancestors inhabited the shores of the bay in (and until) the 17th century. While Europeans who made very early contact with native tribes clearly had difficulty communicating, it was rare—in fact, almost unheard of—for such an English name to be applied to any group of Indians. Much more common was the practice of using the name of a prominent Sachem to describe the whole tribe or using a name applied by a neighboring tribe. This makes the Delaware Indians, to this day, unique.

While Americans after the Revolution became enamored with the use of aboriginal names, the early Europeans considered them heathen and preferred to apply their own. Only out of necessity did they resort to using native appellations. Thus the name "Delaware" was rather casually applied to the Indians who inhabited the banks of that river. The name was descriptive and served the purpose for the Europeans of defining a group of people with whom they began to trade eagerly.

These natives, of course, had their own name for themselves. It was "Lenape" (len-ah'-pay) or "Leni-Lenape," a name meaning simply "the people" or "the true people." Often referred to as a "grandfather" tribe among other Algonquian-speaking groups, the Lenape were sometimes called upon to negotiate peace between warring or feuding tribes. They were not migratory. They had inhabited the Delaware basin for hundreds of years prior to European contact, and their population, by best estimates, numbered some 20,000 in the late 16th century. Their numbers diminished significantly, however, due mainly to disease introduced by the white men, and by the end of the 17th century, only about four thousand remained.

The Delawares, though tenacious, chose in most cases not to fight with European settlers and were subsequently pushed westward for generations until, in 1866, they purchased a district from the Cherokee nation within the Indian Territory of Oklahoma. Most of the remaining tribe live today in and around Bartlesville and Anadarko, Oklahoma. In their own published literature is an explanation for why they continue to use the name "Delaware" to describe themselves:

> The Lenape story is that when the Europeans first arrived a white man kept trying   to ask a Lenape what tribe he belonged to, and he told him "Lenape." For some reason the white man had trouble saying the word properly, and would say "Lenuhpee," "Renahpay" and other mispronunciations. Finally he said "Lenape" correctly, and the Lenape said, "Nal në ndëluwèn! Nal në ndëluwèn!" (That's what I said! That's what I said!).

> The white man heard the DULUWEN part and he said, "Oh, you said Delaware! So you are a Delaware. Now I know what to call you," and the name stuck.

> The Delawares have used the name ever since that time because they knew that   the whites just could not say Lenape properly. Of course, when speaking to each other, Lenape people call themselves "Lenape."[6]

1.   Barbour, Philip L., <u>Pocahontas and Her World,</u> (Boston, 1969), p.76.

2.   Barbour, p.82.

3.   Barbour, p.83.

4.   Vincent, Francis, <u>A History of the State of Delaware</u> (Philadelphia, 1870), p.105.

5.   Stacy, Charles M., "Much Ado About Nothing," *The AATIA Letter*, September 1998, p. 8.

6.   Delaware Tribe of Indians, "Frequently Asked Questions about the Lenape or Delaware Tribe," http://www.delawaretribeofindians.nsn.us/faq.html, accessed 09/13/09.

Chapter 9: Florida

*Because it is evident that any recount seeking to meet the December 12
date will be unconstitutional, we reverse the judgment of the Supreme
Court of Florida ordering a recount to proceed.*

—U.S. Supreme Court, December, 2000

*—Tim Russert correctly predicted in 2000
that the election would "all come down to
Florida"*

The Debacle

Florida is the land of hanging chads and butterfly ballots. Since the
election debacle of 2000 it is a name that strikes fear into the hearts of vot-
ers and candidates alike. The presidential election that wouldn't end began
the night of November 7, 2000, a night which heard news analysts from

virtually every TV network conclude more and more confidently that "it all comes down to Florida." And indeed it did.

And down to Florida went throngs of news crews and hordes of attorneys, filling up hotel rooms at a rate generally only seen there during Spring Break. Finally, on December 13, after a stunning 5-4 decision by the Supreme Court, Al Gore conceded defeat to George W. Bush, brother of then Florida Governor Jeb Bush, after weeks of election controversy. The experience tagged Florida with a whole new reputation and colored Bush's presidency for the next four years.

Of course, before the state was saddled with this reputation, the name "Florida" conveyed many other diverse images—sun-drenched Miami Beach, Cape Canaveral and the space shuttle, the Everglades with its ferocious alligators and mosquitoes, the Keys (from the Spanish *cayos* meaning "small islands"), Dave Barry, Don Johnson, Janet Reno, Jimmy Buffet, Gloria Estefan, and, of course, Disneyworld. It is college students on Spring Break, senior citizens in retirement communities, and names of cities that all seem to be followed by either "Bay" or "Beach."

Florida is also famous for its population of Latin Americans. Dade County, which spans most of Miami, has the highest rate of immigration of any county in the United States; over half of its population are immigrants, according to the 2000 census. While the perception is that all of these immigrants come from Cuba, it turns out that people from many Central and South American countries immigrate to Miami every day. It was, in fact from Puerto Rico that Ponce de Leon set sail in 1513, eventually landing on the American mainland and bestowing on the area the name that has come to symbolize election mayhem.

Juan Ponce de Leon

Ponce de Leon

When Columbus "discovered" America, what he actually found were many of the islands in the Caribbean, as opposed to the side-of-a-barn that is the North American continent. And from 1492 to at least 1513 the exploration efforts of the Spanish and Portuguese were concentrated in these islands and on the search for a water route to the Orient. Coincidentally, in the same year (1513) two significant "discoveries" were made by Spanish explorers—Vasco Nuñez de Balboa crossed the isthmus of Panama and christened the "South Sea," or Pacific Ocean, claiming all land adjacent to it for Spain; and Ponce de Leon made his famous discovery of Florida.

For more than twenty years after Christopher Columbus' voyages there was uncertainty in Europe about the continental nature of his discoveries. Columbus himself went to his grave convinced, at least outwardly, that Cuba was a peninsula of Asia. This, of course, was disproved, as the Spanish continued to explore the islands of the West Indies. And so, when Juan Ponce de Leon went looking for the island of Bimini and the fabled "Fountain of Youth" in 1513, and instead found the continent of North America, he assumed that what he had found was another island.

Ponce de Leon was a Spanish nobleman who joined Columbus on the second of his four voyages to the New World. In 1502 he returned to Hispaniola (the island of Haiti and the Dominican Republic) and eventually was named *adelanto,* or governor of Puerto Rico. While at that post, he heard the natives talk of the island of Bimini, which reportedly contained a fountain with magical healing powers such that an old man who drank from it would regain his youth. Probably more enticing, and more believable, were the stories that the island also contained gold. Ponce obtained from King Charles V of Spain a charter to discover and settle Bimini, a charter that made him governor for life.

The most comprehensive description that survives Juan Ponce's expedition is that of Antonio de Herrera, grand historiographer of America and Castile in the early 1600s. The work is entitled "Decription of the West Indies" and is one of eight sections of a larger work entitled "Historia General de los Hechos de los Castellanos en las Islas y Tierra Firme del Mar Océano" (General History of the Deeds of the Castilians on the Islands and Mainland of the Ocean Sea) originally printed in 1601. Though Herrera's work was published ninety years after Ponce's first voyage to North America, it is considered authoritative because he, unlike other historians of that time, had access to official government documents, presumably including first-hand accounts and journals of Ponce's voyage, documents that today are lost to history.

Ponce departed Puerto Rico on March 3, 1513 with three ships. Three and a half weeks later, on March 27th—Easter Sunday in Spain, commonly called *Pascua Florida* (literally "Flowery Passover")—they sighted land. It was not uncommon in that era for Spanish explorers who discovered new territory to name it for the feast day upon which it was found. In fact, according to George R. Stewart in *Names on the Land*, at least one Spaniard sailing in 1568 along the coast of California used no other means:

> As he sailed still farther north, [Sebastian de] Viscaino showed himself wholly without imagination. He looked in the calendar, or else he asked one of his Carmelite friars, and then he named the place after the saint of that day. So, even without the log-book, a historian can trace that voyage by the names given.

And so on April 2, according to Herrera

> they anchored near shore, in 8 brazas (fathoms) of water. And thinking that this land was an island, they called it La Florida, because it was very pretty to behold with many and refreshing trees, and it was flat, and even; and also because they discovered it in the time of Flowery Passover, Juan Ponce wanted to agree in the name, with these two reasons.[1]

In 1521 Ponce de Leon wrote Charles V of his intention to return to "that island" and create a settlement. "I also intend to explore the coast of said island further, and see whether it is an island, or whether it connects with the land where Diego Velazquez is [meaning New Spain, that part of Mexico which by that time had been occupied by Cortes, discovery of which was claimed by Velazquez] or any other...I shall set out in five or six days."[2] Ponce de Leon did indeed return to Bimini and, in a fight with the natives, received a wound in his leg. He left immediately for Cuba where he died of his injury.

The Line of Demarcation

In 1493 Pope Alexander VI issued a bull (or papal decree) dividing the non-Christian world into halves. The following year the Treaty of Tordesillas was signed by Spain and Portugal, the two benefactors of the papal bull, establishing the line of demarcation at 370 leagues west of the Cape Verde Islands. Because Florida lies west of that line (i.e. in the Spanish half of the world), Spain laid claim to Ponce de Leon's discoveries, no matter if they were islands or continental. On early maps of the sixteenth century, while mapmakers were unsure of *what* Florida was, it clearly was represented as a Spanish holding. Thus, the name "Florida" applied to the North American continent even before the name "America" did*, and it is one of the few surviving names applied by those early conquistadors.

From the time of Ponce de Leon's discovery until about 1560, several Spaniards made serious attempts at establishing colonies in Florida, which is to say anywhere in the southeastern portion of the continent. One of these attempts was made by a royal judge named Lucas Vázquez de Ayllón, who received permission to settle the "land of Chicora" in the early 1520's. "Chicora" was the lyrical name taken from an Indian slave who sparked Ayllón's interest by describing his homeland (actually in what is now South Carolina) as having fertile valleys with abundant gold. Due to disease, starvation, and conflicts with natives, Ayllón's settlement was a fast failure, and "Chicora" turned out to be one in a long series of disappointments for the Spaniards in North America. The most famous of these disappointments was that of Hernando de Soto who, like others including Ayllón and Ponce de Leon, died in the attempt. Spain lost interest in settling Florida until it became clear that another country was trying to encroach on their claim.

In 1562 it was the French who finally got a foothold on the Florida coast. Jean Ribaut claimed the St. John's River for France and built a fortress, which was abandoned a year later. In 1564 the French built Fort Caroline near what is now Jacksonville, a more successful effort, and this time got the attention of the Spanish. Pedro Menendez de Aviles moved into the area with the intention of attacking the French fort and ridding Spain of the French invaders. On September 8, 1565, he established his base of op-

---

The name "America" was introduced by Martin Waldeesmuller's map of 1507, generally accepted as the first widely published map to portray the findings of Columbus, Vespucci, and Cabot as a new continent. But the name originally labeled only the southern portion of the landmass, while the northern "island" is named "Florida". Not until around 1520 did the name "America" consistently apply to both South and North America.

erations in a grand ceremony, christening his new settlement St. Augustine after the name they gave to the river upon which it was founded. The fortress would go down in history as the first permanent European settlement in what would become the United States of America. Menendez' attack on Fort Caroline was gruesomely successful, and all of the inhabitants of the French settlement were murdered at a place that would take on a Spanish name commemorating the slaughter: Matanzas—*massacre*.

Florida Natives

Once the maps began to consistently reflect North America as a continent, the area of what is now Florida, Georgia, South Carolina, Alabama and Mississippi was just as consistently shown as "Florida" or "Spanish Florida," and Spain kept a firm grip on it despite the encroachment of England, France, and later the United States. The effort came at the expense of the natives of the peninsula, who were early casualties of European exploration. During the seventeenth century the Spanish used the mission system to "pacify" the natives, but massive epidemics as well as constant conflict with the Creeks to the north contributed to the destruction of many of the missions and the decimation of the native Florida tribes—the Timucua, Ais, Calusa, Apalachee, and others who were notable for their distinct language stock.

The Seminole Indians, now so famous as the dominant Florida tribe, (not to mention namesake for the mascot of Florida State University) were actually not natives of what is now Florida. The Seminoles were actually Creeks who moved south from current Georgia and Alabama, filling the void left by the decimated Florida tribes. These Creeks migrated into Florida to avoid conflict with the increasingly difficult English settlers in South Carolina, and their numbers increased over the decades as they gave refuge to escaped slaves of African descent and to more and more Creek natives. The Indian Removal policies of the United States in the early 1800's, and the efforts by Andrew Jackson, among others, to enforce them, pushed even more Creeks into Florida. The name *Seminole* derives from the Spanish *Cimarrón* meaning "wild ones" or "free ones." The Florida Seminoles would go on to engage in some of the bloodiest battles, indeed wars, fought by any native tribe in North America in an effort to keep their Florida land.

The Incredible

Shrinking State

About twenty years after the founding of St. Augustine the English set up their colony at Jamestown in what is now Virginia and began to push southward. Almost eighty years later, La Salle would navigate the Mississippi River to its source and claim it for France. Once the

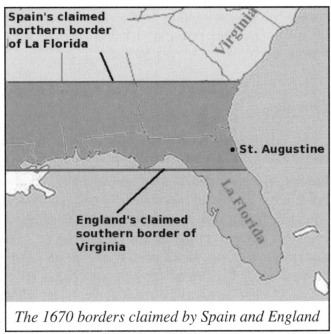

Spain's claimed northern border of La Florida

England's claimed southern border of Virginia

St. Augustine

The 1670 borders claimed by Spain and England

French settlement of New Orleans was established, Spanish Florida was no longer physically connected to Spain's dominion in Texas and the southwest.

The first diplomatic border dispute between Spain and England in North America occurred in 1670 when Spain declared the northern border of Florida to be a line running west from a point in Port Royal Sound. This would have given Spain the entire state of Georgia and the southern tip of South Carolina. England countered with its own claim, placing the southern boundary of its Carolina grant at 29 degrees north latitude, which would have consumed about a third of present day Florida, including the Spanish settlement at St. Augustine.

But if the northern boundary of Florida was fuzzy, the western boundary was even more so, in part because relations between Spain and France were friendly, based on a mutual desire to drive the English off of the North American continent. When La Salle made his attempt in 1685 at placing a French settlement at the mouth of the Mississippi, the Spanish attempted to intercept and stop him (they need not have bothered, as the effort was doomed to failure); but, when Pierre le Moyne Sieur d'Iberville planted a French settlement first at Biloxi, then at Mobile, the Spanish—rather than try to thwart the attempt—were simply relieved that they were so far west of Spain's tenuous position at Pensacola and remained friendly with the French at Mobile for twenty years.[3]

Floridas

Borders were finally established when the British obtained Spanish Florida at the Treaty of Paris in 1763, which ended the Seven Years War in Europe. In one proclamation on October 7, 1763, the English established borders for its new territory and divided it in two. East Florida's northern boundary began at the confluence of the Chattahoochee and the Flint Rivers, went due east to the headwaters of the St. Mary's, and then followed that river to the Atlantic Ocean. West Florida was bordered on the north by the 31st parallel, on the west by the Mississippi River, and on the east by the Chattahoochee down to the Appalachicola, and down the Appalachicola to the Gulf of Mexico. The legacy of this division today is the jag in Florida's northern border where it meets the Chattahoochee River, the same river that marks Georgia's western border. Though these borders would change and be disputed, they closely reflect the current borders for the state of Florida.

One of the most hotly contested border disputes in U. S. history began when, in 1764, Great Britain rather innocently moved the northern border of West Florida from 31° to 32°28' in order to include in the new territory the Natchez district, which was situated in what would become Mississippi. Making this change was a simple formality at the time, because Britain was the recognized "owner" (assuming, of course, that you weren't asking the Creek Indians) of the land both north and south of the changed border. But when the Floridas were ceded back to Spain after the American Revolution in 1783, ambiguous references were made to the northern border in the Treaty of Paris, and so Spain and the United States disputed its placement. The West Florida controversy (see Mississippi) would continue until the signing of the Adams-Onis treaty in 1821, in which Spain ceded the Floridas to the United States.

It was while Florida still belonged to Spain, however, that its eventual borders were finally settled. According to Florida historian Charlton A. Tebeau

" ...When Louisiana became a state in 1812 the eastern boundary was fixed at the Iberville River. In that same year Governor Holmes organized the region between the Iberville and the Perdido as a county of the Mississippi Territory. Though still referred to as East and West Florida and having separate governments, the boundaries of the once extensive Spanish La Florida had now been reduced to the limits of present-day Florida."[4]

Once the United States gained control of Florida one might think the boundaries of the new territory would be more easily settled. But in fact they became perhaps even more complicated with the creation of "Middle Florida" and contentions by some that the entirety of Florida should enter the Union as two or even three states. Some Floridians also maintained that parts of Florida should be annexed by Georgia and/or Alabama, and both of those states extended invitations for Florida to do just that. These disputes continued for some thirty years until the matter was eventually resolved on March 3, 1845, when Florida, borders intact and all the parts of the territory united, became the 27th state to join the United States of America. President John Tyler signed the statehood resolution on the last day of his presidency.

Kathy Guyton

1.   Kelley, James E., Jr., "Juan Ponce de Leon's Discovery of Florida: Herrera's Narrative Revisited," <u>Revista de Historia de America</u> [Mexico] 1991 (111): 31-65.

2.   Weddle, Robert S., <u>Spanish Sea: The Gulf of Mexico in North American Discover 1500-1685</u>, (College Station, 1985), p. 48.

3.   Tebeau, Charlton W., <u>A History of Florida</u>. [Coral Gables, 1971] p. 62.

4.   Tebau, p. 105.

Chapter 10: Georgia

Georgia...Georgia...the whole day through
Just an old, sweet song keeps Georgia on my mind.

> —*"Georgia On My Mind"*
> *Ray Charles*

War, war, war! This war talk's spoiling all the fun at every party this
spring.

> —*Vivien Leigh as Scarlett O'Hara in "*Gone
> With the Wind*"*

The Heart of the South

We see cotton plantations, hear thick, drawling accents, and think of hot, humid summer days and nights and people who are accustomed to them. Georgia is the "Gone With the Wind" state. It's the deep South, conveying images of peaches, peanuts, mint juleps, and the wide, winding staircase at Tara. Images of the Civil War are, in general, dirty, ugly, bloody and depressing, which is perhaps as it should be, and thanks to Margaret Mitchell and David O. Selznick, we have images of the Civil War in Georgia also as a romantic drama, a majestic, epic adventure of human tragedy and triumph.

While the state of Georgia may be quintessentially southern, it also seems the most cosmopolitan of the southern states, due mainly to

Vivien Leigh as Scarlett O'Hara

its largest city, Atlanta. When we're not thinking of Atlanta burning, or Vivien Leigh walking through it as she tends to hundreds of wounded soldiers, we think of Atlanta with highrises, the nation's busiest International airport, the Braves' baseball team, and CNN.

There is also, of course, another Georgia—the one in Eastern Europe. The Republic of Georgia is situated in between the Black and Caspian Seas, bordered on the south by Turkey and Armenia, on the west by Azerbaijan, and on the north by Russia. This Georgia, which has been so called since at least the 5th century A.D., is said to have taken its name from either Saint George, a martyr who is said to have been killed three times, only to be brought back to life each time by the power of God, or from the Greek word *georgos* which means "tiller of the soil." The state, on the othe hand, was definitely named for a British monarch.

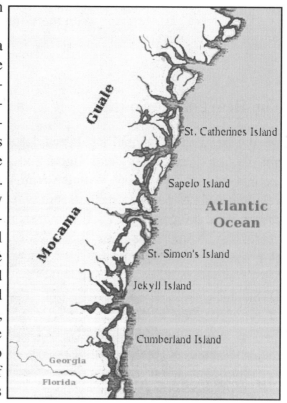

The country of Georgia is about half the size of the American state but has approximately the same population. Interestingly, the Republic of Georgia straddles the Caucasus Mountains, the origin of the Caucasian race. This race, while technically referring to a tribe originating from this relatively small region, has historically come to refer to the entire world population of white-skinned people. How ironic, then, that the U.S. state of the same name as this region is home to the largest U.S. population of African-Americans, which is to say black-skinned people, in the nation.

Guale and Mocama

Georgia was the last of the twelve original colonies[*] to be formed by England and populated by immigrants coming directly from Europe. Chartered in 1732, one hundred and twenty-six years after the first charter of Virginia, Georgia had actually flirted with European colonization long before Jamestown was founded in 1608. But not by the English. In the late 1500's the French and Spanish were clashing on the coast of La Florida as far north as current South Carolina. By 1606 Spanish missionaries had built a series of missions on the coastal islands of Georgia with names more reminiscent of the coast of California than that of Georgia: Santa Catalina, San Buenaventura, San Jose, and San Pedro.

The Georgia coast was roughly divided into two districts by the Spanish. The northern section was called Guale, pronounced "WA-lee," a name which was taken from the island the Spanish labeled Santa Catalina—Guale was the name of the most powerful chief on the island, and the Spanish also used it to refer to the tribe. The southern coast of Georgia was called by the Spanish "Mocama" after the dialect spoken by those natives.

In 1597 a disastrous uprising that resulted the destruction of the missions, took the lives of several Franciscan missionaries in the Guale and Mocama districts. The revolt was termed the "Juanillo" uprising after its rebellious Indian leader. Spain retaliated by destroying native villages, and years of attacks and reprisals followed. Juanillo was eventually killed, and the Spanish authorities felt they had their revenge. They rebuilt, to some extent, the missions of the region, but this never led to Spanish colonization, and the region remained a contested but unsettled zone between the Spanish stronghold of St. Augustine in La Florida and the new English colony of Virginia.

Azilia and Georgina

In 1663 King Charles II created the colony of Carolina just south of Virginia. Initially the borders of the new colony were relatively modest, but two years later they were expanded. Now the southern border of Carolina, by the English definition, engulfed St. Augustine in La Florida. The Span-

---

[*] *The thirteenth colony was Delaware, which was technically part of Pennsylvania until just before theAmerican Revolution.*

ish were understandably alarmed, but the land was still unsettled, and while tensions mounted there were no open hostilities between the two colonies. In 1670 Charles Town (Charleston) was founded in southern Carolina and quickly began to flourish. Now the issue of settling the lands to the south in order to provide protection for Charles Town against both the Spanish and the Indians grew far more important.

Ideas for a separate colony began in earnest around 1700. Carolinians wanted a colony of "farmer-soldiers" who could both make a profit on the land and serve as protection for themselves. Needless to say, while land grants for colonization were coveted, the conditions and the region available were not considered prime, and technically the land was under the ownership and control of the Carolina proprietors (see North and South Carolina). Still, there were interested parties.

The first person to offer a solution was a Scottish baron named Sir Robert Montgomery. In 1717 he proposed the establishment of a colony with himself as governor, but allowing the Carolina proprietors to keep their property rights. Montgomery wanted only the title of governor-for-life and the chance to engage colonists in cultivating silk, wine, olives, raisins, almonds and currants. Montgomery painted quite a rosy picture of the prospects for this new English colony, one which he would call the Margravate of Azilia.

A margravate is, by definition, a border colony or county, military in nature. The word is of German derivation, describing the lands held by a margrave, or nobleman in medieval Germany, who was appointed the task of defending his homeland's borders. Azilia has been called both "a fanciful name of unknown origin" and "a Mesolithic European culture." (While the real definition is elusive, the word is used today as a popular Internet directory.) Montgomery's plans for Azilia were detailed but perhaps a bit too ambitious. Neither he nor the Carolina proprietors could afford the scheme, and the three-year time limit on the establishment of Azilia expired.

Another proposal, made by Jean Pierre Purry in 1724, also failed for lack of financing. A Swiss wine merchant, Purry hoped to develop exactly what the Carolinians wanted—a colony of Swiss farmers who would also act as soldiers to protect the border. He proposed the name "Georgina" in honor of George I, the Hanoverian King of England. While "Georgina" never materialized, Purry did succeed in establishing a small settlement in modern South Carolina, which he called Purrysburg. This colony eventually failed and disappeared from the map, but Purry is forever credited with his enthusiastic advertising of Carolina in his homeland of Switzerland, instigating what would become known as "Rabies Carolinae" or "Carolina Fever."

The colony of Georgia would be created within the next decade, and would serve a purpose very different from those of these initial attempts.

Oglethorpe

The undisputed founder of Georgia was James Edward Oglethorpe, though under closer inspection the idea for the colony may have originated with any of a number of Oglethorpe's colleagues. A member of the House of Commons, Oglethorpe had from 1724 led a fairly undistinguished parliamentary career. But he was moved to action when a dear friend, Robert Castell, died in 1728 in Fleet prison where he had been incarcerated as a debtor. Oglethorpe succeeded in instigating an investigation

General James Edward Oglethorpe

which led to the prosecution of some of the worst prison wardens, but that wasn't enough for Oglethorpe. Working with a philanthropist named Dr. Thomas Bray, he and several associates applied for, and were granted, a colonial charter in 1732 which would be charitable in nature. The idea was to create a place where debtors could be sent, rather than to prison, in the hopes of starting a new life.

The history of this charter and of Oglethorpe's motivations has led to an extremely defensive posture by many Georgia historians. The reputation of the colony as one that was begun by prisoners—thieves, murderers, etc.—has led author after author to deny the allegation unequivocally. They are, in fact, correct in their denials. By the time the charter was granted and colonization began, the focus had indeed changed somewhat. No longer would this be a place for incarcerated debtors; instead it would be home to the "deserving poor." The colony's Trustees chose carefully the first group of settlers who sailed for Georgia in November 1732, and there is no evidence (though evidence has indeed been sought) that there were any convicts among them.

King George II

Oglethorpe named his colony for his king. Britain was ruled by four Georges from 1714 to 1830, all known for their Hanoverian origins and for their seemingly hereditary penchant for passionately hating their respective fathers.

The George that Georgia was named for was King George II who reigned from 1727 to 1760. An accomplished soldier, George II was the last British monarch to lead troops into battle and later survived a threat to his power by Bonnie Prince Charlie, the last of the Stuarts to attempt to reclaim the British throne. George II's eldest son Frederick (with whom he shared a mutual contempt) died without ever assuming the throne, and so in 1760 the monarchy passed to Frederick's son, George III, perhaps the most famous of the Georges and the one who ruled the longest.

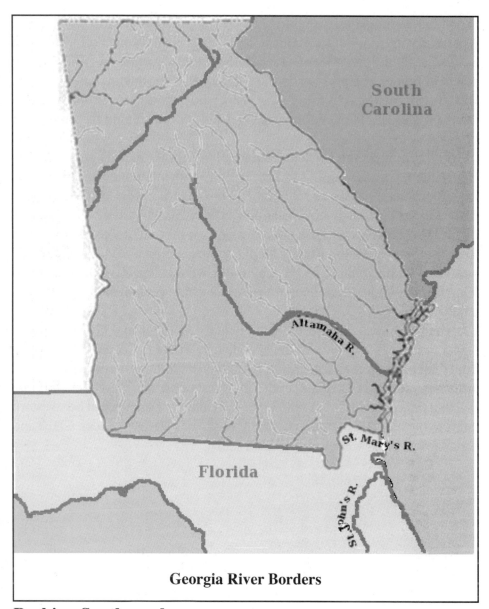

Georgia River Borders

Pushing Southward

While Georgia's northern border was, from the colony's birth, the Savannah River, her southern border was always vague and changing and would not be firmly settled until after the American Revolution. By the time the colony's initial charter was granted South Carolina had divided from the north, and become a Royal province under the control of the monarchy and no longer answerable to its now defunct proprietors. This made it easier for the king to determine borders and to simply slice off a chunk of South Carolina, call it Georgia, and bestow it on Oglethorpe. The original southern border of Georgia was the Altamaha River, though that limitation was virtually ignored by early Georgians who eagerly moved south, establishing trade with the Creek Indians and further threatening the Spanish in Florida.

In 1763, after the French and Indian War, East Florida was ceded to England, making Georgia's southern boundary an internal government matter rather than an international one. The southern border of Georgia was placed at the St. John's River near present-day Jacksonville, but after complaints from the new English governor of East Florida, it was moved north to the St. Mary's. Like virtually all of the other English colonies, Georgia's western border extended all the way to the Mississippi River, even though King George III had forbidden trans-Appalachian settlement by a 1763 decree.

Georgia's delegates to the Continental Congress in 1776 were eager signers of the Declaration of Independence. After the American Revolution, which saw some of its most brutal guerilla fighting in the three southernmost colonies, Georgia was the fourth state to ratify the Constitution, which it did on January 2, 1788. Four years later the state ceded her western lands to the federal government, firmly fixing her western border. Once and for all her borders were firmly settled.

Chapter 11: Hawai'i

Dreams come true in Blue Hawaii...

> — *"Blue Hawaii"*
> *Bing Crosby*

"Book him, Danno."

> —*Jack Lord as Steve McGarrett in*
> "Hawaii 5-O"

Island Paradise

On December 7, 1941, a date which has, as predicted, lived in infamy, Hawaii was not a state. It was a U.S. possession with territory status—much like the U.S. Virgin Islands or Guam today—which contained an excellent harbor that the U.S. had acquired while the islands were still a sovereign kingdom. In the American lexicon, "Pearl Harbor" is not so much a place as an event. For most of us the story of Pearl Harbor begins on the morning of December 7, as if the harbor and the naval base magically appeared on the planet on that date, just in time to be destroyed by Japanese fighter planes.

Morbidly ironic for the purposes of this book is that the Navy named its battleships (the primary targets of the Japanese on that day) after U.S. states, and so most of the ships damaged or destroyed that day had state names: The U.S.S. West Virginia, U.S.S. Arizona, U.S.S. Tennessee, etc. The attack on Pearl Harbor was, of course, monumental in American history; it is one of those rare events that, thanks in part to blockbuster motion pictures, even the most historically challenged of Americans is acquainted with. But the history of the islands themselves remains somewhat obscure.

Of course, when we think of Hawaii it is not usually in the context of something as academic as the study of history. What comes to mind first is "paradise"--warm beaches with gentle breezes, leis and hula dances, exotic vacations in a tropical haven, and totally awesome surfing. But Hawaii is actually rich in native culture. Its isolated location and unique cultural demographic allow travelers to feel as if they've escaped to a far away land, and with a 1,625 mile distance between the islands and the US mainland, they have. Tell someone you're going to Hawaii for a business trip, and you may get laughed at. Tell someone you live there, and make those listening swoon with envy.

It is, perhaps, unfortunate that the state most associated with pleasure and beauty was also the site of one of the most tragic events in our nation's history.

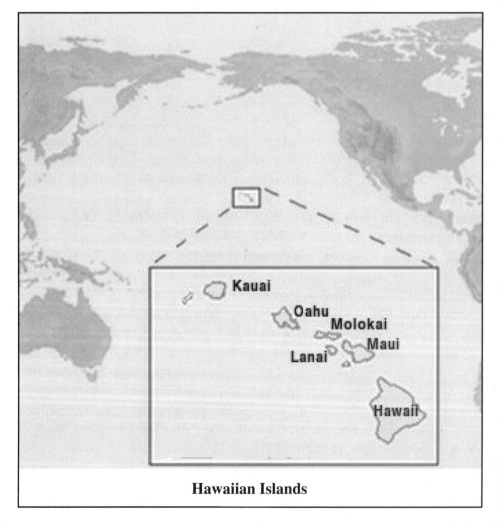

Hawaiian Islands

A Place of Origin

Hawaii is the northernmost archipelago of the Polynesian islands, which include New Zealand and Easter Island. Researchers continue to debate theories about how exactly the islands became populated, but there is consensus on some points. It is generally agreed that hundreds of years before James Cook found Hawaii—a dominant theory suggests around A.D. 350-400—Polynesian sailors from other islands, probably the Marquesas, discovered and settled the islands and formed their own society. It is not clear whether they came intentionally or accidentally or how many people constituted the original settlement, but archaeological as well as language and cultural studies link Hawaii's earliest residents to other Polynesian societies.

The name "Hawai'i" was the word the natives used to identify their home island to early European explorers. The apostrophe represents a glottal stop, a sound made by cutting, and then resuming, the sound of the vowel, as in "uh-oh." This diacritic, called an *'okina* in the Hawaiian language, has historically been somewhat ignored by English writers and speakers, presumably because of the absence of such a marking or speech pattern in our own language. But its absence produces *Hawaii*, which contains the phonetically awkward double *i*, so the 'okina never completely disappeared from the Anglicized version of the word. The "w" in the native language can produce either a "w" or "v" sound when following an "a" making either "Hawai'i" or "Havai'i" a correct pronunciation.

The word "Hawai'i" is believed to be related to "Hawaiki," which is used by natives of New Zealand, the Maori (who share cultural as well as linguistic similarities with Hawaiians), to describe their place of origin, though not necessarily a literal place. The word may mean a specific place or simply the concept of origin.[1] Another theory, based on Hawaiian tradition, holds that the word "Hawaiiloa" was the name of the fisherman who first discovered the islands.

The Hawaiian people had names for all of the islands in the chain, but there was no central government for all of them before contact with Europeans—only feudal societies with local chiefs who periodically warred with each other to gain territory and power. The origins of the names for the islands is not clear, but a common theory is that most, like Maui and Oahu, were named for gods or demi-gods by their earliest inhabitants.

117

An alternate spelling of the state's name, "Owhyhee," was used in the journals of early explorers and survived for decades as a popular method for representing the word. A county in southern Idaho uses this spelling, having been named in honor of three Hawaiian fur trappers who were lost (one was killed, the other two disappeared) in that region in 1819 while trapping game along a section of the Snake River.

Sandwich

The Hawaiian Islands first came onto the international scene during the American Revolution. British Captain James Cook was sailing to the western coast of North America, looking for a water route across the continent, when he stumbled upon

**John Montagu,
4th Earl of Sandwich, 1783**

the tiny island chain. He went ashore on the big island on January 21st, 1778, and was greeted with the curious admiration of some of the island chiefs. Cook was impressed with the beauty of the place, and in his journal several days later he named the islands for his benefactor, Sir Edward Montagu, the Fourth Earl of Sandwich, who presided over the Board of Admiralty back in London and had been instrumental in assigning this voyage to Cook. Cook wrote:

> Of what number this newly-discovered Archipelago consists, must be left for future investigation. We saw five of them, whose names, as given by the natives, are Woahoo [Oahu], Atooi [Kauai], Oneeheow [Niihau], Oreehoua [Lehua], and Tahoora [Kaula]...I

named the whole group the Sandwich Islands, in honor of the Earl of Sandwich.[2]

At the same time that John Montagu, the fourth Earl of Sandwich, was lending his name to these new-found Polynesian islands, he was also lending it to a new food, or rather, a new way of eating his preferred food--salt beef between two slices of bread. The story goes that Montagu was an insatiable gambler who would frequently sit at a gaming table for many hours at a time. So as not to interrupt a run of luck, he began asking for his food to be served between slices of bread so that he could hold his meal in one hand, his cards in the other. Others who gambled with him, presumably just as dedicated to their vice and just as hungry, began asking for the "same as Sandwich," and thus the name of the new culinary contrivance emerged, and the "sandwich" became wildly popular.

In fact, while the name "Sandwich" as applied to the islands (which admittedly conjures up strange images of sandwiches hanging from palm trees or islands between two slices of bread) would fade in time to be replaced with an indigenous title, the name of the food has become ubiquitous, especially in the U.S. Quiznos, Schlotzky's, and Subway can all thank John Montagu for his invention, as can school children worldwide who now have a place to put their peanut butter and jelly.

Cook

Cook and his crew (which, incidentally, included George Vancouver, who would eventually lend his name to Vancouver Island in Canada, as well as William Bligh, who would in later years captain the ship *Bounty* and survive one of the most famous mutinies in naval history) left the islands after only a few days in order to complete their mission. They sailed up the Pacific Coast all the way to Alaska and satisfied themselves that the Northwest Passage did not exist. Then they headed back to the Sandwich Islands.

A year after they first set eyes on the islands, the crews of Cook's two ships, the *Discovery* and the *Resolution*, studied the shores of the Big Bsland of Hawaii for several weeks before finally weighing anchor at Kealakekua Bay on January 17, 1779. They took advantage of their time there, loading up with provisions, engaging in trade with the Hawaiian men, and fraternizing with the women. Among those natives who came aboard to trade was

Captain James Cook

Kamehameha, the nephew of a local chief. Kamehameha would eventually use the metal tools and weapons that he acquired by trading with the Europeans to achieve power over all of the islands.

The British sailors set sail for home in February of 1779 but were quickly turned back after an intense storm caused severe damage to one of the ships. But for that storm, Cook might have lived to reap the rewards that his discovery warranted but instead he was doomed to die in the place he had dubbed "the Sandwich Islands." The natives, who had earlier deified the British explorer as a god of the harvest, resented being enslaved in the repair of Cook's ship. (Imagine!) This caused increasing tensions, which were exacerbated by the theft by Hawaiians of one of Cook's smaller boats. Cook went ashore to try to affect the return of the stolen craft by kidnapping a local chief and holding him hostage, but his tactic backfired, and he was stabbed to death in a confused, bloody clash with the island natives.[3] Cook's crew limped home, the discovery of this beautiful new land now bittersweet.

After Cook

After word of Cook's discovery spread, the Sandwich Islands began to appear on maps in Europe and around the world. Meanwhile, on the

King Kamehameha I of the Hawaiian Islands

islands, Kamehameha used the weapons and boat obtained from the white explorers to expand his reign, conquering virtually the entire chain of islands. He was now recognized as King of Hawaii to the island population and King of the Sandwich Islands to international observers.

Most historians portray Kamehameha as a wise and pragmatic ruler who guided his people into the perilous new world of American and European domination. Others maintain he was somewhat greedy and had a weakness for the luxuries with which he was bribed by white traders. What is certain is that during his rule, with increasing exposure to the rest of the world via merchant ships, the Hawaiian population began to decline dramatically. Rampant infections—including venereal disease and a devastating cholera epidemic in 1804—as well as the oppressive sandalwood trade which effectively enslaved thousands of natives, were among the causes of death for over 100,000 Hawaiians by the time of the king's own death in 1819.

Almost immediately after Cook found them, American interest in the Sandwich Islands was strong. While French, British, Portuguese, and other nations pursued a relationship with the islands, it was American businessmen to whom Kamehameha granted the sandalwood monopoly, and it was Americans who came as protestant missionaries in 1820 to evangelize and "civilize" the natives of Hawaii. The influence that these businessmen and missionaries wielded among the monarchs of the Hawaiian Kingdom can hardly be overstated, but their motives, in many cases, were suspect. White men familiar with international commerce wanted to monopolize, and eventually to own, the natural resources of this tropical paradise, and they clashed constantly with the few white Americans and Europeans who had the real interests of the Hawaiian people at heart. For a hundred years, from the time of Kamehameha I until the downfall of the monarchy in the 1890's, white men with varying motives served as royal ministers and advisers, and in 1840 they were instrumental in the passage of the first Hawaiian Constitution.

During those political power struggles, Hawaii had something of a dual identity. While the name "Sandwich Islands" had been widely used by those outside the islands, it never caught on within the kingdom, where "Hawai'i" or "Hawaiian Islands" was much more common. According to an article by Russell Clement in the Hawaiian Journal of History, it was the 1840 constitution that marked the beginning of the end for the name "Sandwich Islands":

> Officially, then, the 1840 constitution named the islands the Hawaiian Islands. The 1842 constitution reinforced the name and later laws and constitutions consistently follow the 1840 precedent. After 1840, the name Sandwich Islands was slowly replaced by the name Hawaiian Islands.[4]

Americans

In 1876 the U.S. signed a reciprocity agreement with King David Kalakaua of the Hawaiian Islands. With this treaty heavy tariffs were removed from imported Hawaiian sugar produced on Hawaiian plantations. In return, the United States received an excellent still-water harbor on the island of Oahu, which the Hawaiians called Pearl Harbor. Now the land owners in Hawaii, largely naturalized Americans, were more powerful than ever, and cries for annexation to the U.S. became loud and frequent. In 1887 King Kalakaua was forced, under threat of an armed uprising, to sign what is historically called the "Bayonet Constitution" which deprived him, and thus the native Hawaiian people, of much of their political power.[5]

The last Hawaiian monarch, Queen Lili'uokalani, Kalakaua's sister, attempted to curtail some of the power of the American landowners, only to find herself herself surrounded by intimidated cabinet ministers and an il-

Queen Lili'uokalani, last monarch of the kingdom of Hawaii

legally deployed U.S. military. She was forced to yield her authority to the Americans in a relatively bloodless revolution in 1893. A provisional government was established with Sanford B. Dole (yes, the Dole of pineapple fame) as president, and soon the process of annexation by the United States was officially underway. It was temporarily stalled when President Grover Cleveland discovered the coercion, backed by U.S. naval forces, which had forced the Queen's abdication, but the power wielded by annexationists both inside and outside of Hawaii was strong, and Cleveland was unable to assist the queen in regaining her throne.

In 1894 Sanford Dole established the "Republic of Hawaii" and declared himself president. The following year a futile attempt to take back the kingdom for the Hawaiian monarchy ended in violence and bloodshed, and Queen Lili'uokalani was arrested for treason and imprisoned at Iolani Palace in Honolulu for nine months.

In 1898, in a flurry of imperialism, the new president of the United States, William McKinley, and the expansionist Congress annexed Hawaii--as well as Puerto Rico, Cuba and the Philippines. Hawaii was named an official U.S. Territory, and Sanford Dole was appointed governor.

Statehood

"Mr. Vice President," spoke President Franklin D. Roosevelt on December 8, 1941. He continued solemnly, "Mr. Speaker, members of the Senate and the House of Representatives: yesterday, December 7th, 1941—*a date which will live in infamy*—the United States of America was suddenly and deliberately attacked by naval and air forces of the Empire of Japan."

The speech was prescient and inspired. The date has, in fact, lived on in infamy. Several generations after the attack, December 7th is still observed as Pearl Harbor Day, though decades after our nation's vilification of Japan, relations with that country have been normalized and become even congenial and respectful.

At the risk of nitpicking, however, it wasn't technically the United States of America that was attacked by the Empire of Japan. Certainly it was our military forces, our naval base, and our territorial holdings that were devastated by those Japanese bombs and bullets. But that naval base wasn't in the United States at the time of the attack. Pearl Harbor was in Hawaii, and Hawaii wasn't a state.

It was a U.S. territory that had been struggling for statehood for over forty years. That struggle would continue for another seventeen years after the attack on Pearl Harbor, and it would be filled with ironies.

Among the most vocal proponents for statehood within the islands were Hawaii's Asian citizens[6] who wanted more local control over their government. The Asian population was quite large, much larger than the white population, and was composed mostly of Japanese who had been (or were descended from those who had been) imported as labor for the sugar plantations in the 1800's.

Opposing statehood were the very whites who had affected annexation in the first place. Under territory rule these plantation owners, much like the railroad owners on the mainland, received political perks and spoils from appointed governors and judges. After statehood those officials would be elected by the people of Hawaii, and the powerful white land owners would, no doubt, lose the favoritism they enjoyed. Ironically, joining the plantation owners against statehood were an active segment of the native population who wished, more and more futilely, for a return to sovereignty. There is, to this day, a vocal outcry by some native Hawaiians protesting the forced colonization and annexation of the islands by the U.S.

In Congress, biases against statehood hinged primarily on the unwillingness to add such a largely non-Caucasian population to the union. Before and during World War II, this bias was specifically directed at the Japanese Hawaiians whose loyalties were questioned. This racial bias was especially strong following the bombing of Pearl Harbor, after which martial law was imposed upon the islands for three years. Shortly after the war, the concern was directed more toward the growing Communist party in the islands, who were striving hard for fair labor practices for the plantation workers.

After years of machinations by powerful business, political, and military interests, Hawaii was inducted as the 50th state in the union. Dwight D. Eisenhower signed the admission bill on August 21, 1959, a date that is commemorated within the islands with a state holiday every third Friday in August.

1.   "Origins of Hawaii's Names," Hawaii School reports, http://www.hawaiischoolreports.com/symbols/origins.htm, 12/16/03.

2.   Clement, Russell, "From Cook to the 1840 Constitution: The Name Change from Sandwich to Hawaiian Islands," *The Hawaiian Journal of History*, vol. 14, 1980, p. 50.

3.   Dougherty, Michael, To Steal a Kingdom: Probing Hawaiian History (Island Style Press, Waimanalo, 1992) p. 29-41

4.   Clement, p. 53.

5.   Dougherty, pp. 161-162.

6.   Smyser, A. A., "Campaigners for Hawaii's Statehood," *Honolulu Star Bulletin*, March 11, 1999, http://starbulletin.com/1999/03/11/editorial/smyser.html, 7/12/03.

Chapter 12: Idaho

You know, you're gonna have to face it
You're addicted to spuds.

> — *"Addicted to Sputds"*
> *Weird Al Yankovic*

You're living in your own Private Idaho

> —*"Private Idaho"*
> *The B-52's*

An Unusual State of Mind

"The name Idaho induces an unusual state of mind," writes one state historian, who goes on to describe how the word "conjures up visions of openness and vastness, with continually recurring manifestations of nature's versatility."[1] Okay, yeah, and POTATOES.

No matter how gnuine the natural versatility and vast beauty of Idaho is, people hear the state's name and think of a big, brown Russet Burbank potato or perhaps a long, hot MacDonald's french fry. Idaho's association with potatoes is well deserved. The state accounts for over a third of all potatoes grown in the United States each year and lends its name to the most dominant frozen potato products company on the planet--Ore-Ida Foods, Inc. The state's leading agricultural industry was begun by a community of Mormon settlers who moved north from Salt Lake City in 1860 and believed themselves to still be within the borders of Utah. By 1876 these industrious farmers, who by this time were clearly and unapologetically within Idaho Territory, were shipping millions of pounds of potatoes to mining camps all over the west. The region maintained its spud dominance, and to this day Idaho symbolizes the potato industry.

The other strong association with the name Idaho is perhaps an unfortunate one. Besides Boise, one of the most recognizable Idaho place names is Ruby Ridge, a tiny, secluded homestead in the northern mountains. The 1992 confrontation there between the FBI and the reclusive family of Randy Weaver—which led to the shooting deaths of one FBI agent as well as Weaver's wife Vickie, and their 14-year-old son Sam—thrust into the national spotlight a relatively new aspect of Idaho's reputation. It turns out that one of the last regions of the United States to be penetrated and settled by whites had become a haven for white-supremacist groups, often survivalist and paramilitaristic in nature. Idaho is now known worldwide as the U.S. state with a disproportionate population of reclusives ranging from those mildly skeptical of government to extremists who are often belligerently racist and paranoid.

Some people, when they think of Idaho, think first of its odd shape. One historian calls it a "geographical monstrosity," while another quotes *Idaho Statesman* editor John Corlett: "When the great planners in Washington finally got through breaking things up, they left us with a crazy patchwork of a state." While more than half the state is south of Montana, Idaho has a short (about forty-four mile) border with Canada, shorter even than that of Vermont. The state's northeastern border follows the crest of the Bitterroot Mountains, which appear on the map to consume all but a southern sliver of Idaho. It sort of makes you wonder where they find enough farmland to grow all those potatoes.

Bitterroots

In 1805, Lewis and Clark named the Bitterroot Mountains after a small, pink flower, the bitter roots of which were boiled and eaten by local natives. After crossing those mountains into what is now Idaho, the Corps of Discovery passed from the region of the Louisiana Purchase into land which was not only nameless but mysterious. It was one of a dwindling number of areas on Earth that remained unexplored and unmapped by white

Captain Merriwether Lewis and "Captain" William Clark

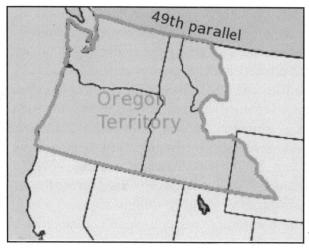

men, though the U.S., Spain and England all laid claim to it.

Great Britain, who held perhaps the strongest international claim, labeled the land "Nova Albion" or "New Albion"— *Albion* being an ancient Celtic name for England—based on maps and journals from Sir Francis Drake's 1577 voyage. Lewis and Clark would soon learn that British explorers traded occasionally from their ships with the natives on the Pacific coast, but had not ventured inland. Spain considered the region part of California, but the Spanish missions on the Pacific Coast extended only as far north as San Francisco Bay, and the days of Spanish exploration and colonization were waning fast. One of the driving reasons for the Lewis and Clark expedition was to lay firm U.S. claim to the enigmatic land that today we casually refer to as the "Pacific Northwest."

The Bitterroot Mountains, the most formidable obstacle faced by the Corps of Discovery, are the historical homeland of the Nez Percé Indians, so named by the French who erroneously believed that tribal members traditionally pierced their noses. Beginning with their contact with Lewis and Clark, the Nez Percé continued for several decades to have peaceful relations with the governments of the U.S. and Great Britain, those two nations having agreed in 1818 to joint occupation of what was becoming more commonly known as "Oregon Country." Of course, "occupation" may be an overstatement, as the craggy, towering mountains of the Idaho panhandle remained intimidating to most white travelers and settlers.

But that intimidation would not last. By the mid-1800's, trappers and loggers discovered the rich resources of those forbidding mountains and found ways to harvest them. While the white population remained sparse, it became clear to the natives as well as to the government that more and more settlers would begin to discover the natural wealth of the region.

In 1846 the Oregon Treaty oficially divided the Oregon Country between Britain and the U.S., extending the U.S./Canada border along the 49th parallel all the way to the Pacific, the U.S. taking the southern section, and Britain the north. Almost immediately the U.S. government began pursuing treaties with the Nez Percé Indians and other tribes of the region to purchase most of the land. When Oregon Territory was created by Congress in 1848 it included the current states of Washington, Oregon, and Idaho. In 1855 the Nez Percé were encouraged to move with other regional tribes to the Umatilla reservation to the southwest, but the tribe indicated that they wished to remain in their ancestral homeland. The Territorial governor agreed to "let" them stay in return for their surrender of about 13 million acres.

By this time in 1860, Mormon settlers began to build communities in what is now southeastern Idaho. Still, the northern, mountainous section of the territory remained the domain of the Nez Percé.

Chief Joseph

Gold was discovered in 1863 near the Wallowa Valley just across the Idaho border in Oregon. White miners began pouring into the region, sparking a dispute between the Nez Percé and the U.S. government. The valley, i.e. the gold, was undeniably within the limits of the Nez Percé reservation in a region considered among their most sacred. In 1870 the U.S. attempted to force the tribe to sign another treaty in which they would give up all but about a tenth of their reservation and leave them with a small fraction of their former homeland.

Tribal elders, who had for years worked amicably with the U.S. government, were outraged. One of these elders was Hin-mah-too-yah-lat-kekt, or Thunder Rolling Down the Mountain, who had changed his name to Joseph after converting to Christianity. He refused to sign the treaty ceding his homeland—

Chief Joseph

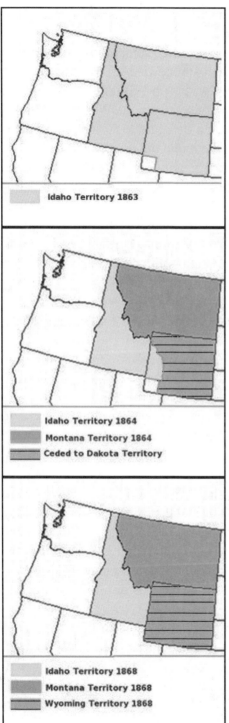

Idaho Territory 1863

Idaho Territory 1864
Montana Territory 1864
Ceded to Dakota Territory

Idaho Territory 1868
Montana Territory 1868
Wyoming Territory 1868

his beloved valley of Wallowa—and he died in 1871, leaving his son, also named Joseph, to lead his people in the fight against the U.S. government. The 1877 war between the retreating Nez Percé and U.S. troops has gone down in history as a series of brilliant, yet ultimately unsuccessful, maneuvers by the Indians who were avoiding being herded onto their assigned Idaho lands. The defining moment in the saga came in Chief Joseph's famous speech of surrender:

"Hear me, my chiefs! I am tired. My heart is sick and sad. From where the sun now stands I will fight no more forever."

Creating Idaho

Idaho Territory was created in 1863 and initially included modern Idaho, Wyoming and Montana. Abraham Lincoln signed the Idaho Organic Act on March 4 of that year, but the story of the name for the new territory goes back even further, originating in what is now Colorado.

In 1859 the Pike's Peak mining camps in the mountains of what would become Colorado held an election to name a delegate to press for their own territory status in Washington D.C. Initially the results indicated that a miner named George M. Willing had been chosen as representative, but after massive fraud was discovered in the balloting, Willing was replaced with B. D. Williams.

Even though he had lost the election, Willing--sometimes called "Doc" Willing due to his training as a physician--proceeded to Washington anyway. It is unclear what his relationship was with Williams, though some adversarial tensions must have existed between them, as Willing continued to represent himself as the "legally elected delegate to Congress from the territory of Jefferson,"[2] *Jefferson* being the name the miners had chosen.

Nevertheless both men, along with a small contingent of supporters, began working for territorial organization, and in April of 1860, a bill was submitted to the House of Representatives for what would be called "Idaho" Territory. It was Williams who pressed for the name, but as will be shown, the suggestion for it came most likely from Willing. On January 30, 1861, the name was discussed in the Senate. Senator Joseph Lane of Oregon objected to "Idaho," but the name was defended by James S. Green of Missouri.

"Idaho is a very good name," said Green, "In the Indian language it signifies 'Gem of the mountains'."

Lane argued "I do not believe it is an Indian word. It is a corruption. No Indian tribe in this nation has that word, in my opinion...It is a corruption certainly, a counterfeit, and ought not to be adopted."

But the name *was* adopted. After Lane's strenuous objections, however, Williams became suspicious and decided to investigate.[3]

A few days later a presumably sheepish Williams asked Henry Wilson, a senator from Massachusetts and future U.S. Vice President, to have the senate bill amended--quickly--substituting "Colorado" for "Idaho." Williams told him that he had discovered that "Idaho" was, in fact, a fraud, a made up word, that it did not mean "gem of the mountains," nor did it mean anything at all. It was a complete fabrication perpetrated by Willing, the backstory to which would not come to light until 20 years later. Wilson was able to get the amendment passed, and the name was dutifully changed to "Colorado."

The explanation for the frantic name change came to light in a letter written to the *New York Daily Tribune* on December 8, 1875. William O. Stoddard, a former aide to Abraham Lincoln and himself no stranger to practical jokes, "explained how his 'eccentric friend,' the late George M. Willing, had coined the name early in 1860. Willing (said Stoddard) often had told the story 'with the most gleeful appreciation of the humor of the thing.'"[4]

So then why....?

So if everyone now knew that "Idaho" was a fabrication, why then was it used to name any state at all? The answer may lie in the all-important euphony of the name. Whether it was Willing or someone else who created the word, it was one that people immediately found pleasing. Even its fabricated definition was agreeable enough that it continued to be used even after its origins were discovered. In June of 1860, a steamboat which would provide service on the Columbia River was christened the "Idaho." A small mining town in Colorado also took the name "Idaho Springs," and to this day, that town's Chamber of Commerce propagates the old "gem of the mountains" definition to explain the name.

By 1863 the new territory east of Washington and Oregon needed a name. It was a huge region, and a name that indicated its mountainous terrain would be appropriate. James M. Ashley, head of the Committee on Territories, proposed the name Montana, and the bill passed through the House of Representatives with that name. Ashley was bitterly disappointed when the Senate then amended the bill and replaced "Montana" with "Idaho."

The source of the change is a bit surprising—it was proposed by Massachusetts Senator Henry Wilson. Now, while there were no doubt members of Congress who had forgotten, or never knew of, the quick name change for Colorado after the name "Idaho" was found to be a fraud, Wilson was most assuredly not one of them. It was Wilson, as noted earlier, whom B. D. Williams had approached in order to change the name of his territory to "Colorado." (Wilson, in an interesting side note, was intimately familiar with the concept of changing names. He had been born Jeremiah Jones Colbath, named for a wealthy neighbor whom his parents hoped would become the boy's benefactor. He changed his name to Henry Wilson shortly after his twenty-first birthday.)

Clearly the name Idaho had survived and prospered in the three years since it was rejected in favor of Colorado. After Wilson proposed it for the new territory in the northwest, another senator, Benjamin Franklin Harding of Oregon, asserted the original "meaning" of the word, "gem of the mountains," and insisted it was appropriate for this new territory. With

Joaquin Miller

very little debate, the name "Idaho" was agreed to, and this time no eleventh-hour reprieve was requested. The bill passed Congress, and Idaho became a huge northwestern territory on March 4, 1863. The next year Montana was separated from it, and Ashley got to use his favorite name after all. President Benjamin Harrison approved Idaho as the forty-third state of the Union on July 3, 1890.

Joaquin Miller

The name Idaho, even after statehood was achieved, did not cease to arouse curiosity and study. By this time William O. Stoddard had given his account of George M. Willing's fabrication of the name, but that story was looked upon skeptically by many.

One of the most famous defenders of the word and its supposed meaning was a California writer/poet named Joaquin Miller. A colorful character, Miller has been called the "Poet of the Sierras" as well as the "greatest liar this country has ever produced." In 1883, writing for a Philadelphia magazine, Miller wrote of his own experience when he first heard the word (or words) "E Dah Ho!" spoken by Indians while he was traveling to the gold fields of the northwest around 1860. Miller tells of a pioneer named Colonel Craig with whom he was traveling and the Indian guide with them who exclaimed "Idahho!" when gazing at the sun dawning over the mountains. Writes Miller, "'That shall be the name of the new mines,' said Colonel Craig quietly, as he rode by his side."[5]

Miller's account, while dramatic, has gradually come to be seen as the product of a very active imagination, though for years his stories were believed and reproduced as fact. There are some glaring inconsistencies with Miller's version of events, however, the most obvious being his attribution of the name to a northwestern tribe of Indians instead of one in the Pike's Peak area where the name was originally proposed. The other conspicuous problem with Miller's, and Willing's for that matter, definition of the word has to do with the concept of a "gem." The idea of an earthen mineral to be mined and used as a valuable trade item is, as one author puts it, "a white man's notion, quite foreign to the thought of...American Indian peoples."[6]

The timing of Miller's story is also suspect. He claims to have heard the word for the first time in 1861, and even proposes that in September of that year he may have been the first to use its current spelling. But the bill to create Idaho Territory was proposed in Congress in April of 1860, over a year before Miller's supposed contribution. Still, scholars familiar with Indian languages have attempted to find a suitable aboriginal derivation, just in case one exists. Even the languages of the Arapahoe and Ute Indians who lived in the Colorado Rockies have been studied, but no such word or phrase has ever been found that might approximate "Idaho" with its alleged definition.

And so it appears that Idaho *is* what it has *become*--a northwestern state with such awesome beauty that the moniker "gem of the mountains" could and does certainly apply. Perhaps, though, the real "gem" is the starchy, brown vegetable that has brought to the state such a prosperous agricultural industry. It seems that no matter its true derivation, the word Idaho now has real meaning.

1.	Peterson, F. Ross, Idaho: A Bicentennial History (New York, 1976), p. 3.

2.	"Letters of George M. Willing, 'Delegate of Jefferson Territory,' With an Introduction by LeRoy R. Hafen," *The Colorado Magazine*, Vol. XVII, No. 5, p. 186.

3.	"Footnotes to History," *Idaho Yesterdays*, v. 8, no. 1, p. 33.

*4.	Idaho Yesterdays*, vol. 8, no. 1, 1964, p. 35.

5.	Miller, Joaqin, "Idahho!," *The Continent*, Vol 111, no. 22, May 30, 1883, p. 689.

*6.	Idaho Yesterdays*, vol. 8, no. 1, 1964, p. 36.

Chapter 13: Illinois

Just got home from Illinois
lock the front door, oh boy!

> — *"Lookin' Out My Backdoor"*
> *Creedence Clearwater Revival*

I drank musty ale at the Illinois Athletic Club with the millionaire manu-
facturer of Green River butter one night

> — *"Chicago Poems"*
> *Carl Sandburg*

The I's Have It

Illinois is one of the "I" states—those three that line up in a crooked midwestern row providing a nice alliterative device for young students of geography to learn their names. Illinois is the long one in the middle, flanked by Iowa to the west and Indiana to the east. Too bad they're not lined up alphabetically.

Illinois is perhaps best known for its largest city. "City of the Big Shoulders," "The Windy City," "My Kind of Town," Chicago is a favorite setting for movies and prime-time television dramas. It conveys images of the wind blowing off of Lake Michigan into Wrigley Field, of Al Capone, the Mayors Daley, the 1968 Democratic National Convention, the Sears Tower, ER, and of course...Michael Jordan and Sammy Sosa. But that's Chicago.

Illinois is in the Midwest, and the Midwest means farms. A large majority of the state is covered in farmland—massive fields of corn owned by wholesome families who drive tractors and wear overalls. That is, of course, the image, but modernization of the agricultural industry has tweaked what once would have been this reality—to say the least. The family farm has been bought up by ADM at foreclosure auctions and the corn fields con-

137

verted to bio-engineered soybeans. The wholesome families more likely work as systems analysts, wear Cubs jerseys and drive Hondas. But the mythical family farm is still the embodiment of the Midwest in the minds of many Americans, even if our mental images admittedly lag a few years — or perhaps decades or centuries — behind reality.

So which Illinois is Illinois — Chicago or the Midwest? Both, of course. They are at once inseparable and irreconcilable. Call it schizophrenia, or call it what the Illinois tourism industry calls it...a cross-section of American culture.

Lincoln

Illinois maintains a strong affiliation with Abraham Lincoln. The state calls itself the "Land of Lincoln," and for all the states that considered that always-a-bridesmaid name* Illinois probably has the most legitimate claim. It was in Illinois where Lincoln served in the legislature and where he debated Stephen Douglas in his losing bid for senator. He was living in Illinois when he won the presidency in 1860.

But it is widely acknowledged that Lincoln was not born in Illinois. In fact, he could not have been because Illinois was not yet a state on February 12, 1809 when Lincoln was born in Hardin County, Kentucky. Illinois wasn't even a territory yet. On the day of Lincoln's birth, it was the western section of Indiana Territory, its white settlers begging Congress for governmental organization:

Indiana Territory (until March 9, 1809)

Northwest Territory

* *Following the president's assassination several territories including New Mexico, Minnesota and Wyoming proposed the name "Lincoln" for their state name, but alas the martyred president was never to be honored with the naming of a U.S. state.*

"...we have been neglected as an abandoned people, to encounter all the difficulties that are always attendant upon anarchy and confusion."[1]

On March 9, 1809, about three weeks after Abraham Lincoln's arrival into the world, the Illinois Territory, by an act of Congress, also arrived.

The French

By that time the name "Illinois" had been used to describe the region— along the Mississippi River, mostly on the east side, north of the Ozark Mountains—for over a century. It was coined by the French, who knew of the Illini Indians as early as 1640. As the French began to push westward from the St. Lawrence River into the Great Lakes region, they became in- terested in reports of a large tribe of Algonquin-speaking people living not too far to the west along a mighty river. They wrote the name "Eriniouai," "Irinions," "Aliniouek," and eventually "Illiniwek."

The first contact between the French and the Illini came in 1666 in what is now Iowa. A map produced in 1667 by Jesuit priests Dablon and Allouez named Lake Michigan "Lac des Ilinois." In 1673 Jacques Marquette and Louis Joliet, the first a missionary and the other an adventurer, explored the Mississippi southward from Lake Michigan further than any European had yet traveled. They took Illini men with them as guides and translators, and also as subjects of study, learning that the term "Illini" referred to several loosely organized bands—the Peoria, Kaskaskia, Cahokia, Michigamea, among others—who lived along the banks of the Mississippi and Illinois Rivers.

A decade later, in 1683, Rene Robert Sieur de La Salle would travel the Mississippi and claim the entire river basin and all its tributaries for France, calling it "Louisiana" for his king (see Louisiana). Because their motivation was primarily trade *with* the natives and religious conversion *of* the natives, the French commonly—more so at least than the English and Spanish—ap- plied native names to the lands they claimed, adjusting aboriginal words to suit their own phonetics. The word "Illini" was that tribe's name for itself, and was made plural by adding "-ek" to the end. "Illiniwek" meant simply "the men" or "the people," but French writers chose to replace the "-ek" ending with the French suffix "-ois," giving us "Illinois," and that oh-so- French silent "s." The French suffix made the word descriptive and is often likened to the English suffix "-ese" as in "Chinese."

But the pronunciation of the word "Illinois" has never been entirely straightforward. A paper published in 2000 by linguist and place-name scholar Allen Walker Read studies the historic variations on the spoken version of the word. Read describes the inclination by Englishmen in the late 19th century to attempt to apply proper French by pronouncing the word "Illin-wah." He discusses the long and continuing competition between the pronunciations "Illinoy" and "Illi-noise" and sites historic variations on spelling that include "Illinoyes," "Illinese," and even "Ylinnesses."[2]

Illinois Country

Illinois to the French was not a county or a district in the 1700's. To them the name described the people more than the land, and so "Illinois Country" was the borderless region one passed through when traveling along the Mississippi from New France to New Orleans, a critical route for French traders. The Illiniwek strongly associated themselves with the French. They traded with them, guided them, and fought with them against both Indian and European enemies. But while the French claimed the Illinois country, they did little to settle it, except to allow their missionaries to engage the Indians and to set up just enough outposts (including St. Louis) to maintain a relatively high profile along the river, giving notice to England and Spain of their claim.

The French claim was not, however, completely unchallenged. The English colony of Virginia, whose charter bestowed upon her a limitless western border, also claimed Illinois Country. But since the French and not the English had control of the Mississippi River, it was not until 1738 that Virginia took official measures to assert that claim. In that year the Virginia assembly created Augusta County, bordered on the east by the Alleghany Mountains and on the west and north by "the utmost limits of Virginia." This was the colony's way of saying that they didn't know precisely what the western border was, but they would keep claiming land until they hit an ocean.

Of course, claiming the land and governing the people in it were two different things. The French had a few settlements in Illinois, but in 1738 the English were just beginning to creep over the Alleghany Mountains into Kentucky. It would be decades before there would be enough English colonists in Illinois to warrant any official government. Illinois Country began

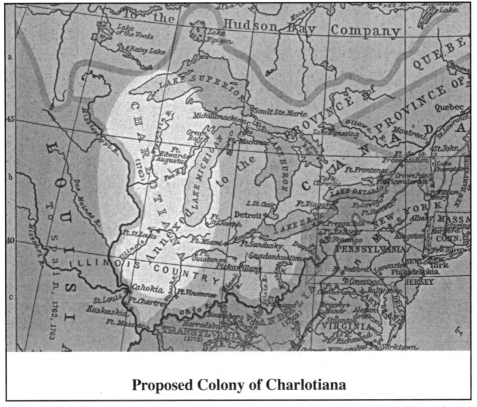

Proposed Colony of Charlotiana

to be referred to by Virginians as the District of West Augusta, differentiated from the County of Augusta, which had an actual governable population.

As English colonists began to move westward, the county names they applied were often geographically meaningless. They usually used names of royalty whose favor was being courted and rarely anything that described the land being named (Augusta was named for the Saxe-Gothe Princess Augusta, married to Prince Frederick, Eldest son of King George II). But "Illinois Country" meant something, though it didn't necessarily refer to the Illini Indians. To the English "Illinois Country" meant French outposts, the Mississippi River, and the frontier of English territory.

After the Seven Years War, or "French and Indian War" as it was known in America, The Paris Treaty of 1763 gave to the English the eastern half of Louisiana from France, and Virginia's claim to the region became internationally recognized. Among the recruitment efforts for settlers to come to "Illinois Country" was a pamphlet that was circulated in Edinburgh, Scotland, proposing the colonization of Illinois country. The specific boundaries would have included the current states of Illinois, Wisconsin and Michigan, and the proposed name was "Charlotiana, in honor of Her Majesty, our present most excellent Queen[3]." Settlers moved in quickly, but instead of encouraging efforts to colonize the region, King George III, Charlotte's husband, in order not to inflame already tense dealings with the western native tribes, issued a proclamation that the region was off limits to colonial settlement, a decree that exacerbated the tensions between colonists and the crown, and eventually helped lead to the American Revolution.

The Americans

During the Revolution few people saw any military or strategic issues in the remote Illinois Country. One exception was George Rogers Clark, a Kentucky frontiersman (his little brother William would, years later, accompany Meriwether Lewis at the head of the expedition to explore the American Northwest). Clark feared for the few American settlements in the Ohio Country, Illinois Country, and Kentucky which were vulnerable to Indian attacks—attacks that were encouraged, and even led by, the British. In 1778 Clark led bold but relatively bloodless movements against British forts at Vincennes, Kaskaskia and Cahokia, in the heart of Illinois Country.

George Rogers Clark

By convincing the mostly French settlers there to join in the revolution against the British, he secured the region for the Americans, drove out the minimal British troops, and reduced the threat of Indian attacks, as the Illiniwek still tended to follow the lead of their French neighbors.

The Virginia Assembly, learning of Clark's victories, wasted no time in reasserting their claim to the conquered region. Illinois County was created on December 9, 1778 from the region of Augusta County on the west side of the Ohio River. Perhaps because the county was created so quickly, the borders of the new Illinois County were vague, and the name was not debated. They simply used the name that they had used for decades, the one supplied by the natives, and altered by the French.

In 1784, after the war ended, Virginia ceded all of her claims to the Ohio Country, including the county of Illinois, to the federal government. The Feds, in turn, developed the Northwest Ordinance (see Ohio) for the purpose of disposing of the Northwest Territory, of which Illinois comprised the southwestern edge. In 1800 Ohio was separated from the rest of the region and given its own territorial status. The remainder of what had been the Northwest Territory was renamed Indiana Territory, and it included "Illinois Country."

But the people of Illinois wanted a separate territorial government and knew that the Northwest Ordinance mandated one. In their impatience to divide themselves from Indiana, the subject of a name was again not debated. Just as Virginia had used the traditional name for their region, so did the settlers, and on March 9, 1809 Illinois Territory was formed.

Portion of Illinois added by Pope Amendment

Don't Forget Chicago

The Northwest Ordinance did not contain a name for the territories it proposed, but it did suggest borders, and those borders were largely adopted when Illinois became a territory. But in 1817, when the residents began to petition for statehood, the territorial representative, Nathaniel Pope, noticed a problem. Pope was the nephew of Daniel Pope Cook (after whom Cook County is named), and he had for two years been lobbying hard to make Illinois a state. Nathaniel Pope proposed an amendment to the enabling act for Illinois that would move its northern border north by about forty miles. The amendment was accepted. Had he not made this proposal, Illinois would have no shoreline on Lake Michigan and would have no clear water route to the East Coast via the Great Lakes. Eight thousand square miles of what is today Illinois, and which currently contains about sixty percent of the state's population—including Chicago and all its suburbs—would have been part of Wisconsin.

Very shortly after the acceptance of the enabling act, Illinois drew up its constitution which was quickly passed by the U.S. Congress. On December 3, 1818, President James Monroe signed the act that created the twenty-first state of the Union: Illinois.

---

1.   Carrier, Lois A., Illinois: Crossroads of a Continent (Chicago, 1993) p.33.

2.   Read, Allen Walker, "The Pronunciation of Illinois," Place Names in the Midwestern United States, Edward Callary, ed., *Studies in Onomastics*, No. 1., (Lewiston: Edwin Mellen Press, 2000), pp. 81-96.

3.   Alden, George Henry, "New Governments West of the Alleghanies Before 1780," *Bulletin of the University of Wisconsin, Historical Series*, Vol. 2, No. 1, p. 12.

Chapter 14: Indiana

"Indiana Jones! I always knew some day you'd come walking back through my door."

—*Karen Allen as Marion*
from "Raiders of the Lost Ark"

Gary, Indiana,
Gary, Indiana,
Gary, Indiana
Let me say it once again.

—*"Gary Indiana"*
from "The Music Man"
Meredith Wilson

Letterman and Hooseiers

Late night television addicts think of David Letterman at the mention of the name Indiana. They might wonder if the city of Indianapolis has gotten around to naming I-465, the highway that loops the city, "David Letterman Highway." They may also wonder how the Ball State Cardinals football team is faring this year. But for others, perhaps those who watch *The Tonight Show*, the easternmost of the three "I" states that define the American Midwest is the Hoosier state, the farm belt, bas-

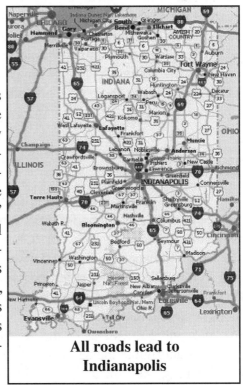

All roads lead to Indianapolis

ketball, and for those of a certain age and disposition, the whole embarrassing episode with Bobby Knight.

And then of course, there's Harrison Ford, Notre Dame, the Indianapolis 500, and a quaint little song from *The Music Man* about Gary, Indiana, that will stick in your brain like *It's a Small World* at Disneyland. For some there is also the image of a young Dennis Quaid and his band of teenaged malcontents, swimming in the quarry and riding their bikes triumphantly in the 1979 award-winning movie *Breaking Away*.

A glance at a road map of Indiana can remind you of Rome--as in, "all roads lead to it," though in this case the roads lead to Indianapolis. Such a glimpse fills you with a comforting sense of pragmatism--the state capital in the geographical middle of the state and sharing its name so intimately, with all of the major highways radiating out from it like a star.

A closer look at that map, however, can give you a bit of a jolt. Indiana has a shore! A coast! Okay, it's not on an ocean, but still...how can a state in the heart of the Midwest have a beach? It's supposed to be land locked and full of wheat or corn or something. And yet, there it is: Marquette Beach on Lake

Indiana's Coastline!

Michigan in Gary, Indiana. This little slice of Indiana heaven sets it apart from the rest of the Midwest. At least...when it comes to water skiis.

Well, Obviously...

The derivation of the name "Indiana" seems so obvious that in searching for it, one tends to find a lot of phrases like "It simply means..." or "It is obviously derived from..." or "Clearly...." It makes sense to assume that the word "Indiana" is directly derived from the word "India" or "Indian," and so it is. These brief assertions are then inevitably followed by a long, detailed description of the possible derivations of the word "Hoosier," Indiana's perennial mascot.

In naming the states of the Northwest Territory, the fashion of using native or aboriginal names was just beginning, and the use of the feminine Latin ending was still in vogue. Whether "Indian" can be considered aboriginal is certainly debatable, but in the minds of early 19ᵗʰ century legislators, the area being organized was closely associated with natives, and their word for native was "Indian." Slap on the Latin ending, and you get "Indiana."

What is not really quite so obvious is that the word *India*, and therefore *Indiana*, takes its original derivation from a Sanskrit word *sindhu* meaning "a river." As early as 893 A.D. King Alfred the Great referred to the area in modern-day Pakistan of the "Indus" river and called its inhabitants *Indikoi*. Eventually the word made its way into Greek and then Latin, and by the time of Columbus' voyages, had become "India," "the Indias" or "the Indies" and was commonly used to refer to all of Southeast Asia. Interestingly, the Indus river headwaters wind through the disputed territory of Kashmir and into China. None of the Indus River flows through what we today call India.

It is also generally acknowledged that the application of the word "India" to the West Indies in 1492 was a mistake, applied by Columbus in the false assumption that he had landed somewhere in southeast Asia. In the journal for his first voyage he writes about the place he named "Indies and its inhabitants who he dubbed the "Indians." Thoroughly debunked is the theory that the word "Indian," as Columbus used it, was originally "El Gente *in Dios*" or "People of God."

Even after Europeans determined once and for all that what Columbus had found was not the Far East but a New World, the names *Indies* and *Indians* stuck. These misnomers so quickly and so thoroughly propagated that for Americans today the word "Indian" is more readily associated with Native Americans than with people from India. Also, we tend to use "Indian" as a noun (he is an Indian) when speaking of Native Americans and as an adjective (he is Indian) when speaking of people from India.

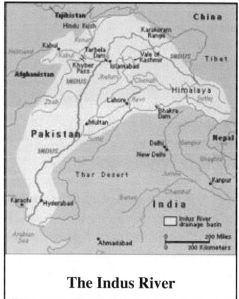

The Indus River

It has been pointed out that while Columbus believed he had found India, he was actually looking specifically for "the noble island of Cipangu," which is to say, Japan. Had he believed himself successful in his quest, the Native Americans we now call Indians might have a different, if still inaccurate, name...and so might Indiana. *Cipangana?*

The First Indiana

The "first Indiana" was actually in West Virginia and is, in fact, sometimes referred to as the "first West Virginia." It was a tract of land procured by a group of Virginia and Pennsylvania land speculators who called themselves The Indiana Company. The leader of the group was Samuel Wharton, son of a successful Philadelphia merchant and friend of Benjamin Franklin.

These men came together with a common complaint—that they had lost valuable property in New York, Pennsylvania, and Virginia during the French and Indian War. They wanted the help of Parliament in reclaiming their losses, but Parliament, noting that the losses were accrued during a declared war, refused, and the petitioners became known as the "suffering traders."

Ever persistent, the "sufferers" formed The Indiana Company, the creation of which is poorly documented. The name may have derived from the intention of the Company to negotiate directly with the Indians in an attempt to acquire land west of the Alleghany Mountains, land which was off limits by order of King George III's proclamation of 1763. At a meeting at Fort Stanwix, New York, in 1768 the suffering traders gained cessions from the Six Iroquois Nations for a section of land between the Ohio and Monongahela Rivers in what is now West Virginia. They called the land Indiana after their company.

Once Indiana was secured, Samuel Wharton and a smaller group of speculators attempted to gain control of a much larger tract of land. They proposed a new colony called either "Pittsylvania" after William Pitt, the English parliamentary reformist, or more likely "Vandalia" for the Germanic tribe of Vandals from whence Queen Charlotte was believed to have descended. Vandalia would have completely surrounded Indiana and consumed most of what is now West Virginia, but Wharton and others engaged in coercive machinations that proved ruinous to the whole venture, and

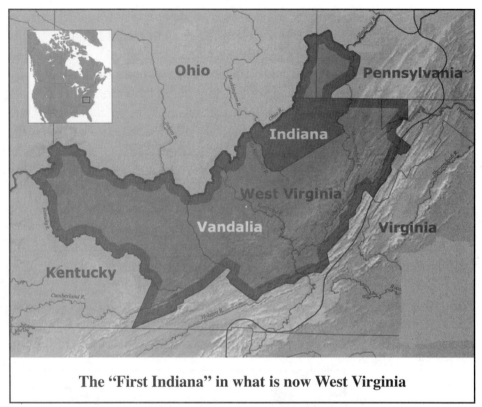

The "First Indiana" in what is now West Virginia

many of the speculators eventually declared bankruptcy. With the Declaration of Independence, the new states vigorously asserted their land claims west of the mountains, only to surrender them willingly to the new Federal Government, and so "Indiana" was effectively liquidated.

The Second Indiana

The name "Indiana" is said to be (clearly, obviously, simply...) a Latin version of "place of Indians." Given that "Indian" was already a Latin version of "Indus," this seems a bit redundant. Still, Latinizing words, that is to say, applying a Latin ending (usually a feminine suffix) to the word for use as a place name, was certainly en vogue during the founding and naming of the nation—Virginia, Louisiana, Montana, America, etc.

Once the Indiana Company was finished with the name "Indiana," it was no longer applied to a place or a group of people. But it was out there, in the consciousness of the new Americans and their government, and it had

151

a particular meaning. While "Indiana" may today signify David Letterman or fields of corn, in the late eighteenth century it still meant Indians. It was probably only a matter of time before the name got applied to a region that was strongly associated with Native Americans, which was virtually any section of the continent that was not yet dominated by white men.

The Northwest Territory was claimed by the United States after the Revolution, and the Northwest Ordinance of 1787 (see Ohio) made provisions for the division of the region but placed no names upon the lands. *Ohio Country* and *Illinois Country* had already long been referred to as such, one for the river which dominated the area and the other for the Natives who inhabited the banks of the the upper portion of the Mississippi River. But the section in between the two was nameless.

When the Northwest Territory began to be divided in earnest, the first bill to address the process drew a line dividing the region into two sections, and naming the eastern section "Washington" and the western section "North-Western Territory." This bill passed the House of Representatives, but the Senate committee that debated the bill didn't care for the names. They removed the name "Washington" and began referring to what is now Ohio as the "Territory North-west of the River Ohio," and they inserted the name "Indiana" for the region in the west.

The name must have made perfect sense to the committee members. Since the end of the Revolution, the U.S., while outwardly claiming to have won the Northwest Territory by conquest over both the British and the Indians, also spent much time and effort acquiring concessions from, and signing treaties with, various Indian tribes who had inhabited the land, perhaps for centuries. After years of negotiation and broken treaties, many native tribes were angered by the usurpation of their lands by the Americans, and they continued to harass settlers and enrage U.S. officials. For the new American government, this was the beginning of a century of handling the "Indian Problem." It would play out over and over again, east to west, north to south, for decades.

In 1805 Indiana's northern border was fixed to create the new territory of Michigan, and four years later, the Territory of Illinois was formed to the west. With no further discussion of a name, Indiana was approved by President James Madison as the nineteenth state of the Union on December 11, 1816.

Despite its name, Indiana today has one of the smallest Indian populations in the country, with fewer than 13,000 people claiming that heritage in the 2000 census. The Midwest in general does not have, nor is it even perceived to have, a concentrated population of Native Americans. This legacy of European domination in the 19th century was perhaps not foreseen by those who placed the named "Indiana." It seems that one subject that tends not to be inspired by the name "Indiana"...is the subject of Indians.

Chapter 15: Iowa

"Is this heaven?"
"No. It's Iowa."

—*"Field of Dreams"*

There's nothing halfway
About the Iowa way to treat you
When we treat you
Which we may not do at all.

—*"Iowa Stubborn"*
from "The Music Man"
Meredith Wilson

Corn

Just as strong as next-door neighbor Wisconsin's association with cheese is Iowa's association with corn... corn-fed cattle, corn-fed chickens, and corn-fed strapping young men. The state's name conjures up images of vast fields of cornstalks drenched in golden sunlight, Kevin Costner ambling through them, an invisible sage whispering in his ear, "If you build it, he will come."

Generations of farming in America's heartland has imbued the name Iowa with a certain wholesomeness. This aesthetic involves hard work, rising before dawn to milk cows and feed chickens, and perhaps squeeze in a little Bible study. One also imagines a cautious, provincial people, proud of their state and their way of life. The mind's eye, of course, sees most of them in overalls, unless it happens to be Sunday.

These proud, independent people are also famous for their primary (pun intended) role in selecting our nation's presidential candidates. Like the first pitch on opening day, the Iowa caucuses in January kick off election season every four years. The event creates front runners and forces resignations, largely deciding for the rest of the country the field of competitors for the White House. While important, this honor subjects the entire state to a barrage of political ads so intense that it is perhaps a privilege the rest of the states do not wish to wrest from the people of Iowa.

When one ponders possible vacation spots Iowa seldom tops the list. In fact it seems almost counterintuitive for the state to have a tourism agency, but in fact they do, and their website is slick and professional. It introduces you to such state attractions as Living History Farms, the actual Field of Dreams, and the world's largest motor home factory, as well as Iowa's many not-so-wholesome casinos. Still, as a tourist destination Iowa has difficulty competing with the untouchable vacation industry of, say Hawaii.

Iowans, one suspects, don't mind.

Albert M. Lea

Albert M. Lea was a twenty-seven year-old lieutenant in the U.S. Army who, in 1835, led a company of dragoons (armed, mounted soldiers) to explore a tract of land on the west side of the Mississippi River that had been acquired three years earlier from the Sauk and Fox Indians. The region, part of the Wisconsin Territory, was commonly called Scott's Purchase after General Winfield Scott, who had negotiated the treaty with the tribes. It was also sometimes called the Black-Hawk Purchase, an ironic name derived from the Sauk elder who, in 1832, led a rebellious band of tribe members into Illinois to attempt to reclaim their homeland.

As punishment for the Indians' "insolence," the United States dictated a treaty to several regional tribes which conferred upon the U.S. this strip of "purchase" land in return for about $600,000. The district was a small tract of land about thirty miles wide, bounded on the south by the state of Missouri, on the east by the Mississippi River, and by an angled line on the west, giving it the shape of a miniature mirror-image of California.

Lieutenant Lea preferred neither of the two commonly used names. He instead chose to refer to the land as the "Iowa District" after the river which "flows centrally through it, and gives character to most of it, the name of that stream being both euphonious [sic] and appropriate...." Upon his return, Lea wrote a short book describing the land in glowing terms: "The general appearance of the land is one of great beauty." Of the white people who were already pouring into the district he wrote,

> "The character of this population is such as is rarely to be found in our newly acquired territories. With very few exceptions there is not a more orderly, industrious, active, pains-taking population west of the Alleghenies [sic] than is this of the Iowa District."

It seems even in 1835, Iowans were cultivating a wholesome reputation.

Lea titled his book *Notes on The Wisconsin Territory; Particularly with Reference to the Iowa District, or Black Hawk Purchase*, and a thousand copies were printed and sold. One hundred years later the book was reprinted, this time with a new title and an "Explanation" at the beginning. It was now called *The Book that Gave Iowa its Name*, an obviously tantalizing label for students of state name derivation. The "Explanation," which appears as a preface or foreword, declares "While the information which [the book] records on the Iowa country in 1835 is invaluable to students of Iowa history, the supreme historical significance of Lieutenant Lea's book is the fact that it fixed the name Iowa upon the country that was to become the Territory of Iowa in 1838 and the State of Iowa in 1846."

Tribe, River, State

"Iowa" is an Indian word whose original meaning has been obscured over generations of language loss and corruption. It has, as a result, assumed an almost comical number of diverse definitions. Among them are "this is the place," "beautiful land," "crossing, or going over," "gray snow," "dusty noses," "something to write with," "one who speaks gibberish," "drowsy ones," "those who put to sleep," "marrow," "squash," and "none such."

Historians and scholars disagree at varying intensities about which definition is correct, some asserting confidently that one of the above meanings is true without mentioning the other possibilities. In 1955 Joseph P. Harrington, working for the Smithsonian Institution's Bureau of American Ethnology, wrote "The Iowa form of the tribal name is 'Ayuxwa,' which means 'one who puts to sleep.'" A Dakota-English dictionary written by Stephen R. Riggs in 1890 and reprinted in 1992 offers the following definition: "i-ó-wa, n. of owa; *something to write* or *paint with, a pen or pencil*." Others, however, acknowledge the conflicting definitions and concede that the true meaning of the word will almost certainly never be known.

To further complicate matters, the Iowa Indians of the 17th and 18th centuries used a different word to describe themselves—*Pahoches* (the "h" is pronounced like the "ch" in the name of the German composer Bach.) This word was used by the Chiwere—a linguistic group that included the Missouri, Oto, and Iowa tribes—of the middle Mississippi, while "Iowa" was used by the Dakota Sioux of the upper Mississippi. But the meaning of the word "Pahoches" is just as unclear as that of "Iowa," and the two may simply be synonyms from different dialects of Sioux. Mildred Mott Wedel, an ethnohistorian who compiled and published a synonymy of names for the Iowa tribe in 1978, conveys the exasperation of scholars in their endeavor to determine a true definition:

> The variety of explanations proffered by the Ioway and other Indians to explain the Chiwere name to Americans makes it quite clear why linguists prefer to view with caution the descriptive meanings or folk etymologies of proper names.[1]

Iowa Indians

But while a meaning for "Iowa" may be elusive, the history of the word and its adoption as a state name is still traceable. In 1676 a French missionary,

Father Louis Andre, wrote of a group of Indians who had come to his mission near what is now Green Bay, Wisconsin. These natives, he reported, were called "Aiaoua" and were visiting their friends and relatives among the Winnebegos who lived near the mission. Historians generally agree that Andre's reference to this tribe is the very first written reference to the Iowa Indians by a European.

Andre, however, was receiving his information about the tribe second- or third-hand. It is believed that Algonquin-speaking Ottawa and Chippewa tribes, those close to Father Andre, borrowed the Dakota name for the Iowas and probably conveyed that name to him. Had Andre been speaking to the Iowa or even the Winnebago Indians directly, he would likely have received the Chiwere name "Pahoches" to describe them.

There is overwhelming evidence that the original (i.e. correct) pronunciation of the word was "Ioway." Indeed, the final "y" was used in the spelling of the tribe's name in at least seven treaties with the U.S. government between 1824 and 1854.[2] According to Wedel, the Spanish were responsible for changing the pronunciation of the final syllable from "way" to "wah." They spelled the name "Ayoa," "Aiaoas," and "Hayuas" during their reign over western Louisiana in the late 1700's. Wedel also explains that anthropologists "have found it useful to use 'Ioway' to distinguish the Indian name from that of the state." She acknowledges, however, that in 1938 the tribe adopted the spelling "Iowa" to match the orthography of the state name.[3]

As early as 1685 the French began to use the name of the Iowa Indians to label the river upon which they lived. Throughout the following centuries the region surrounding the river would be claimed by all three major European powers and eventually the United States. The spelling would change, but the river continued to be named for the Iowa Indians.

In 1778 Thomas Hutchins, an accomplished cartographer as well as experienced frontiersman and Indian agent, mapped the region. His map is considered the first to use the modern spelling of the word *Iowa* (to name the Iowa River), and that map was used in 1803 by Thomas Jefferson and Merriwether Lewis to plan the route for the Corps of Discovery on Lewis and Clark's trek across the North American continent.

Robert Lucas, 1st Territorial Governor of Iowa

Honey War and Slavery

In a familiar pattern, the river of the region took the name of the tribe, and the land, largely by virtue of Albert Lea's little book, took the name of the river. On July 4, 1838 the region became the official U.S. Territory of Iowa.

Iowa was part of the Louisiana Purchase area in 1804, and remained a part of the Louisiana Territory until 1812 when Missouri was carved out and given territory status. In 1816 John C. Sullivan surveyed the northern border of Missouri Territory, defining that area that had been ceded to the United States by the Osage Indians. Sullivan made a minor error in his survey, however, causing the line to be slanted, and so in 1837 a new survey was undertaken by Joseph C. Brown. Brown, unfortunately made an even larger mistake, and designated a fourteen-mile strip in southern Iowa as part of Missouri.

Upon taking office, Robert Lucas, Iowa's first territorial governor, immediately had a border dispute on his hands. Lucas was no stranger to border wars, having served as Ohio's governor during the Todedo War between Ohio and Michigan, which came dangerously close to armed combat (see Michigan). Most disturbing to the Iowans who now found themselves residents of Missouri was that Missouri had entered the Union as a slave state. Many of the people in the disputed region had moved there specifically to avoid paying taxes in a state that supported slavery. If the new boundary held up, they would be forced to move again as a matter of conscience.[4]

President Martin Van Buren selected none other than Albert M. Lea to mediate the controversy. (Ironically, the disputed region was considered by Iowans to be part of their Van Buren County.) Lea studied the situation and submitted four proposals to Congress, each representing a different border configuration. But while Congress debated, some impatient Missouri militiamen angered Iowans by storming north and cutting down three trees which were rich in honeycomb, prized by Iowa farmers as a source of valu-

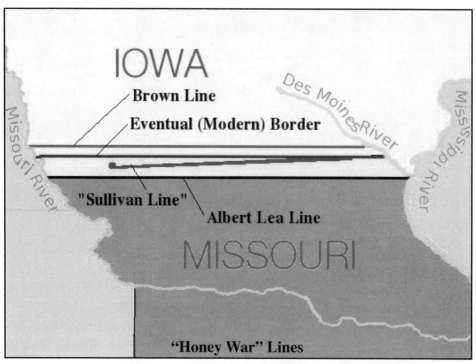

able sugar. Tensions mounted, but fortunately in the end, the trees were the only casualties of what came to be known as the "Honey War." But the dispute would not be finally settled until 1849, three years after Iowa became a state. In that year the U.S. Supreme Court decided that the original "Sullivan line," straightened out except for a tiny notch in the northeast corner, would be Iowa's official southern boundary.

In a complicated set of circumstances, the bill providing for Iowa to create a constitution (the final step toward statehood) changed her borders dramatically, moving the western border from the Missouri River eastward to a longitude that nearly sliced the state in half. Iowans were outraged and refused to act on their own statehood until their original borders were restored. Stephen Douglas of Illinois proposed the compromise that was eventually accepted, moving the western border back to the Missouri River, and placing the northern border at the 43° 30' parallel, instead of following the Mississippi and Minnesota Rivers further north. Boundaries now firmly in place, President James K. Polk signed Iowa into existence as the 29th state in the Union on August 4, 1846.

1.　　Wedel, Mildred Mott, "A Synonymy of Names for the Ioway Indi-ans," *Journal of the Iowa Archeological Society*, vol. 25, 1978, p. 54.

2.　　Wedel, p. 60.

3.　　Wedel, p. 60.

4.　　Wall, Joseph Frazier, <u>Iowa: A Bicentennial History</u> (New York, 1978), p. 32.

Chapter 16: Kansas

"Toto, I don't think we're in Kansas anymore."

—*Judy Garland as Dorothy*
from "The Wizard of Oz"

Carry on my wayward son
There'll be peace when you are done

— "Carry On My Wayward Son"
Kansas

"I'm as corny as Kansas in August..."

—"I'm In Love With a Wonderful Guy"
from "South Pacific"

The Middle

It is a symbol of normalcy, of everything that is familiar to us, everything recognizable as home. We think of Judy Garland as Dorothy with her freckles, pigtails, and checkered dress. We think of rolling fields of wheat, long, straight, dirt farm roads, windmills, county fairs, hard work, and lots of silence. Even city folk find something down right homey about Kansas.

Our image of Kansas is not exactly exciting. Even the major cities of the state—Witchita and Topeka (Kansas City is, of course, mostly in Missouri)—evoke calm. Kansas seems like a place that restless young teenagers want to get out of, and only after experiencing the treacherous world outside her borders can they recognize the beauty and comfort of what they left behind. To some, everything outside of Kansas probably seems like Oz.

Except for an edge along tiny section of the Missouri River, Kansas' borders are a set of four straight lines that proudly surround the geographic middle of the forty-eight contiguous states. That is, of course, another way of saying that people in Kansas (those restless, young teenagers perhaps) who want to leave the United States have to book a longer flight than people who live in any other state.

Apparent political inconsistency is another hallmark of Kansas—as in "What's the Matter With...?" Thomas Frank wrote his bestselling book after the 2000 presidential election about people who vote against their own self interests—as thousands in Kansas had just done. In the introduction he wrote, "People getting their fundamental interests wrong is what American political life is all about." Not all, of course, but, according to Frank, many of those "people" are Kansans.

There is, of course, another image of Kansas that comes to us from the *Wizard of Oz*. It is the foil to that image of utter normalcy that the state conveys: tornados. Kansas lies in the heart of "tornado alley," a vaguely defined section of the country where twisters are most common. The Fujita scale measures tornado intensity, category 5 tornados classified as the most powerful of the lot. Kansas lands are terrorized by this most severe level of twisters more than any other state in the country. A large section of central Kansas is one of the highest risk areas for tornados in the U.S., though an even larger section of her southern neighbor, Oklahoma, shares that distinction. Alabama and Mississippi also have stretches of very-high tornado risk, as do big chunks of Arkansas, Nebraska, and Texas. Nevertheless, when we think of tornadoes, we're more likely to think of Kansas than any other state. Thanks, perhaps, to Dorothy, Toto, and the gang.

Kansas-Nebraska Act

The creation of Kansas was inticrately entangled with the creation of Nebraska, and their formations marked a turning point in the nation's political destiny. After Missouri achieved statehood in 1821 it, quickly became clear that white settlers coveted the land west of the Missouri River. This was land that was now designated "Indian Territory" and on which several reservations had already been established to accommodate eastern tribes who had migrated or been "removed" westward.

In 1845 John O'Sullivan, a writer and editor of a New York newspaper, codified the concept of "Manifest Destiny," writing that, "In its magnificent domain of space and time, the nation of many nations is destined to manifest to mankind the excellence of divine principles." The United States

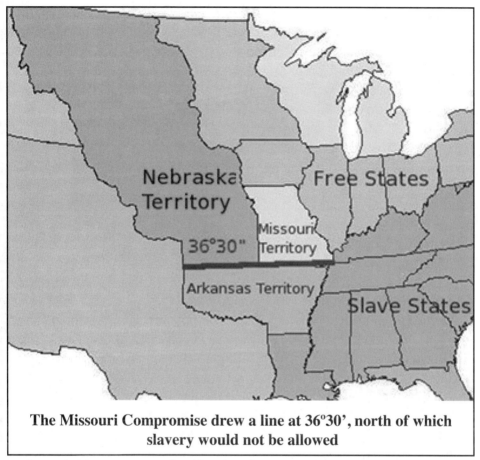

The Missouri Compromise drew a line at 36°30', north of which slavery would not be allowed

embraced this concept as justification for expanding its borders westward, and so the organization into territories of the land west of Missouri quickly became a foregone conclusion for most Americans.

By 1853 several attempts had been made to organize the Territory of Nebraska, but all had failed due in large part to the political controversy surrounding slavery. The Missouri Compromise of 1820 had designated the 36° 30' north latitude—the southern boundary of Missouri—as the line north of which slavery would not be legal. The proposed new territory of Nebraska fell north of this line. Southerners had already "allowed" California to enter the Union without slavery, but they were hell-bent on blocking the creation of any more "free soil."

Stephen Douglas, famous future debater of Abraham Lincoln, took up the cause of Nebraska, but he was pushed and prodded by a senator from Missouri named David Rice Atchison. Atchison was an advocate for the southern states and a staunch supporter of slavery. The Nebraska bill became a way for slave states to push for the repeal of the Missouri Compromise and institute "Squatter* Sovereignty," or as it is more commonly known "popular sovereignty," whereby any new state, regardless of its relation to the 36° 30' line, would be allowed to determine its own status with regard to slavery. Missouri, a slave state, would probably supply most of the settlers to the new territory, and if popular sovereignty were established, those settlers would be able to vote in slavery. The most vocal opposition to the repeal of the Missouri Compromise came from Iowans, many

David Rice Atchison

of whom had moved north from Missouri specifically to *avoid* living in a slave state. Iowa, too, expected to supply settlers to any new territory west of the Missouri River, and these settlers would be "free soilers."

It was Atchison who proposed that the Nebraska Territory be divided, the northern section to be Nebraska and the southern to be Kansas. In this way he could appease the Iowans, virtually giving them their own "free" state to settle, and still achieve his main objective, which was the repeal of the Missouri Compromise and the continued use of African-American slave labor.

Atchison proposed the name *Kansas* to Douglas, taking it from a prominent river in the region. He is said to have claimed that since Nebraska was named after a river, so Kansas should be too. The name was, of course, already in use by the time Atchison proposed it. The city that grew up on the Missouri River at the mouth of the Kansas had been called Westport on the west side of the Missouri, but the ferry landing on the east (Missouri) side came to be known as "Kansas Landing," "Port of Kansas," and eventu-

---

*   *The term "squatter" developed in post-Revolutionary War America to describe those individuals and families who occupied unorganized public land without paying for it. Many conflicts developed between the "squatters" and those who purchased the land from the government.*

ally "City of Kansas." Residents of the town generally referred to it only as "Kansas," and it was becoming a thriving gateway to points west. David Atchison's suggestion of the name was probably influenced by the prominence of this town near what would be the new territory. Once the territory was created, the port city officially changed its name to "Kansas City" to distinguish it from the territory.

Atchison's plan worked, and the bill to create Nebraska now became the Kansas-Nebraska Act, historically better known as a significant step on the nation's road to Civil War rather than an effort that simply organized two territories and set them on the path to statehood.

Bleeding Kansas

Kansas was also set on the path to grisly bloodshed. "Bleeding Kansas" is the graphic term used to describe the territory during the period in the 1850's in which residents of Kansas were supposed to be deciding their own position on slavery. As promised, people moved west from Missouri and Iowa, as well as from places further north and further south, many of them with no intention of settling but hoping only to sway elections. Kansas became a tinderbox.

Among those who moved west were the sons and other followers of the puritan abolitionist, John Brown, followed shortly by Brown himself, and they were among the first anti-slavery warriors to "fight back" against the encroaching proslavery contingent. The close proximity of so

John Brown

167

many violent advocates on both sides of the slavery issue touched off a series of massacres and battles that became a portent for the gruesome, desperate war that lay in the nation's future.

The western border of the Territory of Kansas originally extended all the way to the crest of the Rocky Mountains, and there were many in the region who wanted not only to keep that boundary but to annex part of Nebraska Territory, making the Platte River the northern boundary of Kansas. The Colorado gold rush of 1859 was the major factor in moving Kansas' western border east to 102° longitude, making room for the new Territory of Colorado. Strong efforts to include the Platte River country in Kansas eventually failed.

When, in early 1861, seven states had already seceded from the Union and four others were threatening to do so, the U.S. Congress saw its chance. Now acting as the legitimate government of the United States, but without the southern states to obstruct them, they granted statehood to Kansas as a *free* state. President James Buchanan signed the Act on January 29th, 1861. This served, of course, to exacerbate the tensions between north and south, and four months later the nation was at war.

State of Kaw?

The name that David Rice Atchison proposed for the territory was, as stated, taken from the river. The river, like so many others that had been mapped by Europeans, was named after a prominent tribe living along its banks. *Kansas*, it turns out, is the English plural of *Kansa* or *Kanza*, a Siouan tribe that lived along along the Kansas river at the time of their first meeting with Europeans. The name for the tribe had been spelled many (by some accounts more than a hundred) different ways on maps and in journals from as early as the 1673 expedition of Marquette and Joliet or possibly even earlier. Some believe that the references to the "Escansaques" or "Escanzaques" by members of a Spanish expedition led by Juan de Oñate in 1601 to the village of Quivira were actually the Kansa Indians.

The Kansas belonged to the Dhegiha Sioux group of tribes, a linguistic group that also included the Omahas, Osages, Quapaws (Arkansas), and Poncas. At one time these five tribes were one and migrated westward before contact with Europeans, but from where has never been determined. Some say they could have moved from as far east as the Atlantic seaboard, but more prominent theories suggest a region near Lake Michigan. Sometime before 1673 (the year Marquette and Joliet ventured down the Mississippi), the Dhegiha Sioux divided and separated. Ironically, there is evidence that as late as 1698 the Kansa tribe was still living east of the Mississippi River and may have been driven

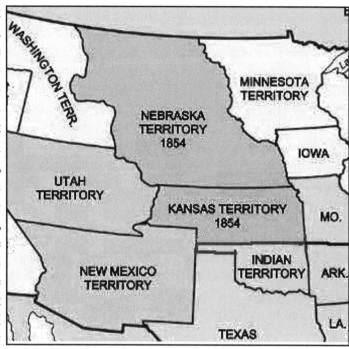

westward by other tribes during the domino effect that the first European contact had on virtually all of the Indians in North America. Had it not been for the push of the Europeans, the "Kansas" River might today be in Illinois.

The 1970's rock band "Kansas," in tribute to their namesake, released a song called "People of the South Wind," acknowledging the widely held belief that the word "Kansas" means "wind people" or "people of the south wind." Ethnologists have noted that other Siouan tribes also contain a "Kansa" or "Kauza" division, a reflection of a certain clan's status within the tribe. While there is strong ethnological support for the interpretation of "Kansas" as "people of the south wind," there are those who support other theories. Kansa interpreter Addison W. Stubbs, writing in 1896, suggests that the word closest to "Kansa" in the tribe's own language was *konza* which meant "plum." He stressed, however, that the name "Kansa" was, to the members of the tribe, simply what other people called them and had no particular meaning.[1]

According to Kansas place-name scholar John Rydjord, the Kansa Indians used the word *Hútañga* to refer to themselves, a name which may be related to the Siouan word *Hu-tam-ya*, meaning "by the edge of the shore."[2]

The name Kansa, used by other Siouan tribes who repeated it to early French explorers, was probably pronounced "Kauza" or "Konza."

There is strong sentiment within the state for the name "Kaw" instead of "Kansas" when describing both the river and the tribe. This shortened appellation is a by-product of the French tendency to abbreviate place names on maps. Historian John Francis McDermott writes

> "The Kansas River for the French was the *Kan*, and even today people speak of that stream as the "Kaw" (sometimes "Caw"), which was as close to the French pronunciation as the Americans could get.[3]"

In fact, the modern tribe maintains its identity as the "Kaw Nation" based in Kaw City, Oklahoma, and while the river still appears on maps as the "Kansas," it is also affectionately referred to, particularly by locals, as the Kaw. It does not appear, however, that anyone has ever suggested applying that name to the state.

1.   Unrau, William E., <u>The Kansa Indians: A History of the Wind People</u> (Norman, 1971), p. 10.

2.   Rydjord, John, <u>Indians Place-Names</u> (Norman: University of Oklahoma Press, 1968), p. 14.

3.   John Francis McDermott, "The French Impress on Place Names in the Mississippi Valley," *Journal of the Illinois State Historical Society*, vol. LXXII, No. 3, August 1979, p. 231.

Chapter 17: Kentucky

Kentucky Rain
Keeps fallin' down...

> — "Kentucky Rain"
> *Elvis Presley*

Kentucky woman
If she get to know you
She goin' to own you

> — "Kentucky Woman"
> *Neil Diamond*

From the Kentucky coal mines...

> — "Me and Bobby McGee"
> *Janis Joplin (Kris Kristofferson)*

Chickens and Horses

In the 1950's Colonel Harland Sanders labeled what would become one of the best kept secret recipes in culinary history with the name of the state in which he developed it. To this day the, word *Kentucky* is likely to call to mind pressure cooked, finger-lickin'-good fried chicken, made with eleven celebrated (albeit secret) herbs and spices, and the white-coated, white-haired honorary colonel whose likeness appears on every box and bucket of it. In the twenty-first century it is conceivable that more people in the world (KFC is franchised in more than fifty countries) know the taste of Kentucky Fried Chicken than could find the state of Kentucky on a map.

Kentucky is also famous for its blue grass, its bourbon, and its family feuds. Bourbon is the term coined for all American-made whiskies, a distilled spirit that originated in Bourbon County, Kentucky, in the 18th

Daniel Boone

Century. Jim Beam, Knob Creek, Maker's Mark, and Wild Turkey are all Kentucky born whiskies, dominating the bourbon industry and served at just about every bar across the country.

The "Hatfields and McCoys," the real-life warring Kentucky families of the 1800's, have become names symbolic of clan warfare everywhere. Simple family clashes between the two erupted into years of property conflicts, love betrayals, and murder. Dozens of family members on each side fell victim to the slaughter, eventually requiring state governors and militia to intervene before a truce was made in 1891, eighteen years after the first dispute.

And even people who don't know an Andalusian from a Thoroughbred know of the Kentucky Derby, perhaps the most famous horse race in the world. The "Run for the Roses" is held every year on the first Saturday in May at Churchill Downs in Louisville, Kentucky. Few sporting events can compare with its tradition and ceremony, not to mention its brevity—the main event lasting no more than three minutes. The first Kentucky Derby was held in 1875, when only thirty-seven of the fifty United States had yet been formed.

Americans know Kentucky as the "Daniel Boone state," the place where arguably the nation's most famous frontiersman hunted and explored. Indeed, mental pictures of coonskin caps and powder horns leap to mind at the mention of the the state's name, as well as images of the Shawnee Indians, Boone's lifetime adversaries. And thanks largely to the efforts of Boone and his ilk, and their efforts to open up the region to settlers, Kentucky would become the first of the trans-montane states to enter the union after the American Revolution.

An "Indian" Word

"Kentucky," often written "Kentucke" in the early days of exploration, is a state whose name origins are shrouded in mystery and controversy. It is clearly derived from a Native American word, but which tribe's language produced it is a matter of speculation. Consider...

Benjamin and Barbara Shearer's book *State Names, Seals, Flags and Symbols* states "The name Kentucky, the Wyandot word for 'plain,' referring to the central plains of the state, was first recorded in 1753."

In *Kentucky Bluegrass Country,* R. Gerald Avey says "...the original meaning of the name of the Cherokee term Anglicized into 'Kentucky' was 'great meadowland'..."

In the forward of that same book however, Thomas D. Clark, a revered Kentucky historian, writes "the Iroquois gave it the name Kentucky, or Land of Tomorrow."

Older histories simply call it an "Indian" word and leave it at that. More recent scholars acknowledge that the exact meaning and derivation of the word is not known, and they might point out that many of the languages spoken by tribes in Kentucky, including the three mentioned above, had Iroquois roots.[*] The general consensus, however, seems to be that the word belonged to one of the dominant native tribes of the region and was used to refer to the area south of the Ohio River.

There is a commonly circulated theory that claims the name "Kentucky" means "dark and bloody ground," but this speculation has been proven false. The myth probably emerged after years of bloodshed between and among Indian tribes, and eventually Europeans as well, over the Kentucky hunting grounds. One Kentucky history book reasons:

---

[*] *As opposed to Algonquin or Muskogean. It was long held that all of the Native languages encountered in eastern North America belonged to one of those three groups, though more recent study shows that premise to be too simplistic.*

175

That legend probably came from remarks made by Cherokee chiefs Dragging Canoe and Oconostota at Sycamore Shoals when Richard Henderson bought what rights the Cherokee had to a large part of Kentucky. "There is a dark cloud over that Country," Dragging Canoe reportedly warned, and Oconostota said to Daniel Boone as they parted, "Brother, we have given you a fine land, but I believe you will have much trouble settling it."[1]

This region may never have been settled by a single group of natives even before European encroachment, at least not for long—a fact that no doubt has generated some of the confusion regarding its name.

Due to the lush woods, gently rolling hills and valleys, and numerous streams and rivers, Kentucky thrived as a deer and beaver habitat. This richness of the land made it a desirable, if not necessary, commodity, and its hunting rights were bitterly fought over by the Cherokee, Iroquois, Shawnee, and other Indian tribes. During the mid 1700's, with the impeding American explorers on their bountiful land, these tribes quickly became frustrated at the existence of yet *another* competitor for the land and its fruits. Yet the Americans' intentions were more commanding than those of the natives in that they not only competed for the guaranteed economic gain, they ultimately intended to settle the land—they wanted to *live* in Kentucky, to *own* it.

A County in Western Virginia

To colonists in the early eighteenth century, "Kentucky" was a vague region in Western Virginia on the opposite side of the forbidding Appalachian Mountains. It was only known to them through the reports of early explorers, hunters, and missionaries as well as by word of the local Indians with whom they traded. Daniel Boone, who began exploring Kentucky in the late 1760's is of course the most famous of these early white adventurers, but there were many others both before and after. They brought back tales of acre upon acre of green pastures, rivers packed with fish, and fur-bearing animals of every kind. Though this area was uninhabited by whites, they regaled their listeners and readers with accounts of menacing Indian tribes who harassed them during their ventures. Ironically, it was these same natives whose name for this coveted land became widely used by the English and other Europeans.

Technically, to the Virginians, the region was part of their vast Orange County formed in 1734 out of unexplored western lands that extended northward to the Great Lakes and westward to the Mississippi River. It was named for William IV, Prince of Orange. In 1738 the county was divided, the western portion becoming Augusta County, named for Princess Augusta of Saxe-Goth, wife of Frederick, Prince of Wales. Their eldest son would become King George III, whose reign would so famously nudge the American colonists toward revolution.

It was in fact King George III who in 1763 made the trans-montane region of Virginia off-limits. By that year the Cumberland Gap, named by Dr. Thomas Walker in 1750 after the Duke of Cumberland, had been established as the easiest path through the mountains, and settlers had begun to trickle westward. In order to buy time to develop a western policy, King George issued a proclamation prohibiting settlement west of the crest of the Appalachians and ordering any of his subjects residing there to move east immediately. Virginians were outraged because they wanted to use the land to pay their soldiers for service in the recently-won French and Indian War. Their anger was somewhat mitigated after hearing of the horrors of Pontiac's Rebellion (1763-65), a brutal and bloody series of battles and massacres be-

Chief Pontiac urging his warriors on in what became known as Pontiac's Rebellion

tween an Indian alliance led by Ottawa Chief Pontiac and British soldiers and settlers in the Ohio River Valley. The war somewhat justified the position of the crown.

In 1770 Augusta County was further divided, and the western portion containing Kentucky became Botetourt County, named for a well-liked governor of Virginia. Two years later, the western lands were once again lopped off and named Fincastle County, either for John Murray, Earl of Dunmore and Viscount of Fincastle, or for his son, Lord Fincastle. Then, in 1776 Fincastle County was broken up once again for ease of administration. The name Fincastle was discarded (possibly because Lord Dunmore was now an unpopular British Military leader in Virginia trying to squash the rebellion), and three new counties were formed: Montgomery, Washington, and Kentucky County, whose northern, southern and eastern boundaries were those we know today as the state. Only the western tip of the state, the land west of the Tennessee River was not part of Kentucky County.

Separation

In 1779 the population of Kentucky County began to change dramatically. Following the war, the government was responsible for paying the mercenaries who had bravely fought its battles. Land ownership was offered to soldiers as payment, and it was not long before they began to move west to claim it. Other settlers, no longer hindered by the British king's proclamation, also poured through the Cumberland Gap by the thousands, so that by 1800 the population of the County was over 200,000.

From the time of its first discovery by colonists, Kentucky was a separate entity from Virginia, partly because of the physical barrier—the Appalachians—that divided them, and partly due to mindset. Virginia was the first British colony, and it was accustomed to being divided. Its northern and southern boundaries had changed drastically since the establishment of Jamestown, when "Virginia" referred virtually to the entire eastern seaboard. By the time the county of Kentucky was formed, it was clear that the western border would change as well to accomodate a new entity in whatever form Kentucky was destined to take. For example, when in 1780 Kentucky County was divided further into three separate counties—Fayette, Jefferson, and Lincoln—they were still referred to collectively as Kentucky.

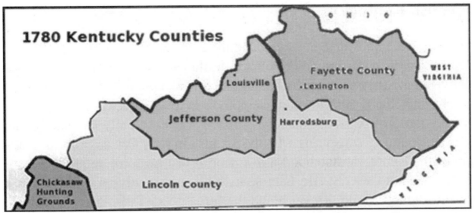

1780 Kentucky Counties

The handwriting on the wall became even clearer in 1783 when the former county was formed into the District of Kentucky, which now made it more administratively independent, and further divided it from Virginia. It had its own court system, but still sent a delegation to the Virginia legislature. But Kentucky also had its own political agenda which, it was becoming clearer, was vastly different than that of easterners. Among its unique problems were the obvious and continuing Indian hostilities, and the politics of navigation on the Mississippi River. Residents were frustrated when these problems were all but ignored by the Virginia, and later the federal, governments.

On December 27, 1784, each militia company in the District of Kentucky sent a representative to the town of Danville for a convention. The only topic on the agenda was the issue of separation from Virginia. There would be nine more conventions over the next ten years as Kentuckians, Virginians, and the federal government debated the matter. There was no precedent yet for adding states to the original thirteen—Vermont would not become the fourteenth state until April of 1791, only a year ahead of Kentucky. However, it wasn't as if the new American government wasn't thinking about the process. The Northwest Ordinance started as a resolution that Congress passed in 1780 to deal with the Northwest Territory. It provided for the lands acquired from the British after the Revolution to "... be settled and formed into distinct republican states."

Spanish Kentucky?

Some Kentuckians, however, had different ideas. A movement led by James Wilkinson, a brigadier general during the Revolution, would have delivered a newly separated Kentucky to Spanish control. Wilkinson lived a notorious life of intrigue, and his motives in the Kentucky endeavor were largely those of personal financial gain. It was eventually learned that he was treasonously conspiring with the Spanish in New Orleans to bribe leaders of the Kentucky statehood movement to instead form an alliance with Spain *against* the U.S. (In later years he would involve Aaron Burr in a scheme which would forever brand the former Vice President as a traitor.) Wilkinson also enticed businessmen of Kentucky to consider his strategy by obtaining trade concessions from Spain, which controlled the Mississippi River. These concessions provided a badly needed outlet for exports from the area and brought to Wilkinson enormous personal profit.

In 1788, when the U.S. once again failed to give Kentucky statehood status, many in the region became increasingly frustrated with the fledgling feds and more enamored of Wilkinson's plan. Serious proposals at the convention in November of that year proposed that Kentucky draft a constitution, declare itself separate from Virginia, and offer the federal government an ultimatum: either accept Kentucky as a separate state, or we will go elsewhere.[2] The proposal failed, however, largely because the Spanish were losing interest, and the Kentuckians no longer had the leverage of a Spain-backed secession. So the District of Kentucky plodded on toward statehood.

Statehood and borders

Finally, on February 4, 1791 Congress passed a bill that would admit Kentucky to the union. State leaders set to work drafting a constitution and selecting representatives, and on June 1, 1792 Kentucky entered the Union as the fifteenth state.

Bordering seven other states, Kentucky found itself embroiled in border disputes that would simmer at varying intensities until as late as 1890. In 1818, however, Andrew Jackson and Isaac Shelby facilitated what would become the most drastic change in Kentucky's borders. Approximately two thousand square miles of land west of the Tennessee River was purchased

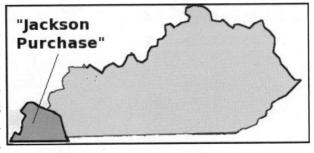

from the Chickasaw In-
dians for three hundred
thousand dollars, and
formed into what is now
the western tip of Ken-
tucky. This region is
bounded by the Missis-
sippi, Ohio, and Tennes-
see rivers (the Tennessee was dammed at this point in 1944 to form Kentucky Lake) as well as the state's southern border with Tennessee—some
twelve miles south of the *rest* of the state's border with Tennessee. This
section of the state is still referred to today as the "Jackson Purchase."

Kathy Guyton

---

1.   Harrison, Lowell H. and James C. Klotter, <u>A New History of Kentucky</u> (The University of Kentucky Press, 1997).

2.   Harrison and Klotter, p. 60.1.

Chapter 18: Louisiana

Way down Louisiana down to New Orleans…

> — *"Johnny B. Goode"*
> *Chuck Berry*

The city that gave us the first American music
The true inspiration and the freedom to use it
Where will we find it again if we lose it

> — *"Where were you"*
> *Jackson Browne*

A Whole Different Country

What's a bayou? What exactly does Creole mean? And why do they call their counties "parishes"? Perhaps more than any other state, Louisiana sometimes seems like a whole different country. Louisiana denizens have their own holiday (Mardi Gras), their own food (Cajun), and their own way of speaking.

It is a small, unpretentious state, buried down south on the western edge of of Dixie. But Louisiana's image is different from other "southern" states—somehow less rebellious and a little more colorful. We think of genteel women like Bette Davis in "Jezebel," or Vivian Leigh in "A Street-car Named Desire," or that 1970's song "New Orleans Ladies" by LeRoux:

New Orleans ladies,
a flair for life,
love and laughter
And they hold you like the night
Holds a chill when this cold wind's blowin'
Them Creole babies,
they strut and sway from dusk till dawn

We think of hot, steamy summers, sultry jazz music, corrupt politicians, and swampy marshlands with lots of mosquitoes. We also think of flavors—andouille, gumbo, crawfish, Tabasco sauce, and anything with Cayenne pepper.

Geographically, too, Louisiana is unique among states. How nice it was of the founding fathers to mold Louisiana into the shape of an "L." No other state has such an obvious mnemonic device to go along with its name. (Why couldn't Vermont be shaped like a "V" or Missouri like an "M"?) But of course, like many states, Louisiana's shape and size are quite different today than when the name was first applied.

Of course, since 2005 there is another word that comes to mind when we think of Louisiana, possibly even our first and most visceral image: *Katrina*. For many of us the images of masses of humanity, primarily people of color, desparately trying to survive both the hurricane and the botched federal response to it, will forever spring to mind at the mention of Louisiana. For a state that would previously have made us think of music, colorful parades, and fascinating history, it is, to put it woefully inadequately, a damn shame.

In the Name of

King Louis XIV

In 1682 Rene-Robert Cavelier, Sieur de LaSalle navigated the Mississippi River to its source, and in so doing handed his king and his country the internationally recognized right to the entire river valley. The French, in the persons of Marquette and Jolliet (see Arkansas and Mississippi), had penetrated the continent as far south as the Arkansas River nine years earlier, but for various reasons their journey is not seen historically as the one which gave France her claim to the North American interior. The most obvious reason, of course, is that they did not reach the Gulf of Mexico as La Salle did. Claiming the region for France was a La Salle's primary objective, so

**Rene-Robert Cavelier,
Sieur de La Salle**

once he reached that point near the mouth of the Arkansas River where Marquette and Jolliet had turned back, he set up the French coat of arms, planted a cross, and declared the land the property of the French king, Louis XIV. (Louisiana is, of course, the state whose history forces us to remember our Roman numerals.) Then La Salle continued to the mouth of the Mississippi and repeated the ceremony, burying a brass plate which read, "In the name of Louis XIV, King of France and of Navarre, this ninth of April, 1682."

Standing on the river banks of what is now New Orleans, La Salle proclaimed,

"On the part of the very-high, very-powerful, very-invincible and victorious Prince Louis the Great, by the grace of God King of France and Navarre, fourteenth of this name..." and declared that he had "...taken possession...*of this country of Louisiana...*" (emphasis added)

It was this act of La Salle's, and the reports and maps produced from it, that Put the name "Louisiana" firmly in the lexicon of geographers, explorers, and missionaries, not to mention monarchs and prime ministers. While not every state can claim so specific an act—even a date, time, and person—responsible for its name, Louisiana can quite confidently claim La Salle's act on the ninth of April in 1682, as the specific origin of its name.

The intrepid explorer went on to describe the extent of the region he was claiming. It included the Mississippi River, all of its tributaries, and a laundry list of items intended to describe what it was his king now owned:

"seas, harbors, ports, bays, adjacent straits and all its nations, peoples, provinces, cities, boroughs, villages, mines, ore-bearing

**Early French Forts
in Louisiana**

earth, fishing waters, salt-water rivers, rivers..."[1]

Obviously La Salle wanted there to be no mistaking that King Louis XIV now owned *everything*.

Of course, in order to keep Louisiana, the French now had to defend it. They quickly (within a couple of decades) established forts at Biloxi, Mobile, Dauphin Island, and Baton Rouge. Finally, in 1718, a site was located closer to the mouth of the Mississippi River where a port city could be built. Jean Baptiste Le Moyne, Sieur de Bienville, established the city of New Orleans as the capital of Louisiana. It quickly became a thriving, multi-cultural trade center of critical importance to France, both politically and militarily.

Which King Louis?

Louisiana is the only state named for a French monarch. (Unless you count Maryland which was named for Queen Henrietta Maria. She was Queen Consort of England, wife of King Charles II, but she was French. She was, in fact, the younger sister of King Louis XIII and the aunt of King Louis XIV.)

Referred to commonly as "The Sun King," because he identified himself with the Greek god Apollo, Louis XIV reigned for 72 years, from 1643 (he assumed the throne at the age of four, when his father died of tuberculosis) until 1715, and he

King Louis XIV of France

still holds the record in Europe for the longest reign of any monarch. His reign was marked by his belief in "absolute monarchy," and when his Prime Minister, Cardinal Mazarin, died in 1661, Louis decided not to replace him but to rule alone. He built the fabulous palace at Versailles and imbued the French court with the lavish excesses that would, less than a hundred years after his death, mark the downfall of the monarchy and help to provoke the French Revolution.

Louis was married to Queen Maria Theresa of Spain, and they had seven children, only one of whom lived to adulthood. Louis also had numerous mistresses, and several bastard children resulted from these extra-marital escapades. One of his (legitimate) grandsons went on to become King Philip V of Spain, a throne which Louis fought to maintain for him in the Wars of the Spanish Succession. One of these, Queen Anne's War, was fought in North America and was responsible for the loss of much of what is now Canada to England.

Louis XIV was succeeded by his great-grandson, Louis the XV, who also enjoyed a long reign, but was destined to preside over the loss of the eastern half of Louisiana to England after the Seven Years War. He died in 1774, relinquishing the throne to Louis XVI, whose reign would be considerably shorter. He and his wife, Marie Antoinette, were beheaded in 1793 during the Reign of Terror that marked the French Revolution. Six years later Napoleon Bonaparte instigated a coup d'état and took control of the new Republic of France, paving the way for France's loss of the *western* half of Louisiana.

The Deal

In discussions of American history, it is difficult to utter the word "Louisiana" without following it by the word "Purchase." In the timeline of events in

Napoleon Bonaparte

187

our nation's history, the Louisiana Purchase is monumental, allowing as it did the size of the United States to double without the "hassle" of a war. Of course, there were wars—they just weren't with the French, whose grip on the land was growing more and more tenuous anyway. These wars were fought with the Indians—the people who occupied the land and who had the most legitimate claim to it.

Actually by the time of the Louisiana Purchase, the United States already laid claim to half of the region that had initially been acquired by La Salle. All of the region east of the Mississippi and west of the Appalachians had been won from France by England in 1763 with the Treaty of Paris that ended the Seven Years War, and then from England by the U.S. after the Revolution only twenty years later. It was the rest of Louisiana, the region between the Mississippi and the Rocky Mountains (excluding Texas, which was a province of New Spain and extended northward as far as Colorado), that changed hands as a result of the machinations surrounding what some call the greatest real estate deal in history.

Volumes, of course, have been written about the Louisiana Purchase, but briefly... France had given the region to Spain in 1762 as thanks for that

country's alliance in the war with England and as a way of keeping England from claiming it as conquered territory. In 1800, Napoleon coerced Spain into giving it back to France with the secret Treaty of Ildefonso. Napoleon had hoped to regain a glorious French empire in North America but, due mainly to massive military setbacks incurred during the Haitian revolution, was unable to send his troops to New Orleans. Eventually he turned his attention to war with England and needed money to finance it. Thus, in 1803 he sold Louisiana to the United States for fifteen million dollars with the intention, many historians assert, of winning it back by force once he was finished with England. Of course, that didn't happen. Instead, France was defeated by the English/Russian alliance at the Battle of Waterloo, and the U.S. went on to consolidate its grip on the North American continent.

Orleans Becomes Louisiana

Thomas Jefferson's now famous idea was to reserve Louisiana for the Indians—those who already lived there, as well as those who were being displaced in the east. Residents of St. Louis (named, by the way, for a different king of France, King Louis IX, who *was* actually a canonized saint), were outraged at such a notion. That city was the "gateway to the west" through which streams of people were already flowing on their way to try to make a living in the new, vast region. Popular dissent won out, and Jefferson's plans for the puchased land quickly began to be reformulated.

In 1804, the Louisiana Purchase was divided. All of the area north of the current northern border of Louisiana was fashioned into the "District of Louisiana;" the "Territory of Orleans" was formed from the remainder. Orleans was comprised of land that is currently the state of Louisiana, excluding what became known as the "Florida Parishes," which was the land north of the Mississippi River, but west of the Pearl River—land that Spain still claimed as part of Florida. The following year the District of Louisiana became the Territory of Louisiana, in preparation for division into new states.

In 1810 the Florida Parishes, along with the rest of West Florida (roughly the current panhandle of Florida, extended west to the Mississippi River), revolted against the Spanish government. The region was settled mostly by Anglo Americans who had, for years, been disappointed that the United States was not more proactive in annexing the region. The Kemper Rebellion, named for three brothers who instigated the revolt, culminated with the

The "Florida Parishes"

raising of a blue flag with a white, five-pointed star in the middle, and declaring the area the "Republic of West Florida." This "Bonnie-Blue Flag" still flies today over many public buildings in southern Louisiana.

A month after the Kemper Rebellion, the U.S. finally claimed the Florida Parishes as part of Louisiana. Spain did not recognize the claim of the United States but had her hands full with the Mexican Revolution, and so was ill equipped to fight the encroachment.

On April 30, 1812, President James Madison admitted Louisiana to the union as the 18th state, but not until a few weeks later, on June 4, was Missouri Territory created out of what had been Louisiana Territory. For just over a month, both a *Territory of Louisiana* and a *State of Louisiana* existed.

And two weeks after *that*, on June 15, America declared war with Great Britain. The War of 1812 was fought primarily over maritime policies and remained a virtual stalemate for about eighteen months. Weary of the costly war, both countries signed the Treaty of Ghent in the Netherlands on Christmas Eve, 1814. Two weeks later, on January 8, 1815, the most famous battle of the war was fought in New Orleans, Andrew Jackson and his army soundly defeating the invading British, neither side having received word of the peace treaty.

Not until 1819, and the signing of the Adams-Onis Treaty between the U.S. and Spain, would the Florida Parishes be secure in their attachment to Louisiana, making the perfect "L" shape a consistent fixture on U.S. maps.

---

1.   Johnson, Donald S., <u>La Salle: A Perilous Odyssey from Canada to the Gulf of Mexico</u> (Cooper Square Press, 2002), p. 112.

Chapter 19: Maine

Third boxcar, midnight train
Destination...Bangor, Maine.

> — *"King of the Road"*
> *Roger Miller*

What a place to live, what a place to die and be buried in!

> —*from* "The Maine Woods"
> *by Henry David Thoreau*

Wild and Fishy

Maine has a quaintness about it, a reminiscence of early America, a small-town, small-farm feeling but with a physical remoteness that renders it as foreign to most Americans as Myanmar or Morocco. Indeed from California, the most populous state, one would have to travel farther to get to Maine than to any other state, including Hawaii. It is the northernmost of the lower forty-eight states and shares a much longer border with Canada than with its only American neighbor, New Hampshire.

Maine makes us think of fishing and of hearty fishermen, of rocky coastlines, old lighthouses, and

Cod fishing has long been an economic mainstay in Maine

lobster traps. The state's history is inarguably tied to the fishermen of its past, who found the waters along its coasts rich with cod. They may have been attracted to the waters off of the Maine shore, but they were not so enthralled with enigmatic Maine shore itself. Even today Maine is perhaps the only state along the eastern seaboard that seems untamed and wild. This image partly stems from a corollary reputation for being constantly cold (July—Maine's warmest month—only averages in the upper sixties). While Maine's quaintness and untamed beauty appeal to Americans, few of us would care to investigate them in the wintertime. Maine is a good place to go camping in the summer, to keep a summer cottage, and to escape the heat of the more southerly states come July and August.

The state shares a trait with Texas, Louisiana, and New York. It's one of those places where "people talk funny." A Maine accent is easily recognizable, its inhabitants using words like *nor'easter*, *steamers* (clams), and *crittah*. Main's denizens say "yah" and "pahk the cah," and in our imaginations, they all sound like the old farmer in the Pepperidge Farm commercial.

For all its remoteness, quaintness, and wildness, Maine is amazingly easy to find on a map. While most of the New England states tend to run together for those who don't live in them, Maine stands out. It's the one

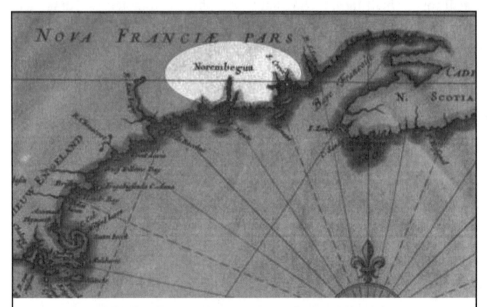

This 1539 Dutch map shows "Norumbegum" (sic) lying in what is now the state of Maine

up in the corner that's almost as big as the rest of them put together. Even children, struggling to learn the states and their borders, find Maine among the easiest to locate and remember. How ironic that this state, with its fishermen so famous for trying to keep their best fishing spots a secret, is so easy to find.

What We Know

Two dominant theories exist regarding the origin of the name *Maine*, but no consensus has ever been reached as to its precise beginnings. The answer to this mystery may lie in new research done by a Maine writer named Carol B. Smith-Fisher. In a newspaper article which appeared in the Bangor Daily News in February of 2002, Smith-Fisher first rather convincingly debunks the two existing theories, and then, also quite convincingly, presents her own. We will present her theory as well later on in the chapter.

While there is little documentation for why Maine came to be named as it is, the details of its exploration and settlement have been prolifically described in books, newspapers, and journals. At the same time the Spaniards in the Southwest were searching for the seven cities of Cibola, the French and Italians eagerly and vainly sought their own fabled land-of-milk-and-honey: the land which Giovanni da Verazzano had called "Oranbega," later appearing on maps as "Norumbega". Paving the way for Samuel de Champlain and Jacques Cartier, Verrazano established the continental nature of the region which on early maps was labeled "Terra Nova" or "New Founde Land," and

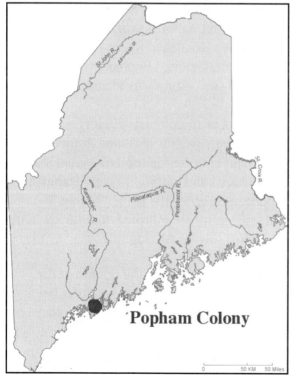

'Popham Colony

Popham's abandoned fort is now a State Park in Maine

was often depicted as in island or islands. In 1615 Captain John Smith explored and mapped the coastline of what the English were by then calling North Virginia. Smith presented to the King of England his new map, which contained the prophetic name "New England."

The first official application of the name "Maine" to the land between the Merrimack and Saga-hadock (now the Kennebec) Rivers appears in a Royal land grant made to Sir Ferdinando Gorges and Captain John Mason by King James I of England on August 10, 1622. The two were businessmen who hoped to profit from the excellent fishing in New England waters by colonizing the coastline. In fact, as early as 1606, under a patent from the Plymouth Company, Gorges had commissioned George Popham to create a settlement in New England. Popham's expedition set out within a year of the Jamestown mission and landed near the mouth of the Kennebec River, establishing the foundation of their colony with a few single huts. Popham, however, died during the extremely harsh winter, and the colony was abandoned the following summer.

While they initially had little success in colonizing, Gorges and Mason took pains to maintain control of their patents and land grants in New England. In 1629 they divided the land specified in the 1622 grant, Mason taking the portion south of the Piscataqua and calling it "New Hampshire" and Gorges taking the northern portion, keeping the name "Maine."

In 1639 Gorges had his Maine grant reconfirmed to him by King Charles I in a document which contains this tantalizing line:

"And Wee Doe name ordeyne and appoynt that the porcon of the Mayne Lande and Premises aforesaide shall forever hereafter bee called The Province or Countie of Mayne and not by any other name or names whatsoever..."

According to Smith-Fisher an explanation has never been found, either in memoirs or letters by Gorges or his descendents, as to why the name "Maine" was so adamantly chosen. And so the speculation began.

Theory Number One

By the time of Gorges' grant by King James I, the land we call Maine was being fished extensively by English, French, Spanish and Portuguese fishermen who were not interested in documenting their travels. On the contrary, they tried desperately (as fishermen still do today) to keep their prime spots secret. Nor were these men interested in colonizing. They wished only to load up their ships with cod, and return home to sell their catch.

According to the first theory regarding the origin of the state's name, these fishermen referred to the mainland as "Mayne" or "Maine." The name was so common among those who frequented the waters that it stuck and was used by Gorges to define the land he chose as his own.

This theory is prevalent among historians and even seems a likely hypothesis unless one considers Ms. Smith-Fisher's argument. She points out that "Maine" with its many different spellings was used up and down the eastern shores of North America (and indeed, on other continents discovered before and since) to differentiate the coast from nearby islands, but only *here* is it proposed that the name rose to the rank of a proper noun. Why, she begs, would Sir Ferdinando Gorges, a devout royalist with an English pedigree dating back to the days of William the Conqueror, choose a name so common and so meaningless?

Why, indeed? Which brings us to...

Queen Henrietta Maria

Theory Number Two

This second theory is certainly in keeping with the regal position of Sir Ferdinando Gorges. It was proposed in 1795 by Maine historian James Sullivan and has been widely accepted ever since. It maintains that the name comes from the French province of Mayne and was bestowed as a compliment to Queen Henrietta Maria, French wife of King Charles I of England.

Henrietta Maria was a fifteen-year-old princess—daughter of France's King Henry IV, and sister to future King Louis XIII—when she married Charles shortly after he ascended the throne. For their first three years of marriage, Henrietta Maria was ignored by Charles, who preferred the company of his favorite courtier the Duke of Buckingham. After Buckingham's assassination, King Charles began to redirect some of his attention toward his wife, and they eventually became openly affectionate.

The queen was widely mistrusted in England, primarily because she was Catholic, and the king's attention toward her was one of many acts which caused suspicion of *him* by his protestant subjects and parliament. (Charles I would go on to provoke Civil War in England, be tried and convicted of high treason, and finally be beheaded.) A royalist like Gorges, however, who was consistently loyal to King Charles and more distrustful of the increasingly powerful puritans in his own country than of the Catholics in France, might well have wished to pay his Queen a compliment. James Sullivan asserted that

> "The territory was then called the Province of Mayne, by way of a compliment to the queen of Charles I who was a daughter of France, and owned as her private estate, a province there, called the Province of Meyne, now called the Province of Maine."[1]

Theory number two, however, is chronologically difficult to swallow. According to a biography of Henrietta Maria written in 1845, the Queen had no connection with the French province of Meyne. Moreover, Smith-Fisher points out that the name "Maine" was bestowed by Gorges in 1622, three years *before* Henrietta Maria became Queen of England in 1625. In fact, in 1622 Charles (who was then Prince of Wales) was engaged to the Infanta Maria of Spain, a marriage that he and his father, King James I, very much hoped for. Not until 1624 did Charles pursue an alliance with France by proposing marriage to the Princess Henrietta Maria.

Theory Number Three

Now we come to Ms. Carol Smith-Fisher's new hypothesis. For her sources she contacted the Somerset and Dorset Historical Society in England. They informed her of a small village called Broadmayne near the Gorges' ancestral home of Shipton Gorges just southeast of Dorchester, England. She further discovered that this village was, in the Domesday (English census) book of 1086, referred to as "Maine" and later divided into Brademaen (Broadmayne) and Parva Maen (Little Maine). The implication derived from Smith-Fisher's theory is that just as Gorges' ancestors settled in (perhaps even founded) the town of Maine in England upon their arrival from France in the eleventh century, so did *he* establish the colony of Maine in North America for the further propagation of the Gorges family.

Naming his new land after the place of his family's estate would be in keeping not only with the times but with Gorges' apparent inclinations for naming of land possessions. He was granted many other patents for land in the new world, one of which he named Lygonia for his mother, Cecily (Lygon) Gorges, and another which he named "New Somersetshire," for the county in which his family estate was situated. His colleague Captain John Mason also honored his home county in England, calling his portion of the granted land "New Hampshire." Years later, in 1634, Sir Ferdinando's nephew Thomas Gorges would name his own Maine plantation "Wells" after *his* family home in England.

Smith-Fisher admits that more proof is needed to verify her theory, but as she eloquently puts it "...does it not ring true that our 17th century English knight would want to bless the future American homeland of the Gorges family with the ancient name of their first English village — Maine?"

So Anyway

Once the grant was made and the name settled upon, all that remained to be determine was *what*, exactly, Maine would be. Gorges' dream was to plant colonies which would engage in fishing, fur trading, and logging, anchoring what he hoped would be the crown jewel in the English colonial empire. While colonies were indeed planted, much of what would become Maine were towns spawned out of the ever-expanding Massachusetts Bay Colony. Settlers searching for freedom from the strict puritan laws of the MBC, or simply wanting land away from the increasingly crowded towns of Massachusetts, spread northward. They generally hugged the coastline of New England and combined with fishing and fur-trading settlements to form firmly planted towns.

In 1640, Sir Ferdinando sent his nephew Thomas Gorges to govern his holdings, and under his judicious leadership, several of the established communities came together to form a tenuous government for their "Province of Maine." By 1651 the Massachusetts Bay Colony began to see that these settlements to the north were "attempting to gain recognition from Parliament"[2] as an independent province. The MBC leaders quickly asserted a contrived control over the region, conceding to the locals a measure of religious freedom and local governmental control in return for their submission to the government of Massachusetts.

That began a tug-of-war between Royal control and that of the Bay Colony. By 1674, Massachusetts had won, creating the "District of Maine of Massachusetts" and governing the region as a province of its own for the next century and a half. During the American Revolution, the English had numerous designs on Maine, one of which proposed taking the territory between the Saco and the St. Croix Rivers, and calling it the "Province of New Ireland," then making it available to loyalists escaping from the rebellious colonies. The plot came to nothing, and the Paris Treaty of 1783, which ended the War for Independence, ended also any claim of the English to the Province of Maine.

In 1819 Maine separated itself from Massachusetts and applied to Congress for statehood. It should have been a formality but instead ran afoul of the slavery debate. Southerners were concerned that the addition of northern, non-slave states would reduce their numbers in the Senate to a minority, and northerners were afraid of the converse regarding Missouri, which was ripe for statehood as a southern, i.e. slave state. On March 3, 1820 the Missouri Compromise was passed, allowing both Maine and Missouri to enter the union, and maintaining the equilibrium in the Senate. Less than two weeks later, on March 15, 1820, Maine became the twenty-third state of the Union, signed in by President James Monroe. Its northern border would not be firmly fixed for another half-century, when the Webster-Ashburton Treaty of 1874 finally determined the line which now separates it from New Brunswick and Quebec.

1. Sullivan, James, <u>The History of the District of Maine</u> (Boston, 1795), p. 307.

2. Judd, Richard W., <u>Maine: The Pine Tree State from Prehistory to Present</u>, (Orono, 1995), p. 64.

Chapter 20: Maryland

Maryland, I'm coming home

> — *"Maryland"*
> *Vonda Shepard*

Don't go back to Rockville
And waste another year

> — *"Don't go back to Rockville"*
> *REM*

'Tweener

Maryland benefits (or suffers, depending on your point of view) from its proximity to the nation's capital. It is known for being one of two states out of which the District of Columbia is carved, but other than that distinction it is a state whose personality may be difficult to get a handle on. Its largest city, Baltimore, comes to mind, but many Americans can't place it withing the state's boundaries—"It's somewhere in Maryland" is about all people can usually tell you. After some thought, one might come up with some Maryland associations such as "the Naval Acadamy at Annapolis," or "the Preakness Stakes at Pimlico Racetracks," but even people who familiar with their Civil War histo-

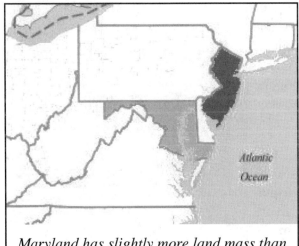

Maryland has slightly more land mass than New Jersey

ry might question whether Maryland fought on the side of the Union or the Confederacy.

Maryland is a 'tweener. It is smack in the middle of the eastern seaboard, and while it sided with the Union during the Civil War, its citizens were passionately divided on the issue, and Maryland had regiments fighting for both sides. (African-American abolitionists Harriet Tubman and Frederick Douglass were both born in small Maryland towns.) It claims over 4,000 miles of coastline, but most of that is along the Chesapeake Bay and its islands; less than half of its shores actually abut the Atlantic Ocean. And while it is generally thought of as a "small" state, that too, is deceiving. It is bigger than New Jersey but smaller than Maine. You could say it is the biggest of the small states or the smallest of the mid-sized ones.

Yet still, this large small state is very diverse. Maryland's highest point is Backbone Mountain at 3,360 feet, and its lowest point is Bloody Point Hole, falling 174 feet below sea level. The highest temperature ever reached in Maryland was 109°F (July 1936) and the lowest trickled in at a chilly -40°F (January 1912), yet Marylanders enjoy a relatively temperate climate most of the time. And when it comes to sports, most Americans might think of baseball great Babe Ruth or the Baltimore Orioles, or pro football team, The Baltimore Ravens, but the state sport is actually *jousting*. Heroes clad in armor, weilding lances, and waving brightly colored banners atop galloping steeds. The medieval tournament has been popular in Maryland for the past 300 years!

George Calvert

Maryland was the undisputed brainchild of George Calvert, a wealthy English courtier in the 1620's whose life was changed dramatically by his conversion to

**George Calvert,
First Lord of Baltimore**

Catholicism in 1625. Calvert had been a favorite of King James I, receiving a knighthood in 1617 and later serving as the king's principal secretary of state. As a member of Parliament Calvert suffered a crisis of conscience when in 1625 that body debated the persecution of Catholics, a religion he had recently espoused. He resigned his seat in Parliament, as well as his secretaryship, but was retained in the King's Privy Council. King James also awarded Calvert an Irish Barony, making him Lord Baltimore of Baltimore, in County Longford, Ireland.

Calvert's interest in colonizing abroad built up for some years. Before his retirement, he served as a member of the London Company, which financed and orchestrated the founding of Jamestown, and as a member of the East India Company, he oversaw British interests in the Far East. In 1620 he initiated his first attempt at colonization in the New World with the purchase of a plantation at Newfoundland. After retiring, Lord Baltimore took his family to the settlement—which he had named *Avalon*—but after a brutal 1628-29 winter, he determined that he might prefer to begin a colony somewhere a bit warmer and not so vulnerable to French war ships.

King Charles I of England

The Catholic Connection

Besides wanting to change the location of his colony, Lord Baltimore's motivations for wanting to colonize also changed. No longer simply a financial venture, Calvert now wanted to establish a refuge for persecuted Catholics and for anyone, for that matter, who was fleeing religious persecution.

King James died in 1625, so in 1632 it was from his son, King Charles I, that Calvert requested a new charter for land further south in Virginia. The King was prepared to grant him this land, which would have encompassed the southern portion of present-day Virginia and northern section of North Carolina. Jamestown residents, however, strongly objected to the establishment of a Catholic haven in such close proximity and voiced their objections rather assertively, so Calvert changed his request to a section of Virginia north of the Potomac River. Apparently King James' esteem for Lord Baltimore had transferred from father to son, and King Charles signed a charter which was written primarily in Calvert's own hand, "leaving only a blank therein for the name of the proposed province."[1]

Lord Baltimore preferred the name "Crescentia," after a Catholic martyr but deferred to His Majesty:

> "The King, before he signed the charter, put the question to his lordship, what he should call it, who replied that he desired to have it called something in honor of His Majesty's name, but that he was deprived of that happiness, there being already land in those parts called Carolina. 'Let us, therefore,' exclaimed the King, 'give it a name in honor of the Queen. What think you of Mariana?' Upon Lord Baltimore's recalling the fact that a Jesuit by that name had written against the monarchy, the King proposed Terra Mariae [Mary Land], which was concluded on and inserted in the bill."[2]

Juan Mariana

The Jesuit who had "written against the monarchy" was Juan Mariana of Spain who, in 1598, published a defense of tyrannicide. He argued, among other things, that it was appropriate for a person to assassinate a king who imposed taxes without the consent of his subjects. After the fatal stabbing of King Henry IV of France in 1610, Mariana's arguments were used as a defense of the assassination. King Henry IV was the father of Charles' bride, Henrietta Maria. It certainly would not do to "honor" the queen by naming the colony after a defender of her father's assassin.

An Appropriate Choice

Maryland, then, was named for King Charles I's wife, Queen Consort Henrietta Maria of France. Besides being the daughter of King Henry IV of France and Marie de Medici, she was the younger sister of France's King Louis XIII. She married King Charles very shortly after his ascent to the throne, when she was only fifteen years old. One of the many controversial aspects of Charles' reign was his wife's Catholicism and her refusal, just like Lord Baltimore, to reject her faith.

The beginning of their marriage was strained and stormy. Charles attempted to exert an awkward control over the young Queen, and she, headstrong and emotional, refused to be controlled. In one instance, Charles sent all of Henrietta Maria's French servants back to France, replacing them with English ones. The young Queen, heartbroken and fiercely defiant, let loose with a tantrum at the end of which she knocked out a window with her bare fists.

After a few tumultuous years, though, the King and his Queen grew to genuinely love each other and together had nine children. Henrietta Maria would eventually attempt to aide her husband in his fight against the Parliamentary forces during the English Civil War, a war which Charles himself was busily provoking by doing things like marrying a catholic princess and granting prime American real estate to a devout Catholic whose expressed intent was to create a Catholic refuge.

The Palatinate

George Calvert died in June of 1632, only a few days after his conversation with King Charles regarding a name for his new colony. It was left, then, to his son Cecilius, or Cecil Calvert, the second Lord Baltimore, to receive the charter and build the new province. The first charter of Maryland was

The Ark and the Dove

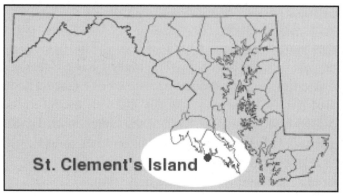

St. Clement's Island

therefore issued in Cecil's name, and he is the one who sent two ships, the *Ark* and the *Dove,* with their cargo of about two hundred colonists and provisions, to begin the colonization of Maryland. The ships arrived at St. Clement's Island on March 25, 1634, and the passengers promptly held Mass to thank God for their safe arrival. March 25th is still celebrated in the state as "Maryland Day."

From its inception Maryland was a "palatinate," which is to say it was

Charles Calvert, Fifth Lord Baltimore

governed by a proprietor—Cecil Calvert until 1675—who had quasi-royal authority. The word "palatine" is derived from Roman times and described a palace guard. In English history, it came to describe a feudal lord who exercised sovereign power over his lands. Lord Baltimore answered only to the King of England and had the power to make laws and grant land however he chose; thus his control was nearly absolute.

Through the end of the seventeenth century, the colony endured a series of power struggles that mimicked those taking place in England between the Puritans of Parliament and the Royalists, who were loyal to the king. When the Parliamentary forces defeated and executed King Charles I in January of 1649, the proprietorship of Maryland was overthrown by Puritans. Then, in 1660, when King Charles II was restored to the throne of England, Cecil

Calvert once again regained control of his palatinate. Calvert's descendants maintained the palatinate until the "Maryland Revolution" of 1689, when Puritans once again took over the government of the colony. But the palatinate was restored one final time when, in 1715 Charles Calvert took the helm as the last Calvert to rule Maryland.[*]

Mason-Dixon Line

It was Charles Calvert, the fifth Lord Baltimore, whose reign oversaw the shrinking borders of Maryland. Like virtually everywhere else in the Colonies, Maryland was embroiled in border disputes on every front but none more pronounced—nor more famous—than the one

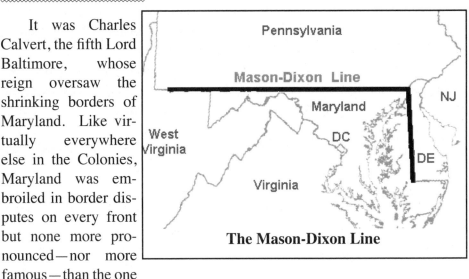

The Mason-Dixon Line

with Pennsylvania and the three sons of William Penn, Jr. This dispute, which Baltimore ultimately lost, was the impetus for some of the most famous and the most creative surveying in America.

The "Mason-Dixon Line" is commonly thought of as the border between North and South, or between Free and Slave states, during the Civil War, but the actual Mason-Dixon Line is the border between Maryland and Pennsylvania. Charles Mason and Jeremiah Dixon, two English astronomers and mathematicians, were hired to determine the location of the boundary between the two colonies, and they did so between 1763 and 1767. They placed stone markers at every mile and larger stones at every

---

[*] *There was, in fact, a sixth Lord Baltimore, Frederick Calvert, son of Charles. Frederick, however, was an aloof proprietor of the colony, and never once travelled to it. He did, however, have official "ownership" of Maryland at the time of the American Revolution, and therefore was, technically, the Calvert who oversaw the family's permanent loss of the colony.*

fifth mile. On the north side of the stones, they laid the arms of the Penns and on the south, that of the Calverts. They also cut down trees, creating a swath divided in half by the border line. This demarcation effectively ended the famous border war between the two families less than a decade before their proprietorships became inconsequential with the American Revolution.

Maryland was the seventh state to ratify the U.S. Constitution, which it did on April 28, 1788. Some time later (an exact date is difficult to determine, though one would have to guess mid- to late-twentieth century), the term "Delmarva" was coined to describe the peninsula Maryland shares with Delaware and Virginia, Maryland consuming the bulk of it.

Delmarva. It's an interesting coinage that compactly reduces to one word the symbolism and sentiment conveyed in the names of an English lord and two English queens. (See corresponding chapters.)

---

1.   Andrews, Matthew Page, <u>History of Maryland: Province and State</u>, (Hatboro, 1965), p. 11.

2.   Andrews, p. 11.

Chapter 21: Massachusetts

I wanna tell you 'bout the town of Stockbridge, Massachusetts, where this is happenin'. They got three stop signs, two police officers, and one police car, but when we got to the scene of the crime, there was five police officers and three police cars, bein' the biggest crime of the last fifty years and everybody wanted to get in the newspaper story about it.

— *"Alice's Restaurant"*
Arlo Guthrie

Feel I'm goin' back to Massachusetts.
Something's telling me I must go home.
And the lights all went out in Massachusetts
The day I left her standing on her own.

— *"Massachusetts"*
Bee Gees

"Baseball is like a poker game. Nobody wants to quit when he's losing; nobody wants you to quit when you're ahead."

—*Jackie Robinson*

Religion

Religion—of all denominations—strongly dictates American culture and societies, more in some states than in others. Utah is known for its Mormons, North Dakota has a decidedly Lutheran bent, Alabama and Mississippi give us Southern Baptists, and Massachusetts is equally identified for its marked Catholic roots. To be fair, the association extends most acutely within the city limits of Boston, but as the dominant city of the state, the link to Catholicism radiates outward. Historically speaking, this religious association could scarcely be more ironic. The Puritans and Pilgrims who

213

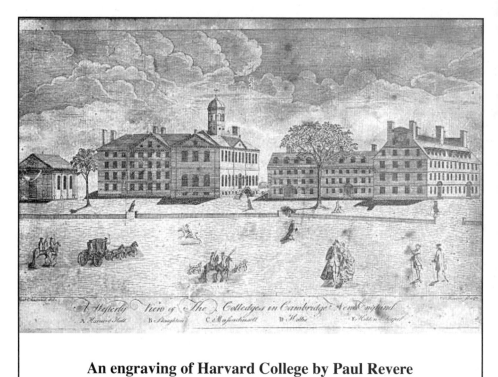

An engraving of Harvard College by Paul Revere

first settled the coast of New England were Protestants escaping the oppression of the Catholic monarchy in England. Yet modern-day Massachusetts supports a Catholic population that is nearly double that of its Protestant population—the result mainly of immigration from predominantly Catholic places such as Ireland, Italy, Poland, and Puerto Rico. Both historically and currently, Massachusetts proves to be a stronghold of religious influence.

When denizens of the Commonwealth of Massachusetts weren't concerning themselves with religious matters, they may have been busy explaining to the rest of the country how they themselves preferred to be named. People from Boston are cleverly known as "Bostonians," but for Massachusetts residents who live outside the city limits, the conversion from state-name to resident-name is a little less clear. Officially, we should be calling them "Bay Staters," a term that seems obvious enough considering we're talking about The Bay State, founded on Massachusetts *Bay*. But this designation feels like something of a cop-out. After all, even Illinois gets away with Illinoisans!

But Massachusetts simply refuses to follow the rules. Rather than finding an appropriate suffix for the 13 letter-long state name—Massachusetts shares the title of the longest name with both of the Carolinas*—yet we can be assured that someone, somewhere, possibly at Harvard, has tried. Massachussians?

Harvard. Including *University* is simply unnecessary. Founded in 1636, the oldest higher learning organization in the country and member of the prestigious Ivy League, Harvard is undoubtedly one of the most famous institutions in the United States. Its austere history dates back farther than most states have existed. It serves as an American emblem for original theories and ideas—the very basis upon which America was founded.

Captain John Smith

If you want to learn more about the name "Massachusetts" a good place to start is with the history of Virginia, because the person responsible for first placing the word "Massachusetts" on European maps was Captain John Smith—the same John Smith of Jamestown fame, Pocahontas fame, Virginia fame. While Smith belongs indelibly to the history of Virginia, his mark on New England, while perhaps not as famous, is at least as heroic—in fact, almost superhuman.

In 1614, after having recovered from a gun-powder accident that forced his de-

Captain John Smith

* *This is, of course, only true if one uses the name "Rhode Island" rather than that state's "official" name. (See Rhode Island)*

John Smith's Map of "New England"

parture from Jamestown, Smith was hired by the Northern Virginia Company to explore the coast of the northern section of the continent, very near where the French were already establishing themselves. Smith explored the coastline from Nova Scotia to Rhode Island, providing his employers and potential colonists with the first description of this land, which he named "New England." However, when Smith attempted to return to New England he was captured by French pirates and kept prisoner on their ship for several months. Ever industrious, Smith used his time in captivity to write "A Description of New England" which he was able to keep with him when he escaped the pirates during a storm and made his way safely to the European mainland. When he got back to England he published the book, and it became a smashing success.

Smith's first mention of the word "Massachusets" was in reference to the people of that tribe, and was not remarkable, "...The others are called Massachusets," he wrote simply, "of another language, humor, and condition." But later he writes of the land occupied by this tribe with glowing praise, "...And then the Countrie of Massachusets (sic), which is the Paradise of all those parts."[1] He goes on to describe the fertility of the land, the agreeable coastline, and the friendly but valiant natives.

When he presented his book and accompanying map to his benefactor, Prince Charles, Smith requested that His Highness "please to change their barbarous names for such English...."[2] The Prince obliged, and covered the map with names taken from his own realm and his own family. Fortunately Smith provided a legend, correlating the native names with their replacements, or as he puts it, the "old names" with the "new names." Among the other names on the list Smith tells us that *Massachusetts Mount* corresponds to *Cheviot Hills* and that the *Massachusetts River* is now the *Charles River*. In hindsight, Charles might need not have bothered. Of the list of "new" names, only three remain today: The River Charles, Cape Ann (named for Charles' mother), and Plymouth.

The Massachusetts Indians

The name "Massachusetts" is Algonquin meaning "at the range of hills" or "people of the great hills." It described the Indians who lived in the area of Massachusetts Bay around 1614 when Smith visited. The hills referred to are the Eastern Upland section of the state, which extends along the coast and inland forty to sixty miles, and is an extension of the White Mountains of New Hampshire. Some historians actually name the precise hill to which "Massachusetts" refers—the Great Blue Hill—in Milton[3]. While it is debatable whether the word referred to that or any particular hill, it is certain that The Great Blue Hill of Milton was at one time inhabited by Massachusetts Indians.

There is, however, no longer a Massachusetts tribe, nor has there been for hundreds of years. Unfortunately, within three years of Smith's exploration the Massachusetts Indians who inhabited and gave their name to the bay area, were decimated by disease. Generally believed to have been Bubonic Plague, the pestilence ripped through the coastal natives at about a 75 percent mortality rate. To make matters worse, the now weakened and vulnerable people were attacked by rival tribes from the north, virtually wiping out the Massachusetts Indians completely. Those who survived were forced to move elsewhere and ally themselves with neighboring tribes.

The villages they left behind were ghost towns, strewn with the bones of unburied bodies. The fields of corn and squash that they had cultivated were completely abandoned. These were the villages which the Pilgrims found when they arrived in 1620, and into which they moved, relieving them of some of the effort of clearing fields and establishing a township. The Pilgrims called their new settlement Plymouth because that's what it said on the map—the map on which John Smith had removed all the native names and had them replaced with more palatable English ones. But the settlers traded with the Indians and soon returned to many of the native names out of necessity of communication. They were familiar, too, with the name "Massachusetts" because while Smith had changed his map, his book had been a best seller, and had, after all, described *Massachusetts* as a "Paradise." And so, once Plymouth was established and new colonizing efforts were developing back in England, "Massachusetts" became a logical place for charter companies to choose to place their colonies.

The Massachusetts Bay Colony

One such company was the Dorchester Company of Adventurers, whose driving force was a Puritan Minister named John White. White was concerned about poverty among the fishermen in his community, and was in agreement with John Smith about the potential solution—colonization in the New World, particularly in New England where the fishing was good. Unlike the Pilgrims of the Mayflower who were religious separatists and whose discontent with the Church of England was complete, the Dorchester company was a

> "company of puritans; but not a puritanic company...a group of public-spirited men who wished to do something for their country, a little for the Indians, somewhat for the fisherman, and a great deal for themselves."[4]

In 1623 the Dorchester Company financed a fishing settlement on Cape Ann called Stage Fort Point. It was a miserable failure but taught

Roger Conant

the adventurers something about colonization, most notably not to expect fishermen to farm and maintain a plantation. A handful of the fishermen, however, including a man named Roger Conant, stayed in New England and built a few thatched houses at a place the natives called *Naumkeag*. The winters were harsh, and they considered moving south to join the colonies in Virginia, but instead they persevered and awaited word from John White.

White, in the meantime, had reorganized the Dorchester Company into "The New England Company for a Plantation in Massachusetts Bay," and the name says it all. With new funding and new leadership, the goals of John White and the investors had changed from underwriting a fishing village to organizing a much more ambitious colony, and they had chosen the place. On March 19, 1628 a patent was granted for

"'all that parte of Newe England in America' lying between parallels three miles north of 'a greate river there, commonlie called Monomack, alias Merriemack,' and three miles south of 'a certen other river there, called Charles river, being in the bottome of a certayne bay there, commonlie called Massachusetts, alias Mattachusetts, alias Massatusetts Bay...from the Atlantick and westerne sea and ocean on the east parte, to the South sea on the west parte.'"[5]

The rivers used on this patent to define the borders were perhaps ill-chosen because of their winding nature, but the only map available (John Smith's) showed only their mouths, and they seemed reasonable enough landmarks at the time. The year after this patent was granted, the colony obtained a Royal charter for the Massachusetts Bay Company, and the village of Naumkeag, where Conant and a few other hardy folk were still living, was officially renamed "Salem"—derived from a Hebrew word meaning "peaceful." In 1630 the town of Boston was founded and very shortly thereafter made the seat of colonial government, but the name "Massachusetts Bay Colony" continued to refer to the villages of Boston, Salem, and new puritan settlements in the area founded under the Massachusetts Bay Company charter.

While the colony at Plymouth had survived for ten years it had not exactly prospered. Its population at the time of the founding of the Bay Colony was probably around 500 and constituted the primary concentration of English people in New England. That would all change abruptly with the "Great Migration" of the 1630's. In that decade the emigration of people—mostly English and mostly Puritan—to the Massachusetts Bay Colony would grow to around 20,000, and the town of Boston would be surrounded by new villages, perhaps the first suburbs of the New World.

Drawing the Boundaries

In 1678 the General Court of Massachusetts purchased the province of Maine (a province they had controlled for two decades) from the descendents of the patent holder, Sir Ferdinando Gorges. This pushed the northern boundary of the Colony into present-day Maine, but the southern boundary was still the Charles River. Then, the following year the province of New Hampshire, which had also been governed from Boston for several decades, was divided from Massachusetts and made a separate royal province. This separated the Province of Maine from its "mother" province of Massachusetts.

In 1684 the Royal Charter of the Massachusetts Bay Colony was revoked by King Charles II, who resented the independence of the New England colonies. His successor, the unpopular King James II, attempted to unite the English colonies in New England as well as New York and New Jersey under the auspices of the *Dominion of New England* with an appointed governor, the tyrannical Edmund Andros. Andros' governorship ended with his arrest and impris-

Sir Edmund Andros

onment after the English throne was wrested from the Stuart monarchs and the reign of William and Mary began in 1688.

In 1691 a new charter united Plymouth with Massachusetts and officially added the province Maine. On February 6th, 1788 Massachusetts became the sixth state of the Union by ratifying the Constitution. Not until 1820 would Maine be severed from Massachusetts and admitted to the Union separately.

1.   Arber, Edward (ed.), "The Travels and Works of Captain John Smith," *Burt Franklin: Research and Source Works Series #130,* (Edinburgh, 1910) pp. 192-205.

2.   Arber, p. 699.

3.   Morison, Samuel Eliot, Builders of the Bay Colony, (Boston, 1930) p. 10.

4.   Morison, p. 28.

5.   Morison, p. 32.

Chapter 22: Michigan

Old Michigan steams like a young man's dreams;
The islands and bays are for sportsmen.

> --from *The Wreck of the Edmond Fitzgerald*
> by Gordon Lightfoot

"Si quaeris peninsulam amoenam, circum spice" (If you are seeking an amenable peninsula, look around you)

> --*Michigan state motto*

Cars and Coastline

There's a bit of onomatopoeia in the name Michigan. Hear it? The firing of the pistons, the roar of the engine, the car rolling off of the assembly line in Detroit or Flint. The name Michigan seems to exude industrialism, factories, and manufacturing. Since the start of the 20th century, and the introduction of the first horseless carriage, a majority of the newly manufactured cars in the United States have been built in Michigan (though admittedly, in recent decades many other states have invited automobile manufacturing plants into their borders, particularly in the southeastern U.S.). Ford, Oldsmobile, and GM all originated in this state, as did the United Auto Workers Union. Detroit, Michigan's largest city, and the tenth largest city in

Henry Ford

Berry Gordy, Jr.

the country, has born the nickname "the Motor City" since the 1940's.

Of course, the more common version of this nickname is "Motown," a word associated with an entirely different industry. Berry Gordy, Jr., the man who founded Motown Records in the late 1950's, once worked on Henry Ford's automobile assembly line. But Gordy would not become idolized for his fundamental contribution to the automobile industry. Instead, he and Motown Records are credited with first introducing the world to such legendary musicians as The Miracles, Marvin Gaye, Diana Ross, The Jackson 5, and The Temptations, and for playing a significant role in the racial desegregation of pop music.

But perceptions of the state of Michigan have largely to do, perhaps more than with its industry, with its geography. It is the only state that is formed out of two completely separate portions of the continent, though probably a little less separate since the opening of the Mackinac Bridge in 1957. The combination of these two peninsulas under one governmental organization is a curiosity to the uninitiated, and sometimes even to the initiated. The northern peninsula—cleverly titled "Upper Peninsula"—makes more sense as a continuation of Wisconsin than part of Michigan, while the main, or southern, peninsula fits more appropriately as part of Indiana, Ohio, or even Canada.

Movements to create a separate state out of the Upper Peninsula, or "U.P.", or to somehow separate it from the rest of the state have brewed at varying intensities almost since Michigan's formation. In the 1800's such movements proposed "Huronia," "Superior," and "North Michigan" as names for a separate state, sometimes including several northern counties of Wisconsin. Oddly, even though they are both peninsulas, it is the upper that is commonly referred to as such. The southern, mitten-shaped, portion of Michigan is rarely called the "Lower Peninsula" or even "Southern Peninsula," though that's exactly what it is.

With borders that touch four of the five Great Lakes in addition to thousands of islands, Michigan, deceivingly, has more coastline than all but one other state (Alaska). The largest of the islands included within her borders is Isle Royale, a roadless national park of an archipelago, sitting much closer to Canada than to either Michigan peninsula.

Like Alaska, Michigan is known for its abundant game fishing. Fishermen (and fisher-women) come from all over the country to cast out into the deep blue waters of one of the sur-

The state of Michigan is made up of two peninsulas. Since 1957 they have been connected by the Mackinack Bridge.

rounding lakes—both great and small, hoping for the opportunity to catch one of the many species of fish found there.

A Stumbling Block

The French were the first Europeans to explore the Great Lakes and the first to map them and place names upon them. They took their own name for Lake Michigan from the Fox Indians, who referred to a neighboring tribe as *Ouinpegouek* or "People of the Stinking Water," a reference to the algae-rich waters near that tribe's home. The French mistranslated the name into *Lac des Puans*, or "Lake of the Stinking People." Fortunately, like their names for several of the Great Lakes, this one would not last.

Later explorers and cartographers would label Lake Michigan *Lac du Illinois* for the nearby Illini Indians, *Lac St. Joseph* for the St. Joseph River to the south, and *Lac Dauphin* for the son of the French king. Finally, a popular map of 1688 used a derivation of the name that had been offered by Father Louis Hennipin, *Michigami*.[1]

Hennipin applied the name he heard used by natives during his explorations, but a precise derivation or definition of the word has proven elusive. It is certainly based in the same root as *Michilimackinac*, which, as an excellent history of the state by Bruce Catton puts it

> "…is a stumbling block for anyone who writes or talks about Michigan. There are innumerable ways to spell it, there is argument over its meaning, and there is no logic whatever to its pronunciation; on top of which, it does not stay put properly as a historic place should.[2]"

Catton dismisses the notion that the name originally meant "great turtle," a persistent myth based on the perceived shape of Mackinac (pronounced *Mak-i-naw*) Island from a distance that has its defenders even today. Catton based his own theory on an interview with an Ottawa Chief who insisted that the name referred to a tribe of people who once lived in the northern tip of the lower peninsula.

George Shankle's reference book on state symbols also reflects the frustration of determining the origin of this state's name:

> "It would be a noteworthy accomplishment indeed, to be able to say authoritatively just who first gave the name *Michigan* to the Territory which now forms the State of Michigan, and from what exact Indian word it came."[3]

The closest we may be able to come is this: the word *Michigan* is derived from some other, probably much longer, Indian word that is likely of Algonquian origin. Based on the language stock of the tribes who inhabited that area during the seventeenth century, *Michigan* is often referred to as an Ottawa or Chippewa word, but that is not provable. What is even less provable is to what someone might have been referring when they used the word. A group of people? A plot of land? A body of water? Or perhaps something else entirely.

Joseph Harrington, author of a Smithsonian report on state names in 1955, asserts unambiguously that the word means "clearing" but the dearth of references to support his assertion makes that definition entirely unsatisfying. Still, the translation "clearing" has become ubiquitous and is commonly offered today as fact. Others claim the word means "lake" or "large body of water," but it is clear that these definitions originated after the word was applied by Europeans to the lake and the land.

Water, Water Everywhere

Michigan's surrounding waters have historically been her life blood as well as her instrument of isolation. Throughout the seventeenth century Europeans (primarily the French) skirted the shores of Michigan, rowing and sailing their boats around the peninsulas in search of that ever-elusive

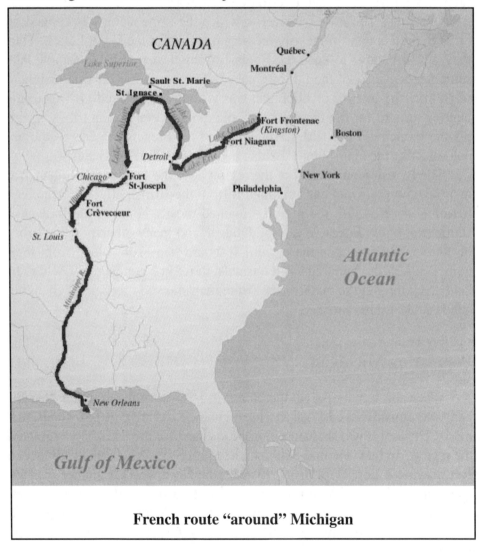

French route "around" Michigan

water route to the other side of the continent. They set up the missions of Sault St. Marie and St. Ignace on the northern side of the straits of Mackinac (the narrow point that separates the two parts of Michigan), but the lower portion was relatively unexplored on the interior, simply because it was just too easy to get around it. The French were primarily trying to get *past* Michigan, and they didn't need to get out of their boats to do it, so on they went, all the way through Wisconsin, and after a short portage, down the Mississippi River to the Gulf of Mexico.

Detroit was built to protect—not the land—but the water routes. The French, who were engaged intermittently in warfare with the English, constructed *Fort d'Etroit* on the river to which the same name was applied, in order to protect their monopoly on the navigation of the Great Lakes. Thus they would be able to keep the Englash from choking off the remote lake settlements in case of the fall of Quebec. But even after the establishment of Detroit, the interior of Michigan was virtually untouched. It was prime hunting ground for the furs being supplied by several Indian tribes, a supply the French did not wish to hinder. And the French, in general, did not colonize like the land-hungry British and, eventually, Americans.

The British won control of the region after the French and Indian War in 1763, and the Americans claimed it from the British after the American Revolution. But still, the region remained mostly home to the Indians— Chippewa, Sauk, Foxes, Wyandot, Ottawa, and many others. While tribes of Native Americans on the eastern seaboard had been forced from their homelands by the hundreds of thousands, those in Michigan still held their land, even though the maps of the white men showed it officially changing hands at least three times.

Populating Michigan

When the U.S. broke up the Northwest Territory the moniker "Michigan" was considered early on as a useful name for one of the new states, primarily because it was the name Europeans used for the lake that dominated the region. In fact, Thomas Jefferson had proposed "Michigania" to label a part of what is now Wisconsin. Instead, the Northwest Ordinance was adopted in 1784, providing for the division of the acquired lands into no more than five, and no less than three, new states. Michigan Territory was carved from the northwestern part of Indiana Territory in 1805, and it remained a territory until 1837, longer than any other in the Old Northwest. Initially Michigan included all of Wisconsin, and after the Louisiana Purchase was made in 1803, her boundaries were extended to the Missouri River. The territory now included all

1834 Map of Michigan Territory showing its boundaries extended all the way to the Missouri River

of what are now Minnesota and Iowa, and parts of the Dakotas.

Still sparsely settled, however, Michigan in the early 1800's was simply too remote and too inaccessible for Americans to flock to, especially when there was plenty of land (and plenty of "Indian trouble") in Ohio, Indiana and Illinois. But then in 1808 John Jacob Astor established his fur trading company, and Michigan was its primary supplier. And then came the Erie Canal.

Hundreds of miles away from each other, New York and Michigan are connected by water—Lake Erie, to be precise. But the route from New York *City*, the state's main seaport, and the lake was either circuitous or overland—either way it was slow. And so, between 1820 and 1825, New York State oversaw the completion of a 363-mile canal from the Hudson River just north of Albany to Lake Erie, which would provide an easy water route for settlers into the Great Lakes region and access to new markets for them to serve and be served by. By 1830 the white population of Michigan Territory was over 200,000—more than ten times that of pre-canal Michi-

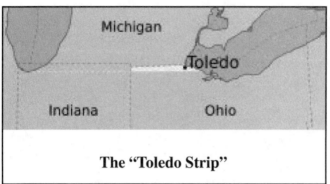

The "Toledo Strip"

gan. The previously insulating waters surrounding Michigan's peninsulas were now flooding her with people.

The U. P. And

Toledo

The reason that the Upper Peninsula is part of Michigan has partly to do with the city of Toledo, Ohio. By the provisions of the Northwest Ordinance, the city of Toledo (or more precisely, its location at the mouth of the Maumee River, a coveted water route) belonged to Michigan, whose border extended east from the southern-most tip of Lake Michigan. But when Ohio achieved statehood, it placed in its constitution a claim on the "Toledo Strip"--a tiny sliver of land created by moving the east end of Michigan's southern border north about ten miles.

This border dispute, known as the "Toledo War," raged for decades and hit its peak when Michigan was lobbying hard for statehood in 1835. As a way of compromising, Congress offered Michigan the Upper Peninsula in return for forfeiting its claim on the Toledo Strip. Michigan refused--the U.P. was considered a wasteland and no substitute for the thriving port city of Toledo. Finally, in 1837, Congress sweetened the pot, offering Michigan a share of a budget surplus of $400,000, to be distributed among all of the states. Territories were not eligible for the cash, so Michigan acquiesced on the Toledo Strip and begrudgingly took the U.P. and the money. Andrew Jackson made Michigan the 26th state on January 26, 1837.

1.   Snyder, Fred, "The Great Lakes - Still Great by Any Other Name," Michigan Department of Environmental Quality, http://www.michigan. gov/deq/0,1607,7-135-3313_3677-15930--,00.html 3/4/03.

2.   Catton, Bruce, <u>Michigan: A Bicentennial History,</u> (New York), p. 11.

3.   Shankle, p. 73.

Chapter 23: Minnesota

"My governor can beat up your governor."

> —*Bumper sticker emblazoned with a picture of Jesse "The Body" Ventura, governor of Minnesota 1999-2003*

"There goes my Minnesota girl"

> — *"Minnesota Girl"*
> *Green Day*

"I'm looking California,
and feeling Minnesota."

> — *"Outshined"*
> *Soundgarden*

True Colors

It is difficult to say the word "Minnesota" without adopting the manner of natives of that state—a sing-songy lilt with the third syllable drawn out and a puckering of the lips: *Min-nuh-suōōō-tuh*. And then it makes us smile.

In fact, just about everything about Minnesota makes us smile: the Mall of America, Former Governor Jesse "The Body" Ventura, Senator Al Franken, and Gophers. Even the nickname of its two largest cities, "The Twin Cities," seems all-together non-threatening, and even pleasing, as if the cities it refers to were two young children who look and dress alike but somehow resent being confused with each other.

The word *Minnesota* is a Dakota Indian word which means "sky-tinted water" or "somewhat clouded water" ("minne" for *water* and "sota" for *cloudy* or *bleary*). One missionary in the 1800's told of having a Dakota illustrate the definition of the word to her by dropping a teaspoon of milk into a glass of clear water. This native was describing the Minnesota River which displays a whitish hue during some spring seasons, when the river swells and the light-colored silt along the banks crumbles into the water.

As one historian notes, a recent advertising slogan has led many to believe that *Minnesota* means "land of sky-blue water." An apt comparison could be drawn to the state's citizenry—calm and placid on the surface, but with the ability to stir the waters and surprise the rest of us, stirring a cool blue into a myriad of surprising colors.

Territory after Territory

The Territory of Minnesota was conceived at the very height of westward expansion in the U.S. After the Northwest Territory had been carved up the into individual states, Manifest Destiny took hold and the organization of the rest of the continent into territories and then states was virtually a foregone conclusion. All that was left to do, in the minds of many an enthusiastic expansionist, was to draw borders and place names. Wisconsin, in 1848, was the last of the Northwest Territories to be granted statehood, but instead of keeping the western border of the territory, the Mississippi River, Congress decided to chop the St. Croix valley in half and use that river as the state's new western edge.

This was done in part due to a pragmatic desire to keep the size of each state manageabe and in part due to a partisan political phenomenon. Once statehood became imminent for a particular territory, congressmen would look westward, salivating at the prospect of adding

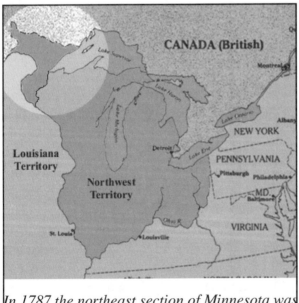

In 1787 the northeast section of Minnesota was part of the Northwest Territory

234

more states, and therefore more representatives in Congress. Democrats wanted to create more Democratic states, and Whigs and Republicans wanted to create more for *their* own party. Slave-holders wanted more slave states, and prohibitionists lobbied for more free states. The same motivations would play out over and over again, notably in the prairie and midwestern states, and was often a major cause of delay in any territory achieving statehood.

The U.S. claimed the land that is now the northeastern portion of Minnesota in 1783 after the Revolution. It was part of the Northwest Territory (for which the Northwest Ordinance was written--see Ohio) and was one of the spoils won from the British and their Indian allies, or at least that was the view of the U.S. government. Technically the region was claimed by Virginia as part of her original charter, but she readily ceded it to the new nation for stewardship under the federal government. The western portion of Minnesota would not be claimed until after the Louisiana Purchase in 1803.

But after 1803 the land was part of a long series of territories. Each time a state was formed by separating an eastern chunk of populated land from an established territory, the new state would usually take the name of the territory, leaving what was left over to be given a new name (and often new borders.) Minnesota, or some of it, had been part of the Northwest Territory, as well as the Territories of Indiana, Louisiana, Illinois, Missouri, Michigan, Wisconsin, and Iowa.

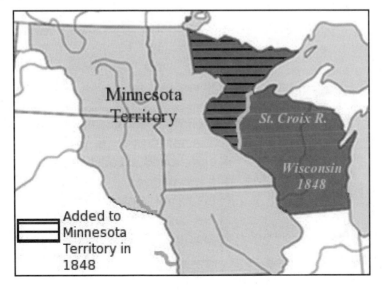

Martin and Brown

"To many easterners *Minnesota* was an almost wholly unfamiliar name," writes one historian, "and they had no idea where the territory really was."[1] It was in 1846, when Wisconsin was still lobbying Congress for statehood, that the name "Minnesota" was proposed for the western portion of the territory that would not be included in the new state. It was possibly the first time most of the Congressmen had ever heard the word uttered, and the person who uttered it was Wisconsin's territorial delegate, a lawyer named Morgan L. Martin. Martin would later claim that, while serving in the Wisconsin legislature he learned the word from a colleague, a former soldier and adventurer named Joseph Renshaw Brown. Unlike Martin, who lived in Green Bay, Brown lived near St. Paul and had served at Fort Snelling. He would have known that the Dakota Indian name for what Americans called the "St. Peter River" was *Minnesota*.

Martin's speech to Congress in 1846 was a plea for statehood for Wisconsin but included a proposal for the "organization of the Territory of Minnesota" as a way of disposing of those lands which would be left out of that state. Dominant in the proposed new territory was the Mississippi River, but that name, alas, was taken. Another prominent waterway was the St. Peter, but that name was inappropriate due to its religious overtones, and besides, Indian names were "all the rage."

Joseph R. Brown

Martin's bill was sent to committee where three other names were suggested for the new territory: "Itasca," "Algonquin," and "Chippewa." *Itasca* has an interesting derivation of its own. It was coined by Henry R. Schoolcraft, the explorer who located the source of the Mississippi River. On his journey, Schoolcraft asked a colleague if he knew the Latin phrase for "true source." The best his friend could come up with was "veritas caput," or *true head*. Schoolcraft took the last four letters of the first word and the first two letters of the second to create "Itasca," and used the word to name the lake he believed to be the actual headwaters of the Mississippi River—once he found it. When Morgan Martin's bill came out of the Committee on Territories, chairman Stephen Douglas referred it to the House with the recommendation that "Itasca," and not "Minnesota," be the name of the new territory.

When the House of Representatives debated the bill, two more names were proposed: "Jackson" and "Washington." At this point Martin suggested that his original name be returned to the bill, and not being able to agree on a replacement, the House passed the bill containing its original name, "Minnesota." The senate rejected it. Two years later Minnesota would gain the territorial status it sought, and by that time, the name was much more popular and so was not debated.

As a territory, Minnesota contained all the land within its current borders plus half of North and South Dakota. Not until it became the 32nd state on May 11, 1858—President James Buchanan affixing his signature to the statehood Act—was the western border moved to its present location.

The Suland and the St. Peter

In 1851 a famous treaty—famous largely for its controversy—was signed with the four bands of Dakota Indians who lived along the Minnesota River. In the *Treaties of Traverse de Sioux and Mendota* these four bands, which comprised a division of the Sioux nation, relinquished their rights to the Minnesota River valley, and the land rush for the *Suland* ("Sioux land") began. Though when the word was coined is not exactly clear, it appeared in newspapers of the time as the name for a vast section of southern Minnesota which was now available to settlers.

Jonathan Carver

Interestingly, in the treaty the name of the river which the Dakota were being asked (many historians say "coerced") to give up was "Minnesota." This is notable because, since the 1600's when the river was first discovered and mapped by French explorers, it had been known as the

St. Peter or St. Pierre River. It was Jonathan Carver, a British explorer and cartographer who spent the winter of 1766-67 near St. Anthony Falls (near modern downtown Minneapolis), who first recorded the name "Menesotor" in his popular book "Travels Through the Interior Parts of North America" and on the accompanying map. But by Carver's time, "St. Peter" was already entrenched as the river's official name.

The fact that "Minnesota" appears on the Treaty of Traverse de Sioux reflects the fact that, in the six years from the time the name was first proposed for the territory, it gained widespread use as the official "American" name of the river as well. Just to remove any confusion, however, on March 6, 1852, the Minnesota legislature memorialized the U.S. president, asking that the aboriginal name be used in place of the traditional "St. Peter" for all official government purposes. An act of Congress confirmed the name change on June 19th of that year.

---

1.   Theodore C. Blegen, The Land Lies Open (Minneapolis, 1949) p. 151.

Chapter 24: Mississippi

In 1814 we took a little trip
Along with Colonel Jackson down the mighty Mississip

> — "Battle of New Orleans"
> *Johnny Horton*

M-I-S-S-I-double S-I-double P-I

> — "Mississippi Delta"
> *Bobbie Gentry*

Why this state?

The Mississippi River touches ten U. S. States on its way from Lake Itasca in Minnesota to the Gulf of Mexico. *Mississippi*, the state, does not claim the longest border with the river (that would be Illinois), nor does it contain the source (Minnesota) nor the mouth (Louisiana). It is not the largest of those ten states (also Minnesota), nor was it the first of the ten to achieve territory or state status (Kentucky). The Native Americans who referred to the river as "Messisipi" were the Chippewas, encountered by French explorers near the southern end of Lake Michigan. The Gulf Coast natives, those who

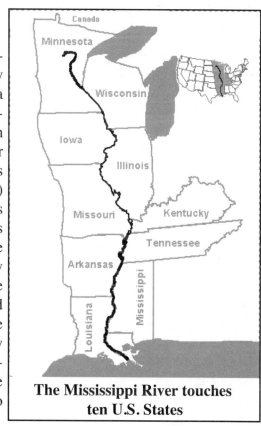

The Mississippi River touches ten U.S. States

actually inhabited what is now Mississippi State, had an entirely different word for the river, "Malbouchia". So how did *Mississippi*, the state, come to bear the name of the mighty Mississippi river?

The answer to that question is vague, but lies in the context of the history of both the river and the state. Indeed, both were known by different names by early European discoverers and settlers—in the case of the river, by *many* different names.

Of course, as a national landmark, it is difficult to beat the Mississippi River in sheer size and volume. Its importance in American history, culture, industry, and commerce is virtually unchallenged by any other natural resource. The mighty river and its banks gave us Mark Twain, riverboats, a massive trade route, and many different tribes of Native Americans who thrived for hundreds, even thousands, of years on her life-giving currents. When combined with the Missouri it is the longest river in North America, and the fourth longest in the world.

The state of Mississippi, however, has a reputation all its own. Besides the obvious "How do you spell that?," the state calls to mind "The South," with all its various images: slavery, the Civil War, southern belles in big hoop skirts, Baptist churches, and thick accents.

One image that Mississippi harbors, though certainly wishes it did not, is that of a poverty-stricken population. It is not an image the state wishes to proliferate, but alas, it need not bother. The state has the highest poverty rate in the country, with many of its western counties—those situated adjacent or very close to the Mississippi River—suffering poverty rates above thirty percent. This has been a misfortune of the state's since the first farmers began to scratch at the land, one that has been burned into our imaginations.

But a 2009 book called "The State of Jones" by Sally Jenkins and John Stauffer reminds us to be careful of our assumptions about Mississippi and its people. It tells the story of Newton Knight, that rarest of creatures, a southern abolitionist who, like his counterpart in the north, John Brown, fought a very personal war not only against slavery, but against bigotry and racism.

For our purposes, it also chronicles the creation of what Knight and his compatriots regarded as a state *separate* from (but within) Mississippi, one where slavery did not exist, and would not be tolerated. And to punctuate their newly created "state," Knight and his men gave it the name of the county they were proud to protect and dominate, creating a new and difficult front for the South in the Civil War.

The Lower Mississippi River

Cabeza de Vaca

Hernando de Soto is generally acknowledged as the first European to discover the Mississippi River. He didn't name it, however, for it already had a name to the Spanish. It was named "Rio del Espiritu Santo" or "River of the Holy Ghost" by Alonzo Alvarez de Pineda who had explored the Gulf Coast in 1519 and applied this name to the mouth of a river he described as "very large and very full"[1]. Later historians guessed that the bay he referred to was actually Mobile Bay.

"Espiritu Santo" appears in 1521 on a map drawn to arbitrate the claims of rival discoverers. On this map the region of the Mississippi belongs to Francis de Garay, governor of Jamaica who had commissioned Pineda's voyage. Garay's dominion was unimpressive by Spanish standards, however, for it was believed to be "too far from the Tropics" to contain gold,[2] and given the riches they plundered from Mexico and South America, Spain wanted virtually nothing else from its New World explorers.

The actual mouth of the Mississippi was likely found by Cabeza de Vaca, the treasurer for an expedition that began in 1527 led by Panfilo de Narvaez. Narvaez was, by all accounts, a brutal and selfish conqueror. He marched his men inland from Tampa Bay where they were molested by natives (not, presumably, unprovoked), and turned back toward the sea. They constructed boats from the hides of their horses and set sail for civilization. Narvaez was never seen again, but de Vaca lived to recount his tale. In it, he describes what historians believe truly *was* the mouth of the Mississippi (though de Vaca had no name for it). In their makeshift boats a few of the survivors attempted to enter the mouth of the great river, but, de Vaca wrote,

"By no effort could we get there, so violent was the current on the way, which drove us out, while we contended and strove to gain the land."[3]

De Soto's efforts were no less futile. His expedition of several hundred men began in 1539, again at Tampa Bay. They marched through the southeastern United States, confronting the natives with almost comical self-importance and belligerence. And when they encountered the mighty Mississippi River it was viewed as an irksome obstacle to be crossed in their quest for treasure, not the majestic waterway that would eventually become such a coveted trade route. De Soto's status as discoverer of the river can only be attributed to the fact that he *must* have crossed it, and the chronicler of his journey, the Gentleman of Elvas, refers to a river which he calls the "Rio Grande" that probably *is* the Mississippi. Arguably de Soto's most compelling claim as the Mississippi's European discoverer is that he was reported to have been buried on its banks.

The Upper Mississippi

After De Soto, the Mississippi went unexplored by Europeans for about a hundred years, after which the French began to close in on its banks in the north. The French explorers differed from the Spanish in almost every way. They were not conquerors but traders and missionaries. They befriended the natives whenever possible (though fought them when they felt it necessary) and generally maintained a healthy respect for their tenacity and willingness—not to mention right—to defend their homeland.

In 1634, French explorer Jean Nicolet journeyed up the Fox River in present day Wisconsin, where he was told by Winnebago tribesmen that there was a river nearby which flowed into the "great water." He did not see the river, nor the tributary which the Indians described, but the "great water" he was told of was the Mississippi River.

The first written instance of the river's current name appears in the *Jesuit Relation* for 1669 to 1670. It was reported by Father Allouez, who had traveled as far as the Wisconsin River, that the "Messisipi," as his Chippewa guides referred to it, was more than a league wide, that it flowed north to south, that the Indians had never traveled to its mouth, and that it was doubt-

Louis Joliet

ful whether it emptied into the Gulf of Florida (meaning modern Gulf of Mexico) or the Gulf of California.[4]

In 1673 a French fur trader named Louis Joliet accepted a commission to explore the "Messipi," translated as the "Great Water" or "Father of Waters." He was accompanied by Father Jacques Marquette, a Jesuit Missionary. The two men explored the Mississippi as far south as the Arkansas River where they encountered Indian tribes in possession of Spanish trade goods. Fearing they would be captured by Spanish forces and imprisoned, the Frenchmen turned back toward Canada. Unfortunately at the end of their journey, Joliet's maps and notes of the expedition were lost in an attempt to shoot a set of rapids in a frail canoe. Joliet himself barely escaped with his life and later tried to reconstruct his journals, but much detail was lost. Marquette's notes were used to fill in the blanks, but he was more a missionary than an explorer, and his accounts were of little consequence except that for some time after the expedition of Joliet and Marquette, the Mississippi River went by Marquette's name for it, "Riviére de la Conception." In one of Joliet's reconstructed maps the Mississippi

Father Jacques Marquette

is referred to as "Riviére Colbert." Jean Baptiste Colbert was a powerful Minister in the court of King Louis XIV and a driving force behind French exploration efforts.

By the time Rene Robert sieur de La Salle navigated the Mississippi to its mouth in 1682 and claimed its banks and tributaries for his King, the river had no less than ten names. Besides those already mentioned it also appeared on Spanish maps as "Rio Escondido," on French maps as "Buade ou Frontenac," the "St. Louis," "La Palisade," and the "River of Louisiana."

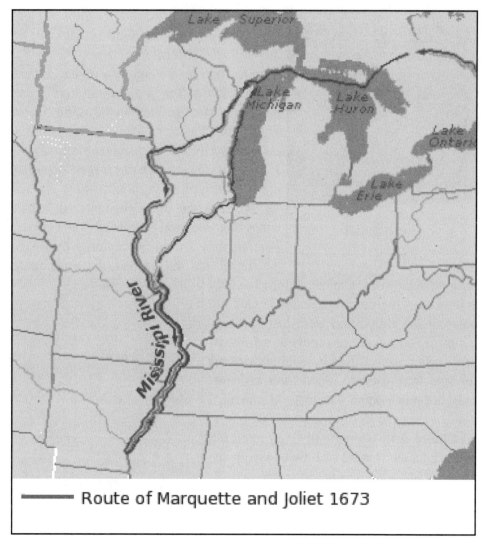

Route of Marquette and Joliet 1673

Other Indian tribes called it "Chu-ca-gua," "Mal-bok-a," and "Namese-si-pon."[5] Even the name by which we now call it had, as one might imagine, countless different spellings since its written form relied upon the phonetic disposition of the writer.

In 1684, Jean-Baptiste Louis Franquelin was the official court cartographer for the French governor-general in Quebec. It was his map which became the standard for French traders and missionaries, and Franquelin chose to use the Chippewa name first recorded fifteen years earlier by Father Allouez. Even though he badly misplaced the mouth of the river and

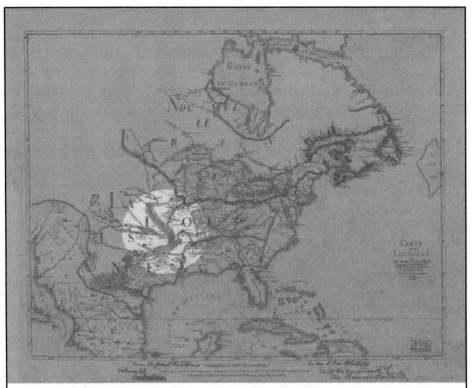

*The heavily flawed Franquelin map correctly shows the
Mississippi River dominating the North American interior.*

made no attempt at its source, Franquelin correctly drew the Mississippi
River dominating the central plains of North America.

Dividing the Land

By 1762, Spain and France had become allies in an all-out world war
against England, one which France was losing. American history calls it the
"French and Indian War," but that name seriously confuses the combatants
(implying that the French were fighting *against* the Indians). The hostilities
were more accurately part of the Seven Years War, a global battle fought
with England and Prussia on one side, France, Spain, Austria and Russia on
the other. The term "French and Indian" refers to the fact that in the interior
of the North American continent, where France and England were the principal powers fighting for dominance, the Indians generally sided with the

French, hoping to drive the land-hungry British back to Europe. Spain gets no billing because her footing on the North American continent was quite tenuous, holding only Florida and a few coastal colonies along the Gulf of Mexico. That however, would change with the war's outcome.

In 1763 the Treaty of Paris was signed to end the Seven Years War, and new borders in North America were established. France, as a controlling power, was removed from the continent, and the land was effectively divided between England and Spain, the border between them being the Mississippi River. England, of course, received the thriving, colonized eastern half of the river basin, and Spain, who was on the losing side of the war, was compensated for more critical losses (namely Cuba), by gaining the relatively unexplored and, at the time, strategically unimportant western half—all the land in between the Mississippi River and the continental divide of the Rocky Mountains.

With the 1763 treaty the mighty river, instead of defining the region of its watershed, uniting its eastern and western banks, now served to divide the land. The river became a dominating border, and remains so today. Every state that touches the river also uses it as a border with a neighboring state. Even at its source, where Minnesota is divided from Wisconsin by a section of the Mississippi, and at its mouth where Louisiana is separated by the Mississippi from the state that bears the great river's name, the river has become, to paraphrase a former U.S. presidential candidate, "a divider, not a uniter."

The West Florida Controversy

By virtue of the 1763 Treaty of Paris, England received Florida from Spain, roughly all of the current state of Florida plus the coastal colonies of the Gulf of Mexico. This included what the British named "West Florida" which "was bounded on the west by the Mississippi River, on the east by the Appalachicola River, on the south by the Gulf of Mexico, and on the north by the northern shores of Lakes Maurepas and Pontchartrain and at 31° north latitude."[6]

In 1764 the British government made a decision that would touch off one of the most complicated border disputes in American history, and it involved the southern portion of the current state of Mississippi.

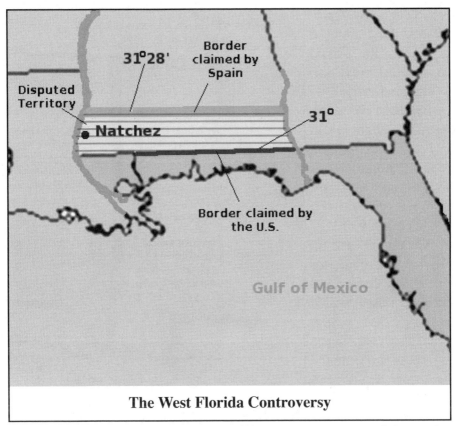

The West Florida Controversy

Finding that the fertile settlements of Natchez fell north of the northern border of British West Florida, the British Board of Trade moved that border slightly northward to 32°, 28'. British West Florida now lay below that parallel, and above it, the British colony of Illinois.

During the American Revolution the colony of British West Florida was a loyalist haven which went unmolested until 1778, when Captain James Willing attacked the settlements in the Natchez District. When France and Spain entered the war on the side of the U.S., Spain quickly took Natchez by force, and at the end of the Revolution, Spain was once again given control of the Floridas.

Thus began the dispute. By the 1783 Treaty of Paris, Britain ceded to the United States the territory between the Appalachians and the Mississippi south to the 31st parallel. She ceded to Spain the colony of British West Florida without reference to its northern border, a border which Britain had moved in 1764 to 32°, 28', to include the coveted Natchez District. Both Spain and the United States claimed the land between 31° and 32°, 28', but

Spain held it by force, and so without going to war again, "the United States could only protest diplomatically."[7]

By the 1790's Europe was caught up in the French Revolution, and the United States was pushing westward full force. Spain felt the encroachment of the Americans, and in 1795 the two countries signed the *Treaty of San Lorenzo* (also called *Pinckney's Treaty*) which gave Americans the right to navigate the Mississippi River, and finally settled—in favor of the United States—the disputed northern boundary of the Natchez District, placing it

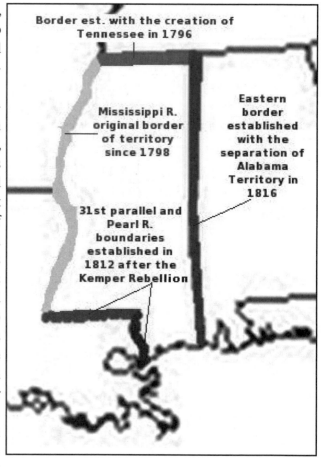

Border est. with the creation of Tennessee in 1796

Mississippi R. original border of territory since 1798

Eastern border established with the separation of Alabama Territory in 1816

31st parallel and Pearl R. boundaries established in 1812 after the Kemper Rebellion

at the 31st parallel. For three years Spain dragged their heels in evacuating the Natchez District, but on March 30, 1798, the last of the Spanish forts was vacated. A week later, on April 7, the U.S. Congress created the Territory of Mississippi.

Territory and State

The borders of the Territory of Mississippi originally bore little resemblance to those of the current state. The western border was the Mississippi River, and along it the district of Natchez was still the most populated region in the new territory. The state of Tennessee marked the northern border, and the Chattahoochee River the eastern. In 1802 the U.S. persuaded Georgia to cede its claim on the lands west of the Chattahoochee, land the U.S. already considered part of the new Mississippi Territory. In 1810 settlers in West Florida rose up against Spanish rule and, in 1812, asked the United States for annexation. The U.S. gave that portion of West Florida between the Mississippi and the Pearl River to Louisiana, and a year later gave to the territory of Mississippi the region between the Pearl and the Perdido. Thus, by 1813 the Mississippi Territory contained all of the land now included in the states of Mississippi and Alabama.

The new territory, from the time of its earliest formation, was already divided economically and socially. The western settlers had become the large cotton plantation owners, while the easterners tended to be smaller farmers of corn and cattle.[8] In March of 1817 the division became official with the creation of the Alabama Territory, and the Mississippi Territory, now with the borders it would carry on to statehood, began the process of electing officials and drawing up a constitution. On December 10, 1817 President James Madison signed the Act that would make *Mississippi* the twentieth of the United States of America.

1.   Severin, Timothy, <u>Explorers of the Mississippi</u> (New York: Alfred A. Knopf, 1968), p. 12.

2.   Severin, p. 12.

3.   Severin, p. 92.

4.   Childs, Marquis, <u>Mighty Mississippi: Biography of a River</u> (New York, 1982), p. 7.

5.   Claiborne, J.F.H., <u>Mississippi as a Province, Territory, and State</u> (Jackson: Power & Barksdale, 1880), p. 32.

6.   Skates, John Ray, <u>Mississippi: A Bicentennial History</u> (New York, Inc., 1979), p.32.

7.   Skates, p. 44.

8.   Skates, p. 68.

Chapter 25: Missouri

It was wonderful to find America, but it would have been more wonderful to miss it.

—Mark Twain

I'm caught up in missing Missouri

— "Missing Missouri"
Sara Evans

Rivers

The story of Missouri is the story of its rivers. Native Americans named them, fought over them, settled on their banks, and taught the French, Spanish, English and Americans all they knew of them. Many Europeans risked their fortunes and their lives upon those rivers, enticed by their size and flow into believing that one of them was the coveted water route from the Atlantic to the Pacific. From the earliest days of European exploration, the rivers movedexplorers and settlers into the middle of the continent, and beyond. La Salle claimed the Mississippi River and all of its tributaries for France; Lewis and Clark and the Corp of Discovery navigated the Missouri from St. Louis to its source, and then crossed the Bitterroots into the mysterious beyond. They

Mark Twain

proved once again the elusiveness of the yearned-for water route across the continent, but still returned to St. Louis true American Heroes.

The name Missouri calls to mind the midwestern quaintness of Mark Twain, the riverboats he dreamed of as a child, and the late 19th century life he painted in story after story about his home state. Huckleberry Finn, Tom Sawyer, and Becky Thatcher are all American icons, as is Twain himself. Like Virginia, Missouri is one of those states that reminds us of our past, so steeped is it in the symbols of Americana.

Just as Twain's stories describe poignantly the division of the nation with regard to slavery and racism, so the story of Missouri tells of a divided people. The state was ground-zero for the slavery issue in the early 1800's, lending its name to the great compromise that many believe forestalled—for better or worse—the Civil War for almost half a century.

On a current map, Missouri still seems somewhat divided. Its two largest cities sit on opposite borders and are shared with their adjacent states.

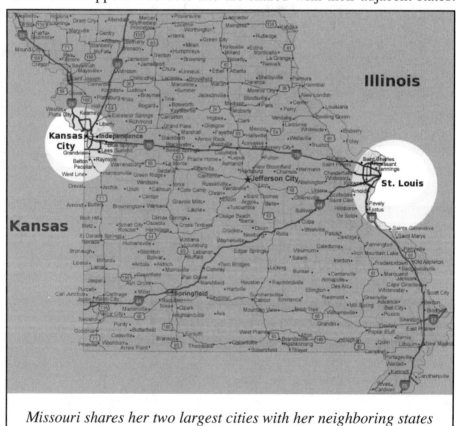

Missouri shares her two largest cities with her neighboring states

St. Louis, historic gateway to the West, is positioned at the confluence of the Mississippi and Missouri Rivers, its eastern section planted firmly in Illinois. Five hours to the west along Interstate 70, at a point where the Missouri River turns north, lies Kansas City, its western section located in its namesake, Kansas. Both of these cities are more quickly associated with Missouri, however, than with the states that share them, because the larger populations of both are, in fact, in Missouri.

In the southeast corner of the state is its "bootheel," a section of Missouri that

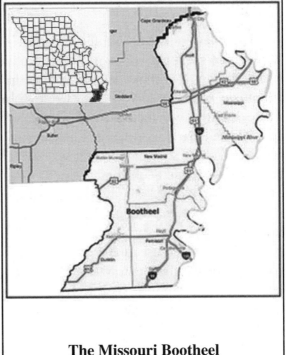

The Missouri Bootheel

looks like what it is. It represents the property claim of a rancher and prominent citizen of the New Madrid section of Missouri Territory in 1812. His name was John Hardeman Walker, and upon learning that his land was south of the 36° 30' parallel that would divide Missouri from Arkansas, lobbied Congress successfully to be included on the north side of the border.

Perhaps it is the influence of Mark Twain. Or maybe it is the history of Thomas Hart Benton, Missouri senator who pushed the concept of "Manifest Denisty." Or his intrepid daughter Jesse, wife of the "American Pathfinder," John C. Fremont, the man who, as governor of Missouri, freed the slaves of his state *before* Lincoln produced the Emancipation Proclamation. Whatever it is, even today Missouri calls to mind the American spirit of adventure and exploration, of our national quest for freedom and self-determination, and of the colorful people who made that happen.

Marquette and Marest

The river which we call the Missouri was called "Pekitanoui" by the Algonquian-speaking tribes of the exploration era. Jacques Marquette, whose Illini guides spoke an Algonquian dialect, was the first European to refer to the river this way when he wrote in 1673 that it joins the Mississippi where "so great was the agitation that the water was very muddy, and could not become clear." For the next half-century the river's name was spelled and pronounced several different ways: Pee-kee-tan-no, Pee-kee-tol-a-ka, Pecha-tan-oke, and Peckatonica, among others.[1] The word Marquette heard from the Illini means "muddy water," and various forms of it appear in other Algonquian dialects, having the same meaning, and referring to the same river.

Marquette also used the word "Missouri" on a map he drew during his voyage. The word appears to signify a village on the Pekitanoui River several miles upstream from its convergence with the Mississippi. The village lies at the mouth of another tributary later named "Grand River." Beginning in the early 1700's Europeans began to refer to "Missouri" (again with various spellings) as the name of the river, the village at the mouth of the Grand, and the people who lived there. Father Gabriel Marest, a French missionary who lived among the Illini around 1712, is often credited with linking the names "Pekitanoui" and "Missouri," and with starting the confusion regarding their definitions. He wrote,

"Seven Leagues below the mouth of the Illinois river is found a large river called the Missouri,—or more commonly Pekitanou; that is to say, "muddy water," which empties into the Mississippi on the West side...it is extremely rapid, and it discolors the beautiful water of the Mississippi..."[2]

This ambiguous statement leaves open the question of which word bore the definition "muddy water," but it is among the first records in which the river was called by the name "Missouri." It has become clear to historians that "Missouri" originally referred to the tribe and their village, and only for lack of a better reference, and an unexplained unwillingness to use the Illini word *Pekitanoui*, began to be used by explorers to name the river as well.

The Tribe

The Missouri were a Siouan tribe closely related to the Oto, Iowa and Winnebago peoples. They called themselves *Niutachi* or *Ne-o-ta-cha* meaning "people who live at the mouth of a river." Some time after contact with Europeans, their numbers were greatly decreased by disease, including whooping cough and smallpox epidemics, and in 1798 the Missouri were further decimated by an attack on their village by Sauk and Fox tribes. The survivors folded themselves into the Kaw, Iowa and Oto tribes, and in 1804 the Oto-Missouris would be the first of several tribes with whom Lewis and Clark would hold a council to introduce the natives of western North America to their "new government." Today the Oto-Missouri tribe numbers about 1300 and are concentrated in Oklahoma near the town of Pawnee.

As early as 1720 another French missionary named Joseph Ignatius Le Boulanger compiled a dictionary of Algonquian terms in which he records the definition of *missouri* as "boat" or "canoe." Later ethnologists recorded the name *emoussulia* or *amassulia* as "boatmen" or "canoemen," and other French explorers sometimes used "les Emissourites" to describe the Indians who lived on the banks of the Missouri River. Father Marquette himself noted in 1670 that the "powerful Nations" who lived along the Missouri did in fact travel in wooden canoes. Thus, the word *Missouri* came to be defined as "he of the big canoe" or "wooden canoe people" or even "village of canoe people."

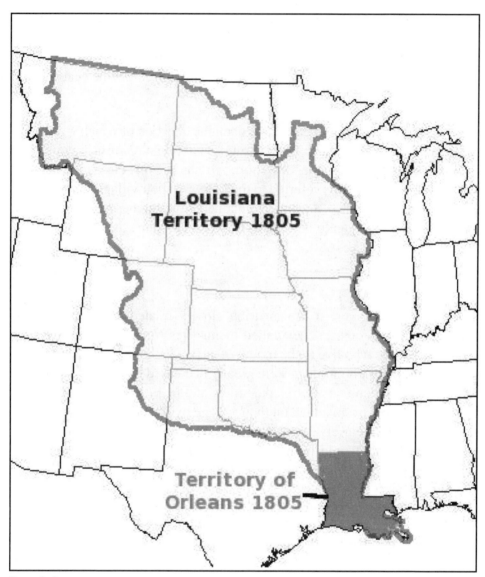

Louisiana

By 1803, when the United States claimed possession of the trans-Mississippi west by virtue of the Louisiana Purchase, the word *Missouri* was entrenched as the name of the river that flowed into the Mississippi from the west, but whose source was not yet known. St. Louis, founded in 1763, was already a thriving fur-trading post and gaining its imminent status as the gateway to the new U.S. possession. But it was not St. Louis, Missouri. The new lands were not yet an official U.S. territory and had no real political or governmental designation. Congress immediately began to struggle with what to do with this vast tract that nearly doubled the size of the country. Thomas Jefferson initially proposed using it as one big Indian reservation including moving European settlers *out*, and eastern Indian tribes *in*. This proposal was short-lived, however, in large part due to objections by French and Spanish settlers in the region, and to the lucrative fur trade emerging in St. Louis, to which white pioneers desperately wanted access.

The whole purchase area began to be called the "District of Louisiana," which was vaguely divided into two parts. "Lower Louisiana," which constituted the current state of Louisiana, and "Upper Louisiana" which was the entire remainder of the purchase area, whose specific boundaries were unknown until well after Lewis and Clark returned from their expedition. In 1805 Lower Louisiana was officially separated at the 33rd parallel and renamed the "Territory of Orleans," while the upper region took the name "Louisiana Territory" for its own.

St. Louis was, by now, the unequivocal "gateway to the west" by virtue of its position at the confluence of the two mightiest rivers in the country. The Mississippi was already well-known and heavily used, but the Missouri was known only to disappear into the "Indian Country," and signified the vast reaches of the new U.S. territory. Lewis and Clark's celebrated exploration of that river, and their return upon it to national exaltations, helped to thrust the name into prominence, associating it with the promise of a new and bountiful frontier.

The Missouri Compromise

In March of 1807, Merriwether Lewis was made governor of the vast Louisiana Territory. He arrived in St. Louis a year later to assume these duties and among his first acts was to invite Joseph Charless to create the first newspaper west of the Mississippi River. The newsman chose as the name for the publication *The Missouri Gazette*. Oddly enough, Charless was among the most vocal opponents of elevating the region's territorial status to statehood, but beginning in 1809, plans were moving forward to do just that.

Missouri's statehood efforts, which began in earnest around 1816, were seriously delayed by the slavery issue. Missouri had been made a territory

Henry Clay proposed the Missouri Compromise

without specifically outlawing slavery, and by the time statehood was officially requested in 1818, the U.S. Senate was equally divided—eleven free states and eleven slave states. Neither side would be able to pass a bill admitting a state without votes from the opposing side and Congress was deadlocked.

Finally, in 1820, Senator Henry Clay of Kentucky, proposed a compromise that would admit Missouri as well as Maine—the former a slave state, and the latter free. Clay would go down in history as the "Great Compromiser" for his proposal.

The compromise also provided that no slave states would be admitted to the union north of Missouri's southern border of 36° 30', except, of course, Missouri. The "Missouri Compromise" many argue, postponed the Civil War for forty years, during which time states were paired off and admitted two at a time as if they were entering Noah's Ark. Thus the status quo was maintained in the U.S. Senate, and the deadlock was lifted.

The act was repealed in 1854, and declared unconstitutional in 1857 in the famous Dred Scott case. But it served Missouri's immediate purpose, and allowed her to enter the Union as the 24th state on August 10, 1821, with the official signature of President James Monroe.

You Say Missouree, I say Missouruh

After several years of debates over land claims, slavery, and suffrage, on June 4, 1812, three days after declaring war on England, James Madison signed legislation elevating the Territory of Louisiana to "second-class" government status, which implied eventual statehood. Two months earlier, the Territory of Orleans had been made a state and usurped the name Louisiana, so a new name was needed for the old Louisiana Territory. *Missouri*, now a popular and dominant name in the region, was rather unceremoniously inserted into the legislation.

However, once the name was adopted as the appellation for the largest territory in the country, a pronunciation debate was touched off. One Missouri historian writes,

> "The new territorial law also authorized a name change: the Territory of Louisiana became the Territory of Missouri. Henceforth, Missouri was to bear the name of the great river that had done so much to shape its history. All that remained was for the people of the territory and later the state to decide how to pronounce it. Was it 'Missouruh' or 'Missouree'?"[3]

The Missouri Compromise drew the slavery boundary at 36°30' and allowed both Maine and Missouri to enter the union.

To the uninvolved, the argument seems a petty one, but the subject of the pronunciation of *Missouri* has sparked as much, if not more, research as the subject of the derivation of the word itself, and it's a debate that continues to this day.

In 2002 Matt Blunt, then Secretary of State for Missouri, sponsored an informal poll at the state fair, asking residents which pronunciation they preferred. While the results indicated that "Missouree" was more popular than "Missourah," the more interesting outcome was the passions which were inflamed by the age-old controversy. The poll sparked letters to editors and the calling of names which were in no way derived from that of the state! Heated tempers aside, however, it appears that Missourians actually love their little debate and do not wish for a resolution—not that there's any danger of one.

1.   Vogel, Virgil J., "The Origin and Meaning of 'Missouri,'" *Bulletin of the Missouri Historical Society*, April 1960, Vol XVI, No. 3.

2.   Vogel, p. 214.

3.   Foley, William E., The Genesis of Missouri: From Wilderness Outpost to Statehood (Columbia, 1989), p. 223.

Chapter 26: Montana

Like Many fly fisherman in western Montana where the summer days are almost Arctic in length, I often do not start fishing until the cool of the evening. Then in the Arctic half-light of the canyon, all existence fades to a being with my soul and memories are the sounds of the Big Blackfoot River and a four-count rhythm and the hope that a fish will rise. Eventually, all things merge into one, and a river runs through it.

— *"A River Runs Through It" (1992)*

"Nobody's Perfect
I gotta work it..."

— *"Nobody's Perfect"*
Miley Cirus, aka Hanna Montana

Anthony 'Tony' Soprano Sr.: *[about his father] He'd been in prison. He was away when I was a little kid. They told me he was in Montana, being a cowboy.*

—*from "The Sopranos"*

The Great Outdoors

Montana is that huge northwestern state that looks like it took a bite out of Idaho. It is a place that, without knowing much about it, people think of as beautiful and inviting. Remember that line in the movie *Hunt for Red October* where Sam Neill says weakly, as he lies dying in the arms of Sean Connery, "I would like to have seen Montana." Most of us have never been to Montana, but it seems like the place you go when you want to disappear into the unspoiled nature of its shining western mountains or the vast rolling hills of its eastern plains. Like Neill's Russian submarine officer, those of us who live in a world starkly different from that which we imagine exists in Montana may find the idea of the state especially enticing. It just sounds peaceful. Maybe it's the name.

Of course, some people hear "Montana" and think not of a pristine wilderness but of a football player—that blond, baby-faced quarterback who could throw on a rope to Jerry Rice. Besides Joe Montana, two other American heroes come to mind: Lewis and Clark. The path of their Corp of Discovery crossed the length of the state both coming and going, along the Missouri and Yellowstone Rivers. To them Montana was part of the undiscovered wilderness of North America, a frontier they were proudly conscious of penetrating.

People may also think of cattle, one of Montana's largest industries. An old truism jokes that Montana has more cows than people, and in fact it does—about three times more. But really, this statistic speaks more to the relatively small population of Montana and to the carnivorous nature of humans—especially humans in the United States. And given the variety of markets Montana's cattle industry serves, the statistic is really not so shocking. Besides a thriving beef production, the state also claims a lucrative dairy industry, as well as being a world leader in providing seedstock— cattle bred for the purpose of...well, breeding cattle.

One thing is for sure. When one envisions Montana, the picture is most certainly one of the outdoors. While we know, rationally, that buildings do exist within the borders of the state, there are none in our mental image. Concrete and steel just don't seem to fit into the picture with all of those mountains, plains, and...cows.

Gold and Vigilantes

After the Louisiana Purchase in 1803 the region of Montana, Wyoming and the Dakotas was commonly referred to on maps as "Indian Country." It was almost completely uninhabited by white people, so Congress largely ignored it while struggling to organize those areas where Americans *were* settling. Then, in 1846 the U.S. signed a treaty with Great Britain continuing the 49th parallel border with Canada all the way to the Pacific Ocean. (It had previously only been recognized as far as the summit of the Rocky Mountains.) And in 1848 the Mexican government ceded all of California and "Eastern California" (Nevada, Utah, and parts of New Mexico, Arizona, Colorado, and Wyoming) to end the Mexican-American War.

Henry Plummer

In 1862 the Civil War fighting began to heat up and so did the Montana gold rush. Of course, it wasn't Montana yet. It was Idaho Territory east of the Rocky Mountains. Prior to that, it had had many official names to the U.S. government. Parts of it had belonged to Washington Territory, Dakota Territory and Nebraska Territory, not to mention its earlier stint as part of Louisiana Territory. But gold-seekers cared nothing of names. Prospectors poured into the mining camps and with them came the lawlessness that historically followed. Vigilance committees, like those created in San Francisco in 1856, were responsible for twenty-two lynchings in the first two months of 1864.

The most notorious of these lynchings was that of a man named Henry Plummer, a gambler and lawman who had come to Idaho to stake a claim in the fevered gold rush. He was hung by a mob in January of 1864 in the town of Bannack, Idaho Territory, for allegedly murdering a hated rival. The historical debate over Plummer's guilt or innocence has fascinated Montanans for over a century and illustrates the murky lawlessness under which the people of the region operated. The citizens in eastern Idaho Territory wanted law and order, and the territorial capital at Lewiston was too far from the mine fields and the eastern plains to be of any use. They decided to appeal to the Federal government.

Edgerton and Ashley

The man sent to Washington to appeal for a new territory was Sidney Edgerton, former congressman from Ohio and known in Washington as a good Republican. Edgerton had been sent to Idaho in 1863 to be the Chief Justice for the territory, but instead

Sidney Edgerton

of going to Lewiston to be sworn into office, he headed to Bannack where miners had recently struck gold, and a lot of it. Rather than establishing law and order for the region, Edgerton and his nephew, Wilbur Sanders, who had been sent along with his uncle as a federal prosecutor, became instrumental in the creation of Bannack's Vigilance Committee—the one that hung twenty-two people including Henry Plummer.

Nevertheless, Edgerton was the man chosen to lead the cause for territorial organization. He left for Washington in January of 1864 and wasted no time looking up his old friend James M. Ashley, chairman of the House Committee on Territories. From 1859 to 1863 the two men had represented Ohio together in the House of Representatives. Edgerton's task was made fairly simple by the fact that the arguments for separating the eastern region from Idaho were sound, and that his political interests were friendly to the Lincoln administration and to Congress which was operating without the southern democrats who had long since seceded. So the process proceeded quickly, as Ashley prepared and then introduced the bill proposing Montana Territory to the House of Representatives on March 17, 1864.

James M. Ashley would, in later years, become known as "The Great Impeacher" for his attempts to impeach and convict Andrew Johnson, believing he had been involved in the assassination of Abraham Lincoln. But this reputation overwhelms many years of state-making which he accomplished as the Chairman of the Committee on Territories. Ashley held this chairmanship from 1861-1869, helping to engineer (and name) many of the western states.

The word "Montana," which is both Spanish and Latin means "mountainous" in both languages, and was a favorite potential state name of Ashley's, one which he dearly wished to apply to any state that contained a section of the Rocky Mountains. He had originally applied the name to what became Ida-

James Mitchell Ashley

ho Territory, but another committee had changed that territory's name to "Idaho," and Ashley was quite disappointed. So when his friend Edgerton asked Ashley to propose a name for this new territory, he immediately suggested "Montana."

Congress

The bill presented to Congress saw little opposition, though there were some details to be worked out, such as the appointment of judges and how much to pay them. There was, however, in the brief congressional debates, some discussion of the name. In the House of Representatives at least one man thought the name "Montana" meaningless until Ashley explained its Spanish derivation and definition. Another delegate offered the name "Shoshone," preferring an Indian name to one imported from a European language. It was pointed out that the word "Shoshone" means "snake," and the proposed name change was quickly abandoned. (The name "Shoshone" is now believed to mean "grass house people," derived from the fact that certain tribes of Shoshone built their homes out of woven grass mats. The "snake" theory, however, persisted for years.) Other members of the House wanted to honor a statesman with the naming of the new territory, and the names Jefferson and Douglas were proposed. But these monikers "...met with little favor in a body dominated by Republicans."[1]

When the measure arose in the Senate, there was still more discussion of the name. Charles Sumner of Massachusetts questioned the name "Montana," claiming it "...strikes me as very peculiar..." and that it "...must have been borrowed from some novel or other." Sumner stated he would prefer an Indian name, a name "from the soil," but when pressed to suggest one, he admitted he did not know the region well enough to do so.

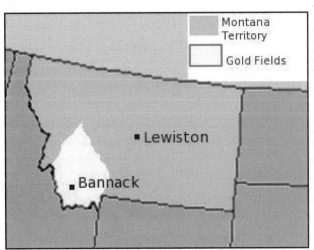

Montana Territory

Gold Fields

• Lewiston

• Bannack

Senator Jacob M. Howard of Michigan quickly responded to Sumner's curiosity about the name "Montana," saying "...I was equally puzzled when I saw the name in the bill, and I ...was obliged to turn to my old Latin dictionary to see if there was any meaning to the word Montana, and I found there was...It is a very classical word, pure Latin. It means a mountainous region, a mountainous country." Howard further championed the name saying "You will find that it is used by Livy and some of the other Latin historians, which is no small praise."

Senator Benjamin Wade, who represented Ohio just as Ashley and Edgerton once did, summed up the entire discussion rather succinctly. Apparently wanting to move on to other topics, Wade noted, "I do not care anything about the name. If there was none in Latin or in Indian I suppose we have a right to make a name; certainly just as good a right to make it as anybody else. It is a good name enough." And that was the end of the discussion on what to name Montana.

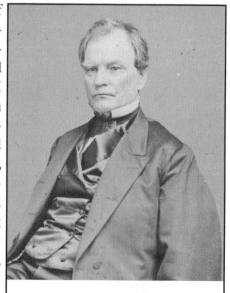

Senator Benjamin Wade

Indians and Statehood

The bill passed Congress fairly easily, and on May 26, 1864, Abraham Lincoln signed the Territory of Montana into existence. The next month he appointed Sidney Edgerton the first governor of the territory. James M. Ashley, the man who named the state, would also serve as governor of the territory a few years later. After leading the fight to impeach Andrew Johnson, Ashley failed to be reelected to the House of Representatives in 1869. As a consolation prize, the new president, Ulysses S. Grant, appointed him to the position of Montana governor, where he served for only one year.

Some irony can be found in the attempt by Charles Sumner to replace "Montana" with an Indian name. Certainly the naming strategy in the creation of most of the western states commonly included aboriginal words,

George Armstrong Custer

preferably—though not necessarily—words that applied to the region being named. But like most members of Congress, and most white Americans, Sumner knew almost nothing of the region he was proposing to name, and what he did know was of the few white Americans who lived there. But a decade after Sumner's feeble attempt to apply an Indian name to the region, Montana would become the site of one of the most famous clashes between white Americans and native Americans—The Battle of the Little Bighorn, also known as Custer's Last Stand.

The Little Bighorn battle marked the pinnacle of strength of the Sioux Nation in their escalating hostilities with the U.S. Army. But it was also the beginning of the end of American Indian wars. Skirmishes continued for the next ten years, but the support of white Americans wasw now with the U.S. army in its attempt to avenge the death of Custer and quell the Indian "threat" once and for all.

By 1888 several western states had languished in territory-hood for over a decade, and Congress was feeling the pressure to grant statehood to them all. An enabling act was passed by that year's lame-duck session providing for the inclusion, pending constitutions and elections, of Montana, Washington, and the two Dakotas. On November 8, 1889, with the swift signature of President Benjamin Harrison, Montana became the 41st state in the Union. One year later final defeat of the Sioux was garnered one state away at Wounded Knee, South Dakota.

1.   Hamilton, James McClellan, <u>From Wilderness to Statehood: A History of Montana, 1805-1900</u> (Oregon, 1957), p. 277.

Chapter 27: Nebraska

"From the town of Lincoln, Nebraska
with a sawed-off .410 on my lap"

> — *"Nebraska"*
> *Bruce Springsteen*

"Ready or Not, Omaha, Nebraska..."

> — *"(Ready Or Not) Omaha, Nebraska"*
> *Bowling for Soup*

"Go Big Red!"

Nebraska's reputation is a bit enigmatic. Some people think of grazing cattle or a Big Mac, as Nebraska has a thriving beef industry. But when it comes to instan images, more of us probably associate beef with Texas or Montana. Corn comes to mind, but its association with that crop cannot rival that of its eastern neighbor, Iowa. Perhaps if Kevin Costner were to make a movie about a corn field in Nebraska...

It separates the fertile farm land of the Midwest from the Rocky Mountain states of Wyoming and Colorado. It sits between the rolling plains of Kansas and the badlands of South Dakota. Nebraska's reputation draws on all of these neighbors to form images of a northernish Great Plains farming state in the heartland of the country.

If Nebraska has a personality of its own, it must surely be associated with football. The whole state lives for football season—at least it seems that way. Consider...

The nickname "Cornhusker" was not adopted by the University of Nebraska as its mascot because of some previous association with the state. It was, in fact, a name that the *state* adopted from the University football team (and other athletic teams) in 1945.

According to the Nebraska Blue Book, the official state song, *A Place Like Nebraska*, contains the line "with cool winding streams / and good football teams..."

The first University of Nebraska football game was played in 1890—only twenty-three years after Nebraska became a state.

With its short, wide panhandle and its curved northeastern corner, Nebraska's shape on the U.S. map is distinctive, breaking up the monotony of all the pseudo-rectangles that surround it. Historically, both the Mormon Trail and the Oregon Trail passed through Nebraska, as it is a convenient state to cross. As one Nebraska history book calls it, "A place on the way to somewhere else."[1]

Fremont

The "American Pathfinder" John C. Fremont

John C. Fremont, the "Pathfinder" of the American West, is often credited with "naming" Nebraska. This reputation is due to a note made in his report on his very first expedition westward in 1842. He wrote,

"Crossing on the way several Pawnee roads to the Arkansas, we reached, in about twenty-one miles from our halt on the Blue, what is called the coast of the Nebraska, or Platte river."[2]

This sentence would indicate that the name for what we now call the

Platte River was not firmly settled in 1842, but despite this particular comment, Fremont refers to the river as the *Platte* in every other reference in the report. Indeed, the exhaustingly long title of the document is "A Report on an Exploration of the Country Lying Between the Missouri River and the Rocky Mountains, on the Line of the Kansas and *Great Platte Rivers*." (emphasis added)

Why Fremont chose to be ambiguous about the river's name in this particular reference is not clear, but his maps of this expedition also use the uncertain label "Nebraska or Platte River." Apparently by the time his journal was transcribed and published, the name Platte had been more firmly decided upon.

Whatever the reason, his ambiguity had some effect. In 1844 an expansionist named William Wilkins, serving at the time as U.S. Secretary of War, submitted his annual report to President Zachary Taylor. It contained the recommendation that the region west of the Missouri River be organized into a territory and that "The Platte or Nebraska River being the central stream would very properly furnish a name to

The Platte River is, in most places, wide and shallow

the territory. Troops and supplies from the projected Nebraska territory would be able to contend for Oregon with any force coming from the sea.[3]" Wilkins' naming suggestion was by no means revolutionary. Three of the four territories—Iowa, Missouri and Arkansas—which had so far been created out of lands obtained in the Louisiana Purchase had been given the aboriginal names of major rivers in their regions, rivers that had originally been named after tribes who lived nearby. While the continent's central plains are not generally known for their dominant rivers, the system seemed to be working and so government officials like Wilkins were disposed to continue it.

The French

But John C. Fremont was not the first to use the name Nebraska. Nor did he apply the name Platte. He was using names which had been previously documented by French explorers more than a hundred years earlier.

Ètienne de Veniard, sieur de Bourgmont, is generally regarded as the first white man to explore the Platte River. He did so in 1714, and noted in his journal, "Higher up the river, one finds the Large river, called Nibraskier by the French and Indians."[4]

But Bourgmont may have been a bit premature. For twenty-five years after his trip, the French explored very little west of the Missouri. Then in 1739 two Canadian Frenchmen, brothers Pierre and Paul Mallet, proposed finding a route to the Spanish settlements in New Mexico by way of the Missouri River. In their attempt, they found and named the Platte River. Chances are they knew of Bourgmont's "Nibraskier" River, but given their circuitous wanderings (they started in New Orleans!), they did not realize that the river they named *Platte* was the same as Bourgmont's *Nibraskier*.

Or perhaps they did. The words actually mean the same thing. *Platte* is French for "flat," while *Nebraska* or *Ni-ubthatka* is an Oto (Siouan dialect) word for "flat, or spreading river." Bourgmont, who had lived among the Missouri Indians for many years and was married to a Missouri woman, would have been accustomed to using the native names for the rivers he found. The Mallets, whose motivations were to find and plunder the Spanish silver mines that they believed existed in New Mexico, would have been more likely to translate the word, using a French name rather than that of the natives. At any rate, the Mallet's name for the river became common on

French maps, and by the time of Fremont's 1842 expedition, Platte was the most widely used name for Nebraska's dominating river.

Stephen Douglas

William Wilkins' suggestion in 1844 to create a new "Nebraska Territory" seemed to make an impression. On December 17, 1844, a bill was introduced in Congress to do just that. The proposed territory included what are now Nebraska, Kansas, the Dakotas, and parts of Colorado, Wyoming and Montana . But unfortunately for Wilkins and other champions of organizing the region, the divisions between north and south, free and slave, were once again affecting territorial politics. The Missouri Compromise had dictated that no slavery would be allowed north of the 36° 30' parallel, and the South, wanting to keep the balance of power in the Senate, would not approve any bill that created a new free state.

Stephen Douglas

For the next ten years, various forces would clamor for territorial organization of Nebraska. The most vocal were the railroad companies who wanted to build a line along the Platte River. But also demanding territorial status were settlers—those who wanted to move into the region, as well as those who were already squatting there in defiance of the law.

It was the railroad issue that most motivated Stephen Douglas. Representing Illinois in the U.S. Senate, he was interested in establishing Chicago as a railroad hub and to this effect lobbied hard to get the Platte River route built. It was Douglas who had introduced the first Nebraska Bill in 1844, and he would continue fighting for the territory for ten years.

Finally, in 1854, all of the issues came to a head. The solution involved dividing the territory and repealing the Missouri Compromise. Douglas and the Republicans agreed to cut off a southern section of what would have been Nebraska and call it "Kansas," thereby creating a territory that southerners were sure they could bring into the southern (i.e. slavery) fold. The bill is the historically significant Kansas-Nebraska Act, though in some

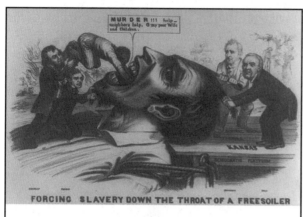

FORCING SLAVERY DOWN THE THROAT OF A FREESOILER

This cartoon, published in 1856, shows Franklin Pierce, Lewis Cass, and James Buchanan holding down a giant Abolitionist, while Stephen Douglas forces a black slave down his throat.

Nebraska history books, it is referred to, with perhaps a tinge of contempt or hubris, as the "Nebraska-Kansas Act."

If Nebraska's fortunes seem historically to be tied to those of its neighbors, nowhere is that more apparent than in the Kansas-Nebraska Act of 1854. It was the creation of Kansas that allowed the creation of Nebraska, and it was Kansas that became the boiling pot that sadly foretold the coming Civil War.

In a final insult (if one is passionate about such things), Kansas was granted statehood in 1861, but Nebraska's would not come until six years later. In the meantime, Colorado and the Dakota Territories were created in 1861 and Idaho Territory two years later (in its original form which included current Montana and Wyoming). Now Nebraska had the borders which define it today, and statehood was becoming imminent. But there was one more hurdle to cross.

The final leg on the march to inclusion as a state was to be unique for Nebraska. It is the only state created since Ohio, that was granted statehood *without* the signature of the sitting president. Andrew Johnson's ostensible reason for vetoing the 1867 statehood proposal was that the state's constitution did not allow suffrage to non-white citizens. This was *baloney*, of course, because Andrew Johnson was a latent racist. He had been a slaveowner before his political career, and fought during his entire presidency against the 1866 Civil Rights Act and against ratification of the fourteenth amendment, which guaranteed the right to vote to all men regardless of race. His conciliatory overtures to the south after the Civil War made him reviled by the Republicans in Congress, leading to his eventual impeachment. Johnson's real motivation was that Nebraska would be dominantly

Republican, and its statehood would provide two more Republican senators to the U.S. Congress, along with three more electoral votes in his looming re-election bid.

Congress, too, was concerned—probably more genuinely so—about the flaw in Nebraska's constitution, so it created a provision in the eventual bill that would only grant statehood if the problem were remedied—that is, if Nebraska guaranteed the right to vote to non-white Americans. The veto issued by President Johnson was of the "pocket" variety – that is, he allowed ten days to pass after the bill reached his desk without signing it. Curiously, a similar set of circumstances was being played out at the same time with regard to Colorado. Johnson received enabling bills for both territories on the same day, but his veto of the Colorado bill was of the traditional variety. Still more curiously, while Congress overrode the veto of the Nebraska statehood bill, on the very same day they did *not* override the veto of the Colorado enabling act.

Thus, Nebraska became a state nine years before its neighbor to the southwest on March 1, 1867, and *without* the signature of the U.S. President. The football rivalry between the two states would just have to wait.

1.   Luebke, Frederick C., <u>Nebraska: An Illustrated History</u> (Lincoln, 1995), p. 7.

2.   Fremont, J. C., <u>The Exploring Expedition to the Rocky Mountains, Oregon and California</u> (Buffalo, 1851), p. 17.

3.   Sheldon, Addison Erwin, <u>History and Stories of Nebraska</u> (Chicago, 1913), p. 232.

4.   James C. Olson and Ronald C. Naugle, <u>History of Nebraska</u> (Lincoln, 1997), p. 31.

Chapter 28: Nevada

"Viva Las Vegas!"

—"Viva! Las Vegas!"
Elvis Presley

Danny: *"You're either in, or you're out. Right now."*
Linus: *"Las Vegas, huh?*
Danny: *"America's Playground."**

—*from "Ocean's Eleven" 2001*

Casinos

The irony is lost on no one—the state with legalized gambling and prostitution, right next door to the one which comes closest to having a state-sanctioned religion. To many, Nevada is an adult Disneyland; for others, it is a waste of space, time, and human energy; and for still others, it is a place of sin and corruption to be avoided and/or converted. People who have never been there may imagine Nicolas Cage and Elizabeth Shue leading their desperate, pathetic lives in 1995's *Leaving Las Vegas*, or the "Flying Elvises" in yet another Nicolas Cage movie, *Honeymoon in Vegas*, or perhaps any version of *Ocean's Eleven*. Nevada's largest city does not want for TV and movie exposure.

Big (monstrous?), lavish (wasteful?), shimmering (gaudy?) casinos with lights bright enough to be seen from outer space—that's Las Vegas. And the rest of Nevada? It's a huge desert with a bunch of smaller Las Vegases dotting the landscape, tiny-to-medium-sized towns that you can always see from miles away because of the massive lighted signs guiding the way

---

* *The website imdb.com claims that this is a mistake, that Las Vegas has never marketed itself as "America's Playground," and that the nickname actually belonged to Atlantic City before Las Vegas became a gambling mecca.*

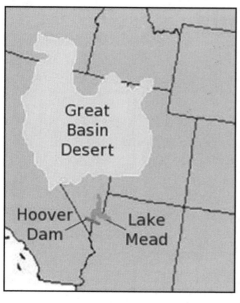

to the casinos. Drive into the state at night on virtually any highway, and the border is unmistakable.

It was in 1931 when Nevada officially legalized gambling, partly in anticipation of a growth in tourism with the construction of the Hoover (Boulder) Dam. In its infancy, the industry was financed by, and intimately connected with, organized crime, prompting many other states not to follow Nevada's lead. Eventually, however, the industry was cleaned up and legitimized and proved to be the tourism magnet that the state had hoped for.

Nevada imparts other images, too. While it is comprised mostly of the Great Basin of the American West, Nevada's natural beauty takes the form of breathtaking plateaus and scenic deserts, and the ominous Hoover Dam and corresponding Lake Mead rival Las Vegas in their inspiration of wonder at man-made monstrosities. There are those who associate Nevada with marriage and divorce, and the ease with which one can come by either within her borders. Still others associate Nevada with nuclear testing and the disposal of radioactive waste. And then there are those who connect the entire state with a sixty-square-mile military aircraft testing facility known as "Area 51," which some believe is the U.S. government's site of choice for examining UFO's and space aliens.

For all its barrenness, Nevada conveys a veritable rainbow of colorful images.

Columbus

In 1848 the state we call *Nevada* was among the spoils claimed by the U.S. after the Mexican-American War. Often referred to as "Eastern California," the region was also commonly referred to on maps as the "Great American Desert" (a term perhaps more commonly associated with the continent's central plains), "Great Basin," and sometimes the "Fremont Ba-

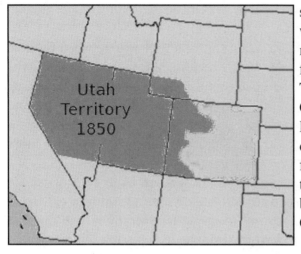

Utah
Territory
1850

sin," after John C. Fremont, who explored and mapped much of the American West for the U.S. government. This massive desert east of California and west of Salt Lake City, was seen as an obstacle to be overcome for fifteen years as prospectors and pioneers crossed its brutal sands on their way to California.

The exception, of course, was the Mormons. They had, since 1847, been settling the Great Salt Lake region of Utah, and for much of that time, lobbying Congress for territorial status, first for their own provisional state of "Deseret," but eventually for whatever form the federal government deemed appropriate. Utah Territory was created in 1850 and included all of current Nevada except for the southern tip. In 1851 a group of Mormons led by John Reese and Steven A. Kinsey established Mormon Station, a trading post near the California border intended to service travelers as they attempted to cross the Sierra Nevada. By fall of the same year, several other settlers joined Reese and Kinsey, and the population grew to perhaps a hundred residents, both Mormon and Gentile. The first attempt to form a territorial government for the region was born out of the "squatter meetings" held by these industrious residents. By the end of 1851 they had drafted a petition to Congress to form a separate territorial government for western Utah, but the petition was never delivered, and the Utah government in Salt Lake City began to take measures to establish law and order in the region. The oldest permanent

Brigham Young

settlement in Nevada, Mormon Station, was made the county seat of Carson County in 1854 and renamed Genoa (Jah-NO-ah) in 1856.

Throughout the 1850's there was a sort of tug-of-war between California and Utah regarding the Carson Valley region. Many of the settlers in the valley were miners who felt they had more in common with the residents of California than with those of their own designated territory. In 1853 and again in 1855, some of these residents petitioned California for annexation, and each time the Utah territorial legislature took measures to assert more control over the region.

In 1857 most of the Mormon settlers in western Utah Territory made a dramatic exodus and returned to Salt Lake City. Heeding a call from Brigham Young, who was preparing to wage the "Mormon War" against government troops, they were told to "bring as much ammunition as possible and to hurry."[1] The Mormons attempted to govern the Carson Valley remotely, but the void of local authorities spurred the next attempt at separation from Utah. On August 3, 1857, a meeting of the remaining residents selected a delegate to present to the U.S. Congress a memorial which requested territorial status separate from that of Utah. The name the squatters chose for their territory was "Columbus," and the capital was to be Genoa.[2]

Some in Congress saw the petition as an opportunity to "compress the limits of the Mormons" and reported on it favorably. James M. Crane, the delegate chosen by Carson Valley residents to deliver the petition to Congress, wrote a letter in February of 1858 suggesting that territorial status was imminent but in an off-hand comment noted that the name for the new territory had been changed to "Sierra Nevada." Meanwhile tensions had eased a little between the federal government and Salt Lake City, and the distraction of the impending Civil War caused the petition to be tabled.

Silver and Gold

The Comstock Lode of 1859 proved to be the impetus for a great migration into the region (as well as an attractive theme for casinos a hundred years later). Most of the new population came not from the east but from the California gold fields to the west. These were seasoned miners accustomed to mining town politics and society. By the spring and summer of 1860 thousands of miners were pouring into the area just north of Genoa to take part in the biggest silver strike in world history. Carson City, formerly a small trading post named Eagle Station, became the new center of government and trade.

In an attempt to establish law and order, the "Gold Hill Mining District" was created in June 1859, but it proved too weak to manage the throngs of new residents. Miners were well acquainted with the mechanics of territory creation, and because they were genuinely dissatisfied with Mormon control, they took every opportunity to press for separation from Utah. In 1861 officials in Salt Lake City recognized the miners' goal and made a last ditch effort to govern the region effectively, providing for the incorporation of Virginia City and moving the county seat from Genoa to Carson City. But it was too little, too late.

Back in the eastern states, the Civil War had been brewing and by 1861 had begun in earnest. With the departure of the southern states from the U.S. legislature, a major obstacle to territory-creation was removed, as the slavery issue was now moot. While it is true that Carson Valley residents had wanted separation from Utah for a number of years, it is also fair to say that once the petition was re-submitted on February 26, 186, it moved through successfully at lightning speed. On March 2, after passing the House, a companion bill passed the Senate and President Buchanan signed it that very day.

A Snow-Covered State?

Juan Rodríguez Cabrillo

It is not clear exactly who inserted the name "Nevada" into the bill creating the territory in 1861. The document was written by Missouri Senator James S. Green but chances are he used the name, or half of the name "Sierra Nevada," which had been proposed four years earlier for the same region. There was already a Nevada City in California, and it was among the oldest mining towns in that state. In fact, some of the miners who had rushed to the Carson Valley after the discovery of the Comstock Lode in 1859 had moved there from Nevada City.

The Sierra Nevada

There is no argument, however, that the name was inspired by the Sierra Nevada, the mountain range that runs along the eastern border of California. The word *sierra* is Spanish for "saw-toothed mountain range," and *nevada,* also Spanish, means "snowy," "snow-covered," or "snow-fall." Juan Rodriquez Cabrillo, a Portuguese navigator who explored the coast of California in 1542 while sailing for Spain, named the snow-covered mountains which he could see far inland *sierra nevada.* Later Spanish explorers wrote of these mountains but not until 1776 did a Franciscan missionary named Pedro Font place "Sierra Nevada" on a map though, as one historian explains, he intended the name to be "descriptive, not specific."[3]

Nevertheless, "Sierra Nevada" became the permanent appellation, and since the first English-speaking Americans began arriving in California the name, according to Guy Rocha, writing for the Nevada State Library and Archives Department of Cultural Affairs, has been misunderstood and mispronounced. Rocha complains of naive attempts to make the words plural, and explains that "Sierra" defines a range of mountains and so is already plural, and that "Nevada" is merely descriptive. "Sierra Nevada Mountains," he continues, is redundant while "Sierra Nevadas" is simply grammatically incorrect.

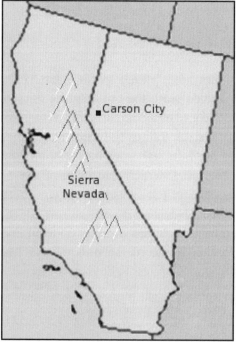

Rocha also points out one of the great ironies in the choice of names for the new territory: the Sierra Nevada is in California. While the original petition for the creation of

Nevada Territory requested a western border along the crest of that mountain range, it was fairly certain that California, which was already a state, would never approve of such a drastic change in her own borders, a change that would decrease her size dramatically and potentially remove rich mineral deposits. The other great irony in the name "Nevada" is that it means "snowy" or "snow-covered," and yet it describes what was acknowledged, even in the 1850's, as the "Great American Desert." Of all of the striking images we may have of Nevada, snow-covered is rarely one of them.

The Telegram

Two days after Buchanan signed the territory of Nevada into existence, Abraham Lincoln was sworn into office as the new U.S. president. He proceeded to appoint all of the administrators for the new territory and among them, in the post of Territorial Secretary, was one Orion Clemens, who moved out west to assume his new position accompanied by his younger, and soon to be much more famous, brother Samuel—a.k.a. Mark Twain.

The issue of the name and the borders for this fledgling territory were not yet com-

Orion Clemens

pletely decided. In 1862 the second territorial legislature adopted a new name, *Washoe*. The Washoe Indians were native to the Carson Valley and Lake Tahoe regions, and while the vague reference "Washoe Country" had been used occasionally to refer to western Utah after the Comstock discovery, no counties were ever officially labeled with that name. Now it was being proposed for the whole territory.

At the first constitutional convention in November of 1863, the issue of a name was debated. The act calling for the convention had already renamed the potential new state "Washoe," but many at the meeting were dissatisfied with the change. Other names were proposed, including "Humboldt" and "Esmaralda," but in the end, the state fathers agreed on the original name of "Nevada." The second constitutional convention was held in March of

1864, and after what one historian calls a "warm debate," the name *Nevada* was decided on once and for all.

In the meantime, Nevada's borders were already changing. Originally her eastern border was set at 116° west longitude, leaving out about a third of the state's modern-day area. Her southern border initially went only as far south as the northern border of Arizona. Gradually, these borders were moved. Twice, while Nevada was still a territory, her eastern boundary was moved eastward. Then, after statehood, another sliver of Utah was given over to Nevada, and the southern section of the state, below the line of 37° north latitude, was also added.

In March of 1864, Congress passed the enabling act for Nevada, and the state legislature set about finalizing their constitution. So as not to waste any time, the entire document was wired to Abraham Lincoln at a cost of $3,416.77 making it the longest telegram ever dispatched to that time. President Lincoln approved it, and the State of Nevada came into existence on October 31, 1864.

1.   Elliott, Russell R., <u>History of Nevada</u> (Lincoln, 1973), p. 56.

2.   Elliott, p. 58.

3.   Farquhar, Francis P., <u>History of the Sierra Nevada</u> (Berkeley, 1965), p. 16.

Chapter 29: New Hampshire

Live Free or Die!

> —*New Hampshire state motto*

"For those of you who are feeling giddy or cocky or think this is all set, I just have two words for you: New Hampshire."

> —*President Barack Obama, during the 2008 presidential campaign, reminding supporters of his loss to Hillary Clinton in the New Hampshire primary*

"Live Free or Die!" New Hampsherites proudly proclaim. Not "Live Free or Fight!" or even "Live Free or Write Your Congressperson!" No, in New Hampshire they don't do anything half-way.

Among the areas in which New Hampshire can claim a unique superlative are

1. It holds the first primary—which is to say, before any other state—of every presidential election season.

2. It has the shortest oceanic coastline of any U.S. state, running only about 18 miles along the Atlantic Ocean.

3. Mount Washington of the White Mountain Range, the tallest peak in the northeastern U.S. (which is a little like saying that your pinky is the largest finger on the far outside portion of your hand), claims the honor of having the "worst weather on earth."

4. It was the first state to lose a native son in the American Revolution.

It was in Hanover, New Hampshire that the prolific, hilarious, and intrepid author, Bill Bryson, first spotted the Appalachian Trail and learned that it runs from Georgia to Maine. Having long been the adventurous type, Mr. Bryson set off to conquer this trail along with his old friend, Katz. From the effort, he produced the exquisitely entertaining book, "A Walk in the Woods."

Our image in the 21st century of New Hampshire is one of colonial and revolutionary America. A place of gentle hills, quaint farms, and fiercely proud people who, despite being the 46th largest state in the country, are intent on making their voices heard in politics and in life. It is a tiny state that refuses to get "lost in the shuffle" as just another New England state. No, New Hampshire raises its hand and says that, "Our people are not afraid, not of being a little revolutionary, and not afraid to tell the nation who we choose to run for president of the country."

It is truly the mouse that, every four years…roars.

Hampshire or Hampton?

New Hampshire is named for the county of Hampshire—birthplace of Charles Dickens, home to Jane Austen, and custodian of the enigmatic Stonehenge—located on the southeastern coast of England. The word Hampshire comes from the Old English words "ham," meaning *home* or *village,* and "shire" or "scire," referring to an administrative district. One history of the English county of Hampshire written in 1909 asserts, however, that the name "Hampshire" is a misnomer, and that the official name of the county is and always has been "Southampton."

" …there seems little doubt that the name is Saxon in origin—

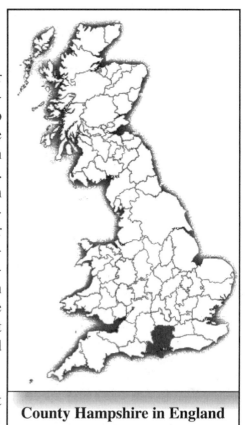

County Hampshire in England

Ham-tun, the home-town or settlement, carrying us back to the... years during which the Saxon invaders...were making good their foothold... *Ham-tun* was the name they gave to their first secure base—Hampton it remained in popular style for at least one thousand years—and the name of the first permanent settlement thus became the name of the 'hinterland' which it dominated."[1]

The Saxon "tun" was indeed a word indicating a farm or settlement and predates "shire," which was a more formal administrative region. In 755 A.D. "Ham-tun scire" appears in the *Anglo-Saxon Chronicle*—a sort of History of the World commissioned by King Alfred the Great of England in the late ninth century. Later the county began to grow and prosper, making it necessary to distinguish between the northern and southern portions. This produced "South Ham-tun shire," and from there the word evolved into "Hampshire" to describe the whole county and "Southampton" which is the name of one of the largest cities in southern Hampshire.

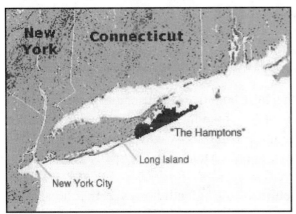

Hampshire or Hampton? The question is academic in England. But if you're in the United States and you want to go to New Hampshire, you go to a state in New England; if you want to go to the "Hamptons," you go to a group of villages on the northern end of Long Island.

Captain John Mason

Captain John Mason, born 1585 at Kings Lynn in the county of Norfolk, England, is described many different ways in the various histories in which he is mentioned: pirate, one-time governor of Newfoundland, heroic naval captain, and successful London merchant. He was all of those things, as well as what he was most famous for: Founder of New Hampshire.

By the age of twenty-five, John Mason had graduated from college, married, and bought himself a nifty little ship which he began using to capture legitimate trading vessels between Norway and Scotland. This was a lucrative business until he was caught in 1615 and forced to surrender his ship and thus his "career."

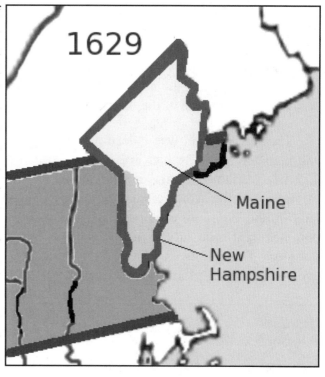

It is stated with authority in some history books that Mason never saw the land which he would "found," but this may not be true. In 1616, with a little help from his friends, he was appointed to the position of Governor of Newfoundland, a post he would hold for six years. During this time he made exploratory excursions westward into what would later become Nova Scotia, Maine, and possibly New Hampshire.

It was not until Mason returned to England, however, that he and his friend Ferdinando Gorges received a grant in 1622—made by the newly formed Council for New England on which Gorges served prominently—for the "Province of Maine" between the Merrimack and Sagahadock (now the Kennebec) Rivers. Within a year, Mason and Gorges sent a man named David Thompson, his wife, and about ten indentured fishermen to establish a settlement and stake their claim. Thompson did exactly that and is a favorite son and source of much pride for the state of New Hampshire. He built a stone manor which he called Pannaway at the mouth of the Piscataqua River, a region Thompson named "Little Harbor" (now the town of Rye). The manor stood for some sixty years and began what would be the third permanent English settlement in the New World after Jamestown and Plymouth.

Back in England, Mason had settled in Portsmouth, Hampshire and established himself as a successful businessman, though he complained in his letters that his colonizing efforts had yet to bring in any money. On the 7th of November in 1629, Gorges and Mason divided their grant amicably: Gorges took Maine north of the Piscataqua, and Mason took the rest and named it "New Hampshire".

Some New Hampshire historians bother to provide a motivation for this name: "It was the home of his family's estate," "he spent many years there as a child," etc. These reasons generally ignore the fact that Mason was born and raised in the county of Norfolk on an estate which had been in his family for several generations, his mother was from Yorkshire, and he did not move to Portsmouth in Hampshire until adulthood. The only available biography of Captain John Mason gives a more plausible, if not very exciting, reason: "...and Mason called it New Hampshire, out of regard to the favor in which he held Hampshire in England, where he had resided many years."[2]

Laconia and Masonia

Attempting to follow the grants and patents distributed by the Council for New England is a frustrating endeavor. As described by one historian, the Council

> "...gave what they never owned, set bounds to that which had never been seen, fixed lines that had never been surveyed and laid the foundation for countless quarrels and much trouble in future years."[3]

Cases in point: Laconia and Masonia.

Shortly after dividing their original grant, Mason and Gorges formed the Laconia Company and applied for a new grant west of (and in fact, overlapping) Mason's New Hampshire. They called the land "Laconia" as it was in the lake region, and also in hopes of finding the fabled "Lake of the Iroquois" and subsequently taking over the fur trade in New England. The endeavor proved impossible because the lake they sought did not exist, however the effort did spawn new settlement along the Piscataqua River.[4] The Laconia Company went bankrupt, but Mason retained proprietorship of some of the land in the Laconia grant.

In 1635 the Council for New England surrendered its charter, and the responsibility for granting land and patents reverted to the king. Mason quickly had his New Hampshire grant confirmed to him and in the same document was given ten thousand acres in what is now Maine which was called "Masonia". Historically speaking Masonia was quickly absorbed into Maine and forgotten, but the document granting the land had the confusing title "Grant of the Province of New Hampshire to Mr. Mason, 22 April 1635, By the Name of Masonia."

John Mason died later that year, leaving his many patents and land grants to his heirs. Years later his eldest grandson would go to New Hampshire to pursue his legal rights to the land.

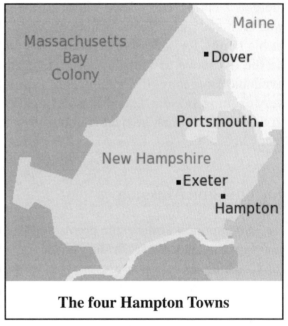

The four Hampton Towns

The Four Towns

By 1640 there were four main "plantations" or towns in the region of the Mason grant. Little Harbor, which was founded by David Thompson and expanded three miles up the Piscataqua River, would later assume the name Strawberry Bank and still later the name Portsmouth. It was joined by Northam— later Dover—a town begun by the Hilton brothers, also under the direction of the Laconia Company. The other two towns were born out of the Massachusetts Bay Colony. One was Exeter, founded by John Wheelwright, who had been expelled from the MBC for heresy and sedition and moved north to found his own settlement. The other was a town settled under the auspices of the MBC at a place the natives called Winnacunnet and which the colonists named Hampton.

These four towns were bound to each other only by their relative proximity and by their tenuous, and perhaps a bit self-conscious, separateness from the imposing Massachusetts Bay Colony. One New Hampshire historian writes,

> "In 1640 the term "New Hampshire" had little or no meaning for the inhabitants of the four plantations. Many probably knew that Captain John Mason had used the name to identify territory included in one of his many patents, but few cared about the legal status of that or other patents granted by the Council for New England. The Council no longer existed, Mason had died, and crown officials were so busy trying to resolve England's internal problems that imposition of effective royal authority in New England seemed unlikely."[5]

In fact by the autumn of 1642 all four towns had applied to Massachusetts for inclusion in *its* government and were accepted as part of the Bay Colony. Mason's heirs, in particular his grandson Robert Mason, had no chance to claim his inheritance during the English Civil War and the reign of the Puritan government of Oliver Cromwell. But after the restoration of the throne to Charles II in 1660, he petitioned the king for redress. At first nothing was done, but Mason persevered, and in 1679 King Charles II declared New Hampshire a Royal Province—separate from Massachusetts—under Mason's proprietorship, meaning he now owned all unsettled land from the original grant and could collect rent from the current landholders. The colony of "New Hampshire" was now firmly planted.

Massachusetts Again

Well, maybe not. Opposition to royal rule and to Mason's proprietorship was strong. Two different governors attempted to enforce English laws pertaining to land tenure and customs, in particular the hated "Navigation Acts" which were intended to force all trade between English colonies to go through England on English vessels so that duties could be collected. The acts were summarily ignored in New England, and no amount of intimidation by New Hampshire's governors could force compliance. Mason, too, was frustrated in his attempts to collect rents or to gain control of unsettled

William III

lands. As a final insult, he was even physically assaulted at the peak of tensions in the colony.

In 1685 a different kind of unrest swept the colony. Those who wished a return to government by Massachusetts had their hopes dashed when that colony's charter was revoked, and the "Dominion of New England" was established—the king's attempt to erase the carefully drawn boundaries and combine all the New England colonies into one carefully managed unit. At this point, confusion ruled among the northern colonies who didn't know if their provincial status existed. To make matters worse, the appointed governor of the Dominion was Edmund Andros, a tyrant who made enemies wherever he governed.

Fortunately the Dominion was short-lived, ending with the Glorious Revolution which brought William of Orange and his wife, Mary, to the throne of England in 1688. Massachusetts now reverted to its pre-Dominion government, but New Hampshire was totally without authority. Even the Mason proprietorship was deprived of its driving force, as Robert Mason died that same year. At this point the four towns came close to establishing their own self-devised, self-imposed government but the Puritans

Mary II

in Hampton feared too much secular control, and the attempt failed. The only solution now available was the reannexation to Massachusetts, and this was done rather efficiently by March of 1690. Once again, New Hampshire ceased to exist.

New Hampshire, at Last

Still, the years of royal government had convinced more and more New Hampshire residents that the colony had an independent destiny separate from that of Massachusetts. The beginning of the eighteenth century brought a sense of optimism for the future of what one official called "little New Hampshire," making separation and self-government a real prospect.

In 1699 New Hampshire petitioned the English authorities to separate it from Massachusetts, while at the same time Massachusetts lobbied for complete control over both. Instead of deciding for either colony, a compromise was instituted whereby the colonies would remain separate but would have the same governor. This solution was surprisingly agreeable to most people, but the tensions between the colonies would ebb and flow for the next forty years.

Finally, in 1741, after a lengthy dispute over the location of the border between Massachusetts and New Hampshire, a border which was unnecessary when the two colonies were governed as one, the English Privy Council handed down a quite favorable ruling for New Hampshire, placing its border south of not only Massachusetts' claim but of New Hampshire's claim as well.

The Proprietorship

In the meantime, the legacy of Captain John Mason continued to turn up like a bad penny for decades. Around 1690 Robert Mason's sons sold the proprietorship to Samuel Allen, an energetic London merchant who had begun to invest heavily in New Hampshire. Allen succeeded in having himself appointed governor of the colony but was frustrated, as Robert Mason had been before him, in his attempts to collect payment or rents from the colonists.

In 1705 a group of representatives from the New Hampshire towns put together an offer to effectively buy out Allen, and Allen probably would have accepted, had he not died on the day after the proposal was made. This morbid but fortuitous turn of events prompted Cotton Mather to remark,

"I cannot but admire at the providence of Heaven, which has all along strangely interposed, with most admirable dispensations, especially with strange mortalities, to stop the proceedings of the controversy about Mason's claim just in the most critical moment of it."[6]

In the 1730's the proprietorship reared its ugly head one last time when John Tufton Mason, a descendant of the Captain, appeared in Boston to stake his claim to New Hampshire. Tufton eventually sold his rights to a group of Portsmouth businessmen who are remembered today as the "Masonian Proprietors." For nearly forty years these proprietors set land policy and granted townships judiciously without attempting to profit unfairly from their powers, and thus the problem of the proprietorship was solved for good.

Statehood and the Western Border

In 1763, with the Treaty of Paris that ended the French and Indian War, the territory west of the Connecticut River was deeded from France to England and was claimed by both New York and New Hampshire. Quickly, however, the residents of the disputed land declared their independence from either colony. In 1777 Vermont's sovereignty was recognized by both claimants, and the borders of New Hampshire were now fixed.

On June 21, 1788 New Hampshire became the ninth state to ratify the Constitution. With New Hampshire, two thirds of the states had now ratified, causing the Constitution to take effect and thereby giving that state yet another source of historical pride.

1.   Varley, Telford and Wilfrid Ball, <u>Hampshire</u> (London: Adam & Charles Black, 1909), p. 3.

2.   Dean, John Ward, <u>Capt. John Mason: The Founder of New Hampshire</u>, (New York, 1887), p. 21.

3.   Hadley, George Plummer, <u>History of the Town of Goffstown 1733-1920</u>, (Concord, 1922), http://www.usgennet.org/usa/nh/county/hillsborough/goffstown/book/chap3.html, created June 28, 2000, accessed July 23, 2009.

4.   Daniel, Jere R., <u>Colonial New Hampshire, A History</u>, (Millwood, 1981), p. 24.

5.   Daniel, p. 38.

6.   Daniel, p. 129.

Chapter 30: New Jersey

'cause nothing matters in this whole wide world
When you're in love with a jersey girl

— *"Jersey Girl"*
Bruce Springsteen

Contradictions

New Jersey, or *"Joisey"* as the stereotype has it, owns a reputation as an industrial, blue collar arm of New York, a reputation rife with images of smokestacks, turnpikes, and organized crime. However unfair, these impressions are pounded out regularly in movies and television, from Marlon Brando in "On the Waterfront" to the new-age crime boss Tony Soprano. The characters and the stories, while irresistible on the screen, foil any possibility for the state to reconcile its image to its well-known nickname the "Garden State."

But then there's Princeton—gorgeous, pristine, and utterly dignified Princeton. There's Atlantic City—flashy, colorful, fun. And there's the Jersey shore. (On the west coast one goes to the beach, but on the east coast one goes to the shore.) Once the images of factories and the mafia are swept away, the name New Jersey easily calls to mind the sound of the Drifters singing "Under the Boardwalk."

Upon its creation New Jersey was among the most ethnically diverse regions in British North America, having not only a large Native American population, but also large Swedish and Dutch communities. Today New Jersey is still among the most ethnically diverse states, and all of those ethnicities live closer together than anywhere else. While New Jersey is the fourth smallest state, it has the 11th largest population. Also, According to

2000 census data the three most densely populated cities in the U.S. are all in New Jersey*.

New Netherland/Sweden

New Jersey's ethnic diversity begins, of course, with the Indians. The Lenape, or Delaware as the English named them, inhabited the banks of the Delaware River upon the arrival of the first European explorers. A Lenape legend holds that when the Dutch arrived they asked only for enough land "for a garden spot," thus conferring the state motto upon the region before states even existed. The legend continues that those Dutch eventually wanted more and more land, and in time the Lenape believed that they would "soon want all their country, which in the end proved true."[1]

Actually the Dutch abandoned their attempt at settling the Delaware River, though they never relinquished their claim to the land, calling everything between the Delaware and Connecticut Rivers "New Netherland." In 1624, to strengthen their defenses against the Indians and the English, they consolidated their colonists at Manhattan which had recently been "purchased" (see New York) by Dutch Governor Peter Minuit. Minuit, however, fell out of favor with his own government, and was recalled to Holland in 1631. In 1638 he sold his services to Queen Christina of Sweden, and led a group of Swedes to the Delaware River to find and purchase land from the Lenape to begin a colony. This one, New Sweden, thrived for almost two decades until the Dutch resolved to challenge the encroachment. In 1655 the Dutch captured New Sweden, once again bringing the area under the control of New Netherland.

Then came the English.

New York/Jersey

In 1664 King Charles II granted all the land that the Dutch were calling New Netherland to his brother James, Duke of York, and sent Colonel

---

* *Union City, West New York, and Hoboken. While Manhattan is more densely populated than any of these, the overall population of New York City, which includes four other buroughs, does not reach the density levels of these three New Jersey cities.*

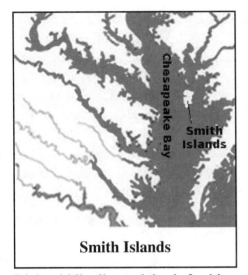

Smith Islands

Lord John Berkeley

Richard Nicolls to claim it for him—by force if necessary. Force, alas, proved *un*necessary when the Dutch governor Peter Stuyvesant surrendered the entire colony (see New York), and Nicolls took over as the new Governor of what he, by prior authority of the Duke, named New York. Part of what Nicolls included in his domain was the region between the Delaware and Hudson Rivers, or modern New Jersey, but what Nicolls didn't know is that while he had been at sea, sailing toward his showdown with Stuyvesant, the king had granted that part of New York to two friends, Lord John Berkeley and Sir George Carteret, calling it *Nova Caesarea* or New Jersey.

Lord John Berkeley had been a financial advisor to Charles II during the years after his father's execution while the English king lived in exile. Carteret had also been loyal to the king, sheltering him on his home island of Jersey for a time, and fighting valiantly, albeit unsuccessfully, to save the island from the control of the Parliamentarians. Carteret's family had for decades held much political control on the island. Sir George, following in his father's Royalist footsteps, even hosted the eventual coronation of Charles II upon the death of Charles I.

Sir George Carteret

For his loyalty the now reinstated King Charles II gave Carteret a gift. He offered Sir George the Smith Islands off the coast of Virginia (now part of Maryland, they are a small group of islands at the southern end of Chesapeake Bay), and Carteret promptly renamed them "New Jersey". His attempt at colonizing them failed, however, when the first ships he sent were captured by Parliamentary forces. Carteret never took possession of the islands.

In 1663 both Berkeley and Carteret were among the proprietors of the Carolina colony, and later both served on the Council on Foreign Plantations which advised the king to seize the Dutch colony of New Netherland. After acquiring the grant for New Jersey from King Charles they sent Carteret's nephew Philip to govern their new estate, but he soon encountered resistance from colonists who had been granted estates by Richard Nicolls. Nicolls, of course, believed he was giving away New York property.

East/West Jersey

By the time the king settled the dispute between Nicolls and Carteret in 1674, Berkeley had given away his portion of New Jersey, now known as West New Jersey, to two Quakers, John Fenwick and Edward Byllynge, who immediately entered into a dispute

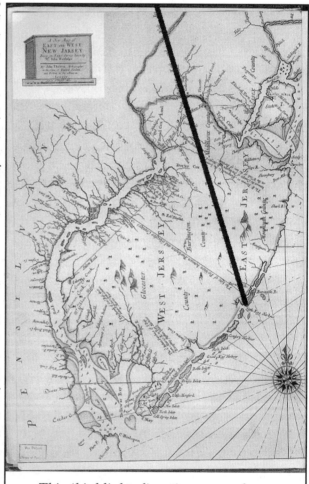

This (highlighted) antique map shows East and West Jersey

over the property. The argument was arbitrated by none other than William Penn who, as payment for his services, took some of the disputed land and started his "social experiment" (see Pennsylvania) in West New Jersey.

Though already owned in two seperate pieces, on July 1, 1676 the colony was "officially" divided in two. The line between East and West New Jersey ran from Little Egg Harbor northwest to a point on the Delaware River just north of the Delaware Water Gap. Commonly in this time the "New" was dropped from the name, and the colonies were referred to as "East Jersey" and "West Jersey."

In 1682 East Jersey was put up for public auction and sold to Penn and some of his associates for 3,400 English pounds, but governing the disparate population was troublesome to the proprietors, and in 1702 the crown reunited the colony, and took back control of it as a Royal Colony. Reunited, New Jersey was placed under the temporary governorship of Edward Hyde, Lord Cornbury, Royal Governor of New York. Lord Cornbury is to this day considered one of the worst royal governors of any American colony. He is charged with having speculated on land while serving as governor and of plundering the public treasury for his personal benefit. This situation was naturally not acceptable to New Jersey, and the colonists clamored for more local control. The king responded, and in 1738 Lewis Morris of Monmouth County was named the first Governor of New Jersey.

Given the territorial dispositions of the Penn family over their colony at Pennsylvania and the similar ambitions of various enterprising governors of New York, it is somewhat surprising that New Jersey remained separate from either of those two colonies. It was, in fact, this proximity to New York and Pennsylvania that in-

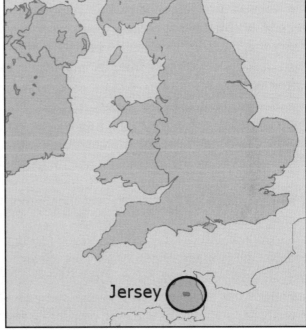

spired Ben Franklin to refer to the state as "a valley of humility between two mountains of conceit." In fact, largely because of its proximity to those two states, two New Jersey cities—Princeton and Trenton—hosted the U.S. Congress in 1784. Not only did New Jersey *not* get consumed by its powerful neighbors, it has the distinction of being the only state which retains to this day virtually the same borders defined in its original royal charter. On December 18, 1787, New Jersey solidified its autonomy, becoming the third state to ratify the Constitution of the United States.

Old Jersey

The island after which New Jersey is named is the largest of the Channel Islands between France and England, and is, in fact, the place where the Jersey dairy cow was originally domesticated. Closer to France, it was once part of the Duchy of Normandy, but to learn the history of its name we must go even further back.

The king in his charter called it *"Nova Caesarea* or New Jersey," perpetuating a long-held, but later strongly challenged, belief that "Jersey" was simply a corruption of the word "Caesarea," the Roman name for the island. "Caesarea" is an obvious tribute to Julius Caesar, under whose leadership the Romans conquered the island. Why this particular island should have been so honored is not entirely clear, especially given that there is no evidence that the Romans actually occupied Caesarea. They placed it on their maps and collected taxes from its inhabitants, but they built no structures or fortresses.

Some time in the fifth century A.D., the Franks moved south and west from Germany and defeated the Romans, driving them out of Gaul. Then, less than a century later, the Bretons (Anglo-Saxons who had taken over the British Isles from the Romans) moved into what is now northern France, and the region became known as Brittany. Jersey, now called Agna or Angia, was influenced by the takeover though not thoroughly consumed, retaining French as the native language.

Around 800 A.D. the Vikings began reeking havoc on the British Isles, France, and Brittany. Their origin was unclear to the Bretons—they knew only that they came from somewhere in the north sea—but their raids each summer were brutal and widespread, burning villages, murdering people brutally and senselessly, and even plundering tombs looking for buried treasure. After a hundred years the Vikings, or *Norsemen,* had come to stay, and the King of France, Charles the Simple, purchased peace in 911 by surrendering to them modern northern France, the region historically known as Normandy (the Normans' Land)[2].

While not originally included in Normandy the island of Jersey was eventually won by the Norsemen, and its name bestowed by them. Whether they used a historical name—"Caesarae" which had been handed down since Roman times—or bestowed a new name from their own language is still debated.

There are two common theories about a possible derivation of the *Viking* word "Jersey." One is the Old Frisian word "gers", which means grass, combined with the common Viking suffix "-ey" meaning island. This would make Jersey "grassy island." The other possibility is the proper Viking name "Geirr," again coupled with "-ey," which then became Geirr's Ey, or Geirr's Island.[3]

1.   Green, Howard L., ed. <u>Words that Make New Jersey History</u> (New Brunswick, 1995), p. 6.

2.   Balleine, G. R., <u>A History of the Island of Jersey</u> (London, 1950), p.27.

3.   Balleine, p. 26.

Chapter 31: New Mexico

"And away I did ride,
Just as fast as I
Could from the West Texas town of El Paso
Out to the bad-lands of New Mexico..."

— *"El Paso"*
Marty Robbins

Texas? Real cowboys don't come from Texas.
We're from New Mexico.

—*The Cowboys (1972)*

Oh, Santa Fe

The New Mexico area has been part of the United States, part of Mexico, the Imperial Spanish viceroyalty of New Spain, and home to the Navajo and Pueblo Indians. Present day New Mexico reflects these deeply rooted histories in its culture and ethnicities. The dominant ancestry group is Mexican, which is nearly double the percentage of the second largest group— Native American. And both of these ethnicities are trailed by single-digit percentages of German, Spanish, English, and Irish.

The topography of New Mexico is breathtaking: towering mesas, endless mountain ranges, canyons, valleys, and infinite highlands. New Mexico truly is a beautiful place to live, and the vast openness and natural beauty make the state a Hollywood hotspot for filming. Motion picture classics like *Butch Cassidy and the Sundance Kid*, *Geronimo*, and even *Oklahoma!* were all filmed in front of natural New Mexico backdrops, and the state has maintained film-maker popularity with more modern works such as *Natural Born Killers*, *Superman*, and *Twins*. Actors Bruce Cabot, Demi Moore, and Neil Patrick Harris were all born in New Mexico, but the surprise might come from another legendary New Mexican, John Denver. Mr. Denver, whose given name was Henry John Deutschendorf, Jr. was born—not in the Mile High City, nor in West Virginia—but in in Roswell, New Mexico.

Santa Fe, capital of the "Land of Enchantment," is a bustling hub of Mexican and Native American art, cuisine, and history and has accomplished the considerable feat of gaining respect as a cosmopolitan city without losing its cultural bedrock. The brilliance of Santa Fe has been captured by many world-renowned artists, but no artist is as closely associated with Southwestern interpretation as Georgia O'Keeffe. O'Keeffe, a Wisconsin-born painter, put New Mexico on the artistic map with her colorful expressions of stunning Southwestern flora.

Mexica

The name "Mexico" is derived from "Mexica" (Me-shee-ka), a people who migrated into the Valley of Mexico in the twelfth century. One tribe of the Mexicas, the Tenochcas, were initially a peaceful people who were reviled by the other tribes of the region for their ritual of human sacrifice. The Tenochcas were forced into slavery by a dominant tribe of the area but proved unmanageable and were eventually released.

An abject people, they were constantly forced onto the worst lands of the area. According to legend, some time between 1300 and 1375 the Tenochcas wandered into the area of a large lake, where they saw an eagle perched on a cactus with a serpent in its talons. They believed this to be a sign, and they chose the area to build their own city, Tenochtitlan, or "place of the Tenochcas."

Once settled, the Tenochcas fortunes changed and they began to dominate the region in a sinister manner, demanding tributes from neighboring villages and tribes, forcing them into servitude, and, most diabolically, using them for

This image, a national symbol of Mexico, depicts the sign interpreted by the Aztecs which told them to build their city on the lake where they saw it.

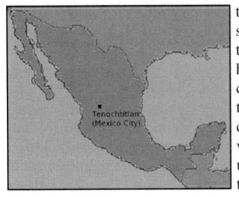

their continued practice of human sacrifice. When the Spanish conquistador Hernán Cortes arrived in 1519, he used the enmity between the Tenochcas—now led by Moctezuma—and their neighbors to his advantage. The chieftains of the villages near the coast where Cortes landed brought him tributes of gold and silver, and indicated that there was more where that came from to the west in Mexico—place of the Mexicas. These people who had been subjected to the cruel domination of the Tenochcas were only too willing to help the Spaniards conquer Moctezuma and destroy his grand city. Thus the European conquerors referred to the city and region of Tenochtitlan as "Mexico," and after his conquest of that region was complete and the city devastated, Cortes rebuilt it, continuing to refer to it as "Mexico."

The Spanish expanded their domination of Mexico northward, now calling the vaster region *Nueva Espana* or "New Spain," and defined separate provinces or kingdoms with their own regional governments. The northernmost region of New Spain was virtually unexplored, but an excit-

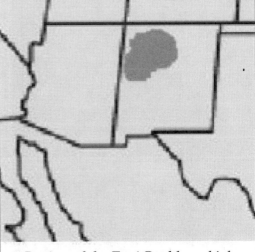

ing first hand account by one explorer was reported to Antonio de Mendoza, governor of Mexico, in 1536. Cabeza de Vaca had spent eight years wandering the American Southwest, along with a handful of other survivors of the Narvaez expedition (see Mississippi). When de Vaca told of rumors of large cities in the north where precious minerals were traded, Mendoza became determined to find them, sending first Fray Marcos de Niza and then Francisco Vasquez de Coronado to explore the territory.

Region of the Zuni Pueblos which Fray Marcos de Niza called "The New Kingdom of St. Francis"

De Niza planted a cross at the Zuni pueblo in what is today New Mexico, and conferred upon the territory the name of "The New Kingdom of St. Francis." Coronado spent two years from 1540 to 1542 looking for the vast wealth of the Seven Cities of Cibola which de Niza claimed to have found, but discovered only the pueblo villages of the Indians.

In 1563 Francisco de Ibarra explored the northern territory for two years. When he returned he claimed to have discovered "The New Mexico," alluding to vast riches like those that Cortes had found in Tenochtitlan, and once again reviving the hope of finding mineral wealth in the region. The name stuck, and the Spaniards began to place "Nuevo Mexico" on their maps as more and more expeditions were sent north in search of the elusive treasures.

Ironically...

The original Mexica Indians who migrated into the valley of Mexico and built the city of Tenochtitlan had come from the remote north. They called themselves Aztecs, meaning "people of Aztlan." The particular location of Aztlan is unknown and widely believed to be a mythical city of origin for this tribe of once nomadic people.

According to legend, a feud arose between two sects of Aztecs—those followers of Huitzilopochtli, their god of war, and those who worshipped his sister, Coyolxuhqui. A civil war broke out, and the followers of Huitzilopochtli won. In his honor, they began to call themselves Mexica, derived from "Mexitli," which was a title for Huitzilopochtli. It was, in fact, from this god that the Mexitli believed the sign of the eagle on the cactus was sent, prompting the building of Tenochtitlan. Ironi-

William Tecumseh Sherman

cally, while the location of the northern region from which the Aztecs originally migrated is not known, it is generally believed to be in the southwest United States—in or very close to...New Mexico.

In 1848, centuries after the Spaniards had defined the province of New Mexico, the now autonomous nation of Mexico ceded the region to the United States in the Treaty of Guadalupe Hidalgo which ended the Mexican-American war. The territory of New Mexico—consisting of what is now New Mexico, Arizona, and part of Nevada—faced a long delay in achieving statehood. The reasons were many and varied but generally derived from an ignorance of, and prejudice toward, the land and its people, the land being mostly desert and the people being predominantly Mexican and Indian. General William Tecumseh Sherman of Civil War fame once commented that the U.S. should declare war on Mexico and make it take New Mexico back![1]

Among the proposals to counter this prejudice were periodic suggestions of new names for the territory—"Lincoln," "Navajo," and "New Andalusia" among them. Ironically, the reason for these proposed name changes was that the word "Mexico," which had so inspired hope and dreams of wealth and prosperity for the Spaniards, was too suggestive of poverty and destitution.

Borders

In 1854 James Gadsden, railroad promoter and American Minister to Mexico, attempted to rectify some confusion in the Treaty of Guadelupe Hidalgo by placing the southern border of New Mexico Territory some thirty miles north of what was its current position. The loss would have cost the U.S. several thousand square miles, including the rich farmland of the Mesilla Valley and a potential site for a transcontinen-

New Mexico
Territory 1861

Gadsden Purchase 1854

tal railroad. Gadsden orchestrated the purchase of the land from Mexico for ten million dollars, cementing the southern border of the United States.

During the Civil War, New Mexico was divided into two separate territories—New Mexico and Arizona. This division, however, was not that which we know today. The region was split horizontally along the 34th parallel, the southern half taking the name *Arizona*. Both territories were governed briefly by Lieutenant Colonel John R. Baylor of the Confederate Army, who had conceived and decreed the division in order to appease the southern ranchers who were more sympathetic to the Confederate cause. But when New Mexico fell to the North after the decisive battle of Glorieta (referred to historically as "The Gettysburg of the West"), the territory resumed its original shape and name under Union control. Congress, now realizing that the region was in need of reorganization, took its own steps in dividing the territory. In 1863 the vertical division of New Mexico became official, with the new territory of Arizona being created out of the western half.

As previously mentioned, statehood was elusive for New Mexico. Opponents tended to be those wealthy land owners who benefited from having appointed officials rather than unpredictable elections. But also opposing statehood were people outside of the region who were prejudiced toward the aboriginal people there. One anecdote on the website for the New Mexico Genealogical Society illustrates how close New Mexico came to achieving statehood early on, in 1850:

> "During an 1876 Congressional debate, Michigan Representative Julius Caesar Burrows, an admired orator, rose to speak in favor of a bill designed to protect the civil rights of freed Negroes. Stephen B. Elkins, New Mexico's delegate to Congress, was not

present for most of the speech, but entered the House chamber just as Burrows was bringing his rousing oration to a close. Unaware of the full nature of Burrows' speech, Elkins shook his colleague's hand in congratulations, a gesture many Southern Congressmen interpreted as support for the civil rights legislation. Elkins' handshake is blamed for costing New Mexico several Southern votes it needed for passage of the statehood bill."[2]

Stephen B. Elkins

On January 6th, 1912, only weeks ahead of Arizona, New Mexico was confirmed as the 47th state of the Union. The statehood act was signed by President William Howard Taft who reportedly, after signing the legislation, looked at the distinguished and proud delegation from New Mexico and said, "Well, it is all over. I am glad to give you life. I hope you will be healthy."[3]

1.   Simmons, Marc, <u>New Mexico: A Bicentennial History</u>, (New York, 1977), p. 133.

2.   Torrez, Robert J., "A Cuarto Centennial History of New Mexico," <u>Official New Mexico Blue Book, Cuarto Centennial Edition, 1598-1998</u>, Office of the New Mexico Secretary of State. (also at http://www.nmgs. org/artcuar7.htm)

3.   Torrez (accessed 10/2/09).

Chapter 32: New York

I want to be a part of it: New York, New York

> — *"New York, New York"*
> *Liza Minelli and/or*
> *Frank Sinatra*

"...it appears, I say, and I make the assertion deliberately, without fear of contradiction, that this globe really was created, and that it is composed of land and water. It further appears that it is curiously divided and parceled out into continents and islands, among which I boldly declare the renowned island of New York will be found by any one who seeks for it in its proper place."

> — *"Knickerbocker's History of New York"*
> *Washington Irving*

New York...State

"New York" refers to New York City. Whereas the phrase "New York City" is almost redundant. If one wants to refer to the state of New York one generally does so explicitly: "New York State."   Not only does "New York" refer to New York City, it refers to Manhattan, otherwise known as "The City." Brooklyn, the Bronx, Queens and Staten Island are all spoken of separately, with their own brand of provincial pride.

**Lower Manhattan in 1660
under Dutch rule**

There are, of course, those who might take offense at this generalization. What about Albany? Syracuse? Cooperstown, for heaven's sake! What about Niagara Falls, the Adirondacks and the Catskills? All are readily and indelibly associated with the state of New York—but there's that word again..."state." Take it away, and what you have is a reference to possibly the most recognizable, the most identifiable place name in the country. And it's not a state.

Such is the blessing and the curse of sharing your state's name with perhaps the most famous city in the world. "New York" immediately sends one's mind to a tiny island covered in slabs of cement, colorful lights, and just over eight million people. For some it stirs the soul with yearning for the cosmopolitan culture, the excitement of its frenetic pace, the endless possibilities for human connection and activity, and for others it evokes fear of crime, terrorism, and simply getting lost in the ocean of people ebbing and flowing through currents of life like the water of its surrounding rivers.

But whatever one's impressions of New York—the state or the city— the words are imbued with perhaps the most emotion-provoking of any state's name. Love it or hate it, fear it or long for it, the feelings are strong and the images crystal clear.

The Dutch

Few stories in American history are as famous as the quaint little number about the Dutch Royal Governor Peter Minuit buying Manhattan from the Indians for sixty guilders or twenty-four dollars. Nowadays, however, historians spend more energy debunking this story than teaching it. They point out that the value of the trade goods has been massively skewed and cannot even be known for certain since no deed or bill of sale has ever been found. They observe that the source of the story is one line written in a letter to the officers of the Dutch West India Company (which had organized the colonization of New Neth-

Peter Minuit

erlands), a letter which wasn't even discovered until 1846. And they note that the natives from whom Minuit purchased the land were the Canarsees who lived in modern Brooklyn and not the Weekquaesgeeks who actually inhabited the island of Manhattan.

Still, the kernel of truth in the story reminds us that New York was originally New Netherland, and that New York City was, naturally, New Amsterdam, and that the colony was the only one of the original thirteen that did not begin as an English holding*. The Dutch claim to the land came courtesy of Henry Hudson, an English adventurer who sold his services to the Dutch who, like everyone else in the world, were interested in finding a water route through the massive—

"Old Peg Leg"
Peter Stuyvesant

and massively inconvenient—obstruction that is North and South America. Hudson, of course, failed. But his attempt during the summer of 1609 gained for the Dutch a solid claim to part of what the English were already calling "Virginia."

The name "New Netherland" was first used in 1614 in a document organizing a group of independent Dutch fur traders who were collectively given a monopoly on trade in the region between the Connecticut River and the Hudson River. By 1624 the Dutch West India Company had supplanted the New Netherland Company, and they began to colonize their holdings in North America which now extended further south to Delaware Bay.

In 1626 Peter Minuit took over as Royal Governor of New Netherland and very quickly made his famous "purchase" of *Manhattan* (an Algonquian word meaning "hilly island"). In order to mitigate the danger of Indian warfare, he then consolidated all of the Dutch settlements onto this tiny island with its most agreeable bay, and called it New Amsterdam. The Dutch fur trade flourished in the 1630's, but the 1640's saw a series of Indian conflicts which, in 1647, prompted the installation of a new governor, the one-legged

---

* *This, of course, depends upon how you count. You could, for instance, claim that New Jersey was settled by Swedes, then the Dutch, and that would be true. But it was the English who named it New Jersey, and separated it from New York. You could also claim, and be correct, that Delaware was never an actual colony, but always part of Pennsylvania until it seceded from that state and Britain at the same time. But by convention, it is considered an original colony, and it was, in fact, controlled by Britain (or at least by a British subject) until the Revolution.*

Calvinist governor-extraordinaire, Peter Stuyvesant. Stuyvesant managed the colony for seventeen years, overseeing a huge increase in its population, but he may be more famous for surrendering it to the English in 1664.

Meanwhile, back in England...

While the Dutch were busy colonizing New Netherland, the English were consumed with Civil War and Oliver Cromwell's rise to power. But it did not go unnoticed in London that the Dutch and their powerful navy were complicating trade for England by disregarding Parliament's Navigation Acts. These laws forbade the American colonies from trading directly with foreign merchants, requiring instead that all trade pass through England on English ships. Despite this the English Parliament was on generally good terms with Amsterdam during the Commonwealth years.

Upon Cromwell's death, the Parliamentarians lost their forceful leader, and the Royalists saw their chance. In 1660 the English throne was restored to King Charles II. Charles, whose father King Charles I had been executed by the Parliamentarians following the English Civil War, made a triumphant return to England to assume the long-vacant throne and with him was his younger brother James, who was promptly made *Duke of York and Albany*.

Old York

York was, and is, a prominent and richly historical city in northern England. Its history (as well as its name) dates back to A.D. 71 when the Romans established a military stronghold at the confluence of the Rivers Ouse and Foss. They called their fortress Eboracum, probably derived from the Celtic personal name Eburos, which many believe was further derived from the ancient British word for the yew tree. The yew, a conifer with a reputation as a resilient, long-lived tree, was sacred to the Celts and can still be found in the churchyards of some old English villages.

When the Anglo-Saxons invaded the British Isles in the sixth century, they made Eboracum, with its walled fortress, the capital of the region, but they confused the Celtic word *Eborus* for their own word *Eofor*, meaning "wild boar." They attached the suffix *-wic*, meaning "place," and the name thus became *Eoforwic* or "wild boar place." When the Norwegian-Irish Vikings settled in the area in the 900's Eoforwic became "Jorvik." The Vikings used "Jorvik" to refer to their entire kingdom in northern England, and only a few short centuries later, *Jorvik* morphed into *York*. The English suffix *-shire* was added to describe the county that had been the Viking kingdom, and so we have the English city of *York* in the county of *Yorkshire*.

The Dukedom and the Duke

In the fourteenth century the tradition began among English royalty of bestowing the Dukedom of York upon the second son of the monarch, which brings us back to Charles II and James*, the first and second sons of Charles I.

Though amazingly forgiving of those who had executed his father, Charles II wasted no time asserting his authority and escalating tensions with the Dutch by giving to his little brother all the land in America between the Connecticut and Delaware Rivers. Now, it's not as if they didn't know that the Dutch had long-since claimed and colonized that particular chunk of North America. Indeed the borders were chosen specifically to match those of New Netherland and in fact overlapped a royal charter which had previously been granted to John Winthrop Jr. of Connecticut. Thus, the king and his kid brother were announcing to Amsterdam their claim to Virginia...all of Virginia, and had the Dutch taken the announcement seriously the most recognizable place name in the coun-

**James II of England,
VII of Scotland
(formerly Duke of
York and Albany)**

---

*   *Because James' grandfather had been "James I of England,
VI of Scotland," when* this *James ascended to the throne, he was dubbed
"James II of England, VII of Scotland."*

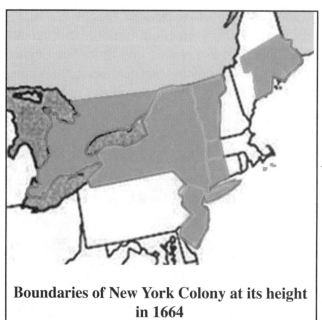

Boundaries of New York Colony at its height in 1664

try might now have a Dutch, rather than English, origin.

As it was, Peter Stuyvesant braced for an invasion by the English, but he was told by the West India Company leaders not to worry—the small fleet of English ships carrying about five hundred soldiers and led by Colonel Richard Nicolls was instead on its way to Boston to quiet the ever-troublesome Puritans. Stuyvesant was therefore wholly unprepared when Nicolls appeared off Long Island and demanded the immediate surrender of New Amsterdam. Stuyvesant was willing to fight, but the burgomasters of the colony, important land-owners and merchants who made up a kind of "city council," agreed not only that the fight would be futile but that the terms offered by Nicolls were fair—indeed generous. They eventually convinced Stuyvesant to surrender, which he did on August 29, 1664, the day Richard Nicolls officially took control of the region in honor of

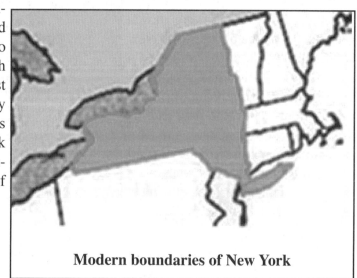

Modern boundaries of New York

his patron, the Duke of York, and the city and colony of *New York* were born.

As royal charters went, New York was a remarkably large region to have been offered in a single grant, but then New York was different. It was the only charter which was not bestowed as a gift from the king but concocted as an international political maneuver. It was also the only grant of land which was already substantially populated by Europeans. The task, then, once the colony was secured, was not to colonize but to govern.

The borders of New York were unwieldy and far-flung, including not only the former New Netherland but all of Long Island (the northern half of which had previously belonged to Connecticut), the land west of the Connecticut River, eastern Maine, and the islands of modern Nantucket and Martha's Vineyard. The largest change in borders happened before Nicolls even arrived in New Netherland. On June 24, 1664, James, Duke of York, bestowed upon two supporters, John Berkeley and Sir George Carteret, the land south of the Delaware River which he named New Jersey. The borders with Connecticut were eventually settled by giving back to Connecticut most of the land west of the Connecticut River but keeping all of Long Island. This accounts for what now looks like a rather odd border, New York having only a few short miles of coastline on Long Island Sound but owning all of Long Island, which reaches northward nearly touching Connecticut.

The colony was already a thriving business center when the English took it, and that may explain the reluctance of the English governors to censure the Dutch or discourage their trade. Indeed, one of the reasons for conquering the province was its potential for wealth, badly needed (but in fairness, *always* badly needed) by the monarchy. James, Duke of York, became King of England in 1701, and the ducal proprietorship of New York was immediately converted to royal province, but New York's fortunes would quickly be tied to those of the other colonies.

By the time of the Revolution, New York was one of the few colonies whose economy was robust enough to support the war. The City was already a metropolis (albeit by 18th century standards), and served as the nation's capital for a short period after independence was declared.

On July 9, 1776, the New York provincial congress declared its independence from England. New York ratified the U.S. Constitution on July 26, 1788, making it the tenth state in the Union.

Chapter 33: North Carolina

Her mom and dad went down to Charlotte
They're not home to find us out…

> — *"Brick"*
> *Ben Folds Five*

In my mind I'm goin' to Carolina…

> — *"Carolina In My Mind"*
> *James Taylor*

Standing Apart

Nerds think "Research Triangle." Sports fans think "Tar Heels" or possibly "Duke." North Carolina is perhaps the only southern state that doesn't immediately make one think of slavery, the Civil War, and antebellum houses, though certainly all of those existed in North Carolina. Maybe it's that word "North." Or maybe it's because, compared to its neighbors to the north and south, North Carolina seems unassuming, subdued, somehow less "southern." In fact, in some quarters it has assumed the famous Ben Franklin quote that was originally meant to describe New Jersey: "A valley of humility between two mountains of

Wright Brothers:
Orville on the left,
Wilbur on the right

conceit." It is a state that has moved on from its past and emerged with a reputation as modern, new, fresh.

Indeed, one of North Carolina's major sources of pride is its claim to the accomplishments of the Wright Brothers. "First in Flight" refers to them both—the Wright Brothers and the state of North Carolina. Kitty Hawk is one of those places in the United States that people know—they know why it's famous, even if they don't know exactly where it is. While Orville and Wilbur have undergone scrutiny and even some disparagement in recent years (modern scholars debating heatedly whether they were really the first to fly an aircraft), the state clings to them and their history, but it is a symbiotic relationship. They help each other—North Carolina props up the Wrights in their times of trouble, and the brothers link North Carolina indelibly to technological advances in aviation.

North Carolina has another important historical claim to fame. The very first attempt at English colonization in North America was the ill-fated Roanoke Island settlers in 1587, otherwise known as the "Lost Colony." Sir Walter Raleigh, who held the patent for Virginia, sent the colonists not to Roanoke Island but to Chesapeake Bay, but his orders were countermanded by the Portuguese pilot Simon Fernandes, who was anxious to rid himself of the colonists and get back to raiding Spanish ships. Fernandes forced the group off at Roanoke Island, where they attempted to make a go of it. Their fate robbed North Carolina of the first English Colony, but gave it one of the most famous mysteries in American History. Of course, had the Roanoke colony succeeded, North Carolina might now be known as Virginia, Spain might never have gained such a foothold in Florida, and the whole eastern seaboard—indeed all of the Americas—could look a lot different on maps today.

Close, but no Cigar

Alas, the stand-alone name "Carolina" was simply not meant to be. It seemed destined for success when monarch after monarch was honored by it, but its history, and that of the two states which now share the name, is filled with near misses. Attempts at starting settlements failed, were driven back by storms and hurricanes, or were thrown off course and wound up in Virginia or Florida. Then, when it finally stuck as a place name in North

America, the region it described was too big for it. So, just as the land was divided, so was the name.

The name Carolina was intended to remind us of King Charles—*Caroluus* being the Latin version of "Charles", and *Carolina* being a feminine form of Caroluus. The question is...which King Charles? Three monarchs vie for that distinction, and most histories of the word mention all three: King Charles IX of France, King Charles I of England, and his son, King Charles II. All three became the namesake for some plot of land in America, but only one—King Charles II—is specifically tied to the states of North and South Carolina.

The Three Kings

King Charles IX of France was the earliest of the three, and was only twelve years old when his subjects set out boldly for "La Florida." They aimed to take it from the Spaniards by settling the lands that Spain had virtually ignored since staking its claim in 1513. But while he did have a section of land in North America named in his honor, it wasn't necessarily the region we now call The Carolinas. The explorer who honored Charles IX was

Jean Ribaut who in, 1562, sailed to the mouth of a river he named the River of May, now called the St. John's. Ribaut claimed the land in honor of King Charles by erecting a stone marker bearing the arms of the monarchy.

Ribaut, however, was not simply naming a colony, he was naming the land. Just as the English had "Virginia" and the Spanish had "La Florida," the French deemed "Carolina" their dominion in North America (*southern* North America, that is, as they already had a foothold in what is now Canada), however large or small it turned out to be.

King Charles IX of France

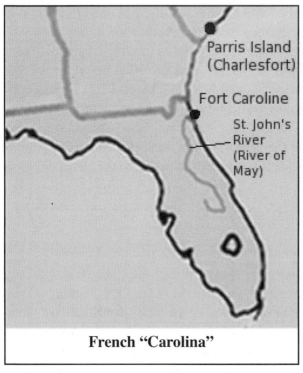

Parris Island
(Charlesfort)

Fort Caroline

St. John's
River
(River of
May)

French "Carolina"

Leaving the stone pillar on the beach for other Europeans to see from their ships, he then sailed north to what is now Parris Island, South Carolina, and instructed his men to build a small fortress. This he named Charlesfort, also in honor of his king, lest there be any mistake as to whom Ribaut was working for. Charlesfort was abandoned after eighteen months, but a new French fort was later erected at the Florida site. This one, called "Fort Caroline," was destined to suffer a gruesome ending at the hands of the Spanish in 1565 (see Florida), and French Carolina ended with it. But France would have its North American empire. Almost a hundred years later another French king, Louis XIV, would have almost a third of the continent named for him.

Which brings us to Charles number two. In 1629 King Charles I of England granted the region south of Virginia to his attorney general Sir Robert Heath. The borders of the grant stretched from 31 to 36 degrees latitude (very close to the borders of the current Carolinas), and as with many of the royal grants in America, from the Atlantic Ocean to the "South Sea," or Pacific Ocean. The king named the land "Carolana" after himself and included in Heath's charter the powerful "Bishop of Durham" clause. In England, Durham County was situated on the northern border with Scotland, and its proprietor, or Bishop, was charged with protecting England from invasion by the Scots. The placement, naming, and powers of the proprietor of Carolana represented a southward push from Virginia. Clearly, King Charles was giving notice to the Spaniards in Florida of his claim to "Carolana" and his intention to defend it.

King Charles I of England

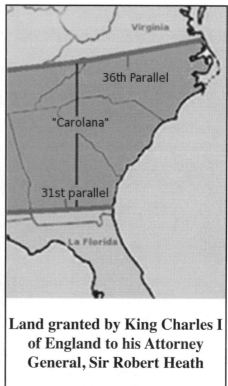

Land granted by King Charles I of England to his Attorney General, Sir Robert Heath

Heath made an unsuccessful attempt to colonize Carolana then transferred his grant to Henry Frederick Howard, Lord Maltravers, in 1638. Maltravers, the grandson of the Duke of Norfolk, was successful in creating the county of Norfolk in Carolana but no more successful than Heath had been at colonizing. Still, it was clear to settlers in Virginia that the lands to the south were considered by the king to be part of his domain, so the governor of Virginia began granting land south of that colony's border, in what they referred to as the "Southern Plantation."

In 1649, King Charles was executed by the Parliamentarians, and royal patents in America came to a halt. Many loyalists found refuge in Virginia, and the Southern Plantation began to swell with new settlers. A new name was applied: Albemarle County Colony, and it may have had as many as 500 settlers by the time of the Restoration in England.

Thus, we arrive at Charles number three. When King Charles II, who had been living in exile on the European continent, was restored to the throne in 1660, he wasted no time granting patents for new colonies in America. He granted New York to his brother, New Jersey to his friends

Berkeley and Carteret (see New Jersey), Pennsylvania to the son of a major supporter, and Carolina to a group of eight proprietors who had been loyal during his exile.

The group of Carolina proprietors are notable here for the names they placed upon the region:

Edward Hyde, Earl of Clarendon (Clarendon County)
George Monck, Duke of Albemarle (Albemarle Sound, County)
William Craven, Earl of Craven (Craven County, N.C. and S.C.)
Anthony Ashley Cooper (Ashley and Cooper Rivers)
Sir George Carteret (Carteret County)
John Lord Berkeley (Berkeley County, S.C.)

The last two of these would practically abandon their claim to Carolina in favor of a new grant to the north. Sir William Berkeley, who was governor of Virginia at the time of the grant, and Sir John Colleton of Barbados rounded out the group of proprietors.

The grant was made in 1663, and then expanded the following year to include all of the land north to the Virginia border, including what the proprietors named Albemarle County (to Virginia, the aforementioned "Southern Plantation") which was quite heavily populated and which Virginia claimed as her own, touching off a border dispute between the two colonies. The southern boundary was also moved, and

King Charles II of England

its new placement near Cape Canaveral, Florida, engulfed the established Spanish settlement at St. Augustine. Like his father, Charles was challenging the Spanish.

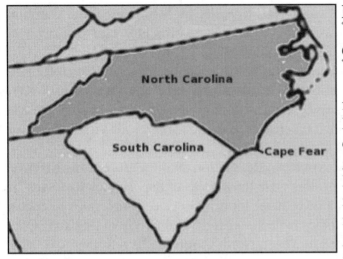

Division and Independence

Also like his father, Charles II's Lords Proprietor had difficulty settling and governing Carolina. It became clear almost instantly that not only was the region too large for a single government, but that it was divided geographically into a northern and a southern section. The southern region (see South Carolina) would not be finally settled for several years, and the northern section was full of settlers who resented the Proprietors and the series of rather corrupt governors whom they installed in Carolina. The settlers believed themselves either Virginians or true pioneers, independent and rebellious.

The southern boundary of North Carolina, therefore, was established earlier and more easily than the northern border. In 1691 Philip Ludwell was selected Governor of Carolina, and as such he would reside in the now revitalized southern city of Charles Town. He was, however, to select a deputy governor for the northern section of the unwieldy colony, and he did so with care and discretion, selecting men who brought relative prosperity to "North Carolina," as it came to be called.

Eventually, however, this situation proved chaotic, and to remedy the problem with a single document, the Lords Proprietor made the division between north and south official and permanent. On January 12, 1712 they commissioned a governor of North Carolina "independent of the Governor of Carolina." The name "South Carolina" would routinely be used from then on to describe the southern region, but interestingly it was the North, the larger section, which would give up the sole use of the name in order to gain its separation from the southern region.

Cape Fear had always been the point of division between the two colonies, and the actual border would not be determined until 1735, but once it was surveyed the line was agreed to easily by North and South Carolina. Both states, however, would have much more difficulty with their opposite neighbors in settling disputed boundary lines.

North Carolina's border with Virginia had been a source of resentment for over half a century before it was finally resolved. By order of King George II a group of surveyors were commissioned. They ran the line correctly according to the 1665 charter, and once and for all Virginia gave up its claim to Albemarle County in North Carolina.

By the time of the American Revolution, North Carolina was eager for independence. Its legislators were the authors of the "Halifax Resolves" in April of 1776 which, among other things, directed its delegates to concur with those of other colonies in declaring independence from England. Once the revolution was over, however, North Carolina was reluctant to join the Union. It was twelfth of the thirteen colonies to ratify the Constitution (ahead of only Rhode Island), which it did on November 21, 1789.

Chapter 34: North Dakota

[Dakota] is a name at once suggesting greatness and broad domain. And a careful review of its history must satisfy one that a substitute should never be given. And it is no wonder that the people throughout the length and breadth of the Territory, as with one voice said: "Let them bear the ancestral name! A name whose every letter seems an unwritten chapter in the history of that powerful nation, from whose hands we adopted her; with all the legends, wild romances and fascinating traditions—an ancient jeweled-chain—which must be kept: A legacy for her children.

> — *"Once Their Home: Our Legacy From the Dakhkotahs (sic)" by Frances Chamberlain Holley*

"Don't come, unless you're prepared to stay."

> *—Garrison Keillor on North Dakota*

It Can't Snow All the Time

When you think of North Dakota and its continental climate location, it is difficult to picture anything else but snow. Not only does it snow—and a lot!—but once the snow arrives in late fall, North Dakotans can expect it to stick around until spring. Maybe it's the ice storms or the polar fronts, the blinding blizzards, or the blood-drenched snow of the infamous *wood chipper scene* from 1996's Oscar winning "Fargo"; but whatever the mental image, if there's snow involved, North Dakota probably isn't very far from your mind.

Summers in North Dakota can also exhibit the drastic variations created by the continental climate, yet are typically mild and receive ample precipitation. This summer weather, joined with vast, fertile soil, permit North Dakota to be the country's largest producer of barley, sunflower seeds, and durum wheat. In fact, in the summer months, the rolling snow-covered prairies are transformed into seas of bright burnt yellow, as sunflower farms take over the land. North Dakota truly is a perfect example of the beauty of nature's climactic extremes.

Aside from the obvious—weather, agriculture, the widely popular progressive radio phenomenon *The Ed Schultz Show*—North Dakota is also (uncommonly) known for its cuisine. Knoephla soup, lutefisk, Kuchen, lefse, Fleischkuekle—these are not genus classifications for prehistoric organisms or the names of small, blink-through towns in unfamiliar European countries. They are in fact popular dishes of German and Scandinavian cuisine. In the late nineteenth century, the territory of North Dakota experienced an influx of Scandinavian emigration that has shaped, molded, and simmered the modern North Dakotan culture.

Moving

It is not difficult to trace the word "Dakota" to its origins. What is more difficult is tracing the application of the word to the land it now names, for it is not as simple as saying that the two states bearing the name "Dakota" were so called because they were inhabited by an Indian tribe of that name. In fact, before any European had met a Dakota Indian, they had a different name for them, a name that would describe them, their brethren, their language, and the language of many other tribes in North America.

The French, who in the early 1700's first explored the western Great Lakes region, traded among and were allied with the Chippewa Indians who were concentrated in northern Michigan and Wisconsin. The Chippewa, sometimes called Ojibwe, spoke an Algonquian language and were in the precarious position of being surrounded by enemies. To the north and east were the Iroquois, a powerful, dominating foe, in part because they obtained guns through their trade with the Dutch. And to the south and west were the people they called "naudiwisiweg" meaning "little snake" to differentiate them from the more awesome Iroquois. The French recorded the name as "naudiwisioux" and later shortened it to simply "Sioux."

When ethnologists began classifying Native Americans by language, they discovered that the Siouan language was spoken by tribes all over central North America. The still-accepted inference is that wherever and however the Sioux people began as a culture, several groups divided from them before or during their move westward from the East coast of North

America. Some moved south and became the Iowa and Kansa tribes, while others moved north and further west and became the Mandan and Hidatsas. The main group of Sioux moved west along the southern edge of the Great Lakes through Michigan and Wisconsin to Minnesota.

The Sioux, it turns out, were a highly organized nation of people. They trace their history (though not necessarily their origins) to a time just before the arrival of Europeans. During this era, the early 1500's, they lived mainly in the east between the Appalachians and the Atlantic. If they weren't already rather nomadic (and indications are that they were), the coming of the white man caused them and virtually every other group of people living in North America to move, and move a lot. By the 1700's, before they had even seen a European, the Sioux were living in the Mille Lac region of Minnesota, though some groups had broken off and become enemies of their former tribe. The Sioux referred to them as hohay or "rebels," and it was several of these tribes—the Mandans, Hidatsas, and Assiniboin—who would dominate central and northwestern North Dakota.

Migration routes of some Siouan tribes

Allies

The Sioux called themselves Oceti Sakowin or "Seven Council Fires," referring to the seven divisions of the nation. These seven divisions are

The Lakota Sioux became expert horsemen, lived on the plains, wore headresses of feathers, and hunted bison.
Painting by Karl Bodmer

grouped by the three similar dialects they speak. Four of the Council Fires are Santee Sioux who spoke the Dakota dialect. Two are Yankton Sioux, and spoke Nakota. The third and largest by far is the Teton Sioux group who spoke the Lakota dialect. The dialect is important in distinguishing between the three divisions, and often the tribes would refer to themselves by the language they spoke. As is indicated in the names of the dialects, often words were identical for each dialect except for the substitution of the letters d, l, and n. Thus the word for "thank you" in Dakota is pidomiye; in Nakota it is pinomiye; and in Lakota the word is pilomiye.[1]

The word Dakota (as well as Nakota and Lakota) means "ally," but is often translated as "friend". "Ally" is more appropriate, however, because while all of the members in the seven councils became increasingly different in their culture and lifestyle, they remained allied with each other and had many common enemies, not least of all the encroaching Europeans.

Of the three, the Lakota became the tribe that epitomizes the stereotypical Plains Indian of American folklore. They took advantage of the newly introduced beasts of burden brought over by the Spaniards in the early 1500's—horses. They moved onto the prairies, became extremely nomadic, lived in easily-moved teepees, wore headdresses of feathers, were expert horsemen, hunted buffalo, and were fiercely defensive of their territory, especially with regard to white men. The Lakota dominated the Missouri River in what is now South Dakota and also hunted the southwest corner of North Dakota.

The Yankton-nai, a division of the Nakota Sioux, lived and hunted in south-eastern North Dakota. In the central part of the state, however, the place where the Missouri River turns west, were the permanent villages of the Mandan and Hidatsa tribes. These villages 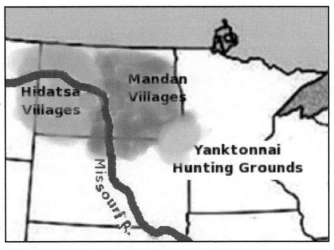 were well known trading centers, frequented by the French, and known to Americans by the time of the Lewis and Clark expedition. In fact, once the Louisiana Purchase created a new frontier for the U.S., the northern section of it was frequently referred to as "Mandan Country."

Ironically, the Dakota were the only division of Sioux who did not migrate into what are now North and South Dakota. The Santee, or Dakota Sioux, were less nomadic than their brethren. When the Chippewa forced them from the Mille Lac region in Minnesota, they moved south only a short distance to the Minnesota River, maintaining their woodland and agrarian ways, and relying little, if at all, on the buffalo of the plains. While they defended their territory, the Dakota were also less warlike than the Lakota and Nakota and were therefore better known to the Americans who quickly moved into the region following the purchase of Louisiana.

For, this reason during the first half of the 1800's, the name Dakota was often used to refer to the entire Sioux nation, a legacy that has largely endured to this day. But the region that would become Dakota Territory did not yet have a name and was certainly not yet called "Dakota." In fact, the word, while not completely obscure, was not by any means ubiquitous. In his journal in 1803, William Clark wrote "This great nation, whom the French have given the nickname of Sioux, call themselves Dakota-Darco-tar."[2] The fact that Lewis and Clark felt compelled to report this indicates that the name "Dakota" was not entirely familiar to them, nor to those to whom they were reporting.

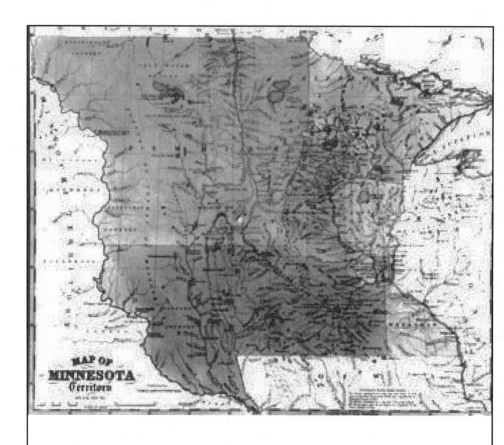

This 1852 map shows the counties of Minnesota Territory which extended from the Mississippi to the Missouri River

The Dakota Land Company

In March of 1849, Minnesota was given territorial status with borders that extended to the Missouri River, which is to say, it included half of what are now the states of North and South Dakota. A few short months later, the county of Dakota was formed in Minnesota Territory, the name taken from the Indians who in fact occupied much of the land at the time. The county included the bustling city of St. Paul and extended westward all the way to the western territorial boundary. This was undoubtedly the first point at which North and South Dakota could claim their name; however, four years later the county was divided up, and Dakota County Minnesota shrunk to a few square miles surrounding the city of St. Paul.

The connection between the county and the future states, however, would continue. In the 1850's it became clear that the imminent statehood for Minnesota would involve lopping off the western portion at the Red River. On May 23, 1857, a group of St. Paul businessmen who saw the handwriting on the wall were granted a charter by the Minnesota territorial legislature "with full powers for the purchase and entry of lands and the establishment of townsites."[3] They called themselves the Dakota Land Company, and though they were formed in Dakota County, Minnesota, their object was the land west of the Red River Valley, which would be left out of the new state once it was admitted. They sent a group of settlers to form a township on the Big Sioux River, but when they arrived, they found a town already established. The Western Town Lot Company of Dubuque, Iowa, had beaten them to the punch only weeks earlier and had claimed the choicest spot on the river, which they named Sioux Falls. Not to be outdone, the Dakota Land Company simply claimed the adjoining 320 acres and called their township Sioux Falls City.

The motivation of The Dakota Land Company is critical. While most of the history books allude to it, one book asserts rather blatantly that "From its very beginning the company was a financial venture of the Minnesota Democratic Party."[4] The goal of the company, then, was to gain territorial status for the region, and insert its own members as delegates and government officials, giving the Democrats complete control over a huge new territory, as well as more power in congress. The actual settlement of the land was secondary. Put another way "The Dakota Land Company...attached more importance to political organization than to immediate growth."[5]

This point is hilariously illustrated by the story of the first territorial elections held in the region. Once Minnesota achieved statehood in May of 1858, the thirty or so citizens of Sioux Falls determined to form a legislature, thereby sending a message to Congress of the need for governmental organization. And so that there could be no confusion about who was putting forth the effort to organize the region, the Dakota Land Company began referring to it as "Dakota Territory" and organized the elections rather creatively:

> ...on the morning of election, the whole population organized into parties of three or four, elected each other judges and clerks of election, and then started off with their teams in various directions for a pleasure trip, and whenever a rest was taken, which

occurred frequently, an election precinct was established, and the votes not only of the party but of their uncles, cousins, relatives and friends were cast, until as a result of the election the total vote rolled up into the hundreds, and was properly certified to.[6]

Similar antics of the Dakota Land Company are rampant in the history of the territory. Between 1858 and 1861 its agents formed "paper towns," reported on phantom surveys, and began their own newspaper—*The Dakota Democrat*—which routinely reported the grossly exaggerated population of the area. A few short months after the "election" of 1858, an agent of the Dakota Land Company named Alpheus G. Fuller, who had been chosen to represent the territory to the U.S. Government, appeared before Congress declaring himself the delegate from the "Territory of Dakota."

Late in 1860 a bill was introduced to organize a portion of the region along the Red River into the Territory of Chippewa. The request for this organization came from the citizens of Pembina, an old trading town near the Canadian border, and the only concentrated non-Indian population (though many of the residents were part Indian) in the northern section of the region. This bill failed, but the following year, under the guidance of the now Republican administration in Washington, the Dakota Territory was finally formed out of what are now North and South Dakota and the entire state of Montana.

The Rest of the Story

While the Dakota Land Company had failed in its political goals (i.e. making North Dakota a new territory safe for the Democratic Party), it had succeeded in imprinting upon the region the name which it would carry to statehood. Like most state names, the spelling of the word would not be finally settled upon for decades. Dacota, Dacotah, and Dakotah all appear in the Territorial Papers—in bills and memorials to Congress as well as various correspondence and newspaper articles, and often one document would contain different variations of the spelling. But the name was settled upon, and the work toward statehood now commenced in earnest.

Statehood, of course, involved division, and so the rest of the story of the naming of the Dakotas will be told in the chapter on South Dakota.

1.   Tweton, D. Jerome and Theodore B. Jelliff, <u>North Dakota: The Heritage of a People</u>, (Fargo: North Dakota Institute for Regional Studies, 1976), p. 16.

2.   <u>The Journals of Lewis and Clark</u>, Chapter 1, *Setting Forth*, http://xroads.virginia.edu/~HYPER/JOURNALS/LEWIS.html, accessed 7/25/09

3.   Schell, Herbert S., <u>Dakota Territory During the Eighteen Sixties</u> (University Research Fund, 1954), p. 11

4.   Lamar, Howard Roberts, <u>Dakota Territory 1861-1889</u> (Yale University Press, New Haven, 1956), p. 42.

5.   Schell, p. 12.

6.   Baily, Dana R., <u>History of Minnehaha County, South Dakota</u>, (Sioux Falls: Brown & Saenqer, Ptrs., 1899), accessed at http://files.usgwarchives.org/sd/minnehaha/history/bailey/chap1.txt, 7/25/09.

Chapter 35: Ohio

Tin soldiers and Nixon's coming
We're finally on our own
This summer I hear the drumming
Four dead in Ohio

> — "Ohio"
> *Crosby, Stills, Nash, and Young*

Q: What's round on both ends, and hi in the middle?
A: Ohio.

> —*Old Riddle*

North, West, South, or East

Despite the fact that Ohio is named for the "beautiful" river that creates its southern border, the state's name often conjures up images of industrialization, steel and rubber factories, and smokestacks piercing the horizon. And Ohio's city names may be even more evocative of the blue collar ethic that fuels such gritty development: Dayton, Cleveland, Cincinnati, Columbus, etc.

Up until the 1970's Ohio was known more for the pollution of its rivers than for their beauty. The PBS series *The States* discusses the many fires that burned on the Cuyahoga River, fires that were fueled by the sheer tonnage of pollution in the river. These conflagrations, it turns out, had a silver lining. Because of the dramatic dumping of toxic waste into the state's waterways, the environmentalist movement was galvanized with the Federal "Clean Water Act" and the creation of the Environmental Protection Agency. The rivers of the state were cleaned up, and Ohio could once again take pride, knowing that its namesake was represents nature's beauty and not man's folly. We owe a humble thanks for these new ideas on the environment.

PBS also reminds us that Ohio calls itself the "Mother of Presidents," having provided seven of our nation's leaders. But given who those seven were, it is not, perhaps, a title Ohio truly wishes to embrace. William Henry Harrison gave his inaugural speech on a cold, rainy day and died of pneumonia only thirty-two days later. Ulysses S. Grant led the Union to victory over the South in the Civil War, but is known for running one of the most corrupt presidential administrations in history. James Garfield was the second president to be assassinated after Lincoln, and William McKinley became the third president to be murdered in office. (Being killed while in office is, of course, not their fault, but it does lend itself to a rather morose legacy.) Lastly, William Howard Taft was, famously, the fattest president we have ever had.

Ohio is also known for its farmland and its football. While the cities of Ohio convey an industrial theme, a little over half of Ohio's land is farmland. And one thing that both the city dwellers and rural folk can agree on is a passion for their football teams: the Hawkeyes and Buckeyes, the Browns and the Bengals—all can claim an enthusiastic base of proud Ohio football fans.

Ohio was the first of the states formed out of the Northwest Territory. It sits in the far southeast corner of that massive tract, won by the U.S. after the American Revolution. Its norther border is south of all of the other states carved out of the Northwest Territory. To westerners, Ohio is "eastern," and to southerners it is "northern," all the while remaining the easternmost of the "Midwestern" states. Make sense?

The Iroquois

In the late 16th and early 17th centuries, the French explored much of the eastern coast of Canada and the St. Lawrence River and established trading posts in order to obtain valuable furs from the Indians of the region. The French, under Samuel de Champlain* allied themselves with the Hurons, long-time enemies of the Iroquois. The Iroquois, whose native land was in the region of New York State, began trading with Dutch settlers, eventually obtaining muskets and iron tools from them in order to effectively battle their Indian enemies as well as the hated French.

* *Though no contemporary portrait of Samuel de Champlain exists, several posthumous portraits (like the one above) were painted or drawn.*

Samuel de Champlain

Around 1650 the Iroquois (or, more accurately, the Europeans who traded ravenously for furs) depleted the supply of fur-bearing animals in the area they inhabited, and so moved south and west to the lush Ohio River Valley. Using their newly obtained weaponry, they easily overtook the indigenous tribes of the region, tribes who were already weakened from diseases which had been spread to them by European explorers and missionaries. In what came to be known as the "Beaver Wars," because of the beaver and deer pelts so coveted by the aggressors, the Iroquois easily defeated and pushed out Ohio's native tribes and claimed the land for the Iroquois Confederacy — not for habitation but for hunting and fishing.

The River

"Ohio", the Iroquois word for the river which ran through the region they now dominated, was thus adopted by Europeans. The meaning of the word is mildly disputed. The French, who continued an adversarial (to put it gently) relationship with the Iroquois, translated *Ohio* into "La Belle Rivière" — "the Beautiful River." Historian R. E. Banta interprets the French translation further: "Not *a* beautiful river, mind you, but *the* beautiful river, with no fear that it might be confused with any other." Banta goes on to say that the French may have misunderstood the exact meaning of the Iroquois word. Later linguists have translated *Ohio* as "The Great," "The White" or "The Sparkling."[1]

Given old and current descriptions of the Ohio River, the French translation seems entirely appropriate. But more than being a beautiful river, the waterway, its banks, and the valley in which it is situated — called informally "Ohio Country" until the end of the Revolutionary War — was a strategic jewel for the Indians, the French, the British and the Americans. Not surprisingly then, the beautiful Ohio River and the region to its north and west were the sites of battles, skirmishes and grisly massacres for many years to come.

The river began to appear on maps around 1669, and descriptions of it renewed widespread anxiety that a trade route to the Orient may yet be found. Renè Robert Cavelier Sieur de La Salle explored the Ohio River, but whether or not he was the first European to do so is a matter of speculation.

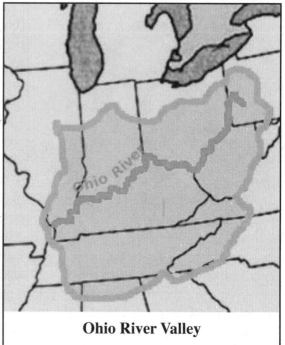

Ohio River Valley

The Territory

When the Ohio Country became a territory, it was not called "Ohio Territory." It was referred to instead as the "Northwest Territory," and included what is now Ohio, Indiana, Michigan, Wisconsin, and Illinois. The Northwest Territory was created after the American Revolution out of lands ceded to the United States by Great Britain. The question of what to do with those lands was being answered, however, while the war was still in progress, by a resolution adopted by Congress on October 10, 1780:

> *Resolved*, that the unappropriated lands that may be ceded or relinquished to the United States, by any particular states...shall be disposed of for the common benefit of the United States, and be settled and formed into distinct republican States, which shall become members of the Federal Union, and shall have the same rights of sovereignty, freedom and independence, as the other States...[2]

The lands referred to were, at the time, claimed by the British, the Indians, and even by some of the original colonies, like Virginia and Pennsylvania, whose original charters included lands "from sea to sea." After the war, the defeated British relinquished their claim on the territory. The Indians, who had for the most part sided with the British during the conflict, were coerced into giving up the Northwest Territory based on the American claim to have defeated the British and their Indian allies.[3] Congress attempted to cloak its coercion in legality by signing dubious treaties with several of the Indian tribes, but the reality for the future would be a bloody struggle between Indians and settlers.

In 1787 Congress passed the Northwest Ordinance of 1787, a document whose significance in U.S. history rivals that of the Constitution. It formalized the 1780 resolution, allowing new lands to be formed into territories, and then equal states, rather than satellite provinces of the Union.

Thomas Jefferson was one Founding Father who was actively attempting to design a procedure for organizing the Northwest Territory into American states. In the now-famous Jefferson-Hartley map of the region, he not only divided the land into fourteen new states (some historians interpret it as up to seventeen), he proposed names for them as well. Sylvania, Michigania, Metropotamia, and Chersonesus were among the classical names proposed,

The now-famous Jefferson-Hartley map of 1784

and they sound kind of silly to our twenty-first century ears. But in truth, they were no more silly than, say, "Indiana" or "Montana."

One other name that Jefferson proposed was "Washington," in an obvious homage to our first president. It was actually inserted as one name for what would be the first territory created when the Northwest Ordinance was being debated in

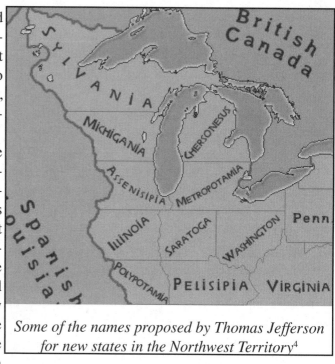

Some of the names proposed by Thomas Jefferson for new states in the Northwest Territory[4]

Congress. But when it actually came time to break up the Old Northwest, "Washington" was replaced with "Ohio" in the eastern, most populous region, and "Indiana" became the name for the remaining territory in the west. *Washington* became a county of the sixteenth state and remains so today.

The Seventeenth or the Forty-Eighth State?

For over a century Ohio's statehood, or more accurately, the date on which statehood was conferred, labored under the most extreme confusion. One writer, a former Governor of Ohio, James Edwin Campbell, makes a convincing case in one article[5] for five different dates upon which Ohio could have entered the union, none of the five contradicting the others. His point, which comes through loud and clear, is that when Ohio was being populated, largely by former soldiers from the Revolution, there was no clear procedure for new areas to be granted statehood. The Northwest Ordinance proclaimed it possible but did not lay out a definitive process.

348

Therefore, Ohio's statehood could be asserted as

1) April 30, 1802, the day the Continental Congress passed the Enabling Act authorizing Ohio to elect representatives and draw up a constitution.

2) February 19th, 1803, when President Jefferson signed an act approving Ohio's constitution and boundaries.

3) March 1st, 1803, when state officials were inaugurated and judges were appointed.

4) March 3rd, 1803, the date Congress reviewed and accepted revisions to the state constitution of Ohio.

5) Or last, but not least, on August 7, 1953, when Ohio Congressman George H. Bender introduced a bill in Congress, specifically to admit the state of Ohio into the Union.

This last one, while odd, is actually true. In 1953, the year of Ohio's sesquicentennial, a rider on horseback delivered an act to Congress in Washington D.C., which accepted the statehood of Ohio retroactive to March 1st, 1803 (the date most commonly agreed upon as the date of Ohio's admission into the Union as the 17th state). It was signed by President Dwight D. Eisenhower.

1.   Banta, R. E., <u>Rivers of America: The Ohio</u> (New York, 1949), p. 8.

2.   Knepper, George W., <u>Ohio and Its People</u> (Kent, 1989), p. 47.

3.   Knepper, p. 51.

4.   Penny, Jordan, "248 – Friends, Polypotamians, Countrymen!," Strange Maps, http://strangemaps.wordpress.com/2008/02/25/248-friends-polypotamians-countrymen/, accessed 9/15/09.

5.   Campbell, James Edwin, "How and When (?) Ohio Became a State," *Ohio History*, vol. 34, p. 29.

Chapter 36: Oklahoma

Oooo-OK-lahoma!
Where the wind comes sweeping down the plains!

> — *"Oklahoma"*
> *Rodgers & Hammerstein*

You're the reason God made Oklahoma
And I'm sure missin' you.

> — *"Your the Reason God Made Oklahoma"*
> *David Frizzell*

Sooners

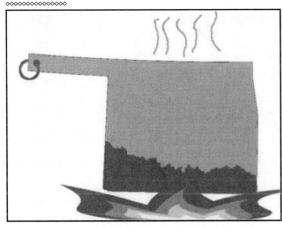

Oklahoma is one of the more uniquely shaped states. When looking at a map, its borders closely resemble a cooking pot or large frying pan. Oklahoma's unique panhandle shape unnaturally extends its borders west, joining the bordering states of Texas, Arkansas, Missouri, and Kansas with small slivers of Colorado and New Mexico. However diverting Oklahoma may seem, Oklahomans take themselves pretty seriously. Well, at least if you can define seriousness by college football.

Like its northern neighbor Nebraska, college football reigns supreme in Oklahoma. The Division 1 Oklahoma University Sooners and Oklahoma State University Cowboys both average over 60,000 fans at *each* football game. Some professional teams can't even claim fan support at that level. And with nine other college and university teams competing within the NCAA (two more of those in Division 1), it is no surprise why *Sports Illustrated* has deemed Oklahoma schools to be among the top institutions for college athletics in the United States.

Officially, Oklahoma is considered a southern state because of its position south of the 36th parallel, but more generally it lies between the Midwest and Southwestern regions. Oklahoman culture is clearly a product of its history and geography. Due largely to the forced migration of many native tribes from east of the Mississippi River instituted by the federal government of the 1820's and 1830's, Native American ancestry runs deep in Oklahoma. Sixty-seven tribes are represented in the state and over twenty-five different native languages are spoken to this day. The state mammal is the American Bison, and pow wows and other cultural events are frequently held throughout most Oklahoma cities and counties.

"Oklahoma!" was a smash hit on Broadway when it opened in 1943

During the cattle-drive years of the 1860's and 70's Oklahoma was in the middle of the action. Massive herds of cattle were driven along cattle trails from Texas to Kansas, crossing what was then still largely referred to rather unceremoniously as "Indian Country," even though the name for the territory, *Oklahoma*, had been adopted in 1866. Conflict arose between the cowboys and ranchers who drove the herds, and white farmers who had migrated to Oklahoma with the promise of free land. Land was allocated on a "first-come first-served" basis, and many settlers refused to wait until they were officially granted access to claim their homesteads, crossing the territory lines *sooner* than their law-abiding counterparts. "Sooners" became the nickname for these new Oklahomans, eventually becoming the official nickname of the state.

While conflict with the Indians was rare during this period, the resentment between the farmers and ranchers often reached a fevered pitch. And while this territorial feud was certainly nothing to sing about, it did give us the legendary musical stage play, "Oklahoma," the first of many collaboration efforts by the incomparable duo, Richard Rodgers and Oscar Hammerstein.

Removal Treaties

The "Indian Removal Treaties" of the early 1800's were about as indelicate as the name implies. They were documents by which the United States claimed the authority to move the Five Civilized Tribes (Cherokee, Choctaw, Chickasaw, Creek, and Seminole) out of their homeland in the southeastern U.S. and into a region west of the Mississippi which had recently been acquired in the Louisiana Purchase. These treaties were often the cause of severe factionalism within the individual tribes, because in virtually every case at least some of the members were understandably loathe to leave the land of their ancestors, land that their people had inhabited for generations and that was considered sacred, while others were anxious to peacefully escape the encroaching white settlers.

To make matters worse, while the treaties may have been entered into in good faith on the part of the Americans (though clearly this was not always the case), the execution of the terms resulted in tragic suffering. Volumes have been written about the "Trail of Tears," the path—actually there were several routes—taken from Indians' homelands north through Tennessee into Arkansas, and later Oklahoma. Terrible winters were endured, and sickness took many lives. The dead were buried along the trail and given a short funeral ceremony, after which the torturous journey continued.

Those who refused to travel the Trail of Tears suffered as well. The Seminole tribe chose to fight the Americans rather than be forced from their home. The ensuing Seminole Wars were ugly and inglorious, and all but decimated the tribe. Many of those who survived the war were eventually transported, some in manacles, a few hundred at a time, to the west.

*Some of the Trail of Tears routes used for
"Indian removal" to Oklahoma*

The Cherokees, the first to sign a removal treaty, were initially removed to a region in northwestern Arkansas, but white settlers were already pouring into that area. Almost immediately after arriving, the Indians began to experience the same difficulties that had driven them from their homelands. Before the problem could fester, the government appropriated what is now the entire state of Oklahoma minus the panhandle as "Indian Country," and took responsibility for keeping white settlers out of the region. After the Cherokees, over about two decades in the 1820's and 1830's, the remaining tribes from Georgia, Florida, Mississippi and Alabama crossed the Trail of Tears into what was commonly called "Indian Territory".

This rather embarrassing moment in U.S. history finds its relevance to the naming of the state of Oklahoma, largely because of the Treaty of Dancing Rabbit Creek. That was the removal treaty in which the Choctaw tribe agreed to relinquish their lands in Mississippi in exchange for land west of the Mississippi River. In the treaty, the Choctaw refer to themselves several times as the "Choctaw Nation of Red People," or, in their own language, "Oklahoma".

Indian Country and the Civil War

The Civil War brought about more factionalism among and between the tribes of the Indian Territory. The Choctaw and Chickasaws formed alliances with the South early on, but the remaining tribes were sharply

354

divided. Eventually all five tribes plus some smaller tribes now residing in the region signed treaties with the Confederacy, which promised them more autonomy than the current U.S. government.

Though Indians fought on both sides of the Civil War, when it ended the tribes were forced to answer for their written alliances with the South. By siding with the Confederacy they had forfeited (in the U.S. view) any treaty that existed with the United States, and at the Council of Fort Smith in 1865 the U.S. made known to the Indians the terms of peace which would be imposed upon them.

Allen Wright

In the Spring of 1866 the Five Civilized Tribes sent delegations to Washington to sign formal treaties with the United States based upon agreements

Reverend Allen Wright

made at Fort Smith. Representing the Choctaw was, among others, Reverend Allen Wright, a full blood Choctaw who had traveled the Trail of Tears. His mother had died on that journey, and his father shortly after arriving in Indian Territory. Allen Wright, whose Choctaw name was *Killihote*, was raised by Reverend Cyrus Kingsbury, a Presbyterian missionary, and later went on to distinguish himself as a statesman within the Choctaw tribe.[1]

One of the terms of the Fort Smith agreement had been that the Indian nations would attempt to consolidate themselves, and so at the 1866 negotiations the question arose "What would you call your territory?" Allen

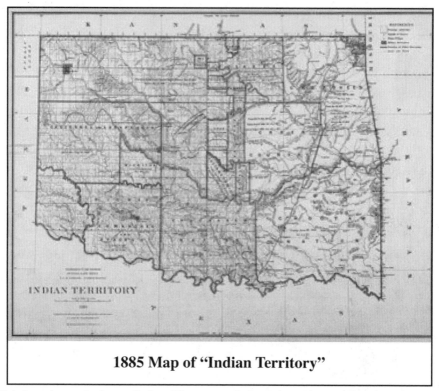

1885 Map of "Indian Territory"

Wright, the scholar of the Choctaw delegation, immediately responded "Oklahoma."

The word "Okla" means *people* in Choctaw, and the word "homma" or "humma" means *red*. Therefore, the name must have seemed naturally fitting to Allen Wright who had no doubt studied the Treaty of Dancing Rabbit Creek, and who was accustomed to referring to his people as the "Choctaw Nation of Red People."

While there were some grumblings among the other delegations they had more to do with the fact that Wright had given his answer so decidedly and so quickly, without consulting with the tribes or even with the other delegates. But while there was some general disgruntlement, no one was prepared to offer an alternative name for the new territory, and so "Oklahoma" stuck.

Four treaties were signed in 1866: one with the Choctaws and Chickasaws, and one each with the other three tribes. The first occurrence of the word "Oklahoma" in any U.S. Document appears in the Chickasaw-Choctaw treaty of 1866 in a section providing that, in the event that the tribes are consolidated under one government, the Superintendent of Indian Affairs should be the chief executive, and should have the title "Governor of Oklahoma."[2]

Twin Territories

The Indians, however, were to be squeezed once more, even within the confines of what was intended to be Indian Territory. As more and more settlers moved west and ranchers began to covet the grazing lands of Oklahoma, the Federal government opened the unassigned lands to non-Indian settlement. The panhandle region was added in 1890, and even more white settlers moved into the new territory, primarily in the western half.

As the division between the Indian reservations of the east and the white settlers of the west became sharper, they began to be referred to in a rather ironic manner. "Indian Territory" or "Indian Country" was the region in the east with the large Native American population and the majority of the reservations. Oddly, the root of the word that described them, "Indian," was the name created by Europeans on the false assumption that the Carribean Islands were the Indies of the Orient (see Indiana). On the other hand, the name used to label the western lands, those populated mostly by whites, was "Oklahoma," the name the Choctaw used to refer to *themselves*.

The term "Twin Territories" was codified with the publication of a magazine called *Twin Territories: The Indian Magazine*. It described itself as "the only publication of its class in the Indian Territory, and named in honor of both the Indian Territory and Oklahoma."[3]

During the 1890's and early 1900's the efforts to gain statehood for either or both of the Twin Territories gained strength, and out of those efforts were developed four possible strategies:

1. Joint or single statehood for one state made up of both territories,

2. Two seperate states, statehood for each territory,

3. *Piecemeal absoption*, meaning that Oklahoma would become a state, and Indian Country would be absorbed little by little as agreements were made with each tribe, and

4. The granting of statehood to the white settlers in "Oklahoma," and leaving the Indian Country to persue its own destiny.[4]

In 1905, in a bid for the second of these options, the Five Civilized Tribes of the Indian Territory developed a Constitution and presented it to the U.S. Congress along with a request for statehood. This time they would call their state "Sequoyah." The effort failed, however, and it became clear that there was a vast preference in the U.S. Congress for the single-state plan.

Indeed, the following year Congress passed the Oklahoma Enabling Act, providing for the combination of the Twin Territories into one state of "Oklahoma." On November 16, 1907, our 46th state entered the union with the signature of President Theodore Roosevelt.

1.   Dale, Edward Everett, <u>History of Oklahoma,</u> (New York, 1948), p. 185.

2.   Thoburn, Joseph B., <u>A Standard History of Oklahoma,</u> (Chicago, 1916), p. 382.

3.   Pennington, William D., "Twin Territories," *Encyclopedia of Oklahoma History & Culture,* (Oklahoma Historical Society), http://digital.library.okstate.edu/encyclopedia/entries/T/TW003.html, accessed 08/20/09.

4.   Gibson, Arrell Morgan, <u>Oklahoma, A History of Five Centuries,</u> (Norman: University of Oklahoma Press, 1981), p. 192.

Chapter 37: Oregon

I met him on the cliffs
of Twin Rocks, Oregon...

> — *"Twin Rocks, Oregon"*
> *Shawn Mullins*

Well Portland Oregon and sloe gin fizz
If that ain't love then tell me what is
Well I lost my heart it didn't take no time
But that ain't all I lost my mind in Oregon

> — *"Portland, Oregon"*
> *Loretta Lynn*

The "New" Oregon Trail

Young children, upon hearing the word "Oregon," may think of that piano-like instrument in the church balconey. But to the rest of us Oregon is that Pacific Northwest state full of people who have a serious bias against Californians, even though much of the state is populated with displaced... Californians. If any state has a "slam the door behind you" policy, it is Oregon—at least with regard to its southern neighbor. The flood of immigrants and refugees northward from the increasingly over-populated cities of California travelled what has been called the "New Oregon Trail" and is famously resented by those who thought to do it first.

But Oregon, to most of us, calls to mind the state's plethora of natural resources rather than the people who move in to exploit them. Oregon's geography is perhaps more varied than any other state. While known for its rainfall, there is also a place in western Oregon called the "Great Sandy Desert," part of the Great Basin of the American West.

With such diverse geography it is not surprising that Oregon is famous for its natural resources: abundant timber, hundreds of varieties of fish,

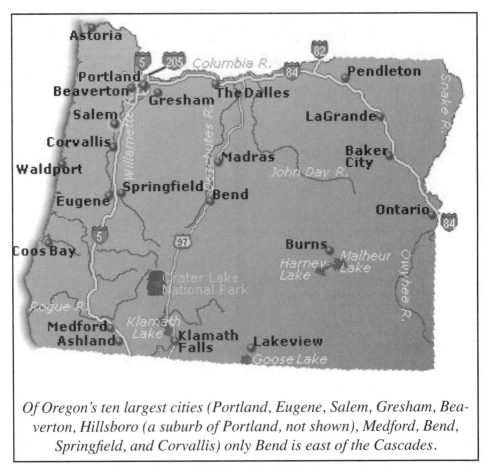

*Of Oregon's ten largest cities (Portland, Eugene, Salem, Gresham, Bea-
verton, Hillsboro (a suburb of Portland, not shown), Medford, Bend,
Springfield, and Corvallis) only Bend is east of the Cascades.*

minerals and gems, and even rich farmland. There are also those resources
we think of in terms of recreation: Mount Hood, the Snake River, Crater
Lake, the Columbia Gorge, and the beautifully named Cascade Mountains.
And then there's the rain...lots of rain. The southwest coast of Oregon, one
of the wettest regions in the country, can receive over a hundred inches of
rainfall per year, and on any given winter day, it is more likely to rain than
not.

If the arid regions of the southwest part of the state are sometimes left
out of descriptions of Oregon, it is perhaps because most of the people who
live in the state live west of the Cascades. Nine of the state's ten largest
cities line up along Interstate Five, which threads its way in between the
mountains and the ocean all the way from California to Washington along
the...ahem...New Oregon Trail.

Pick a Theory

Oregon is unique among state names because even its language of origin is not entirely clear (i.e. there has been no consensus as to whether the word is Euro-American or Aboriginal-American), and thus any "meaning" has been blurred, distorted or entirely lost.

There is, however, no shortage of theories. Among the most popular is that the word *Oregon* is derived from the Spanish word *oregano*, referring to a spice (oregano, marjoram or sage) that grows wild in the northwest. The Spanish indeed explored the northwest coast in the late 1500's, but there is no record that they referred to the region by the name Oregon or anything similar.

Another widely held theory is that the word derives from the French word *ouragan* meaning "storm" or "hurricane." This idea stems from the belief that the Columbia River was once called the "River of Storms" by French traders.

Still another theory proposes that the word is connected to the Spanish word *oreja* meaning "the ear." This one appears to derive from the big ears of the natives encountered by Spanish explorers. However, as one historian notes, "...the Spaniards themselves have left no record of the kind; nor has it been noted, so far as we are aware, that the ears of our Indians were remarkably large."[1]

One more theory holds that the word is a corruption of "Aragon," a province in Spain, the name of which might have been dropped upon the natives by Spanish explorers as a substitute for Spain and repeated to English and French traders up to a century later.

All of the above theories are contradicted by the fact that the first written instances of the word in any letters or publications found thus far indicate specifically that the word is Indian, not European. One of the only definitions that has arisen (until recently, as will be shown) as an aboriginal derivation is a Siouan word which means "a casket" or "plate of bark." This definition, however, is also suspect being simply the result of looking up, in an early vocabulary for a particular tribe, a word that the compiler had spelled "Oragan."

The Grease Trail

Efforts have been made in recent years to find a more plausible indigenous meaning for the word, and an article published in 2001 in the *Oregon Historical Quarterly* supplies a very likely candidate.

The article, "Ourigan: Wealth of the Northwest Coast" by Scott Byram and David G. Lewis, proposes convincingly that the word is derived from a kind of fish oil that was produced and traded by the coastal Indians of the Northwest in the 1700's (and, indeed, is still produced and sold today). The native word for the fish *Thaleichthys pacificus*, a variety of smelt, was *ooligan*, a name that is also applied to the oil which can be extracted from the fish. This oil, used for preserving food, waterproofing canoes, and even treating illnesses, was an extremely important trade good of several northwest tribes. It found its way eastward across the Rocky Mountains on what Byram and Lewis refer to as the "Grease Trail," where it was traded to tribes of the northern plains.

The article even describes the phonetic transition from *ooligan* to *oorigan* or *ourigan*:

> "The western-most Cree speakers used the [r] sound in place of the [l], and thus [uligan], or *ooligan*, would have been pronounced [urigan], or oorigan."

It was the Cree, as well as the tribes with whom they traded and fought, who, according to Byram and Lewis, conveyed the name eastward to French and Spanish explorers in the 1700's.

Which River?

In 1765 the word begins to appear in historical texts, in particular in letters of an English explorer named Robert Rogers. Rogers petitioned King George III in that year to explore the interior of North America by way of what he was sure would be the elusive Northwest Passage, or water route to the Pacific Ocean. In his request, Rogers specifically mentioned a river which he claimed the Indians called the "Ouragon." His petition was denied, but in a subsequent petition seven years later, he referred to the same river, this time spelling it "Ourigan." The route Rogers specified in his request, Byram and Lewis say, followed a trade route established by the western Cree. The conclusion then is that Rogers got his information directly from this native tribe or from the writings (or even possibly information transferred only orally) of someone else who had spoken with them. Rogers' reference to this "Ourigan" River, which he also called the "River of the West," is generally believed to be the first written instance of the word.

According to early scholar T.C. Elliot, it was Rogers who imparted the word "Ourigan" to Jonathan Carver. Carver, an Englishman, acted as cartographer for an expedition organized

Capt. JONATHAN CARVER.
From the Original Picture in the Possession of J.C. Lettsom M.D.
Published as the Act directs by B. Turner N° 21 near S. Faconville Bedford Sq. 28 1780.

Jonathan Carver

by Rogers and eventually gained fame as an explorer in his own right. After an extensive exploration of parts of what are now Minnesota and Wisconsin, Carver published a book in 1778 called *Travels through the Interior Part of North America,* which became vastly popular. In it he used Rogers' spelling "Ourigan" to refer to a western river which he had learned of from natives during his explorations.

It has long been assumed that the *Ourigan* river to which Carver and Rogers referred was the Columbia. Captain Robert Gray, the first American to sail around the world, found and explored the Columbia River beginning in 1792. He named it for his ship, the *Columbia Rediviva,* and his explorations would become the basis for the American claim to the region. Byram and Lewis, however, matched descriptions and latitudinal coordinates given by Rogers more closely with the Fraser River, which runs through Canada's British Columbia. Regardless, it is probable that, even given the popularity of Carver's book, the name "Oregon" was not widely used in 1792, given that Gray did not, apparently, even consider using that name for the river he found.

Still, when Lewis and Clark, and vicariously Thomas Jefferson, explored the northwest in 1804-06, they referred only occasionally to the Oregon River. Maps of the time, which were largely based on scant explorations of the coast combined with information gleaned from native tribes of the northern plains, often depicted both a Columbia and an Oregon River.

Nova Albion

As for the name of the land, Spaniards, of course, referred to it as part of California (a fate worse than death for some modern-day Oregonians), and staked their claim on the basis of explorations by Greek navigator Juan de Fuca in 1592 and Spanish explorer Sebastian Vizcaíno in 1603. These explorers, however, who were primarily interested in finding a water route across the continent,

Sir Francis Drake

John Jacob Astor

rarely got out of their boats to look around, much less to establish any kind of settlement or colony.

The most universally recognized claim to the Pacific Northwest was England's by virtue of the clandestine 1577-1580 circumnavigation of the globe by Sir Francis Drake. During this voyage, Drake landed on the northwest coast—though the exact location of this landing is the subject of heated debate among regional historians—and named the land "Nova Albion." "Albion" was a common reference to England, and can be traced to times when the Romans occupied the British Isles. The word is derived from the Latin *albus* or "white," and referred to the white cliffs which are prominent on the south-east coast of England, and which at least one of Drake's crewmen noted on the western coast of North America as well. After Drake's voyage was made public, the name "Nova Albion," or "New Albion," was commonly used on maps—even occasionally on Spanish maps—to name what is now Oregon, Washington, and British Columbia.

Drake was knighted by Queen Elizabeth in 1581 upon the ship in which he had made his famous voyage, the "Golden Hind." Even though Drake's name for the region didn't stick, it is perhaps fortunate that he did not choose to use Gray's method of naming the land after his sailing vessel!

Very shortly after the Louisiana Purchase, even before Lewis and Clark returned from their journey, Americans began to move westward and encroach upon New Albion. In 1811 John Jacob Astor financed a venture which consisted of two expeditions, one by land, the other by sea. On behalf

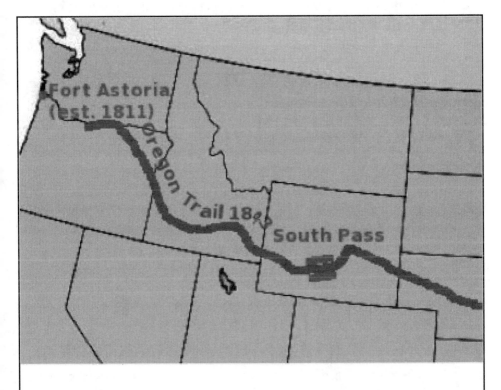

Route of the original Oregon Trail and the location of the South Pass

of his American Fur Company he sent the ship *Tonquin* around Cape Horn to Vancouver Island. Its crew then established Fort Astoria on the banks of the Columbia River. He also sent an overland crew, only some of whom survived the grueling journey to make it over the Rockies to Fort Astoria.

Hostilities between the Americans at Fort Astoria and local natives, as well as with the British once the War of 1812 had begun, caused the ultimate failure of Fort Astoria. Several of its founders, led by Robert Stuart, abandoned the site and began the long journey east over the mountains. In October of 1812, having almost starved to death along the way, this small band of men discovered the South Pass, a route through the intimidating Rockie Mountains which was substantially easier than had as yet been found. When they returned, they reported this route to Astor who considered the information about the South Pass proprietary, and was able to keep it secret for twelve years.

In 1824 the South Pass, a wide valley that interrupts the craggy peaks and ridges of the Rocky Mountains in what is today southern Wyoming, was rediscovered by Jedediah Smith and made public. This revelation would lead the way to increasingly larger waves of settlers over the next three decades into Oregon and northern California. Eventually this route, from the east—usually beginning in St. Louis—to the northern Pacific coast, became known as the "Oregon Trail."

Grass Roots

In 1817 William Cullen Bryant, then a completely unknown poet, published his breakthrough work "Thanatopsis*." By this time the great river in the Northwest was commonly called the Columbia on maps and charts, but Bryant had read his Jonathan Carver and chose to use "Oregon":

> " ...Or lose thyself in the continuous woods,
> Where rolls the Oregon, and hears no sound,
> Save his own dashings—yet the dead are there..."

The poem, a solemn, hundred-line piece about the marriage of nature and death, which Bryant had written five years before its publication when he was only seventeen years old, became vastly popular, as did Bryant him-

---

*   *Actually his father sent it in for publication, having found it in his son's desk.*

self. He went on to become an editor of the *Saturday Evening Post*, and a famous abolitionist, who had some influence on Abraham Lincoln. Perhaps less importantly, he also had some influence on the word "Oregon."

Within a year after the publication of Bryant's poem, a school teacher and writer in Massachusetts named Hall Jackson Kelley began to zealously advocate the exploration and settlement of the Northwest. In 1829 Kelley was instrumental in creating the "American society for encouraging the settlement of the Oregon Territory" and went on to write books and pamphlets reflecting his enthusiasm, among them "A Geographical Memoir of Oregon," which strongly advocated populating what was more and more frequently referred to as "Oregon Country."

Hall Jackson Kelley

Meanwhile

In 1818, in order "...to prevent disputes and differences amongst themselves," the United States and Great Britain agreed to jointly occupy the country "...on the North West coast of America, westward of the Stony Mountains...." No name was given to the land which was still very sparsely populated by whites. The agreement, which was originally intended to last only ten years, was extended indefinitely in 1827.

In 1819 the U.S. signed a treaty with Spain that set the northern border of California (i.e. Spanish Territory) at the 42nd parallel, the modern border between California and Oregon. Within two years, bills began to be submitted to Congress for the formation of a new territory. The first was proposed by John Floyd of Virginia on January 18, 1822, and named the potential new state "Origon Territory." The politics of the next three decades with regard to this region have filled fat history books, but it is clear that by 1822 the name "Oregon" (though a correct spelling was not yet agreed upon) was the decided favorite, at least to Americans, for what they were sure would eventually become a U.S. territory.

On May 2, 1843, a provisional government was established at the town of French Prairie by American fur traders and other civilians for the independent "Territory of Oregon." The leaders of the movement were initially divided over whether they wanted independence or annexation by the United States. The quest for annexation ultimately prevailed, and the aforementioned provisional government went into effect. On June 15, 1846, the Treaty of Oregon was signed between the U.S. and Great Britain establishing the 49th parallel as the now continuous border between British Canada and the U.S. On August 14, 1848, the U.S. created Oregon Territory, leaving much of the provisional government intact. Oregon then became a state on Valentine's Day, February 14, 1859. President James Buchanan signed the Act, making Oregon the thirty-third state to join the union.

----

1.   MacArthur, Lewis M., <u>Oregon Place Names</u> (Portland, 1944), p. 3.

Chapter 38: Pennsylvania

"...From the heightening Alleghenies of Pennsylvania, let freedom Ring..."

—*Martin Luther King, Jr.*

"We are the second oldest state in the Union because too many of our young people are leaving Pennsylvania. They are leaving Pennsylvania behind for opportunities elsewhere."

—*Governor Ed Rendell of Pennsylvania*

Father and Son

One need not be a history buff to know the derivation of the name *Pennsylvania*. While Americans have a famously diminished knowledge of their own national history, most could probably tell you that Pennsylvania is named for William Penn. Many could even tell you who William Penn was. But what many Americans may not know is that, technically speaking, Pennsylvania was actually named not for William Penn, famous founder of the colony and preserver of religious freedoms, but for his father, William Penn...Senior.

Here's something funny...Think about Pennsylvania State University. I know, I know, nobody calls it *Pennsylvania* State University, and anyway, why would the mere mention of the Keystone State's flagship university set you to guffawing? It's only funny in that American history, name nerd kind of way. But when people speak of that particular institution, they call it *Penn State—Penn* being short for *Pennsylvania*. But in actuality, the word *Penn* isn't short for anything. It is the word *Pennsylvania* that was newly created—out of the name *Penn*. So when one says "Penn State" one is shortening a word that was lengthened to create the state name (actually the colony name) in the first place.

Of course, when we hear the word "Pennsylvania" we also think of the Amish with their plain, buttonless clothing and horse-drawn carriages, of the smokestacks and steel factories in Pittsburgh, and of the Americana and history scattered throughout Philadelphia. Movies like *Witness*, *The Deer Hunter*, and *National Treasure* are filled with these Pennsylvania icons.

But perhaps the most socially relevant film to feature this somewhat conservative, working-class state was 1993's *Philadelphia* with Tom Hanks and Denzel Washington. The movie broke through the proverbial anti-homosexual glass ceiling by being the first major motion picture to unstereotypically portray a gay man who is realistically and sympathetically dying of AIDS, allowing the City of Brotherly Love to lead the way in de-stigmatizing this important social health issue.

The Experiment

Pennsylvania, as already mentioned, calls to mind Quakers or Amish, with their horse-driven carriages and simple, black clothing that hasn't changed in roughly three-hundred years. This image is, of course, appropriate because the colony was originally founded to accommodate this particular group of settlers from Europe. Religious tolerance and equality among all men were the cornerstones of the "experiment" that William Penn and his friends wished to implement—to see if a society could live without hierarchies in politics, society, or religion; to see if people really could consider others their equal in all aspects of life. Pennsylvania, the experiment, was of course wildly successful, its beliefs and values spilling over into the other colonies. Here was

Amish people are sometimes referred to as "Pennsylvania Dutch"

an example, if perhaps a bit extreme, for the American Revolutionaries to show the world what they were fighting for. Here was a lifestyle available nowhere else on Earth, and even though some Quakers were among the first "conscientious objectors," refusing to fight in any war, their new freedoms were, to others, worth fighting to save, and possibly even worth making the ultimate sacrifice.

Of course, for other reasons too, Pennsylvania reminds us of those revolutionary days, the heady times of Benedict Arnold, Benjamin Rush, and Betsy Ross. We think of Independence Hall, and of the Liberty Bell. We think of Benjamin Franklin strolling the streets of Philadelphia, his own newspaper tucked under his arm.

Moving ahead chronologically, Pennsylvania gave us early coal-mining and steel production. And still further along we get Penn State, the Nittany Lions, and Katherine Hepburn and Cary Grant in the incomparable *Philadelphia Story*.

If the name "Pennsylvania" brings to mind a single theme, that theme must be "Americana."

A Brief Summary

William Penn, the younger, grew up during a time of severe religious persecution that had its roots in King Henry VIII's break with the Catholic Church and creation of the Church of England in 1534. Some saw the dispute with Rome as an opportunity to "purify" their religion—to abolish the sacraments and abandon the traditions and ceremony of the Roman Catholic Church and reform Christianity into a religion based solely on scripture. The Puritan movement spread throughout Europe and produced several extremist sects, most notably the Pilgrims and, later, the Quakers.

Henry's daughter, Queen Mary— "Bloody Mary" to her detractors—restored Catholicism and executed protestant ministers. Her reign was brutal but

William Penn, "Jr." at 22

mercifully short, lasting only from 1553-1558, during which time many Reformation leaders fled into hiding in Europe. They returned when Henry VIII's younger daughter, Elizabeth I, ascended to the throne and reverted the country back to the National Church of England. Queen Elizabeth I practiced somewhat more restraint with respect to the Catholics than her half-sister had shown with Protestants, opting for some tolerance of religious diversity. Elizabeth I lived a long time, long enough to see the Church of England grow and become deeply entrenched. It was during her reign that the Puritan movement became popular and widespread.

Her successor, King James VI of Scotland and I of England, was less tolerant of Catholics but also succeeded in alienating Protestants by refusing to recognize the importance of a largely Puritan parliament. His major contribution to the religious landscape was the commissioning, at the request of the Puritans, of the King James Version of the Bible. He passed

Oliver Cromwell

down his theories, and in fact his treatise (*Basilicon Doron*, 1598) on the Divine Right of Kings, to his son Charles I, who took the throne in 1625.

By this time the political situation in England was fractious and volatile. Even if Charles I had proved a capable and diplomatic leader, the task of unifying the disparate religious sides and governing his subjects would have been difficult. Charles I, however, was proud and obstinate and eventually thrust the country into Civil War, primarily over his disagreement with Parliament over whose authority—his or theirs—was supreme. Charles I was beheaded in 1649 by Cromwell and the Parliamentarians, and his son Charles II lived in exile until 1659. During that time, England was governed by Oliver Cromwell and his chosen members of Parliament. Cromwell, a Puritan, proved schizophrenic in his religious tolerance, allowing Jews and non-Anglican Protestants freedom of conscience but harshly persecuting Irish Catholics.

It was into this climate that William Penn, Jr. was born in 1644, and the religious turmoil in England would only grow and diversify further. As Penn emerged into adulthood, he enraged his father by rejecting his birthright of privilege and society and adopted the faith of the Quakers.

Admiral Sir William Penn—William Penn's father

Sir William Penn, Sr.

Though he was a monarchist at heart, William Penn, the elder, was also a pragmatist. He fought for the Parliamentary forces during the English Civil Wars of the 1640's and later for Oliver Cromwell and the Commonwealth of England against international foes. In 1655 following a severely botched offensive on Hispaniola*, Penn was arrested and remanded to the Tower of London. It has been speculated that Penn was involved in intentionally losing the battle or that he made some effort to offer his ships to the exiled King Charles II, but more likely the blundered battle was simply that. Though he was released after questioning before the Council of State and after offering a full apology, he no longer sailed for the Commonwealth but retired to Ireland with his family, including his oldest son William Jr..

When Oliver Cromwell, Lord Protector, died in 1658, the Commonwealth lost its most forceful and influential leader, and the Parliamentary government weakened. William Penn, Sr. was elected to a seat in the House of Commons, and within two years, King Charles II returned to London

---

* *in the West Indies, the island which now is divided between the Dominican Republic and Haiti, though in the 1600's it was the Spanish Colony of Santo Domingo*

from exile to take his place on the throne of England, a throne which had been vacant for over a decade. It is clear that Penn had been loyal to his King during the exile, for he went to Holland with a fleet of thirty-one ships to bring him home. Before the ships returned to England—in fact shortly after boarding the vessel which would carry him—Charles II knighted William Penn.

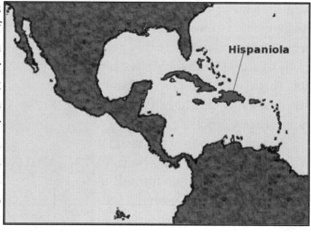

The Quaker Movement

George Fox, founder of the Quaker movement

William Penn, the son, was a serious, often brooding, child. He was educated at Oxford, as was customary for the sons of courtiers. During his adolescence, he was touched by the preaching of Thomas Loe, a follower of George Fox, founder of the Quaker movement.

Fox, the lowly son of a weaver, was extremely intelligent and eloquent. In 1647 he experienced a personal revelation and began to preach non-violence and equality among men, a truly revolutionary philosophy during those times of forced religious subjugation and serious attention to rank and class. The Quaker label was applied to Fox and his followers even before their official name, "The Society of Friends," was settled upon. In

1650, Fox told a justice of the peace to "tremble at the word of the Lord", who in turn sarcastically called him a Quaker and imprisoned him for his preachings. The label stuck and survived its derisive beginnings until the Friends began using it to refer to themselves.

Ironically it was Penn's father, Sir William, who had invited Thomas Loe into his home at Macroom, Ireland, to speak to a small gathering. Both father and son were moved to tears by Loe's preaching[1], but the younger William Penn would go on to adopt the preachings of Loe and Fox and become their most famous benefactor. His father, Sir William, like many in England, was as confounded by the Quakers as he was angry with them. Their absolute refusal to acknowledge a system of rank, whether that of royalty, secular authority, or even within their own community, was simply foreign and therefore threatening to the establishment.

In another ironic twist, it was Penn Jr.'s lofty position in that establishment which allowed him to become something of a liaison between the King's authorities and the Quakers. He successfully secured the release of Friends who had been imprisoned for their beliefs in England and in Ireland. He was also able (albeit with more difficulty and with his father's help) to keep *himself* out of any extended stay in prison, though after his father's death he did spend six months in Newgate, a revolting prison of the times.

Though Penn's father sharply disagreed with his son's radical beliefs he was apparently resigned to them by the time of his death in 1670. Penn, Jr., inherited his father's estates (not because of any reconciliation, but due to the laws of primogeniture), and many of his other possessions, including a cherished gold medal that had been bestowed upon him by Oliver Cromwell for his service in the Parliamentarian Navy.[2]

The Colony

For the next decade, William Penn promoted the teachings of George Fox (often in Fox's company, as well as other leaders of the movement). He traveled through Holland and Germany, acquiring converts and debating his antagonists. He wrote prolifically, usually in response to attacks on the Quakers.

During these years, Penn and his colleagues dreamed of starting a new country, a new society, where freedom of conscience would be the foundation. It would be interesting, they believed, to see if men could live hap-

pily and peacefully in such a society, and in 1675 William Penn found himself on the verge of an opportunity to create just such a place. He was asked to arbitrate a land dispute in North America between two members of the Society of Friends who had come into some land in the province of New Jersey. The result of the arbitration granted several Quaker leaders, Penn among them, a portion of the province, and they set about creating the frame of government under which those lands would be occupied. They stipulated not only religious freedom, but elected officials, jury trials, and an end to imprisonment for debt. When the first group of colonists to test this social experiment arrived in the New World in 1677, they settled the town of Burlington on the Delaware River, a town that succeeded and prospered and eventually encompassed all of West New Jersey.

Because of this success, and because of growing intolerance of Friends in England, Penn requested from King Charles II a much larger grant of land in New England in 1681. His specifications were not for the prime coastal territories which were already increasingly populated, but for the wilderness west of New Jersey. He needed space, space for as many adventurers as wanted to participate in the social experiment like that of West New Jersey.

Land grants like these were political plums, however, and Penn, though his family had been friendly with the Stuarts, was not exactly high on the list to be granted Royal favors. But Charles II was politically savvy. He wanted to rid himself of the political opposition that the Quakers presented, but he knew his own party would resent the granting of a North American colony to a leading Quaker. Penn and Charles II came up with a resolution that was nothing short of ingenious. Instead of "granting" the territory to William Penn, the king would offer it to him as payment for a debt which the monarch had incurred from Penn's father, Sir William. The actual debt was of the sort that were rarely repaid by kings, but its existence was serendipitous to both parties, allowing Penn his dream of a new country, and allowing the King to send shiploads of Whigs to America where they could not effectively oppose him.

The final charter for William Penn's American colony was presented on March 4, 1681. It included confusing language about the boundaries of the colony which would cause a disagreement between Penn and Lord Baltimore of Maryland for the rest of their lives, and even between their heirs, but it named William Penn absolute proprietor of the country, beholden only to the king. As for the name of the colony, William Penn explains in a letter to an old friend, Robert Turner:

> "...this day my country was confirmed to me by the name of Pennsylvania; a name the King would give it in honor of my father. I chose New Wales, being, as this, a pretty hilly country, but Penn being Welsh for a head, as Penmanmoire in Wales, and

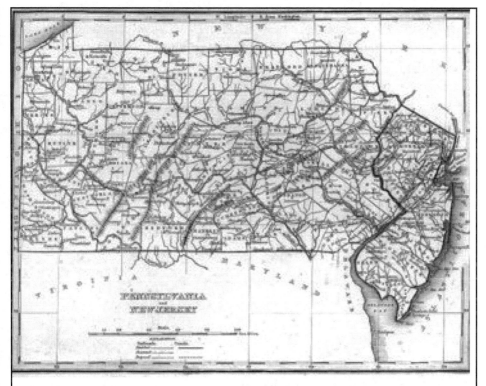

William Penn was not interested in the prime coastal areas that were being rapidly settled, but in having plenty of land for as many settlers as wanted to join in his grand experiment.

Penrith in Cumberland, and Penn in Buckinghamshire, the highest land in England, called this Pennsylvania, which is the high or head woodlands; for I proposed, when the Secretary, a Welshman, refused to have it called New Wales, Sylvania, and they added Penn to it; and though I much opposed it, and went to the King to have it struck out and altered, he said it was past, and would take it upon him; nor could twenty guineas move the under secretary to vary the name; for I feared lest it should be looked on as vanity in me, and not as a respect in the King, as it truly was, to my father, whom he often mentions with praise."[3]

William Penn made only two trips and spent a total of less than five years in his "new country," but his influence over it was profound. He insisted upon paying the natives before inhabiting any land, and he included them in his policy of self-government. They were allowed to settle grievances in court with a jury that included settlers and natives. It is generally accepted that William Penn's humane dealings with the natives of Pennsylvania allowed the colony's settlers to live peacefully among them for decades.

William Penn died July 30, 1718. His later years were unfortunately plagued by illness and financial troubles, but his legacy in the United States is almost unblemished. Thomas Jefferson called William Penn "the greatest law-giver the world has ever produced." Pennsylvania ratified the U.S. Constitution on December 12, 1787, becoming the second state in the Union after Delaware.

1. Peare, Catherine Owens, <u>William Penn: A Biography</u> (Philadel-phia, 1957), p. 23.

2. Peare, p. 126.

3. Peare, p. 215.

Chapter 39: Rhode Island and Providence Plantations

"She came from Providence, the one in Rhode Island..."

—"The Last Resort"
The Eagles

"Brian: We're quite a pair of partners,
Just Like Thelma and Louise.
'cept you're not six feet tall
Stewie: Yes and your breasts don't reach your knees.
Brian: Give it time.
We're off on the road to Rhode Island.
We're certainly going in style."

—*TV Show* "The Family Guy"
"We're Off on the Road to Rhode Island"

It's Small

The smallest of all of the United States has the biggest name. Official-ly, it is "Rhode Island and Providence Plantations"—that's approximately one letter for every 38 square miles, compared to 126,000 square miles per letter for Alaska.

It is a state famous for its smallness, indeed proud of its smallness—or should we say *smallestness*? In fact while it boasts many superlatives—first to declare independence from England, last to sign the Constitution, first to ban the importation of slaves—it is fair to say that being the state with the least land mass distinguishes Rhode Island more than any other feature or achievement. Rhode Island contains only five counties. It has half the land mass of the second smallest state (Delaware) and only a little more than the city of Los Angeles. It is about the size of Utah's Great Salt Lake,

385

its longest section of interstate (I-95) runs only thirty miles, and it would get lost inside Yellowstone National Park. One of the state's nicknames is, in fact, "Little Rhody."

Of course, for such a small state Rhode Island has plenty to distinguish it. There is the harbor town of Newport, onetime frolicking ground of the dynastically wealthy. Around the turn of the twentieth century, no matter how much wealth you had amassed, if you

Engraving by Martin Heemskerch of an imagined version of the Colossus of Rhodes

weren't seen around Newport, R.I., hobnobbing with the likes of Lady Ascot and the Vanderbilt family in their majecstic estates and tony mansions, you simply hadn't made it. Some may think of yacht-racing, the sounds of halyards clanging in a marina, of sailboats easily coasting along its shores.

But Rhode Island is remarkable for an even more noble reason. It's founder, the intreped writer and self-made scholar, Roger Williams worked tirelessly to make the colony a place of *true* religious freedom, a quality he found sorely lacking in Massachusetts in the 1630's. (More on Mr. Williams later.)

But no matter your image, when it comes to Rhode Island, the overwhelming feature is that of being, at least where *size* is concerned, decidedly non-overwhelming.

Rhode Island...

Rhode Island is, in fact, an island. (The state, however—as will be discussed more in depth later—is made up of both the island and the surrounding mainland.) Situated snugly in Narragansett Bay, the natives, Narragansett Indians, called it "Aquidneck" which simply meant "at the island"

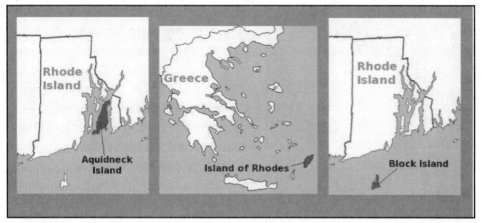

Rhode Island · Aquidneck Island · Greece · Island of Rhodes · Rhode Island · Block Island

or "at the floating mass." This Narragansett name was actually used by the earliest Rhode Island settlers and never completely faded from usage. In fact, today the island is commonly referred to as "Aquidneck," leaving "Rhode Island" free to describe the entire state.

One of the two dominant theories about how Rhode Island came to be named holds that the Italian explorer Giovanni da Verrazano who navigated the bay in 1524, named it for its similarity in size and shape to the Greek island Rodhos or "Rhodes." The Greek island, in turn, has two competing theories about the origin of *its* name. The first is that it was named for a Greek nymph called Rhodes, who was the wife of the island's patron God, Helios—the sun god. The other theory is that its name derives from the ancient Greek word for rose and describes the abundance of flowers on the island. Home of one of the seven ancient wonders of the world, the Colossus (now *there's* a word one does not immediately associate with smallness)—a massive bronze statue of Helios that was destroyed by an earthquake in 226 b.c.—Rhodes does indeed bear similarities in shape to Aquidneck.

A variation on the Verrazano theory is that it was Roger Williams, the undisputed founder of Rhode Island, who actually applied the name "isle of roses" to Aquidneck, referring to it being "bedecked by

Roger Williams, founder of Rhode Island

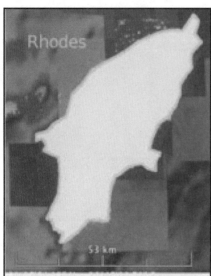

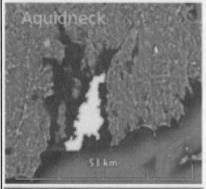

A Comparison of the three islands and their relative sizes and shapes.

rhododendrons."[1] In another digression lies the theory that Verrazano, on his 1524 voyage, was actually describing Block Island, but that Williams and his colleagues confused it with Aquidneck, and applied the name erroneously. This theory springs from the writings of Verrazano himself: "...an island in the form of a triangle, distant from the mainland ten leagues, about the bigness of the Island of Rhodes."[2]   Verrazano named this island "Luisa," after the mother of his benefactor, King Francis I of France. Block island is the correct distance from the mainland to fit this description, and is in fact shaped like a triangle. Aquidneck, on the other hand, lies within the bay itself, nearly touching the mainland.

While it is impossible to know—five centuries later—to which island Verrazano was referring, the most likely conclusion (and the most popular theory today) is that it was Block Island that he named Luisa, and that any similarity of Aquidneck to Rhodes is coincidental.

Ninety years after Verrazano, Narragansett Bay was explored by a Dutch navigator named Adriaen Block. He is not only the namesake of Block Island, but the source of the second dominant theory about the origin of the name "Rhode Island." In this version, after sailing around the largest island in the Bay in 1614, sometime after he had founded and named Block Island for himself, Block recorded the name of his discovery as "Roodt Eylandt" (Red Island), due to the "fiery aspect of the place, caused by the red clay in some portions of its shores."[3] Those who espouse this theory believe that the anglicizing of "Roodt Eylandt" is a much easier leap than the dropping of the "s" from "Rhodes."

...And Providence Plantations

The origin of "Providence Plantations" is not nearly so obscure as that of the name "Rhode Island." It was bestowed by Roger Williams, the afore-mentioned founder of the colony, in 1636 after his banishment from Massachusetts Bay Colony for having

> "...broached and divulged divers [sic] new and dangerous opin-ions, against the authority of magistrates...and yet maintaineth the same without any retraction[4]."

Williams was a true pioneer in the concept of separation of church and state. His "divers [sic] new and dangerous opinions" were basically three-fold:

> 1) that the King had no right to give away lands in the New World that belonged not to him but to the Indians,

> 2) that the magistrates should not have authority over the reli-gious beliefs that a man held, and

> 3) that "whole nations and generations of men have been forced... to pretend and assume the name of Jesus Christ which only be-longs...to truly regenerate and repenting souls."[5]

While his tolerance for other religions was not necessarily greater than that of some of his contemporaries, his firm belief that religious law should not govern civil matters was absolutely novel and pure heresy at the time.

Williams was encouraged by John Winthrop and John Winslow, gover-nors of Massachusetts Bay Colony and Plymouth respectively, to go to Nar-ragansett Bay after he was banished from their colonies. They knew that the bay was just beyond the borders of the Plymouth colony, from which Williams was exiled, and that it was south of the MBC charter, so that no

Massasoit

English claim existed to that land. They also knew, as did Williams himself, that it was the home of Massasoit and Canonicus, sachems of the Wampanoag and Narragansett tribes, with whom Williams had become friends.

While Roger Williams took the advice of his friends and settled in the Narragasett Bay area, he was not the first Englishman to do so. William Blackstone, another escaper of religious persecution, had settled there about a year before Williams moved in. He built a home near a river (now called Blackstone River) and called it "Study Hill" where he read prolifically and ministered to the Indians. But Blackstone "cannot be considered a real founder of the State. He gathered no band of colonists about him...."[6] Clearly, Blackstone's preference for reclusiveness kept him from vying for the title of "founder."

Williams, on the other hand, gratefully purchased property from the Narragansetts for the specified purpose of founding a plantation (village) for himself and his followers. Once banished from the MBC in 1635, Williams was allowed to remain at Salem, where he was living with his family, on the condition that he not preach his heresy to other church members. He found this impossible, however, and was sentenced to be deported to England, but instead he fled south to Narragansett Bay. He was joined by a small group of followers the next spring, and they settled along the Seekonk River. Informed by Winslow that they were still within the bounds of Plymouth Colony, they removed—with the help of the Narragansetts—to an area on the mainland at the mouth of two rivers, the Moshassuck and the Woonasquatucket at the northern tip of the bay. He named the place Providence

> "from the freedom and vacancy of the place and many other providences of the most holy and only wise."[7]

Forming a State

In April of 1638, John Clarke and William Coddington, two former MBC residents, established the town of Pocasset at the north end of Aquidneck. The town was later renamed Portsmouth and into it moved Anne Hutchinson, another exile from MBC, who, like Williams, had been banished for her heretical teachings. Coddington, in a disagreement with Hutchinson, left in May of 1639 to found the community of Newport at the opposite end of the island. Eventually the towns united under one governorship, and in March of 1644, the general Court of Election ordered that "the ysland commonly called Aquethneck, shall be from henceforth called the Isle of Rhodes, or RHODE ISLAND."[8]

The phrase "Aquednetick, called by us Rode-Island" appears in a letter from Roger Williams to John Winthrop in May 1637[9], but no clarification is given as to *why* they renamed it. In fact, in many subsequent letters from Williams, he uses the aboriginal name of the island, but it is also the case that much of Williams' correspondence is lost to us. Regardless, it is clear that the name "Rhode Island" was in at least limited use by its English residents very shortly after they arrived.

Anne Hutchinson on trial for preaching heresy

At the time the court handed down the decree to change the name of their colony, Roger Williams was in England securing a patent for Portsmouth, Newport, and Providence Plantations. He returned in September of 1644, with the patent he received from the Earl of Warwick, titled "The Incorporation of Providence Plantations, in the Narragansett Bay, in New England." It makes no mention of any island, neither Aquidneck nor Rhode. However, by the time Williams requested and received *royal* confirmation of this patent in 1663, the name Rhode Island seems to have been settled upon to apply to the entirety of the area, including Providence on the mainland, and the island of Aquidneck/Rhode. In July of that year King Charles II granted a charter for "Rhode Island and Providence Plantations."

Revolutionary Rhode Island

On May 4, 1776, a full two months before the Declaration of Independence was drafted and signed, Rhode Island became the first of the colonies to declare itself independent from the British royal and parliamentary rule. Shortly after the rest of the fledgling country followed suit, Rhode Island codified its official name when, on July 18, 1776, the General Assembly at Newport resolved that

> "the style and title of this government...shall be the State of Rhode Island and Providence Plantations."[10]

As for the boundaries of the state, one state history points out that for such a small area—1084 square miles—the boundaries took an agonizingly long time to settle. The book quotes Rufus Choate, a Massachusetts politician, who declared that Rhode Island's borders

> "might as well have been marked on the north by a bramblebush, on the south by a bluejay, on the west by a hive of bees in swarming time, and on the east by five hundred foxes with firebrands tied to their tails."[11]

The final establishment of the border with Connecticut was settled by King George in 1728, but the border with Massachusetts proved more difficult to determine. The dispute eventually went to the U.S. Supreme Court and wasn't firmly settled until 1887.

Once the American Revolution was won, Rhode Island was the last (13th) of the colonies to ratify the Constitution. It finally did so on May 29, 1790, after receiving assurances that the Bill of Rights would be adopted as law.

1.   "Rhode Island State History," http://www.negenealogy.com/ri/ri_history.htm, accessed 7/25/09.

2.   Wroth, Lawrence C., The Voyages of Giovanni da Verrazzano 1524-1528, (Yale University Press, New Haven, 1970), p. 137.

3.   Arnold, Samuel Greene, History of the State of Rhode Island and Providence Plantations, (D. Appleton and Co., New York, 1859), p. 17.

4.   Easton, Emily, Roger Williams: Prophet and Pioneer, (AMS Press, New York, 1969), pp. 168-169.

5.   Easton, p. 164.

6.   *Rhode Island: A Guide to the Smallest State* (Writers program, Rhode Island, 1937), p. 32.

7.   Easton, p. 179.

8.   *Rhode Island: A Guide to the Smallest State*, p. 44.

9.   LaFantasie, Glenn W., The Correspondence of Roger Williams, (Brown University Press, 1988), p. 73.

10.   LaFantasie, p. 44.

11.   LaFantasie, p. 36.

Chapter 40: South Carolina

"Just a little bit south of North Carolina
That's where I long to be
In a little brown shack in South Carolina
Someone waits for me."

> — "Just a Little Bit South of North Caro-
> lina"
> *Dean Martin*

"From South Carolina
To San Francisco
I'm always waiting here
Outside of this door"

> — "From South Carolina"
> *Her Space Holiday*

SOUTH Carolina

Fort Sumter, South Carolina

Of all of the "southern" states the only one that contains the word "south" in its name is the smallest of them all, South Carolina. The word "south," in our historical and geographical lexicon, is almost synonymous with the Civil War, slavery, Reconstruction and the Civil Rights Movement. "South" signifies the struggle of black people in America to overcome oppression, a battle that climaxed with the Civil War...which started in South Carolina.

While South Carolina does not have a monopoly on retaining its southern flavor, it does seem that a few southern states have tried hard to slough off their relationship to the Civil War era, to leave behind their connections to slavery and to the bitter conflict which that peculiar institution provoked. But South Carolina may never do so, nor may it ever want to. South Carolina uses its connection to the history of "The South" to frame its own reputation.

Of course, South Carolina's relationship to the Civil War is not just philosophical or ethereal. It is tangible. It is full of dates, places and people—real history. On April 12, 1861 Fort Sumter in Charleston Harbor was seized by Confederate troops, marking the beginning of the Civil War. Sherman's famous march to the sea burned a swath through South Carolina that branded it with the brutality of the war for posterity. And in the late 20th century the confederate flag took center stage in a controversy over whether its presence flying over the South Carolina statehouse was appropriate.

Writing in late 2009, the name *South Carolina* conveys other meanings besides its connections to southern heritage. In particular, those who follow politics closely are aware of the sordid scandals that seem to be plaguing the state's politicians. First, Governor Mark Sanford gave new meaning (to the delight of late-night talk-show hosts) to the phrase "hiking the Old Appalachian Trail." And as if the sex scandals are not enough, in the Fall of 2009 South Carolina Representative Joe Wilson was reprimanded by the U.S. House of Representatives for shouting "You Lie!" at President Barack Obama, interrupting an important speech to a joint session of Congress. For some, of course, Joe Wilson's actions—rather than being a scandal—were simply another display of the state's natural tendency to rebellion.

But besides a few unfortunate news stories, and besides its renown as a still-rebellious southern state, South Carolina is also distinguished by a famous native son, beloved by many late-night faux-news fans. Steven Colbert, talk-show host extrordinaire, has created such a perfectly sardonic persona, that his personal politics are the subject of dinner-table debate nation-wide. Leave it to South Carolina to produce such an enigmatic-yet-still-lovable character.

King Charles II

In 1566 the Spanish built a fort on Parris Island off the coast of what is now South Carolina. They named it, and the settlement that grew up around it, Santa Elena, and for twenty years it was the Spanish capital of La Florida. The settlers endured constant clashes with local natives, and in 1576 the fort 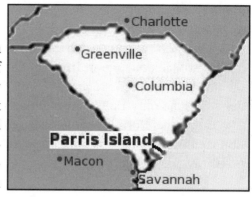 was actually destroyed and rebuilt. With the encroachment of the English on the eastern seaboard, Spain finally abandoned Santa Elena in 1587 and moved their capital down the coast to St. Augustine.

For the next eight decades, the area of South Carolina saw no attempts at settlement by Europeans, but that changed when the Virginians began to push southward. Because South Carolina shares an intimate history, not to mention a name, with its northern neighbor, a lot of information about the name "Carolina" is contained in the chapter on North Carolina. But briefly, the name Carolina was bestowed on the colony by King Charles II in 1663, and he named it in honor of himself. *Carolina* is the feminine form of the Latin *Caroluus*. The word has its origins in the germanic lnguages as "Churl" which referred to a common man, specifically *not* royalty. The name gained a higher status with the success and fame of Charlemagne, and became appropriate for naming princes and kings. When those kings then used their own name for land that they claimed, it was generally converted to the Latin feminine (as in "Louisiana" and "America").

The use of the name by Charles II was not merely a matter of ego. King Charles, the rightful heir to the English throne, had been living in exile since his father's execution in 1649. Many of his loyal subjects had worked tirelessly for years to see that the king was eventually restored to the throne in 1660 after the death of Oliver Cromwell and the weakening of Parliament. The eight people to whom he granted Carolina were among those who had given him back his kingdom, and this was his way of rewarding them.

But the eight proprietors were mostly absentee landlords (with the exception of William Berkeley, governor of Virginia) and had much difficulty colonizing their new province, especially in its southern region. It was almost immediately clear that the colony was too massive for one governor to manage, and until about 1670, when Charleston was firmly established (an earlier settlement at Charleston—or Charles Town— had failed in 1667 because of lack of support from England and troubles with the local natives) the northern section of Carolina—the region just south of the Virginia border—was the only European-populated area.

But while North Carolina was populated primarily by virtue of migration southward from Virginia, the southern region would be colonized purposefully and deliberately.

The Barbados Connection

The island of Barbados in the Lesser Antilles of the West Indies was England's stronghold in the Caribbean Sea. Settled in 1627, it began to flourish with the introduction of sugar cane as a cash crop in the 1640's. Large plantations worked by African slaves coupled with a worldwide demand for sugar, rum and molasses made a handful of Englishmen massively wealthy.

One such man was Anthony Ashley Cooper, first Earl of Shaftesbury, and one of the eight proprietors of Carolina. Ashley convinced the proprietors to finance a colony of settlers who would be primarily immigrants from Barbados, and would export the island's socio-economic structure— which is to say the plantation/slave system—to mainland North America.

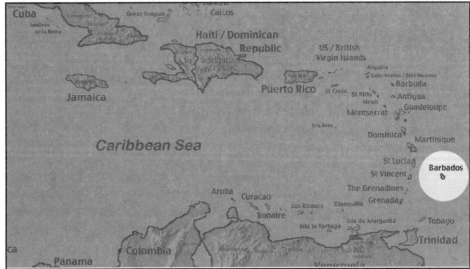

The settlement that Ashley and the proprietors founded was Charles Town or Charleston, also named after their king, and it flourished. Unlike the northern section of the colony, which was sparsely populated over a wide region, Charleston was a hub of economic activity and soon became a thriving city. The Barbadian influence was strong. Nine of the early parishes of South Carolina were named after regions of Barbados.

The hedonistic nature of the island society was also derived from the West Indies. The materialistic culture was driven by the wealthy plantation owners whose competitive quest for wealth differed from the gentleman farmers of Virginia.

**Sir Anthony Ashley Cooper,
1st Earl of Shaftesbury**

According to one historian, "Material success, not character or honor, was the measure of an individual's worth. And how a person acquired wealth was not important."[1]

While the English maintained a slight plurality of the European population, immigrants from other countries were attracted to the Charleston region by virtue of the liberal laws set forth in Carolina's Fundamental Constitution. This was a document written by John Locke, then a personal secretary to Ashley, which provided for religious freedom, naturalized citizenship for aliens, property rights and land grants, among other rights and privileges which were intended to attract settlers.

Not lost on the European population was the fact that the importation of African slaves was increasing the black population at an alarming rate. This was of some concern to

John Locke

leaders of the colony, not out of any regard for the African people, but out of concern for the safety of the white population in the event that the blacks could no longer be "controlled." But the benefits of slavery to the plantation owners still outweighed their fears of slave revolt, and in 1720 the black population had officially grown larger than that of the whites. In some parts of the colony, the black population reached almost eighty perscent.

Division

The division between North and South Carolina was surprisingly congenial and apolitical. In fact, the two colonies had greater border disputes with their opposite neighbors than with each other. This was largely because it was the proprietors themselves who divided the colony. In 1691 they changed the commission of Governor Philip Ludwell from "Governor of that part of Carolina that lies North and East of Cape feare" to "Governor of Carolina," whose capital was in Charleston.[2]

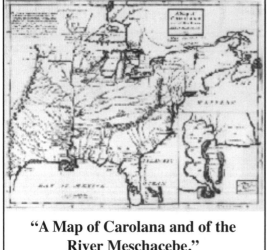

"A Map of Carolana and of the River Meschacebe."

Final division came in 1710 when it became clear that the northern residents of Carolina were too far from Charleston to participate in their own government. The proprietors appointed a new governor of "North Carolina," "independent of the Governor of Carolina." Clearly, it was the southern portion of the colony that retained the right to the name "Carolina," but the division between north and south had been so natural and so gradual that the name "South Carolina" was also natural, and so it stuck.

All that was left was to draw a line between the two halves, and that was done fairly seamlessly in 1765, just in time for the beginning of the American Revolution movement. South Carolina can be said to have moved into independence on March 26, 1776. On that morning the last Provincial Congress was held in Charleston, and after adjourning, the same men returned that afternoon for the first legislative session of the South Carolina General Assembly. Official statehood would come after the American Revolution and the drafting of the U.S. Constitution. South Carolina was the eighth state to ratify it, which they did on May 23, 1788.

Whatever happened to Carolana?

As noted in the chapter on North Carolina, a grant of land called "Carolana" was made in 1629 to Sir Robert Heath, attorney general to King Charles I. That grant was sold by Heath's heirs to Daniel Coxe, physician to King Charles II. Coxe attempted to claim the land by sending his son to America in 1702. His son, also named Daniel, returned to England with a map of the explored region of his father's claim. The grant included all of the land between 31 and 36 degrees latitude between the Atlantic Ocean and the "South Sea," or Pacific Ocean, which by now included the already thriving colony of Carolina. One assumes that had Coxe successfully promoted his land, he would have had a boundary dispute on his hands, pitting his claim, which had come from Charles I, against the Carolina Proprietors whose land had been granted by Charles I's son, Charles II.

A map entitled "A Map of Carolana and the Meschacebe" was published in 1722 along with a promotional book inviting adventurers and settlers to the region, but Coxe was never able to colonize the vast grant. In 1769 his descendants exchanged "Carolana" for a portion of the Mohawk Valley in New York State. The map has remained of interest to this day because it is the first English map of the Mississippi Valley. Coxe used it to promote his notion of "symmetrical geography," and it was used by Lewis and Clark in planning their expedition to the American Northwest.

1.   Edgar, Walter, <u>South Carolina: A History</u>, (Columbia, 1998), p. 37.

2.   Edgar, p. 2.

Chapter 41: South Dakota

"Henceforth, with paths diverging, North and South Dakota can no more walk together. But, with honesty of purpose, exalted aims, and hallowed recollections to stimulate, they will never forget that they are still Dakota."

> — *"Once Their Home: Our Legacy From the Dakhkotahs" by Frances Chamberlain Holley*

He said, "I hope to God she finds the good-bye letter that I wrote her But the mail don't move so fast in Rapid City, South Dakota."

> — *"Rapid City, South Dakota"*
> *Kinky Friedman*

Allies

Dakota means "ally" in the language of the Dakota Indians. It is perhaps appropriate then that the name belongs to two states — states which, like siblings, share a common history. Often referred to as "sister states," North and South Dakota were simply "the Dakota Territory" up until their concurrent statehood in 1898, when they were separated upon entering the union. While they have since developed their own identities, their histories are inextricably linked, espe-

The Dakotas were one territory up until statehood in 1898

The most recognizable places in South Dakota—Mount Rushmore, the Badlands, Deadwood—are concentrated in the Southwest corner of the state

cially with regard to their names.

Unlike its sister state, however, South Dakota has cultivated an image conducive to its lucrative tourism industry. The Black Hills, Mount Rushmore, the Badlands, and the gambling town of Deadwood are all easily associated with South Dakota. Admittedly all of these tourist destinations are concentrated in the southwest corner of the state, but they are fundamental to its image and are an important reason why South Dakota has never sought to change its name, as its northern ally has contemplated.

South Dakota is also strongly associated with Native Americans and their struggle with white settlers and the U.S. military in the late 19th and 20th centuries. The aforementioned Black Hills were a sacred homeland of the Sioux tribe. Besides being the site of Mount Rushmore with its all-American connections and history, the Hills are also home to the in-progress, and just as massive, sculpture of Crazy Horse, the famous Lakota warrior.

Also in South Dakota is the battleground of Wounded Knee Creek, where the final armed conflict of the Lakota Sioux with U.S. troops took place. About 300 Sioux were killed in a short, confused conflict that most historians label "Wounded Knee Massacre."

This painting by artist Frederick Remington used soldiers' accounts to depict the opening moments of the massacre at Wounded Knee

The chapter on North Dakota discusses the history of the name "Dakota" up until territorial status was applied in 1861. This chapter, then, will describe the division of the territory and the decision to share the name once statehood was imminent.

Lincoln Territory

The first agitation for separation from Dakota Territory came from the Black Hills region—that same region that is now so important to the tourism industry of South Dakota. In 1874 gold was discovered in these hills, and miners flooded the area; these miners were veterans of the gold fields of California, Nevada, Colorado, and Idaho, and who were familiar with how to establish a mining-town government. In 1877 a convention was held in Deadwood where delegates to Congress were elected and a name for their new territory was selected: Lincoln.

Proponents of this division eventually selected Sheridan City to be the capital of the new territory and managed to gain support in Congress, but not enough. Though the movement continued for years, no bill ever passed in Congress, and the "Territory of Lincoln" never materialized.[1] Still, the miners in the Black Hills and the citizens of the towns that supplied them, namely Yankton and Vermillion in the southeast (Yankton was the Dakota territorial capital), felt increasingly distant from the rest of the territory, and continued lobbying for separation and immediate statehood.

North vs. South

As for the north, its settlers had their own motivations for wanting separation but not until after 1873. Before that year the economic ties of the very sparsely populated north—whose settlements consisted of Pembina and the Red River valley region—extended east to St.

Until 1873 the most heavily populated region of North Dakota was in the town of Pembina and the Red River Valley

Paul and north to Canada. But in 1871 the Northern Pacific railroad was granted an enormous swath of land to build a track from St. Paul all the way to the west coast. By 1874 the track extended to the "end of track" town of Bismarck on the Missouri River, but the bottom had dropped out of the U.S. economy, and the Northern Pacific Railroad needed to find ways to make a return on its investment without laying any more track.[2]

The extreme overbuilding of railroads, especially those of the Northern Pacific, are largely to blame for the Panic of 1873, a depression which began with the failure of a prominent Philadelphia bank, followed by the collapse of the Vienna stock exchange. The economic turmoil affected not only the U.S. economy, but that of Europe as well. The depression lasted five years, during which time the railroad company moved furiously to import farmers to the northern region of the Dakota Territory as a way of providing a transportation market for itself.

Oliver Dalrymple

One farmer whose assistance the railroad companies sought was Oliver Dalrymple, a Minnesota attorney who had gained a reputation as a very successful wheat farmer. That success had earned him the nickname "King of Wheat," and when approached by General George Cass, president of the Northern Pacific Railroad, to help draw famers into northern Dakota, Dalrymple obligingly moved there from Minnesota. The influx of "bonanza farmers" who heard of Dalrymple's success helped achieve the goal of the Northern Pacific and made Bismarck the undisputed center of the agricultural industry in the northern section of the territory.

Wheat farmers and railroad agents in the north, miners in the south. This was the way the regional affiliations broke down, and as the mining industry began to feel the powerful influence of the railroads, they complained (somewhat justifiably) of political persecution by outside interests. For in 1878, every railroad in Dakota was owned by an out-of-territory company.[3]

Capitals

In 1879 delegates from the north officially, though unsuccessfully, requested that the territorial capital be moved from Yankton to Bismarck. This was a touchy subject for the powerful political forces in Yankton, and one which they had dealt with before. In 1862 George M. Pinney, Speaker of the first Assembly, was thrown through a closed window for his failure to support Yankton as the capital.

George M. Pinney was once thrown through a glass window because he failed to support Yankton as the capital of Dakota.

Later, in 1883, the powerful Bismarck forces pushed a bill through the legislature to create a capital removal commission, whose job would be to scope out possible new sites for a capital. The commission was to meet in Yankton within thirty days of its creation or lose its mandate. But the commission had some rather creative opposing forces, as historian Howard Roberts Lamar explains:

"...the Yankton citizens still had hopes of halting the entire scheme by preventing the commission from meeting within the city limits. The three members of the Yankton commission were carefully watched; any suspicious gathering was reported, and the local members of the commission were openly threatened with violence."

After some time, the Yanktonians thought they had succeeded in stopping the removal of the capital. But unbeknownst to them, a slow-moving train had rolled through the city early one morning containing the members of the commission, allowing them to officially organize and assume their duties.[4]

The capital issue was finally resolved in favor of Bismarck in 1887, but only through the machinations of a corrupt territorial governor named Nehemiah G. Ordway. Ordway was indicted by a grand jury for irregularities—including bribery in the process of moving the capital—and removed as governor in 1884. Still, his influence continued, and in 1887, the funds were released to move the capital to Bismarck. Ordway, who owned much property in Dakota Territory, would continue even after his removal as governor to lobby Congress against statehood for Dakota, and against division.

The attempts to move the capital were the most obvious signs of irreconcilable differences between north and south. It was now clear that division was not only inevitable, but desired by both sides. But it wasn't divorce. It was more like two sisters marrying into different families.

Nehemiah G. Ordway

Division

In 1885 the strong statehood forces in southern Dakota grew tired of lobbying Congress for admission and took matters into their own hands. They convened a convention at Huron and drew up a ballot for a popular election to be held south of the forty-sixth parallel. In November of that year the citizens of southern Dakota declared themselves to be the "State of Dakota," and they elected a governor, adopted a constitution, and selected Huron as their capital.

The northern Dakotans immediately objected to the choice of names chosen by the southerners, claiming that the name "Dakota" had been made famous by its own brand of wheat. At any rate, the U.S. Congress was unimpressed, and continued to refuse admission, favoring a one-state plan (on the advice of Ordway, among others).

In November of 1887, a popular election was held within the territory on the question of division. To the surprise and dismay of division and statehood advocates, the north opposed division by a huge margin, and the south favored it only slightly. Blame was immediately placed on the influence of the railroads, even accusing the Northern Pacific of "fixing" the election.

Divisionist leaders mobilized quickly, exposing to Congress and to Dakotans the corrupt motives of the railroad companies and one-state advocates. Most of the nefarious reasons against separation and statehood had to do with land speculation and keeping control of government offices through bribery and graft*.

To try a new tack, southern Dakotans proposed a new idea. Instead of lobbying for statehood only for themselves, they began to advocate immediate statehood for both halves of Dakota. While all of this

President Benjamin Harrison

activity was helpful in garnering support for their cause, the statehood proponents truly won their fight when Indiana Senator Benjamin Harrison, a long-time supporter of Dakota statehood (and division), won election to the U.S. Presidency.

Seeing the handwriting on the wall, a now lame-duck Congress beat Harrison and his supporters to the punch. On February 22, 1889, Congress passed admission bills for North and South Dakota.

Still Sisters

The concept of sister-statehood was one that President Benjamin Harrison took seriously. On November 2, 1889, when the proclamations for statehood were prepared for him to sign, Harrison felt the need to avoid the appearance of favoritism by allowing neither state to claim that it had been chosen to enter the union *first*. Therefore his Secretary of State, before presenting him with the statehood documents to sign, covered the text and shuffled the papers. Once the President's signature was applied, the papers were again shuffled—this time by a different person.

---

* *These reasons would play out in many territories where the government officials were appointed, and therefore easier to control through corruption. Once statehood was granted the officials of the state would be elected, and much more difficult for law-ignoring land-speculators to control.*

The effort had the desired effect. No one knows which state entered the union first—which was 39th and which was 40th. However, by virtue of its name North Dakota, the undisputed alphabetical leader of the two, generally appears before South Dakota in lists where such detail matters.

1.   Lamar, Howard Roberts, <u>Dakota Territory 1861-1889</u>, (Yale University Press, New Haven, 1956), p. 165.

2.   Lamar, p. 191.

3.   Lamar, p. 192.

4.   Lamar, pp. 204-205.

Chapter 42: Tennessee

I remember the night and the Tennessee Waltz
Now I know just how much I have lost
Yes, I lost my little darlin' the night they were playing
The beautiful Tennessee Waltz.

> — *"Tennessee Waltz"*

Oh remember my darling
When spring is in the air
And the bald headed birds
Are whisp'ring ev'rywhere
You can see them walking
Southward in their dirty underwear
That's Tennessee Bird walk

> — *"Tennessee Birdwalk"*
> *Jack Blanchard and Misty Morgan*

Middle?

Geographically Tennessee is divided into three sections: East, West and Middle, and Tennesseeans aren't the only ones who know this. It is part of the state's geographical identity. But when you think about it, no other state has such a well-defined "middle." Almost all have "Norths", "Souths", "Easts", or "Wests", or some combination of these directions, and some large states like Texas and Montana have "Centrals", but even the other long, thin states like Florida and California don't refer to their central regions as "middle." Tennessee does.

These three divisions, while seldom delineated on maps, are almost as important to people of the region as the delineation between the states themselves. One state history book asserts

"Tennesseeans...seldom identify their home state by its name alone. Their usual response: 'I live in West Tennessee,' or 'My home is in Middle Tennessee,' or 'I'm from East Tennessee.' This is no idle conversation gambit...It is a statement of geography which is also a condensation of history, a reminder of sociology, a hint of cultural variety shaped by geographical fact..."[1]

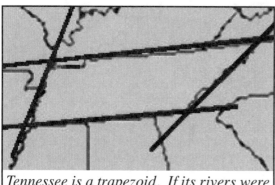

Tennessee is a trapezoid. If its rivers were parallel it would be a parallelegram, or possibly a rhombus.

Looking at Tennessee on a map forces you to remember your geometry. Is it a trapezoid or a parallelogram? Whatever it is, it is almost four times as long as it is wide—432 miles by 110 miles—with unnaturally straight lines on the north and south, and roughly parallel diagonal rivers marking the ends. It looks a little like Kentucky was plopped on top of it and squashed it.

A Cherokee Town

There is evidence that Hernando De Soto explored portions of Tennessee in 1540, and another Spaniard, Juan Pardo, crossed through about 25 years later. The Spaniards barely noticed the natives of the region, except to steal from them and kill them, but Pardo's expedition did note the name of one of the towns through which they passed—Tanasqui. Was this the same village that the English and French would recognize centuries later as an important city of the Cherokee nation? Of course, we'll never know, but certainly this is the first instance of *this word* being applied to *this region*. Not finding cities of gold as they had in Mexico and Peru, the Conquistadores, mercifully, did not stay long in the area, and Tennessee remained relatively untouched by Europeans for the next century.

By 1673, however, the state was virtually crawling with Europeans. Okay, not exactly crawling, but ironically, after a hundred years of isolation from whites, both ends of Tennessee saw Europeans creeping in upon

414

its borders at virtually the same time. In the west, the French adventurers Marquette and Joliet were paddling down the Mississippi River, possibly stopping near the modern city of Memphis. The same year, maybe even on the same day, two Virginians, Gabriel Arthur and James Needham, were climbing to the top of the Great Smoky Mountains in eastern Tennessee, and peering into the lush hunting grounds of the Cherokee, Creeks, Chickasaw and Shawnee. Of these tribes the Cherokee were the most prominent in the region.

By the early 1700's the English in Virginia and both Carolinas were trading regularly with the Cherokee Indians on the other side of the Appalachian mountains. They called these natives "Overhills" and referred to the river on which they lived as the "Cherakee River," or sometimes as the "Tennasee River," after one of two villages situated in a sharp bend in the river. It is believed that the other village, "Chota," was much smaller during the first two decades of the 1700's, but that it gradually grew quite large, and eventually enveloped Tenase (there are as many as twenty different spellings) until the latter eventually disappeared from the map. Alas, any further archaeological study of the site of the village of Tenase is impossible, as it was inundated by the creation of the Tellico dam in 1979, the same dam that made the tiny, endangered snail-darter famous in the 1970's. Anyway, by the middle of the eighteenth century the name "Tennessee" was in common usage among the English to describe a vague region and a river just over the mountains.

An excellent article by Bill Baker which appeared in the *Tellico Times,* entitled "The Origin of Our State's Name," describes the history and possible definition of the word. While some believe it means "big spoon," a more likely meaning, according to Baker, is a combination of two popular theories: that it is a derivation of a Yuchi Indian word meaning "meeting place" or that it is a Cherokee word which means "bends." The Cherokee language, Baker says, is

James Glen

415

notoriously vague, but the suffix "ee" was commonly used to refer to a place, so if "Tennessee" meant "the bends place," it may very well have meant a place where the river bends. And if it referred to a place in the river where it bends so sharply that it comes back upon itself, the name "meeting place" now also makes sense. As for its spelling, Baker says that it was probably James Glen, Royal governor of South Carolina from 1738 to 1756, who gave us the modern spelling of "Tennessee," using its current form in much of his official correspondence in the 1750's.

Watauga...and beyond

By the early 1770's several groups of colonists had traversed the Smoky Mountains and settled into hunting and farming. But it was a perilous place to live. The British government had surveyed a section of land beyond which colonists were forbidden to settle, and the Watauga River settlement, as well as two other small groups of settlers, had crossed that line. The British government simply refused to acknowledge the settlements, and though they were not made to move, they were given no governmental authority, no lawmen and no laws.

So they created their own. The Watauga Association is proudly described by Tennessee historians as the first attempt at real self-government by Europeans in the New World. They set up a five-person legislative council, and elected a sheriff, a clerk and some other officers. They made their own agreement with the local natives and governed themselves successfully for approximately three years. Lord Dunmore, governor of Virginia, raised an eyebrow, writing that this enterprising group of people set "a dangerous example to the people of America, of forming governments distinct from and independent of his majesty's authority."[2]

With the outbreak of the American Revolution in 1775, the Watauga Association changed its name and its form to the "Washington District" (yes, for George Washington) and the following year requested annexation by North Carolina. This was achieved, and the Watauga settlements now became "Washington County" in the state of North Carolina.

In 1779 the community of Nashborough Station was founded in Middle Tennessee, named for a Revolutionary War hero named Francis Nash. Residents of this, and a few surrounding communities, all founded by a colonizer named Richard Henderson, signed a document called the Cumberland

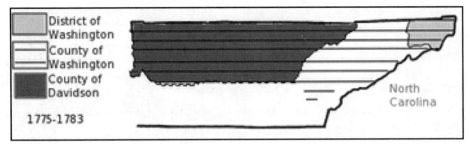

District of
Washington

County of
Washington

County of
Davidson

North
Carolina

1775-1783

Compact which declared themselves separate from the state of North Carolina and outlined their own government. But the Cumberland pioneers had a difficult time the first two years and were relieved when they, too, were annexed by North Carolina as Davidson County.

Name changes now came fast and furious. In 1786 Nashborough was renamed Nashville, and Davidson County was divided to create Sumner County. Two years later, those two counties were further divided to create Tennessee County, and the three of them were designated the Mero District, a form of flattery toward the Spanish governor of Louisiana, Don Estevan Mero (also spelled *Miro*), who was threatening to bar American shipping on the Mississippi River.[3]

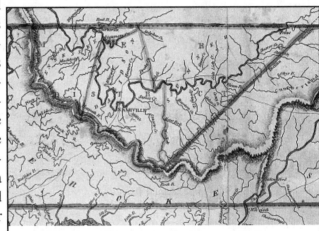

The "Mero District" of what would become Tennessee. It was made up of Tennessee, Davidson, and Sumner Counties.

Franklin

Meanwhile, back in east Tennessee, more counties and several towns had been created to accommodate an influx of settlers there as well. Now, safely tucked into North Carolina's domain, these towns became stifled and restless once the Revolution ended, as they no longer needed the mother state's protection from the British.

In 1784, before the Northwest Ordinance had been designed to dispose of western lands, the residents of what was now being commonly called "Tennessee Country" made the decision to request statehood under the leadership of John Sevier. When North Carolina ceded its transmontane lands to the federal government a constitution was adopted by the citizens of this region, Sevier was elected governor, and a name was decided upon: Franklin.

Interestingly, the preamble to Franklin's constitution refers to the name of the new state as "Frankland."[4] This may have been a simple mis-

John Sevier

spelling or a cute play on words, but the name adopted by the petitioners was indeed Franklin and was intended to honor Benjamin Franklin.

Later that year, however, North Carolina rescinded its cession of the lands, and Franklin once more reverted to Washington, Greene, and Sullivan Counties. Its residents were not pleased, and Sevier entered into a war of words with the North Carolina government, which at its peak threatened Civil War if *Franklin* was not granted independence. But instead of taking up arms, the people of Franklin appealed to the new federal government for statehood. When that effort failed by a slim margin, Franklin ratified their own constitution and began to function as a separate state without sanction from either North Carolina or the federal government.

Unfortunately, Sevier proved to be a contentious leader, and there was much infighting among the elected officials of Franklin. Still, the "state of Franklin" managed to exist for four years. Eventually, poor relations with local Indian tribes coupled with the serious efforts by North Carolina to bring *Franklin* back into the fold proved the end of this independence movement. In 1788 the mother state pardoned all of those who had "seceded," and Franklin quietly faded back into Washington, Sullivan and Greene counties of North Carolina...from whence it had come.

Statehood

Only a year after the Franklin movement ended, North Carolina finally (it was next to last among the thirteen colonies) ratified the U.S. Constitution. By mutual desire of the state, the feds and the transmontane residents, North Carolina once again ceded her western lands. This time for good. Now this rebellious community was an issue for the federal government, to the relief of virtually everybody.

In 1790 Congress created the "Territory of the United States, South of the River Ohio," more commonly called the "Southwest Territory." This name would imply a much larger region than the thin strip that is the state of Tennessee, but in fact it included only what would become that single state. What is now Kentucky was a county of Virginia and was excluded from that state's cession agreement with the U.S. South of Tennessee were lands that were claimed by Georgia, which would not be ceded until 1802. So the Southwest Territory consisted only of the North Carolina cession.

Unlike its counterpart, the Northwest Territory, it was fairly clear that the Southwest Territory would not need to be divided. In fact, federal officials were disappointed to learn how little public land had become available when it obtained the region. But like the Northwest, the Southwest also had to bide its time and work through the process of becoming a state, waiting for Congress to establish procedures for doing so. The Northwest Ordinance had outlined the steps, but making them a reality took time.

In 1796 delegates from the Southwest Territory met in Knoxville to frame a constitution. Included in this group of delegates was the future president, Andrew Jackson, and tradition holds that it was he who suggested the name "Tennessee." However, the name was already being used to describe the whole state, due largely to an essay called "Short Description of the Tennessee Government," written in 1793 by Daniel Smith and republished in 1795 with an accompanying map. Smith was a long-time resident and prominent leader of the Cumberland Basin region that included Tennessee County and had been active in the region's push for self-government, including the "Franklin" statehood movement. At any rate there appears to have been no serious debate concerning the now popular name for the region, and so *Tennessee* it would be.

Congress debated Tennessee's statehood in May of 1796, working out the kinks in the process, and finally agreed to admission on May 31. President Washington signed the statehood bill the next day, and so on June 1, 1796, Tennessee became the sixteenth state to join the Union.

1.	Dykeman, Wilma, <u>Tennessee: A Bicentennial History</u>, (New York: WW Norton, 1975), p. 3.

2.	Caldwell, Mary French, <u>Tennessee, the Dangerous Example: Watauga to 1849</u>, (Nashville, 1974), p. 29.

3.	Bergeron, Paul H., Stephen V. Ash, Jeanette Keith, <u>Tennesseans and their History</u>, (Knoxville, 1999), p. 36.

4.	Bergeron, et al., p. 40.

Chapter 43: Texas

The stars at night
are big and bright
(clap, clap, clap, clap)
deep in the heart of Texas

— "Deep in the Heart of Texas"

There's a yellow rose in Texas,
I'm goin' there to see

— "The Yellow Rose of Texas"

Big State, Big Pride

Few states can be caricatured like Texas. Just choose your stereotype: oil wells, cowboy boots, NASA, country music, small towns, big hair, funny accents, tumbleweed, the Alamo, barbecue. From *King of the Hill* to *True Stories*, from *Walker—Texas Ranger* to *Giant*, Texas provides television and movies with a perfect setting for the outrageous, the obscure, and the unbelievable. As Bugs Bunny puts it while watching carrots spew from an oil derrick, "Anything can happen in Tex-ayuz."

Like those of the more populous states—namely New York and California—the name "Texas" evokes emotion and passion at its very utterance. But unlike the others, there is very little hint

The Alamo in San Antonio

of sophistication or of the cosmopolitan with Texas. Say "New York" or "California," and one can immediately understand—though not necessarily sympathize with—the allure, the magnetism that attracts all those millions of people who choose to make them their home. It is something about the excitement, the opportunities, the modernity. But the name *Texas* inspires no such excitement. It, instead, seems to exude a quaintness, an aw-shucks down-hominess that to some is comical and unappealing, but to others is inviting, warm, and attractive.

For native Texans, the pride in their state is possibly the fiercest in the land. Texans wear popular t-shirts emblazoned with the Lone Star flag and the word "Secede" underneath (even *before* Governor Rick "Good-Hair" Perry made his famous threat of secession regarding the 2009 economic stimulus package). The study of Texas history is mandatory in the state's schools, taught even before that of the nation. There is a downright haughtiness in the twangy Texas accent which sounds, at its thickest, laughable to the ears of a Yankee but is imperceptible to another Texan.   From the food—be it barbecue or Mexican—to the music—be it live rock and roll or country music on the radio—to the cowboys—both real and wannabe— Texas is nothing if not proud.

This state pride has an interesting quirkiness. One of the features for which Texans exude a fervent pride is the state's size—Texas has more land mass than any of the other contiguous states. (One can imagine the collective sinking of hearts when Alaska joined the Union.) This makes for an incredibly diverse geography, not to mention population, and a befuddling question about that passionate Texas Pride. Consider...

****

—**East Texas**, covered in pine trees and dotted with lush forests and lakes, is populated much like its neighbor, Louisiana. A large African-American population connects East Texas with "the South" and all of the antebellum, plantation-owning, civil-rights-fighting images that the South conveys.

—Several **metropolitan areas**—Dallas, Fort Worth, Houston, San Antonio, among others—offer a legitimate "big city" feel and a genuine cultural diversity inherent in such urban areas.

—**Central Texas**, or the "hill country," is often associated with George W. Bush, even though he grew up in New England and only purchased the Prairie Chapel Ranch near Crawford in 1999, when he was running for president.

—**South Texas**, near Brownsville and all along the border with Mexico, has, as one might imagine, a large Latino presence. And given that Texas' history is so closely associated with that of Mexico, this is not surprising. While the image of "illegal aliens" is difficult to overcome, it is, in the case of south Texas, largely erroneous. A population that may be called "Latino", because they speak Spanish and have dark skin and eyes, actually have lived in south Texas since long before it became an independent republic in 1836.

—South Texas also has its own string of **islands**. Legitimate tropical sandy beaches with blissfully warm gulf waters and plenty of vacation homes and condo-filled resort towns for Spring Break crowds.

—**West Texas** is decidedly "oil" territory, and the Panhandle, often pictured as barren and deserted, is actually quite productive farmland.

—And then there is **Austin**, the "jewel" of Texas, famous as the live-music capital of the world, and the state's politically progressive haven.

****

So the question must be asked, "What is it that Texans are so proud of?" Is it the thick piney woods of the east or the tumbleweed deserts of the west? Is it Padre Island or Dallas? Is it the ethnic diversity or the football teams? Whatever it is it exists only within the borders of the state, and any Texan will tell you that you just have to be born there to understand.

The Indians and the Spaniards

The word "texas" (tejas, tayshas, texias, techan, teychas—like many state names, there were dozens of different spellings before one emerged as dominant) was used by the Hasinai Indians who inhabited a small section of east Texas in the mid-1500's when the Spaniards first made contact. The Hasinai spoke a Caddoan language (a derivative of the Sioux language family) and were among the more socially advanced tribes of the area[1]. The word "texas" meant "friends" or "allies," and the Hasinai used it to refer to several other tribes in the area who were friendly to them and loosely organized against the Apaches to the west.

They also used "Tejas!" as a greeting, "Hello, friend!," so the possibility that it was the first word heard by any European from natives of this region is not far-fetched, though it is not clear when the Spaniards first heard the word uttered. Cabeza de Vaca had wandered through much of Texas and near the villages of the Hasinai during his seven-year trek (see Mississippi), ending at Culiacan in 1536. Then in 1542, what was left of Hernando de Soto's expedition after their leader's death explored a section of east Texas in an attempt to find a route back to Mexico. It is not clear if any of these explorers encountered the Hasinai or heard the word "Tejas," but it would be over a century before the word was recorded and applied to the region it now names.

It is certain that the greeting "Tejas!" was made when the Hasinai were met by a group of Spaniards led by an explorer named Alonso De León and a missionary, Father Damián Massanet. They had gone into the area of the Sabine River in 1689 to determine the extent of French encroachment into what the Spaniards considered to be New Spain. The Spaniards were looking, in particular, for Fort St. Louis, the ill-fated settlement established by La Salle on the Texas coast, which had been destroyed and most of its inhabitants killed by Karankawa Indians. It was Massanet who recorded the word "Tejas" in his report, erroneously using it as the name for the Hasinai Indians.

This was a confused translation. "Tejas" was the word the Hasinai used for their friends and allies. *Hasinai*, meaning "the people," was how the natives actually referred to themselves. But in what would become a pattern of misunderstanding between Native Americans and Europeans, the Spanish used "Tejas" to refer not only to all of the regional tribes but to the land as well. The extensive *Handbook of Texas Online* describes how another Spanish missionary, Francisco de Jesus Maria, attempted to correct the Massanet translation. It explains that the natives of that region did not constitute a "kingdom" as Massanet had reported, did not call themselves "Tejas" (but "Hasinai"), and that the tribal leader whom Massanet had referred to as "governor" was not a head chief. The Spaniards attempted to integrate these corrections into their official documents, but the name "Tejas" had been fixed upon the maps and did not fade easily. The Spaniards continued to refer to the region as the "Empire of Tejas" and considered it part of Mexico in New Spain.

The Spanish Province

of Tejas

During most of the 1600's, Tejas was a mysterious region to the Spanish, as it represented the furthest reaches of Mexico, the frontier of their domain,

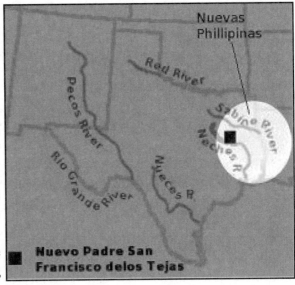

but not worth settling unless it was in danger of being occupied by another European nation. *We don't want it, but we don't want anyone else to have it either* was a common theme among the powerful European nations with regard to the two continents they had stumbled upon. From 1690 to 1693, the Spanish attempted to build missions in the land of *Tejas* in order to keep an eye on the encroaching French, but disease and Indian hostilities forced them to abandon the region. They burned their buildings, scoped out the area to make sure the French weren't horning in, and left, noting for future attempts that colonists and fortified presidios must accompany any efforts at settlement in Tejas.

In the early eighteenth century, during a lull in hostilities with the French, Spanish missions began to spring up along the Neches River in east Texas, one at "a point almost within cannon shot of the French outpost at Natchitoches on the Red River[2]." One of the missions was named

José de Escandón

Nuevo Padre San Francisco de los Tejas, but Spain had applied a more official name to the province: "Nuevas Phillipinas" in honor of the Spanish King, Phillip V. These missions constituted Spain's still rather tenuous hold on the region, and even though some maps recognized its new name, the most common label was still "Tejas."

With the renewal of hostilities came a French invasion sometimes referred to as the "Chicken War." During the French capture of the first Spanish mission, as the story goes, the loud squawking of excited chickens produced enough mayhem to allow the escape of a Spaniard layman who was then able to warn the other missions of the approaching French, allowing them to evacuate. Two years later, however, the Spanish—under San Miguel de Aguayo—retook the missions with authority, supplying them with new troops and colonists and asserting a powerful presence which did not go unnoticed by the French. For his efforts Aguayo was named governor of the newly created Spanish "Province of Tejas."

While the rest of North America was busy with the American Revolution, the Spanish were eagerly colonizing Tejas. Thousands of settlers moved into the region, the northern border of which was, vaguely, the Red River (though Spain claimed virtually all of western North America after France ceded Louisiana to her in 1762). The southern border of the province of Texas was the Nueces River, not the Rio Grande. This division was affected by José de Escandón, a tireless colonizer of the region, who named the province south of Texas *Nuevo Santander* after his home province of Santander in Spain. The area between the

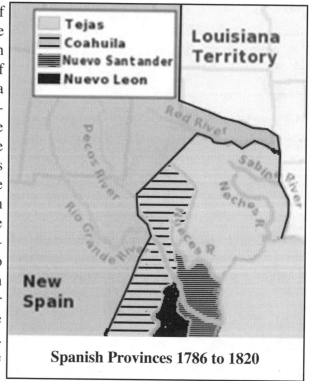

Spanish Provinces 1786 to 1820

Nueces and Rio Grande Rivers was less heavily populated than either Texas or southern Nuevo Santander, though the region, commonly called the "Nueces Strip," would eventually be bitterly disputed by the U.S. and Mexico. Western Texas was part of the Mexican province of Coahuila but was, and still is, sparsely populated.

Anglo Colonization

After the American Revolution, U.S. citizens began moving into Texas, many with political ambitions and dreams of seeing Texas become a U.S. dependency. To that end, they fought largely on the side of the revolutionaries during Mexico's War for Independence from Spain, which began in 1810. In 1812 a revolutionary commander named Bernardo Gutierrez de Lara helped drive the Spanish from Texas, and on April 17, 1813, he declared Texas an independent state which formed "a part of the Mexican Republic to which it is inviolably joined[3]."

Stephen F. Austin

Well, perhaps inviolably, but not, as it turns out, permanently. The state lasted only four months, after which the Spanish authorities, who took back power, began a form of ethnic cleansing designed to drive all Anglo-Americans out of Texas.

It was around this time that the pronunciation of the word "Texas" began to change. The "x" in the name is an artifact of the Spanish language (that is, the language of Spain, as opposed to that of Mexico). The same sound was produced by the Mexican "j", one of the differences between the two closely related languages. Europeans saw "Texas" on early maps created by the Spanish, and would have pronounced it Teks-uz, even though the Spanish pronunciation was Tay-hoss. It is clear that the pronunciation followed the original Spanish spelling, and only when the Mexican language morphed was the "j" commonly inserted in place of the Spanish "x".

Despite Spanish efforts, the flood of U.S. citizens into Texas would not be stopped. Unable to stem the tide of immigrants, in 1820 Spanish officials opened Texas up to any "foreigners" who would respect the laws and constitution of the monarchy. An American colonizer, Moses Austin, asked the viceroy in San Antonio for permission to plant a colony of 300 American families in Texas. A former "subject" of Spain, as he had previously lived in Spanish Missouri, Austin was supported by friends in

Haden Edwards

the Spanish government. His request was granted, but when he died shortly before the colonists were set to begin their journey, his son, 27-year-old Stephen, had to assume his leadership role and continue the effort without him. Unfortunately for Stephen F. Austin, not only did he have to prove his legitimacy as heir to his father's claim, but when, in the summer of 1821, Mexico finally won her independence from Spain, he had to renegotiate that claim with the new government. Both of these he did successfully, and the winter of 1821 saw the beginnings of his massive colonizing effort. Other colonizers or "empresarios" also brought Anglo-Americans to Texas, but none were as successful as Austin.

In 1824 Mexico combined the old Spanish provinces of Coahuila and Texas into one Mexican state with the cumbersome—if obvious—name of "Coahuila-Texas."

The Republic of Texas

The movement for Texas independence began with the Fredonian Rebellion of 1825-26. Haden Edwards was an empresario who angered Mexican officials by demanding that settlers who already occupied land in the section of east Texas that Mexico later granted to him either move out or pay him for their land. This was a clear breech of the Empresario Agreement, but Edwards forced the issue. When the government officials attempted to censure him, he declared his territory, which included the city of Nacogdoches, an independent republic called "Fredonia." Edwards attempted unsuccessfully to gain allegiance from the native Cherokee Indians but did get support from the settlers he had brought with him and from a few other Anglo settlers in the region. When eventually faced with Mexican troops, Edwards fled to the United States, but the incident polarized factions in Texas and made the Mexican government suspicious of Anglo colonizers.

Another issue that began to divide Anglo-Texas from Mexico was slavery. On September 15, 1829, Mexican President Vicente Guerrero issued a proclamation of emancipation for all slaves. The edict was barely noticed in most of Mexico, but in Texas it caused such an uproar that the state was excluded from the proclamation, and slavery continued.

The following year, the Mexican government, so alarmed at the enormous number of immigrants to Texas from the U.S., created the *Law of April 6, 1830*, which stated that "Citizens of foreign countries lying adjacent to Mexican territory are prohibited from settling as colonists in the states or territories of the Republic adjoining such countries." While this outwardly prohibited colonization in Texas by Americans, and did slow its rate, loopholes were found, and often the law was simply ignored. And so still the Americans came to Texas...

Meanwhile the U.S. government, under Presidents John Quincy Adams and Andrew Jackson, were openly coveting Texas. Adams asserted that the Louisiana Purchase extended south all the way to the Rio Grande River, and both presidents offered money to Mexico to negotiate a "more suitable" boundary for the U.S. The monetary offers were declined, but the overtures compounded the suspicions of the Anglo colonists by the Mexican government.

Finally, in 1835, the citizens of Texas revolted and began to form their own independent government. The Texas Revolution was relatively short, lasting only about seven months. The Mexican army suffered about 1500 casualties, while Texas lost some 700 souls, including virtually all of those fighting the famous and futile battle of the Alamo. The war ended with the Battle of San Jacinto on April 21, 1836. This final showdown was actually a surprise attack perpetrated by Texas General Sam Houston on Mexican President Santa Anna's forces as they took their afternoon siesta, and it famously lasted only eighteen minutes. During the battle, Santa Anna disappeared and was immediately sought by the victorious Texans:

> "Santa Anna shed his ornate uniform to elude discovery. It was not until he was saluted as "El Presidente" that suspicion was narrowed. Unfortunately for Santa Anna, it was well known that he wore silk underwear. So, when it was discovered that this same person who had been saluted was also wearing silk underwear, the Texans knew they had captured Santa Anna[4].

Annexation

There were—and are—many who believe that the revolution was a conspiracy by Texans to wrest the state away from Mexico in order to deliver it to the United States. Many Texans were open about their desire for annexation to the U.S., and the government of the new Texas Republic, led by President Sam Houston, wasted no time in voting to request that annexation. But the process was delayed somewhat, in part because treaties between the U.S. and Mexico hindered it.

Finally, however, on February 29, 1845, after an existence of almost ten years, President James K. Polk signed the legislation annexing the Republic of Texas as the 28th state in the Union. Upon entry, this newly acquired land included parts of Oklahoma, New Mexico, and a sliver of Colorado. In 1850 Texas agreed to sell to the U.S. the lands north and west of its modern-day borders for the sum of $10 million. The northernmost border of Texas lies at 36 degrees, 30 minutes, the line that had previously been established by the United States as the border between slave and non-slave states. Only about fifteen years after entering the Union, Texas would secede from it with the rest of the South during the Civil War.

A little known (outside of Texas) provision of the annexation agreement of 1846 gave the state the right to divide into as many as five smaller states. This was considered a possibility just prior to the Civil War in order to give the South more votes in the Senate. The reality, however, was that much of northern Texas sympathized with the North, and the plan may have backfired, so it was never undertaken.

To this day the state claims the right to divide itself, and there have been outspoken proponents of doing so, citing the state's huge size, as well as geographical and cultural differences. Even today, newspaper editorials and web articles advocate the so-called "Great Divide," or the division of Texas into five smaller states. Most of them are tongue-in-cheek, but occasionally a serious suggestion is made, usually by someone mad-as-hell, and using it as more of a threat than an actual proposal, as was the statement by Governor Perry mentioned at the beginning of this chapter. Given Texas pride and tradition, it seems an unlikely scenario. Still...you have to wonder what they might call them.

1.   Magnaghi, Russell M., "Hasinai Indians," <u>The Handbook of Texas Online</u>, http://www.tsha.utexas.edu/handbook/online/articles/view/HH/bmh8.html, 2/23/02.

2.   Richardson, Rupert N., Adrian Anderson, Earnest Wallace, <u>Texas: The Lone Star State, 7th ed.</u> (Upper Saddle River, 1997), p. 29.

3.   Richardson, et al, p. 52.

4.   "Battle of San Jacinto," <u>Wikipedia, the Free Encyclopedia</u>, http://en.wikipedia.org/w/index.php?title=Battle_of_San_Jacinto&oldid=224147615, Date of last revision: 7 July 2008, Date retrieved: 12 July 2008.

Chapter 44: Utah

Utah! People working together.
Utah! What a great place to be.
Blessed from Heaven above.
It's the land that we love.
This is the place!

> —"Utah! This is the place!"
> *The state song as of 2003*

Land of the mountains high, Utah, we love thee!
Land of the sunny sky, Utah, we love thee!
Far in the glorious West, Throned on the mountain's crest,
In robes of statehood dressed, Utah, we love thee!

> — "Utah, We Love Thee"
> *The previous state song, now the official*
> *state hymn*

Mormons

Whereas with some states we find our perceptions and impressions to be wrong, exaggerated, or overly stereotypical, the association of Mormons with Utah would be difficult to overstate. (No pun intended.) Over seventy percent of Utah's population is Mormon. The state's symbol, the beehive, is derived from the Book of Mormon and is said to signify work and industry. Nearly all of the state nicknames—"The Deseret State," "Land of Saints," "The Mormon State," refer to the church and its liturgy. Utah's history is very much the history of the Mormons, and Utah's present reality is Mormonism.

At times, it seems, the affiliation with the Latter Day Saints to Utah is downplayed for political reasons. The connection of a religion, particularly one that is often characterized as "cultish," to such a secular entity as a state,

The beehive, a symbol taken from the Book of Mormon, is featured prominently in the state seal of Utah

is distasteful to many Americans. For those people the struggle with "separation of church and state" could not find a more poignant battlefield than Utah. In Utah the Mormons are in control—of the Church and of the State. For some it is galling, but for most, within and without, it is simply the way it is.

Still "Utah" can mean other things to people: spectacular canyons and rock formations, the Great Salt Lake, Zion National Park, and awesome skiing. It's the heart of the American West, still something of the untamed wilderness toward which the Mormon's directed their pilgrimage, and still very much a land of the Indians.

But Briefly...

By the 1840's the carving up of the American West into individual states was practically inevitable. To some extent the Mormons knew this, and proceeded accordingly. The emigration of Mormons to the Great Salt Lake region was calculated, organized, and controversial. They were led by Brigham Young, heir to Joseph Smith's congregation, and they believed that they would settle in an area that would one day exist within the United States. The storied history of Mormonism, while important to the creation of Utah, is well-documented, voluminous, and plagued with controversy, and it need not be detailed here. However, some details about the evolution of Mormonism help explain the creation, and even the naming, of Utah.

In 1844 Joseph Smith, Jr., the founder of the congregation, was brutally murdered along with his brother, both shot to death by Church

Joseph Smith, Jr.

antagonists while locked in a Carthage, Illinois prison cell. Smith's alleged crime was that he had vandalized the printing facilities of a local newspaper that routinely printed anti-Mormon stories, though the official charge against him was "treason".

Shortly after Smith's murder Brigham Young, formerly one of several leaders among the Mormons, emerged as the new President of the Church, and in 1847 led approximately 16,000 followers out of the Mississippi Valley to the Great Salt Lake in what was then commonly referred to as Eastern California.

Brigham Young

The region was controlled by Mexico but coveted by the United States, and the two countries were embroiled in a war which would decide the political destiny of western North America. With the emergence of Manifest Destiny there was every reason to believe that all of the continent north of the Rio Grande would soon come into American possession one way or another.

In Great Salt Lake City*, the Mormons founded a thriving colony that was governed by the Church in religious and secular matters. The success of the colony has historically been attributed both to its brand of communal enterprise, as well as its isolation in the desert, but this isolation would last only long enough for them to become well established. On February 2, 1848 the United States and Mexico signed the Treaty of Guadalupe Hidalgo

---

* *It was Brigham Young who lent the "Great" to the name "Great Salt Lake". In time that appellation would fade (though not completely), and Young's "Great Salt Lake City" would simply be "Salt Lake City".*

which ended the war and gave to the U.S. what is commonly called the "Mexican Cession," which included parts of Wyoming, Colorado, New Mexico, and Arizona, and all of Utah, Nevada, and California. Almost simultaneously, on January 24th of the same year, gold was discovered at Sutter's Mill in Coloma, California. These two events had the effect of ending the isolation of the Mormons, as thousands of people moved west to seek a quick fortune in gold.

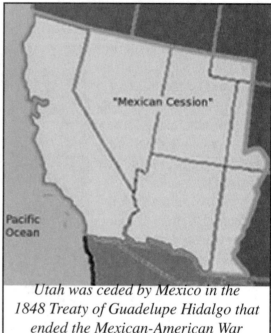

Utah was ceded by Mexico in the 1848 Treaty of Guadelupe Hidalgo that ended the Mexican-American War

The Mormons knew that eventually they would have to deal with a federal government, either American or Mexican, but Brigham Young and the Church leaders were divided on whether or not to immediately petition Congress for territorial status. Young's nephew wrote in October of 1848 "...If we send a written petition there, we may expect that some sycophant of an office seeker will...take from us our rights as free men..."[1] Congress too, was ambivalent for a while about organizing portions of the ceded territory, tabling a motion to do so on January 3, 1849[2]. But in May of 1849 the Mormons did send a petition asking Congress for recognition as a territory.

The State of Deseret

"Deseret" was the name the Mormon's chose for their new territory. It is taken directly from the Book of Mormon, "And they did also carry with them deseret, which, by interpretation, is a honeybee; and thus they did carry with them swarms of bees..." The borders of the land they requested were enormous, including all of "Eastern California": virtually all of present day Utah and Nevada, almost all of Arizona, about half of Colorado,

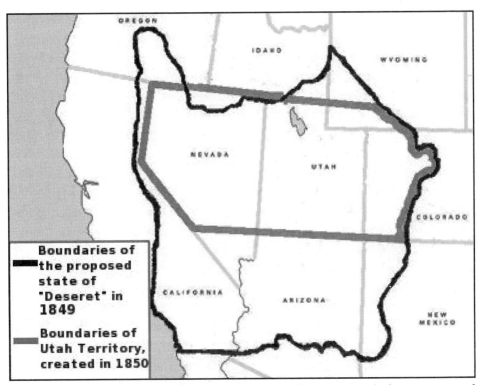

Boundaries of the proposed state of "Deseret" in 1849

Boundaries of Utah Territory, created in 1850

southern California including San Diego which was to be their seaport, and corners of New Mexico, Wyoming, Idaho, and Oregon.

The petition for territory status, however, was never presented to Congress. Before the Mormon delegate had the chance, the Church leaders changed their minds again, and decided to try a different method. They would organize their own state government (much of which was already in place), and then ask for admission to the union as a fully formed state. Their reasons were fairly pragmatic. Territories relied upon the federal government to appoint most of their officials—including their governor—and to create many of their laws. The Mormons were adamant that they retain control of the community they had founded, that they be able to elect their own governor, and create their own laws. They drafted a constitution, elected a governor (Brigham Young) and a General Assembly, and declared themselves the provisional state of Deseret in July of 1849. Then they sent another delegate to Washington who would work with the original delegation to try to achieve statehood for Deseret.

Sentiment in Washington ran the gamut. There were those who fully supported the Mormons, either defending or ignoring the obvious religious influence on such a large tract of land. But there also some who were vehemently opposed, not only for the religious reason per se, but for the practice of polygamy which was ubiquitous in the Mormon community. Those in the middle had concerns about allowing the religious group to dictate territorial policy, but admired the Mormons' fortitude, and were, to some extent, grateful at the prospect of an American foothold in a land they had just fought a war to gain possession of, a land admittedly unattractive to most other settlers.

For the Mormons some form of governmental organization was becoming necessary. The miners headed for California were pouring across the American West, and the Salt Lake community was now a midway point for the flood of prospectors on their way to the gold fields. The Latter Day Saints found themselves in the precarious position of wanting federal authority over the intruders, but not wanting to remove their own church authority. What they really wanted was the federal legitimization of their own self-imposed, religious government.

But that wasn't likely to happen. The Mormons, for instance, were not a litigious society. Their church bishops presided over civil matters in the same capacity as judges and juries. That was a system that the U.S. Congress simply could not sanction. Also the prospect of having any governor imposed upon them was unthinkable to the Mormons. They wanted Brigham Young, and would accept no other.

"Utah"

The Smithsonian report of 1954 on state names asserts that the name "Utah" is derived from a White Mountain Apache word "Yuttahih" which that tribe used to refer to the Navajo Indians[3]. The report explains that the word means "one that is higher up" and that the Navajo did indeed live at a higher elevation than the Apache, but that the Spaniards who learned the word mistook it to refer to the Utes who lived still higher.

While most references define "Utah" as "those who live higher up," "mountain people" or something similar, others insist that the name actually means "meat eaters," and still others, "Land of the Sun." Some believe the word is derived not from the Apache language, but from Navajo, or even from the Ute language itself. This last assertion is unlikely. The Ute name for themselves is "Nuche" which, like most self-references of na-

Jedediah Smith

tive American tribes, simply means "the people." While the actual definition and derivation of the word is somewhat disputed, what is certain is that it was first recorded by Spanish missionaries who explored the area in the late 1770's, and wrote it as "Yuta" or "Yuutaa." Settlement of California by the Spanish, and indeed the Mexicans after they won their independence, was limited almost exclusively to the west coast of the continent, so until the Americans became interested, the name "Utah" was almost unknown, and rarely applied to any specific region. In the 1820's William Ashley and Jedediah Smith, two of the earliest pioneers of the region, explored much of northern Utah, and came into contact with what Ashley called the "Eutaw" Indians, engaging in trade with them. Largely through the efforts of Ashley and other traders/explorers the name became more prominent on maps of the west.

By 1850 the territory-creating machinery in Congress was in motion and would not be derailed. Congress considered it their duty to organize the Mexican cession without regard to the Mormons' request, but in the end the Latter Day Saints gained a modicum of satisfaction through their efforts in Washington. Dr. John M. Bernhisel was the chosen lobbyist for the Mormons, and he worked tirelessly to convince even the most antagonistic congressmen to legitimize their government.

It was Thomas Hart Benton, Bernhisel reported, who "disliked the name of Deseret, which to him was repulsive [Benton was an outspoken opponent of the Mormons] and sounded too much like Desert." Stephen Douglas, although a supporter of the Mormons, agreed and preferred the name "Utah," saying he would insist on that name for any new state or territory. Douglas also suggested that the massive borders for the provisional state would never be acceptable to Congress, and suggested they be curtailed.

Thomas Hart Benton

The Organic Act for the Territory of Utah was passed September 7, 1850, and President Millard Fillmore signed it two days later. While substantially smaller than Deseret, Utah was still quite large, including the current states of Nevada, Utah, half of Colorado, and a small part of Wyoming. On the questions of the name and the borders, the Mormon's submitted their "quiet acquiescence...for the time being" and were satisfied by having their own slate of nominees accepted into key government positions, i.e., they got Brigham Young as their governor.

Still, the Mormons were not happy about the name change:

> "The congressional liking for the name of Utah was not shared by the inhabitants of Deseret... Utah was one of the several forms of the name for the Ute Indians, who were regarded by the mormons (sic) with a little fear, more pity, and a great deal of contempt."[4]

As far as the federal government is concerned, that was the end of Deseret. But the Mormons were not entirely satisfied with their lot. They were indignant that California, with a much smaller white population, was admitted as a state. Bernhisel wrote to Brigham Young "...Should not a nation...cherish those who are endeavoring to render her most sterile and barren domain productive..."[5] The next few years saw several attempts at memorializing Congress for statehood, but the federal government, now embroiled in issues that would lead to the Civil War, would not be bothered by the pleas of this religious "sect" whom many in Congress disliked and distrusted.

The War and the end of Deseret

Specific events led to serious conflict between Utah and the federal government, but more generally there was a clash of philosophies. The Mormons who had settled the region believed it their right and duty to govern themselves, while Congress and the President assumed the duty was theirs. It was, in its purist form, a state's rights issue, a question of republicanism versus federalism, the same differences in governmental philosophy that divided Thomas Jefferson and Alexander Hamilton almost one hundred years earlier, a difference that the United States still struggles with to this day.

But the religious aspect of it, while a common theme in American colonization, muddied the waters on both sides. The Mormons had moved to Utah not only to enjoy freedom of religion, but to allow themselves to be governed by their church. The U.S Congress saw this as a usurpation of federal authority, the Mormons as freedom of religion. Under these conditions a conflict was almost inevitable, and it came in the late summer of 1857. Dissatisfied with the "dictatorial" leadership of Brigham Young, and appalled at the Mormons' practice of polygamy, in 1857 the president sent Colonel Albert S. Johnston into the territory to establish a new territorial government. Bracing for an "invasion by a hostile force" the Mormons attempted (and succeeded to some extent)

Colonel Albert S. Johnston

to stall Johnston's progress into Salt Lake City by burning some of their wagon trains full of supplies. This defiance of the U.S. Government is often referred to as the "Mormon War," and it culminated in the grisly Mountain Meadows Massacre in which almost a hundred settlers from Arkansas and Missouri were viciously murdered.

The people of Utah reluctantly accepted Johnston's imposed government, and a new peace followed. But the Mormons still held out hopes for Deseret. In 1862, they called a constitutional convention, and elected a general assembly for the "State of Deseret." Sometimes called the "Ghost Government of Deseret," this body was unprecedented, and would never be replicated in any other state. It was a second legislature, and a second governor (Brigham Young), whose main function was to echo to the inhabitants of Deseret the laws and provisions which were passed by the territorial legislature of Utah. In this way the Mormons asserted their own control over themselves, while not stepping on any federal toes. In the meantime, memorials to Congress for statehood continued. This ghost government met yearly until 1870, when it rather mysteriously ceased to exist.

Deseret's Last Stand

Still lobbying for statehood, Utah's borders had been squeezed to their current boxy shape by 1872. In that year its citizens held a constitutional convention to try to further their progress in achieving statehood. By this time there were many Mormons who wished to move on. They wanted statehood that was sanctioned by Congress and the president, rather than their own ghost government. They set about addressing the real sticking points, the biggest was the issue of polygamy, but also being debated was the name.

Those who favored changing the name from *Deseret* to *Utah* in their own constitution argued "...the name Deseret might be made a basis of prejudice by persons opposed to the State movement." These were sage words, indeed, for the Mormons had enough obstacles to overcome in convincing Congress to grant statehood. The polygamy issue alone alienated a majority of the congressmen to the prospect. The name Deseret was entirely associated with Mormon liturgy, and that fact alone would likely make it distasteful to Congress, no matter how euphonious it was.

Opponents of the change, on the other hand, argued that the name Deseret was entirely unobjectionable, was dear to the petitioners, and was easy to spell, unlike "Utah." This last point is debatable, but was a common argument for many a name proposed for a territory or state. In a vicious attack on the alternative, opponents argued that Utah "...referred to a dirty, theiving, insect-infested, grasshopper-eating tribe of Indians."[6] But the argument that Deseret was better because it did *not* originate with an indigenous tribe was counterintuitive. Congress routinely used aboriginal names in their creation of territories and states, and were hardly likely to change that pattern in favor of a name with a clearly religious slant.

One delegate recommended a new name, "Argenta" referring to a chapter of Masons in Utah, but in the end the delegates voted to retain "Deseret."

For Congress the problem of Utah was a sticky one. The residents wanted and needed statehood because the territorial system was simply not sufficient. Court cases were piling up for lack of judges, and the people could not legally appoint their own. Meanwhile, the population continued to grow. The problem was not the name (Congress had no intention of replacing the name Utah with Deseret), but polygamy was an absolute showstopper. Until the proposed state constitution included a full condemnation and outlawing of bigamy and polygamy, Congress would not even consider statehood.

The polygamy issue so consumed the efforts to become a state that the name issue faded from the public debate. By 1896 both issues had finally been decided. Polygamy was against the law, and the name of the state would be Utah. On January 4 of that year President Grover Cleveland at last made Utah the 45th state of the Union.

---

1.   Morgan, Dale L., <u>The State of Deseret</u>, (Logan, 1987), p. 25.

2.   Morgan, p. 25.

3.   Harrison, Clifford Dale, <u>The Explorations of William H. Ashley and Jedediah Smith</u>, 1822-1829 (Lincoln, 1991) p. 386.

4.   Morgan, p. 82.

5.   Morgan, p. 85.

6.   Morgan, p. 113.

Chapter 45: Vermont

*"When I was in high school I moved from the big city to a tiny village of
500 people in Vermont. It was like The Waltons!"*

— *Actress Daphne Zuniga*

Pennies in a stream
Falling leaves, a sycamore
Moonlight in Vermont

— *"Moonlight in Vermont"*
Margaret Whiting

Maple Syrup and Teddy Bears

Vermont makes people think of maple syrup and quaint bed and breakfasts, which is appropriate, because that's what Vermont wants people to think of. Maple syrup and tourism are two of the state's biggest industries. In 2001, Vermont produced 26% of the nation's maple syrup, more than any other state. They generated over half a million gallons of the pancake condiment—that's more than a half gallon for every resident of the state... and production was way down that year.

Some other things come to mind when one hears the name "Vermont." The state animal is the Morgan Horse; a popular breed cherished by equine enthusiasts for its versatility and level headedness. The Morgan Horse is also one of the earliest (and few) breeds developed in the United States. There are those who think of skiing, though that would be easterners. Residents of Colorado and Utah might have difficulty associating skiing with a state whose tallest peak rises no higher than 4,400 feet. Sometimes teddy bears come to mind, thanks to The Vermont Teddy Bear Company, one of the world's largest manufacturers of the cute and cuddly stuffed companions. Still others might think of Vermont as a haven for progressive politics; certainly Vermont's history was shaped by strong, independent-minded people who established a precedent in the state for breaking from the pack and forging new ground.

Benning Wentworth and Ethan Allen

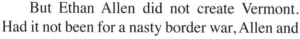

But one does not have to reach far back into the historical consciousness to associate the name Vermont with the name Ethan Allen. Ethan Allen, the company, might be famous as a maker of fine furniture, but Ethan Allen the man has a slightly more nuanced reputation. Allen was the leader of the Green Mountain Boys, a band of men who fought not only for American independence from Britain during the revolution, but at about the same time fought for Vermont's independence from New York and New Hampshire.

Ethan Allen

But Ethan Allen did not create Vermont. Had it not been for a nasty border war, Allen and his colleagues would probably have been quite content as citizens of New Hampshire or New York, which is what they believed themselves to be until around 1775. Credit for the creation of Vermont falls more appropriately

Benning Wentworth

to a man whose methods, upon closer review, were like Allen's—colorful, if not suspect.

Benning Wentworth, "an unscrupulous man who craved power, riches and pomp,"[1] became governor of New Hampshire in 1741. In 1749 he began granting land west of the Connecticut River, even though the border with New York was being officially disputed. The first of these grants he rather audaciously named Bennington and set it on the west side of the Green Mountains—close to the New York border, as he saw it, but well beyond it by the measure of George Clinton, governor of New York.

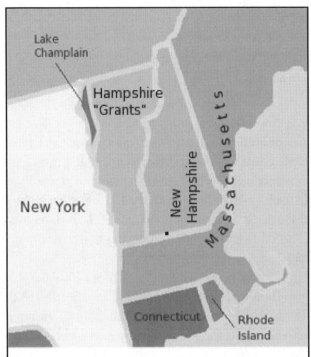

The "Hampshire Grants" were claimed by both New Hampshire and New York.

By 1764, when the king confirmed that the land in question—between the Connecticut River and Lake Champlain—belonged rightfully to New York, Wentworth had granted 138 towns covering about three million acres and keeping about 65,000 acres for himself.[2] Also known as the "Wentworth Grants," they came to be more famously coined the "Hampshire Grants," or simply "The Grants," and were being aggressively settled.

Since many of the Hampshire grants overlapped grants made by New York, a series of ejection suits began to be filed by the "Yorkers." In 1770, nine of them were due to be heard by the New York Supreme Court, and the Hampshiremen organized themselves for a legal fight. Known originally as the Bennington Nine, they elected Ethan Allen as their leader, and Allen went to Connecticut to hire a lawyer to defend them. The Bennington Nine lost the suits, due partly to a conflict of interest on the part of Chief Justice Robert Livingston, and afterwards Ethan Allen refused to accept a bribe by Livingston's operatives to convince the Bennington grantees not to oppose New York's authority. Allen's refusal of this bribe proved to be a pivotal moment in the formation of Vermont.

Ethan Allen returned to Bennington and organized a band of about 200 men who called themselves the Green Mountain Boys. Their goal was to protect their land titles and to oppose—by force if necessary—the authority of New York. The exploits of the Green Mountain Boys are legendary and voluminous. What they wanted initially was to have their land grants confirmed to them, no matter which colony or state claimed jurisdiction, but by 1775 this seemed no longer an option. In that year Allen wrote a letter to the governor of Connecticut suggesting independence for The Grants.

Independence

Early in the American Revolution, Ethan Allen was captured by the British, leaving the Grants to continue their struggle without him. Embroiled in two wars for independence, The Grants' residents decided in 1776 to form a "separate district," and in their January 1777 Declaration of Independence, chose to call themselves "New Connecticut." This name was quickly dropped, however, since a Pennsylvania community had already chosen the name for its own.

On April 12, 1777, a radical propagandist from Philadelphia named Dr. Thomas Young sent a letter addressed "To the INHABITANTS of VERMONT, a Free and Independent State, bounding on the River CONNECTICUT and LAKE CHAMPLAIN,"[3] urging them on in their fight for independence. Young, called by one historian "America's first professional revolutionist," also suggested that Vermont use as a model for its government the new federal Constitution which had been adopted in Pennsylvania. At the next convention of citizens of The Grants, a new constitution based on Young's suggestion was adopted, and the name used by Young—*Vermont*—was also agreed upon

By 1778 The Grants had declared independence, ratified a constitution, and elected a president of what they were calling the Republic of Vermont, and all this in the middle of the American Revolution. So brazen were the actions of the Vermont people that even some towns on the New Hampshire side of the Connecticut River requested, and were welcomed, to join them. Now the Green Mountain Boys were in conflict not only with New York, but with New Hampshire as well...not to mention with the British.

The tumult created by Vermont's Declaration of Independence, and now, it would seem, territorial ambitions, continued until 1791. For the remainder of the Revolution the new republic's destiny—whether as a state in the new United States or as a colony in the British Empire—was unclear. But by 1791 certain factors came together—primarily the agreement to terms with New York and the imminent acceptance of Kentucky as a southern state—to allow the Republic of Vermont to be accepted as the fourteenth state in the Union, and on March 4 of that year, it was.

The first state to enter the Union after the original thirteen colonies, Vermont paved the way for other new states to enter. Kentucky was accepted the very next year, and Ohio would enter as the first state to be created from the Northwest Territory in 1803. But as was the case for Kentucky and Ohio, the action of voting Vermont in as a state was a bit unorthodox, since the process of state admittance had not yet completely congealed.

Vermont was voted in by the U.S. Congress, and President Washington's signature was, at that time, not required. The Act approved by Congress proclaims that, "…the said State, by the name and style of 'the State of Vermont,' shall be received and admitted into this Union…"

Okay, but why "Vermont"?

Dr. Thomas Young is generally given credit for applying the name "Vermont" to the fledgling state, and to be sure it was after he suggested it that the name took hold, but *why* he suggested it is unclear. Tradition holds that the name had been in limited use to describe the region for years before Young used it, but there are differing (if not mutually exclusive) stories as to how it originated.

The one dating back the furthest is attributed to Samuel de Champlain, an explorer who first entered the region in 1609, lending his own name to the lake that marks the western border of Vermont. One popular book (and corre-

Samuel de Champlain

sponding website) on state names asserts that "Vermont is an English form of the name that French explorer Samuel de Champlain gave to Vermont's Green Mountains on his 1647 map."[4] This assertion is attributed to a Smithsonian report from 1955 written by John Harrington, and has been widely proliferated in books and on hundreds of websites. But while Champlain

451

may well have noted the Green Mountains on a map, he certainly did not do so in 1647, because he died in 1635.

In his excellent bicentennial history of Vermont, Charles T. Morrissey describes the most colorful and probably most famous story of the origin of the name. It involves an Anglican clergyman named Reverend Samuel Peters who published his own account of the tale in 1807. Peters claimed he was traveling through the region in 1763 performing baptisms, when he decided to baptize the entire state.

> "Peters...and his party in the late fall ascended "a high mountain, then named Mount Pisgah, because it provided to the company a clear sight of Lake Champlain at the west, and the Connecticut River to the east, and overlooked all the trees and hills in the vast wilderness at the north and south." While pouring a bottle of spirits on a rock he dedicated the wilderness with "a new name worthy of the Athenians and ancient Spartans—which new name is Verd Mont, in token that her mountains and hills shall be ever green and shall never die.

Peters, however, was known for telling lies, and his tale was largely disbelieved, despite his fierce defense of it. Morrissey continues:

> "Peters insisted that his claim was valid, and he insisted that he named the state Verd Mont, for Green Mountain, not Vermont, which translates from the French as "Mountain of Maggots." Piqued at his critics he curtly observed: "If the former spelling is to give way to the latter, it will prove that the state had rather be considered a *mountain of worms* than an ever green mountain!"[5]

While some history books claim that the phrase "Verd Mont" was in use well before Peters claimed to have conferred it, they offer no specific written reference. Technically, it is not even proper French. "Green mountains" stated correctly would be "monts verts," which does not easily morph into "Vermont." But the two French words, whoever applied them, are certainly the ones which formed the state's name. Perhaps the person or people who first used them were not native speakers of French.

Morrissey writes that the matter was complicated by the discovery of a 1774 map of Sherbourne, Vermont. It shows Killington Peak, the second highest mountain in the state, labeled "Mount Pisgah." Atop this mountain, on a clear autumn day, one is in fact able to see both Lake Champlain to the west and the Connecticut River to the east. Perhaps, Morrissey concedes, Peters was telling the truth after all.

1.   Robertson, Doug, "The Story of Ethan Allen (1738-1789), A Right to Liberty," <u>From Revolution to Reconstruction...and What Happened Afterwards</u>, http://odur.let.rug.nl/~usa/B/allen/allen01.htm, Last updated 3/6/2003, retrieved 7/30/09

2.   Morrissey, Charles T., <u>Vermont: A Bicentennial History</u> (New York, 1981), p.71.

3.   Wardner, Henry Steele, <u>The Birthplace of Vermont: A History of Windsor to 1781</u> (New York, 1927), p. 357.

4.   Shearer, Benjamin F. and Barbara S., <u>State Names, Seals, Flags, and Symbols</u> (Westport, Connecticut; London: Greenwood Press), p. 16.

5.   Morrissey, p. 70.

Chapter 46: Virginia

Homesick, tired, all alone in a big city
Why should everybody pity me?
Nighttime falling, and I'm yearning for Virginia.

> — *"Sleepy Time Down South"*
> *Billie Holiday*

But Virginia, they didn't give you quite enough information

> — *"Only the Good Die Young"*
> *Billy Joel*

She never comprimises,
Loves babies and surprises,
wears high heels when she exercises
Ain't that beautuiful
Meet Virginia

> — *"Meet Virginia"*
> *Train*

"Virginia is for Lovers" (...of History)

Original, archetypal, earliest, authentic, the first... No matter which descriptor you use, when it comes to states, it is clear you're probably talking about Virginia. Even today, this maiden state is perhaps best known as the *original* of the original thirteen colonies. Essentially, early American history is Virginia history, and the state features some of the most historic sites in the country.

When exploring Virginia, it is important to note that there are two very distinct regions: northern and southern. Due to its close proximity to Washington D.C., northern Virginia is comprised mostly of suburbs, and

Monticello

its industry is hi-tech and scientifically oriented. And contrary to what many American's might believe, the Pentagon is actually located in Arlington, VA—a fact that corrects many references to the 911 terrorist attack on that building as being an attack on *Washington D.C.*

Southern Virginia is considered just that: a southern state. Tobacco fields cover a generous portion of the southern counties, and coal mining and other mineral extraction are common industries.

Aspects of Virginia's rich history can be attributed to the original colonists' European influences, particularly in the areas of art and culture. The genius of one of Virginia's most famous architects—and third American president—Thomas Jefferson can still be seen today. Monticello, Jefferson's Palladian masterpiece home, and the Virginia State Capital building are probably the two most noteworthy structures designed by this Founding Father. However, for those who find classical European architecture a bit too stuffy for their tastes, Virginia offers numerous design styles, from modern contemporary to Georgian to…prehistoric. At Enchanted Castle Studios in Natural Bridge, Virginia, a local artist has been credited with building the world's most accurate replica of Stonehenge…in foam. Visiting this faux phenomenon may not feel as humbling as, say, trekking across the English countryside to see the real thing, but nonetheless, it's a Virginian visionary marvel.

The Virgin Queen

Virginia was the sight of the first English settlement in the New World, and who better to name it for than England's reigning monarch, Queen Elizabeth I—the Virgin Queen. (The Latin word for virgin is virginius. "Virginia" is its feminine form.) The Queen's nickname was not intended as a judgment of her character—though it does lend itself to some rather

Elizabeth I, the "Virgin Queen"

lurid historical investigation. Rather the use of the name *Virginia* seems to have been carefully considered by the Queen herself:

Everything with this politic woman meant something. The permission to use her name was not mere coquettishness, not only the suggestion of romance which, genuine enough in that day, it has come chiefly to signify for us. It was, like everything with her, an intensely personal act, calling attention to an aspect of her personality which, if not unique in a ruler, was an unforgettable element in her fame. But it was also politics: a characteristically ambivalent notice to the world that she personally was involved as well as the Crown of England, her good name pledged. It was therefore an unmistakable underlining of her claim, which could not chivalrously be disregarded, a warning to others to keep off.[1]

Was She or Wasn't She?

The delicate question of whether or not Queen Elizabeth I was actually, technically and officially a virgin is to this day a matter of curiosity to historians, and the answer seems to be an un-

**Robert Dudley,
Earl of Leicester**

457

qualified "maybe." Anyone who has seen the award winning 1998 movie *Elizabeth* can only conclude that the Virgin Queen was not only *not* a virgin, but that she carried on a very public and very sexual affair with Sir Robert Dudley, Lord of Leicester. An exquisite performance by actress Cate Blanchett notwithstanding, the movie is clearly based on extreme speculation and even then beautifully embellished.

To be sure, the Queen and Leicester, even in their own day, prompted (and even appeared to enjoy) widespread speculation about the exact nature of their relationship. But certain historical facts legitimize the possibility that Elizabeth truly was the Virgin Queen. Not the least of these is her own declaration: "...although I love and always have loved my Lord Robert dearly, as God is my witness, nothing improper has ever passed between us."[2] This statement is rendered more profound because it was uttered while she was sick with smallpox, and believed she was on her deathbed.[3]

Other convincing arguments have been made that Elizabeth certainly had the psychological profile of being extremely averse to the institution of marriage. Though a beautiful young woman at the time of her succession to the throne, and though that made her one of the most coveted and courted women in history, she may have been, at least subconsciously, deathly afraid of pregnancy and childbirth. Given the circumstances of her mother's death (Anne Boleyn was beheaded when she "failed" to produce a male heir for her husband, King Henry VIII), and the death of her first stepmother a few days after giving birth to Elizabeth's half-brother Edward, one can hardly blame her for having some severe, unresolved issues surrounding marriage and childbirth.[4] And given that the only certain method of birth control in the sixteenth century was abstinence, the title

Sir Walter Raleigh

458

of "Virgin Queen" begins to seem more likely.

A Close Call

The name Virginia was bestowed by Sir Walter Raleigh, a courtier, poet, and adventurer, who himself never actually voyaged to North America—some say because he was such a favorite of the Queen that she would not tolerate his absence for such a long period of time. Raleigh's half-brother, Sir Humphrey Gilbert, was granted by the Queen the original patent for establishing an English colony in America, and upon his death in 1583 Walter Raleigh inherited that patent. Raleigh organized an expedition in 1584 led by Philip Amadas and Arthur Barlowe which landed in July of that year on the coast of what is now North Carolina.

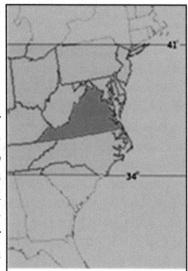

The original Virginia Company Charter granted the colony all of the land between the 34th and 41st parallels, virtually the entire mid-Atlantic seaboard.

Amadas and Barlowe met Granganimeo, the brother of the local Indian chief or *weroance*, and attempted to communicate with him and his followers. This communication was, under the circumstances, fairly successful, except with regard to the name the natives used to refer to their country. "For when some of my people asked the name of that Countrie," Raleigh would later write, "one of the Salvages (sic) answered *Wingandacon*." The native, it turned out, had simply not understood the question, and so had replied with a polite, off-hand comment which was eventually translated as "You wear good clothes."[5]

And so, until Queen Elizabeth I allowed her unofficial title to be applied to it, the first English colony in the new world was known as "Wingandacon." The spelling took a variety of forms, including *Wyngandecora, Wingantekoy, Wingane Dehoy,* and *Wingan deCoy,*[6] but by the fall of 1584 "Wingandacon" began to appear in official English documents, as well as in those of the Spanish government, as the name of England's potential first North American colony.

Virginia Dare

Just as Queen Elizabeth I bestowed her name upon the new country, so did the country bestow its name upon Virginia Dare, the first English child to be born and baptized in the New World. The baby Virginia was the granddaughter of John White, governor of the ill-fated first English colony on Roanoke Island. She was only a month old when White left his daughter, her family, and the other potential colonists at Roanoke to return to England for supplies.

Because of war with Spain White did not return to Roanoke for three years, and by then the colonists were gone, leaving precious few clues to their whereabouts or fate. The "Lost Colony" at Roanoke Island (which is actually in North Carolina) lives on as one of the most intriguing mysteries in American History. The name of Virginia Dare lives on also—as a part of that mystery, and as the very first American of European descent.

Motherhood

Despite the oxymoronic implications, Virginia is often referred to as the "mother" of the United States, given that it was this original colony that was divided and subdivided to create most of the other eastern states. But despite its status as "original" colony, Virginia was nowhere near the first state of the U.S. Not even close.

Largely because of the debate over slavery, and more specifically, how slaves would be counted for census purposes when it came to allocating seats in the House of Representatives, Virginia held off ratifying the Constitution until July 25th, 1788. That makes it tenth in the chronological list of states.

The debate that caused the delay was finally settled in favor of the "three-fifths" rule, which, while allowing slaves no rights as citizens, did count them as three-fifths of a person for census purposes. This ruling gave Virginia the largest original complement of Representatives in the House, thus it was apparently worth the wait for the "mother" of colonies.

To this day Virginia and three other states* maintain their status as "Commonwealths." While there is technically no difference between this distinction and that of a state, the word connotes a government that is given

* *The others are Massachusetts, Pennsylvania and Kentucky.*

by the "consent of the people" or for the "*common wealth* of the people" rather than by royal fiat. One wonders if Queen Elizabeth I would still give her consent...or her name.

1.   Rowse, A. L., <u>The Elizabethans and America</u>, (London, 1959), p. 35.

2.   Wilson, Derek, <u>Sweet Robin: A Biography of Robert Dudley, Earl of Leicester, 1533-1588</u>, p. 136; Jenkins, Elizabeth, <u>Elizabeth and Leicester</u>, (Panther, 1972), p. 89.

3.   Wilson, p. 89.

4.   Taylor-Smither, Larissa J., "Elizabeth I: A Psychological Profile," *Sixteenth Century Journal XV*, No. 1 (1984), 47-72.

5.   Stick, David, <u>Roanoke Island: The Beginnings of English America</u>, (Chapel Hill, 1983), pp. 46-47.

6.   Stick, pp. 66-67.

Chapter 47: Washington

"I can't believe it," said the tourist. "I've been here an entire week and it's done nothing but rain. When do you have summer here?"

"Well, that's hard to say," replied the local. "Last year, it was on a Wednesday."

—*old joke*

"I cannot tell a lie, father, you know I cannot tell a lie! I did cut it with my hatchet."

—*From* "The Cherry Tree"
by Mason Locke Weems in his book,
Life of George Washington; with Curious
Anecdotes, Equally Honorable to Himself,
and Exemplary to His Young Countrymen

George Who?

A hundred years ago the name Washington might have inspired the image of the father of our country. Today it is more likely to make us think of a monolithic software company run by the richest man in the world, or the wildly famous purveyor of coffee whose ubiquitous corner-front stores can be fount anywhere in America.

Of course, multibillion-dollar corporations aside, the name "Washington" produces other images, too. Apples, for one. The state produces more than half of the "eating apples" consumed in the U.S. And rain. Washington is among the wettest and foggiest of all the states, the western coastal region sometimes going weeks without a clear day. Also Mount St. Helens. In 1980 the world was fixated on images of the cataclysmic destruction caused by the sudden eruption of this volcano." And can anyone hum the theme song from *Frasier*?

And speaking of *Frasier*, that massively popular spin-off from *Cheers* sets itself in Seattle, the state's largest, and arguably most well-known, city—though not, to the surprise of many, its capital. (Olympia.) And along with the enormously successful TV sitcom, the coffee, the Space Needle, the Seahawks, and, well, the rain, Seattle-ites may attribute part of the fascination with their city to one particularly unusual Seattle institution: Grunge music.

Properly coined the "Seattle Sound", this cult-culture music scene started small, in garages and among a young, ecclectic, and fiercely loathe-to-be-labled youth, and then exploded in the mid-1980's. It permeated the mainstream music of the world with its legions of longhaired and defiant adolescents, who rejected the "Me Generation" icons of their elders in favor of the angst-filled teen anthems of Nirvana, Pearl Jam, and Alice in Chains. And it all started in Seattle, in Washington, our only post-revolution state named for a specific person.

Pacific Northwest

Washington was carved out of the Oregon Territory and shares many of the same dimensions and geography of its southern neighbor. This creates a common dilemma for young geography students, the problem of being unable to remember "which one is on top." Well, Washington is indeed the one on top, and the two of them, along with—and this point is debatable—a portion of Idaho, make up the Pacific Northwest, a name notable for its imprecision.

One might think that the phrase "Pacific Northwest" is redundant. After all, Washington and Oregon are in the northwest corner of the country (excluding, of course, Alaska, which not everyone does). The fact that the Pacific Ocean lies to the west of them seems irrelevant. The problem is the word "northwest" and the evolution of what it has come to mean.

After the American Revolution, the Northwest Territory

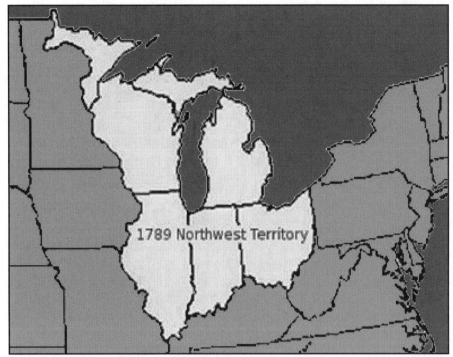

1789 Northwest Territory

was all the land west of the Appalachian Mountains, north of the Ohio River, and east of the Mississippi River. The Northwest Ordinance of 1787, one of the defining documents of our nation, was written for the purpose of organizing this massive region, which the United States claimed from Britain and her Indian allies after the war. A few years later, however, in 1803, the Louisiana Purchase was made, and the Northwest Territory wasn't so *northwest* anymore. It was more *midwest*, and so that is the word that began to describe it.

But by 1848 the United States officially laid claim to all the land between the Atlantic and Pacific Oceans, from the 49th parallel south to a still-fuzzy (but close to its current placement) border with Mexico. Now the term "midwest" didn't even seem appropriate, but it was fairly cemented and stuck relentlessly. That meant that the word "west" must mean everything west of "midwest." And so our geographical vocabulary had to expand.

The middle of the country became the "central plains," except for Texas, which is no doubt a "western" state. (Oddly, Texas is rarely described as "southern," even though it certainly went the way of the South in the Civil War, and it's southern tip is south of every other "southern" state ex-

cept Florida.) Other western states are Colorado, Wyoming, Utah, Nevada, Montana, California, and most of Idaho. The "Southwest" is Arizona and New Mexico. California eventually became synonymous with "west coast," leaving only the two states north of it to find their geographical distinction. "Northwest" by now had not only been appropriated by the midwest but realistically could describe a quarter of the country, way too broad a term to be useful to, say, your average meteorologist.

And so arrive at "Pacific Northwest." It is a descriptive phrase, accurate, and even euphonious. And most importantly for our discussion, it is where Washington is.

Which Washington?

When speaking of Washington, one often feels the need to distinguish it from our nation's capital, and so, as with New York, we say Washington *State* to distinguish it from the city with the same name. This is a source of angst for many a Washingtonian, as well as for a few place-name historians:

> ...the duplication was one of the most unfortunate events of our naming-history...the two Washingtons (not to mention all the smaller ones) have grown steadily in importance, necessitating an ever more frequent and tiresome mention of "Washington State" or "Washington, D.C." The two initials have become attached to the name of the nationl capital like an ugly parasitic growth.[1]

But interestingly the name "Washington" was bestowed in part to *avoid* such confusion.

As with "Lincoln" and "Jefferson," the name "Washington" was often proposed as a state name. In fact, one of the very earliest states created by Congress very nearly bore that name. When the Northwest Territory (that is, the first Northwest Territory, not the Pacific Northwest) was initially divided, before a name was finally settled on for what is now the state of Ohio, the name proposed for the remaining portion of the territory was *Washington*. After committee debate, it was changed to "Indiana." Then, in 1817, the Mississippi Territory and again in the 1840's the Minnesota Territory both had the name "Washington" proposed for them, but it never stuck.

When the residents of what was, in 1853, called "Northern Oregon"—that section of the Oregon Territory north of the Columbia River—petitioned for organization as a separate territory, they proposed the name "Columbia" for themselves. It was Richard H. Stanton of Kentucky who, when the petition was read in the House of Representatives, suggested

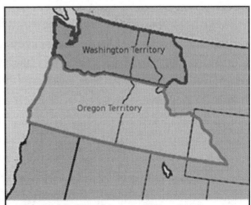

In 1853 Washington Territory was separated from Oregon Territory at the Columbia River.

467

changing the name to "Washington." He argued that there was already a "District of Columbia," and that using that name for a new territory would be too confusing. Historian Terence Cole wrote an excellent article in 1994 for the journal *Columbia* lamenting the naming of Washington, and in it he points out that Stanton had close ties to D.C.—he was born and raised there, and as a congressman used his chairmanship of the Public Grounds Committee to fight for the building of the Capitol dome which became known as "Stanton's Monument."[2]

Alexander Evans, U.S. Representative for Maryland pointed out a flaw in Stanton's argument. He noted that countless places in the country already honored Washington, and that "our geographical nomenclature has become such a mass of confusion that it is almost impossible, when you hear the name of a town to know in what part of the world it is, much less to know in what part of the United States it may be found." Evans' argument was followed by a suggestion from Stephen A. Douglas, the chairman of the Committee on Territories, that instead of "Washington," the new territory be named "Washingtonia." It probably sounded just as silly to Congress in 1853 as it does to us today, and so the suggestion was ignored.

When the debate was over, the long-dead father of our country had won the day. "Washington Territory" was signed into existence by President Millard Fillmore on March 2, 1853.

You Named it What?

Still, opposition to the name raged on. James M. Ashley, a powerful representative from Ohio who served three terms as the chairman of the Committee on Territories, led the charge. Ashley presided over the creation of many western territories and was often passionate about how to name them: "My purpose was to give each territory a euphonious name...and at the same time use a word that should appropriately describe the topography of the country." Hisorian Cole writes that if Ashley had had his way, the name "Washington" would have been erased from the map in the 1860's.[3]

Indeed, Ashley was not alone among congressmen. During the debate about the naming of Wyoming in 1868 Representative Charles Pomeroy from New York lamented the naming of Washington Territory. In response to suggestions that the proposed territory of Wyoming be named instead "Lincoln," Pomeroy said, "We have never had any state named after any man, however good or great. We have the Territory of Washington, to be sure; but when it becomes a state I doubt very much whether it will be called the State of Washington."

Pomeroy was, of course, mistaken. Delaware, the Carolinas and New York were all named after men, and Virginia and Maryland were both named for women. No doubt he was excluding them based on the fact that Congress was not responsible for those names, but this does not make his assertion any more correct.

Regrets over the naming of Washington continued even after statehood. Washington novelist Nard Jones wrote in 1947,

"There was a great galaxy to choose from. Names like Quillayute, Pysht, Chewelah, Klickitat, Washougal, Snoqualmie, Okanogan. Names wasted on streams and waterfalls, mountains and towns.... I mean only to say that I think we would be handsomer in Indian feathers or a coonskin cap than in a cocked hat."

In the 1990's the state tourism department of Washington adopted the self-conscious slogan "The Other Washington" as an advertising gimmick to distinguish it from that "other" one on the east coast. After all these years Washington seems to have finally made peace with its home in the "Pacific Northwest"—home to Microsoft, Starbucks, and a brand of music all its own.[4]

Boundaries

Washington did indeed take its name on to statehood, but statehood did not come until 1889. Washington remained a territory for thirty-six years, longer than all but five other states, during which time its borders were debated and changed more than once.

The northern border, the one with Canada, was actually settled just before Washington was separated from Oregon. In 1846 the U.S. signed the Or-

Nard Jones

469

egon Treaty with Great Britain, which extended the 49th parallel border between the U.S. and Canada from the Rocky Mountains all the way to the west coast, except for the southern half of Vancouver Island, which Britain fought successfully to keep. In return, the British gave up any rights to what they called New Albion or Nova Albion (Latin for New England), what we call Washington and Oregon. This agreement inflamed those Americans in the Pacific Northwest, whose militant motto had become "Fifty-four forty or fight," referring to their wish to move the northern boundary of Oregon Territory all the way north to the southern tip of Alaska. But the treaty avoided yet another war with Britain, at a point when America itself was becoming severely divided over slavery.

Washington Territory's southern and eastern boundaries were also disputed, mostly in an effort by Washingtonians to maintain or increase their population. An attempt by Oregon to annex the Walla Walla region was successfully fought off, and once Idaho was created, Washington's eastern border was fixed at -117.5° longitude.

These are the borders that Washington carried to statehood along with its self-conscious name. In November of 1889, Benjamin Harrison created with the brevity of his signature four states within a span of nine days—North and South Dakota on the 2nd, Montana on the 8th, and Washington—as if it hadn't waited long enough—on the 11th. It was the forty-second state in the Union.

---

1.   Stewart, George R., <u>Names on the Land</u>, (New York, 1945), p. 288.

2.   Cole, Terrence, "The Other Washington: The Naming of Northern Oregon," *Columbia*, Fall, 1994, p. 7.

3.   Cole, p. 8.

4.   Cole, p. 8.

Chapter 48: West Virginia

Almost Heaven, West Virginia
Blue Ridge Mountains
Shenandoah River

> —*"Take Me Home, Country Road"*
> *John Denver*

*"So I had Cheneys on both sides of the family, and we don't even live in West Virginia...You can say those things when you're not running for re-election."**

> —*Vice President Dick Cheney, 2008*

Mountains

West Virginia is virtually synonymous with "mountains". We think of the Alleghany and the Blue Ridge Mountains and the pioneers who explored them all the way to Kentucky. We think of the coal mines that stretch from West Virginia's western valleys north into Pennsylvania. West Virginia shares its history with those states that share its mountains. Of course we also think of John Denver—almost heaven, mountain mama, and all that. What we tend not to associate with West Virginia are the colonial plantation owners of its parent state, Virginia.

West Virginia's name says a lot. Virginia, originally the English name for the whole eastern seaboard, was

Blue Ridge Mountains

---

*   *Vice President Cheney was widely, and understandably, chastised for his attempt at humor and within hours produced a public apology.*

473

accustomed to being divided.   During colonial times, chunks were broken off routinely to create new colonies, and later territories, all around it. What is different about West Virginia is that it divided *itself* from Virginia during the Civil War, after the eastern, midwestern, and southeastern states were well established. By 1860 the borders in America's eastern region *seemed* firmly established. But Virginia had a natural dividing line—the mountains that separated its genteel farmers from its western settlers. By the time war broke out between the states, that natural division caused irreconcilable differences.

"West" Virginia tells the story, not of consensual division of a state, but of secession. North and South Carolina and North and South Dakota all share names, connoting correctly the mutually beneficial divisions that pulled them apart from one another. But West Virginia, we can tell by what we call it, is the product of reluctant division. Virginia remained Virginia, but those who disagreed so strongly with its secession from the Union in 1861 broke off. They would be a new state with a new name, but they considered themselves Virginians, too, and deeply regretted that they could not keep the name. That, however, was the price of acting on their collective conscience.

West, Western, Transmontane Virginia

The bicentennial history of West Virginia written by John Alexander Williams contains the following footnote:

> "Before West Virginia became a state in 1863, the terms "western Virginia" and "West Virginia" were used interchangeably to describe the entire western half of Virginia, that is, all Virginia territory lying west of the Blue Ridge Mountains. The new state, however, took about two-thirds of this territory, which creates a problem of nomenclature...

And not a *small* problem. Williams continues,

> "when writing about present West Virginia in its prestatehood days. In this volume, "western Virginia" and "West Virginia" are used interchangeably, but only to refer to that territory now

included in West Virginia. Traditional western Virginia (present West Virginia plus present west-central and southwestern Virginia) is called "transmontane Virginia."[1]

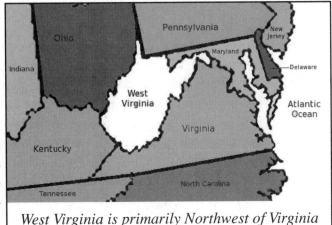

West Virginia is primarily Northwest of Virginia

At least part of what Williams is talking about is that West Virginia isn't exactly west of Virginia. It is northwest of Virginia, and truth be told, more north than west. That is, all of West Virginia is north of Virginia, but all of Virginia isn't east of West Virginia. He is also saying that most, but not *all*, of Virginia west of the Allelgheny Mountains became West Virginia. Okay, maybe Williams says it better, but the point is it can be a little difficult to talk about.

The geography is important, though, because long before the Civil War the state's physical features were dividing it. The wealthy plantation owners in the east were making all the rules, such as those that required substantial land ownership before a person could vote. This excluded the majority of settlers in the mountains who did not own the land they lived on, or if they did, it wasn't enough. There were also problems of taxation, the easterners making it easier on themselves by taxing their slaves at only ten percent of their recorded value, creating a larger tax burden for those in the west. Still, these were political problems that the state was trying to work through.

In the 1820's and 30's rumblings of division began in earnest. Abolitionism began as a political movement, and western Virginia was a hotbed of activism. Businessmen of the region supported abolitionism, not entirely on moral grounds, but largely because they felt slavery was taking jobs away from whites in the state who desperately needed work. But separation from Virginia was still a drastic concept, and so to appease the westerners and quiet their calls for separation, the General Assembly worked to improve the representation for those across the Alleghanies, and build up the western infrastructure.

Kanawha?

The election of Abraham Lincoln divided the state of Virginia just as cleanly as it divided the rest of the nation, and the process of creating a new state from the western counties moved at lightning speed, at least compared to other, more conventional state-making efforts. On April 17, 1861, the Virginia legislature voted to submit a secession bill for popular vote, and the delegates from the western part of the state walked out of the convention. Two months later, when the Civil War fighting was underway in earnest, those western delegates met to form the Restored Government of "New" Virginia, which was quickly recognized by Lincoln as the legitimate government of the state. In August, the Second Wheeling Convention approved an ordinance creating a new state out of portions of Virginia, and named it *Kanawha*.

"Kanawha" was the name of two rivers, as well as a large county, central to the proposed new state. The name derived from an Indian word, probably from an Algonquin-speaking tribe—Delaware or Shawnee perhaps. The true derivation is unclear because when the earliest white settlers arrived in West Virginia, there were almost no natives living there. Early explanations for this dearth of Indian settlements centered on the decimation of natives by disease, but the region was also fought over, and the Iroquois to the north had asserted their dominance and driven out the tribes who had once called the region home. As near as anyone can tell, the name "Kanawha" meant "place of white stone" in reference to the large salt deposits in the region.

The Debate

On November 26, the Constitutional Convention for what would become West Virginia began, and about a week into it, on December 3, the state's name was debated. Harmon Sinsel, a carpenter from Taylor County, was the first to object to the new, native-language-based name. His comments were passionate and illustrated the heartache of the times. He said, in part, "I am a Virginian; I was born and raised in Virginia, and I have ever been proud of the name. I admit that Virginians have done wrong—that many of them in this rebellion have disgraced themselves; but that has not weaned me from the name."[2]

His objections were followed by a more pragmatic one. An attorney named Peter Van Winkle pointed out that the name already applied to a county in the new state, and that it would be imprudent for the state to share the county's name. He highlighted the problems of postal delivery and the fact that no other state bore the name of any of its own counties. (Which wasn't true, and Van Winkle was corrected later in the debate.)

Peter Van Winkle

The discussion was lengthy. The delegate from Kanawha argued that the name had already been decided upon, and that this body had no right to change it. Another attorney rebutted this, saying that his constituents who had voted for the creation of a new state *had* objected to the name *Kanawha* and had requested that he attempt, in this convention, to have it changed. The arguments were full of protestations of loyalty to the union and the hope of finding a name that would convey that sentiment. Eventually, the names "Western Virginia" and "New Virginia" were proposed, prompting a passionate response from Daniel Lamb of Wheeling:

"Sir, I have been an inhabitant of western Virginia for thirty odd years. During that time what have we received here but oppression, and outrage I may say, from the State of Virginia... Are we still to retain the name? Are we to change everything in Virginia but the name? Shall we make a change in everything—in all the essentials—and yet stick upon this slight matter? Shall we proclaim in the very act which this Convention is now about to adopt that we feel grateful for the favor of the State of Virginia as heretofore bestowed upon us? No, gentlemen, no! I want to cut loose from these recollections. I want to have the new State, not merely in substance, but even in name."

The discussion lightened up, however, when a delegate admitted that one of the objections he had to "Kanawha" was its difficult spelling, and another suggested that "Loyal Virginia" might be an appropriate compromise. Cutting to the heart of the matter, Peter Van Winkle noted,

"If you make an agreement with eastern Virginia that after the division takes place, one is to be called East and the other West, or one is to be called Old Virginia and the other New, there might be less impropriety in it; for then it would indicate a division of territory, but, sir, under any circumstances they are to retain the name. They are to be Virginia and we are to be Little Virginia or New Virginia, or West Virginia, or some other soubriquet which is to degrade us in comparison with them.

"West Virginia" was eventually proposed by Chapman Stuart, a 41-year-old attorney from Doddridge County, saying "...It is familiar all over this broad land of our country—West Virginia. Something attaches to the name that ennobles us in the eyes of the country."

There were other names proposed, and the debate finally came to a vote. The matter of a name was decided with the following vote count:

"Augusta" - 1
"Alleghany" - 2
"Western Virginia" - 2
"Kanawha" - 9
"West Virginia" - 30

West Virginia

The U.S. Constitution states that any portion of a state wishing to secede from its "parent" state must receive permission from that parent. This was obviously not going to happen, as the secession was occuring during the Civil War, but the problem was solved rather easily. Because Lincoln had recognized the Restored Government of Virginia, formed by western Virginians, as the state's legitimate one, the government of eastern Virginia technically had no say in the matter. The Restored Government essentially granted itself permission to secede, and the matter was settled.

In early July of 1862, the U.S. Senate debated the admission of West Virginia to the Union. They focused mainly on matters of slavery and did not discuss the name, though some of the senators clearly struggled with using its new moniker, calling it instead"Western Virginia" or "Northwestern Virginia" at times. The vote to admit West Virginia was 23 to 17, and so it became the 35th state in the Union—provided, of course, that the Union was ultimately preserved.

The Enabling Act was signed by President Abraham Lincoln on New Year's Eve, December 31, 1862, but that was not the final step in the process. The Enabling Act provided for statehood on the condition that the new state's constitution contain language that would eventually abolish slavery. The West Virginia legislature went back to work and added this provision. Finally, Lincoln read a proclamation on April 20, 1863, that would confer statehood in sixty days time. Thus, the official date of statehood for West Virginia is June 20, 1863.

1.   Williams, John Alexander, <u>West Virginia: A Bicentennial History</u>, (New York, 1976), p. 3

2.   West Virginia Archives and History, "'What's in a name?' The naming of West Virginia," *A State of Convenience: The Creation of West Virginia*, an On-Line Exhibit, http://www.wvculture.org/history/statehood/statename.html, last accessed 11/5/09.

Chapter 49: Wisconsin

"Cheese!!!, Gromit! CHEEEESE!!!"

—Wallace and Gromit

"The last ingredient in the recipe is da Vinci's model of a helicopter. On display for three days only in the Louvre in Paris. As opposed to the Louvre in Wisconsin?"

—Hudson Hawk

The Cheese State

Wisconsin means cheese...and cows, which produce milk to make cheese...and Green Bay Packers, whose fans wear foam cheese on their heads. Cheesecake, cheese balls, Cheetohs...if Cheese Whiz was a dairy product it, would be made in Wisconsin. Wisconsin is home to the Wisconsin Specialty Cheese Institute. The University of Wisconsin at Madison offers a short course in Cheese Technology. Three of the state's nicknames refer to its dairy industry: the Dairy State, America's Dairyland, and, of course, the Cheese State. Wisconsin is in that Garrison Keilor part of the country that makes us think of Norwegian Lutherans and bachelor farmers. The uninformed perception is that some time in Wisconsin's early history, the land was so conducive to dairy farming that all of the dairy farming immigrants to the U.S. moved there to engage in the traditional family occupation.

Well, almost. Actually, the early immigrants to Wisconsin were wheat farmers. In the early 1800's, Wisconsin produced a large

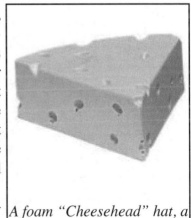

A foam "Cheesehead" hat, a common sight at Green Bay Packers football games

percentage of the nation's wheat, until diseases, mineral depletion, and falling wheat prices forced the Wisconsin farmers to diversify.

With the land spent from years of over-planting wheat, the farmers found that it made good grazing land for dairy cows. The dairy industry grew quickly but still asserted only regional dominance. Around the mid 1860's, the dairy farmers in Wisconsin began to organize into professional associations.[1] It was this consolidation of marketing and technological expertise that allowed Wisconsin to dominate the cheese and butter markets.

Beer is the other commodity strongly associated with Wisconsin—though primarily only with the city of Milwaukee—and the industry that produces it developed in a similar way to that of cheese. Beer makers in Milwaukee were forced, because of the relatively small population in that region, to look to outside markets to sell their beer.[2] The organization of marketing strategies and technology efforts—as opposed to any natural regional advantage—was what made Milwaukee, Wisconsin the "Beer Capital of the World."

The River

As with many states, Wisconsin takes its name from the river that winds through its heartland. The earliest mention of the name "Wisconsin" is traced to 1672 and to two French adventurers, Joliet and Marquet. Joliet wrote of a river he called "Miskonsing" that he followed with a group of natives, who had told him of a much greater river they called the "Missisipi." Other French explorers and traders exploited the region for

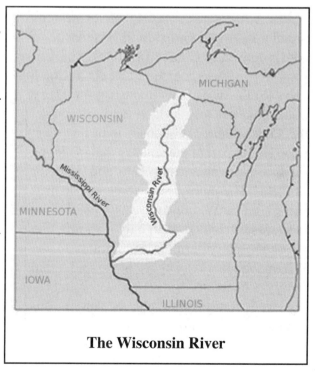

The Wisconsin River

its furs, labeling the river on maps with variations on the same name Jolliet had used. Eventually the initial "M-" was replaced with "Ou-" (the closest thing the French language has to a "W"), which was said to more closely mimic the Indian name. The French traded for furs with natives along the "Ouisconsin" and used the river as a route to the Mississippi, but its banks were not permanently settled by the French.

This map shows the proposed region of "Charlotiana" in 1763

The name "Wisconsin" was barely known to the British who, by virtue of their victory in the French and Indian War in 1763, now claimed the region as their own. The banks of the river were considered part of "Illinois Country," which some British subjects were anxious to colonize.

In1763 a pamphlet was circulated in Edinburgh, Scotland, that laid out a new colony called "Charlotiana,"[3] after Queen Charlotte, the young bride of King George III. Charlotiana would have encompassed what are now the states of Illinois, Wisconsin, and Michigan. But instead of granting the colony, King George forbade it, as well as any other new colonies west of the Alleghanies, until a policy of negotiating with the Indians could be developed.

In 1766 a surveyor and war veteran named Jonathan Carver set out to explore Wisconsin for England. Carver, guided by natives, canoed down what

Judge James Doty

he called the "Ouisconsin" River as it wound its way around the modest Baraboo Range. Shortly after Carver's explorations, the name "Wisconsin" began appearing on maps with its modern spelling, as well as several variations.

As for the word's meaning, there are books and web sites that assert a certain definition of "Wisconsin" with great confidence. The most authoritative of these sources claim one of two different meanings for the word: 1) that it is a Chippewa word for "grassy place" or 2) that it is an Indian (of unspecified linguistic stock) word for "a gathering of waters," referring to the fact that the river's source contains many tributaries. The second of these definitions may stem from the fact that the Winnebago Indians called the same river "Neekoonts-Sara," meaning "gathering of waters" or "gathering river."[4] Most historians agree, however, that the origin of the word "Wisconsin" is lost, and that it continually defies attempts to derive its true meaning.

Last, but not Least

After the American Revolution, the land which now constitutes Wisconsin was part of the Northwest Territory, or "Old Northwest," which the new United States of America now claimed. The Northwest Ordinance of 1787 provided for this region—the land west of the Alleghany Mountains, north of the Ohio River, and east of the Mississippi River—to be divided into no less than three, no more than five, new territories, and eventually states. Wisconsin would be the fifth, and last, of these, and would not be named a territory until well after the Louisiana Purchase in 1803. So besides the Northwest Territory, the land we call Wisconsin was also eventually part of Indiana, Illinois, and Michigan Territories.

Wisconsin was finally divided from Michigan Territory in 1836, largely through the efforts of a federal judge named James Doty. Doty was said to have favored the name "Chippewau," and others suggested the name "Huron," but "Wisconsin," the name of the region's dominant river, became the favorite. Though Doty fought hard to maintain what he believed was the most authentic spelling of the word (i.e., closest to the native pronunciation) by changing the "c" to a "k," and though "Wiskonsan" and "Wiskonsin" appeared in some documents, "Wisconsin" was the final form approved in the Organic Act for the territory on April 20, 1836.

Borders

The Northwest Ordinance recommended borders for the states that would be created, but by the time it was Wisconsin's turn, the United States was a substantially larger country, and Manifest Destiny was just beginning to take hold. The organization of territories and states was no longer an experiment, but an established process, and it was clear that states would be formed out of more than just the "Old Northwest," but also out of lands west of the Mississippi River, and possibly beyond even the Rocky Mountains.

Wisconsin's first iteration as a territory began when Michigan achieved statehood. Now officially "Wisconsin Territory," it included what is now Minnesota and much of the Dakotas. What it did not include was Chicago, which had been tacked on to Illinois at the last minute of its organic process by moving the "recommended" northern border north about 60 miles. (See Illinois.) James Doty had been troubled by the maneuver, but as one history book puts it,

> "Generations of pious Badgers have since congratulated themselves that the congressional interference placed turbulent Chicago in Illinois."[5]

Also not attached to Wisconsin was that section of land to the north and east of the Menominee River extending all the way to Lake Superior, the section that had been included in the state of Michigan when it was created. We call it, of course, the Upper Peninsula, and why it is part of Michigan, and not Wisconsin, is not immediately clear by looking at a map. In fact, it's not clear at all unless one happens to live there; and sometimes not even then. The U.P. is discussed at greater length in the section on Michigan, but generally because Michigan and Illinois were created first, and because of Wisconsin's small population, its edges were whittled away by other states and territories with more political power.

Not insisting on Chicago or the U.P. had one fortunate effect on Wisconsin. The legislation creating the new territory

> "sailed through Congress smoothly...accompanied by the usual hyperbole about the hazards of lawlessness and Indian depredations from which this new status would somehow shield the intrepid pioneers."[6]

485

Before statehood, Wisconsin's border with Minnesota had also to be decided. The Northwest Ordinance, which still guided the organization of the region, stated that no more than five states were to be created out of the Old Northwest. But when it came time to draw the western border of Wisconsin, there were strong arguments for placing it at the St. Croix River instead of the Mississippi, as had been specified in the Ordinance. Opponents argued the illegality of this border, asserting that Minnesota constituted a sixth

The Northwest Ordinance stipulated that the Northwest Territory be divided into no less than three, no more than five new states.

state within the Northwest Territory, but the objections were relatively weak and short lived, and the desire for statehood stronger than the desire for the entire St. Croix valley.

Wisconsin statehood finally came on May 29, 1848 with the signature of President James K. Polk. It was the thirtieth state in the union, and its birth marked the end of the Old Northwest. From then on, the Northwest Ordinance was a historical guideline—a precedent, but no longer a law. Wisconsin completed the puzzle of the eastern United States. Except for West Virginia, Wisconsin was the last state to be created east of the Mississippi River, and from 1848 on, the state-making efforts of the nation turned to the far West.

1.   Gibbens, Jeff, et al, "A Brief History of…Economics in Wisconsin," http://www.scils.rutgers.edu/~dalbello/FLVA/background/economics. html, created 5/17/2000, accessed 7/30/2009

2.   "Why Milwaukee?" BeerHistory.com, http://www.beerhistory.com/ library/holdings/milwaukee.shtml, accessed 7/31/2009

3.   Alden, George Henry, "New Governments West of the Alleghenies Before 1780," *Bulletin of the University of Wisconsin*, Historical Series Vol 2, No. 1, p. 12.

4.   "Traditions and Recollections of Prairie Du Chen," *Collections of the State Historical Society of Wisconsin*, vol. IX, p.301.

5.   Nesbit, Robert C., Revised and updated by William F. Thompson, Wisconsin: A History, (Madison, 1989), p. 122.

6.   Nesbit, p. 123.

Chapter 50: Wyoming

Out on the trail night birds are callin
Singin their wild melody
Down in the canyon cottonwood whispers
A Song of Wyoming for me

> — "Song of Wyoming"
> *John Denver*

Clay Carroll: Not many men would have the guts to close down a historical monument.

John O'Hanlan: What historical monument is that, Mr. Carroll?

Clay Carroll: The Cheyenne Social Club - that's the historical monument!

John O'Hanlan: The Cheyenne Social Club is a...

Clay Carroll: It was there when there wasn't a railroad for 300 miles. It withstood prairie fires and Indian attacks. And the first ounce, O'Hanlan, the first ounce of gold discovered in this territory was spent wisely and well at the Cheyenne Social Club. And you? You come up here from Texas and close it down!

> — "The Cheyenne Social Club" *1970*

People-less

Wyoming of the twenty-first century has a reputation as a playground for the rich and famous. Movie stars and multimillionaires outdo each other trying to acquire the most land closest to Jackson Hole (named for David Jackson, a fur-trapper in the 1820's). One reason for this is, no doubt, Wyoming's allure as a state with wide, open spaces and big, blue skies, which is to say people like to go to Wyoming because Wyoming doesn't have a

Cheyenne Frontier Days in 1922
Photographer: Ralph Doubleday

lot of people. As a matter of fact, Wyoming has never had a large population. Even before Europeans, the region supported relatively few Indians, largely because buffalo did not thrive as well in Wyoming as they did to the south and east. Wyoming, according to the most recent U.S. Census, has the smallest population of any state in the union, smaller even than Rhode Island or Alaska, and since celebrities have begun buying up "ranches" by the thousands of acres, it is likely to remain that way.

Of course, even more than rich celebrities, Wyoming makes us think of Cowboys and the old west. But unlike the Texas cowboy image—rough, loud, perhaps more prone to violence—Wyoming's cowboy is solemn, probably alone (given the state's dearth of...well, people), and serene. Wyoming perpetuates the old-west image with its Cheyenne Frontier Days celebration, one of the most famous rodeos in the world. Rodeos began as informal competitions among cowboys as a way to show off their ranching skills. Over the years, rodeos developed into popular community entertainment events that highlight ranching culture and industry, and there is no better place for this identity to thrive than Wyoming.

Wyoming has another claim to fame, at least for those people who know where it is. Yellowstone National Park, the nation's—indeed the world's—first and oldest national park, occupies the northwest corner of the state, carving out yet another 3,472 square miles of Wyoming where people generally don't live. Every year the Park experiences around three million visitors hoping to time Old Faithful just right or to possibly catch a glimpse of a grizzly bear or wolf in their natural habitat. So, to put it into perspective, this single tourist attraction draws six times more people to the state every year than the number of people who actually live there.

Pennsylvania

The story of Wyoming's name begins in Pennsylvania, specifically in a small valley of the Susquehanna River basin near Wilkes-Barre. The Algonquin-speaking Delaware Indians called the place something like *mscheweamiing* which meant "large prairie place" or "big flats." The missionaries of the 1700's had difficulty with the name (go figure) and shortened it to "Wayomik."

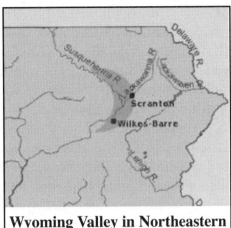

Wyoming Valley in Northeastern Pennsylvania

In 1754 Connecticut asserted its claim to the valley by virtue of their Royal charter, which described the colony's western border as the "South Sea," meaning the Pacific Ocean. Boldly ignoring the conflicting claims of New York and Pennsylvania, the Susquehanna and Delaware Company of Connecticut purchased the valley, which they called "Waioming" or "Wyoming," from the Iroquois Indians and made plans to settle it. Eight years later, they began to do so, but conflicts with Indians made the process troublesome and time consuming. By the mid 1770's the Wyoming Valley had several villages of "Connecticut Yankees" protected by a few small forts.

Thomas Campbell

The American Revolution then saw an event that would thrust the name "Wyoming" into the national consciousness. With most of the men off fighting the war, one of the forts—called Forty Fort—was attacked on July 3, 1778, by a group of about 400 British soldiers and Loyalists and 700 Seneca and Cayuga Indians. Having won the battle, the attackers engaged in what has gone down in history as the "Wyoming

Massacre" in which hundreds of settlers were brutally executed. As horrible as the massacre was, it became more graphic with each retelling, as the story radiated in all directions and frightened other settlers out of Pennsylvania and the Ohio Valley. In 1809, a Scottish poet named Thomas Campbell memorialized the massacre with his poem "Gertrude of Wyoming," which became quite popular.

A monument to honor those who perished in the massacre was completed in 1830. About that time, thanks largely to the popularity of Campbell's poem, Wyoming became a popular name for new cities and counties. Pennsylvania, New York, and Virginia (in what later became West Virginia) all created counties using the name, and at least five states and one Canadian province used the name for newly incorporated cities. But as "Wyoming" became more and more popular, the meaning of the word, and indeed the memory of the massacre, began to fade.

The Two Ashleys

The region that would become Wyoming began to be explored shortly after the Lewis and Clark venture of 1803-06. Fur trappers and traders were among the most prominent explorers of the area, and one of the most famous of these was General William H. Ashley. Between 1822 and 1826, Ashley operated a fur trading company with his partner Andrew Henry and hired such Mountain Men as Jedediah Smith and David Jackson to trap furs in the northern Rocky Mountains and to engage the natives of this region for purposes of trade. Ashley and Smith kept journals of their explorations, which became the basis for much geographical knowledge of the region during the 1800's. Of course, when Ashley was exploring, there were very few place names to which he could refer. In his narrative, he refers to many of the rivers by name, but in other places struggles to find a point of reference for the area he is describing:

> Our situation here was distant six or eight miles north of a conspicuous peak of the mountains, which I imagined to be that point described by Major Long as being the highest peak and lying in latitude 40 N., longitude 29 W.[1]

James M. Ashley

From 1831 to 1837, William Ashley served as a Congressman from Missouri (which at that time included modern Wyoming), using his extensive knowledge of the western natives in his work on the Committee on Indian Affairs. It is unclear if General Ashley has any connection to the naming of Wyoming, but he is integral to Wyoming's early history, and poses a fascinating mystery as to the origin of the state's name because of...well, his name.

You see, his last name is the same as that of another Congressman, James M. Ashley, who was born in Pennsylvania around the time that William Ashley was traipsing through the Wyoming Rocky Mountains. It is not clear if the two men were related, though chances are there was at least a distant familial connection. James Ashley's father John was born in Virginia a few miles from where William Ashley was born, and only two years later.

James M. Ashley was known as the Great Impeacher for having initiated impeachment proceedings against Andrew Johnson[*]. Ashley, a staunch abolitionist, opposed Johnson on many civil rights issues and had become convinced that Johnson was involved in the assassination of Abraham Lincoln. Johnson was impeached, but not convicted, and Ashley's role in the proceedings doomed him to the loss of his congressional seat in the elections of 1868.

The Johnson impeachment virtually consumes James Ashley's biography, but he did do other things while he was in Congress. In particular,

---

* *There were actually two attempts to impeach Andrew Johnson. The first failed quickly in 1867, but the second succeeded. Johnson was accused of violating the* Tenure of Office Act *by having fired his own Secretary of War, William H. Stanton. Though the House of Representatives voted to impeach, the Senate found the President "not guilty," and Johnson remained in office. The* Tenure of Office Act *would, in 1926, be declared unconstitutional by the Supreme Court.*

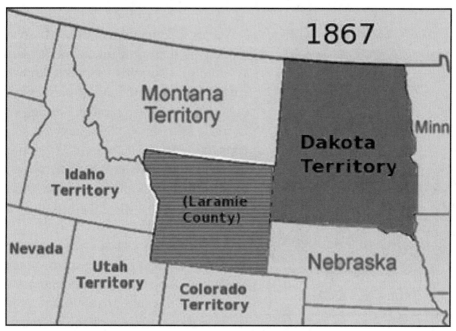

he proposed the new Territory of Wyoming in 1865. The Congressional Record entry for this proposal is the earliest mention of the name *Wyoming* being used to describe the region the state now occupies.

Ashley's motives in proposing the creation of Wyoming were suspect. He was intent on mitigating the power of Brigham Young, whose lofty position in Utah was the source of much angst for many congressmen. One means of suppressing the Mormons was to decrease the size of their territory, and Ashley's proposed new territory took a sizeable chunk out of Brigham Young's domain. This effort to organize Wyoming Territory did not succeed, but it did propose the name that would ultimately be used.

The name Wyoming was a natural choice for a newly proposed territory. It was certainly becoming popular—a township in Ashley's home state of Ohio had just adopted the name when it incorporated in 1861—and it originated in the state where Ashley himself was born...Pennsylvania. In the 1860's it was common for new territories to have aboriginal names— Dakota, Minnesota, Kansas, Nebraska. And given that Ashley had never visited the region for which he was proposing territory status, and that he knew very little about it, almost any Indian name would do. *Wyoming* was popular. It was being applied to towns and counties all over the east...why not this new *western* territory?

James or William?

By 1867 the population of Wyoming was growing relatively quickly, thanks in large part to the construction of the Union Pacific railroad that passed through a southern strip of the state. Officially the entire region was Laramie County in western Dakota Territory, but unofficially the name Wyoming was beginning to take hold, thanks primarily to the efforts of a newspaper publisher named Legh R. Freeman (more on him later).

In 1868 the new territory of Wyoming was once again proposed in Congress, this time for more pragmatic than political reasons. Several thousand people now lived in the region, mostly in Laramie and Cheyenne, and Dakota Territory was too large to govern them. They wanted separation, and Dakota, who had political problems of her own, wanted to be rid of them.

In June of 1868 the senate debated several amendments to the bill creating Wyoming Territory, one of which would change the name to "Lincoln." During the debate, which lasted for some time, several other names were proposed as well including Cheyenne, Shoshoni, Arapaho, Sioux, and Pawnee—all names of Indian tribes from in or near the region—as well as Platte, Big Horn, Yellowstone, and Sweetwater—names of regional rivers.

The debate became heated in certain places, but one exchange stands out:

Mr. NYE: In my opinion, if the name is to be changed at all, from what the committee proposed, it had better be Wyoming.

Mr. SUMNER: I ask the chairman if the name of Wyoming is not found in the Territory?

Mr. YATES: No, sir; it belongs to Pennsylvania.

Mr. SUMNER: I know, originally; but then what suggested this name for this Territory?

Mr. DOOLITTLE: It was suggested by General Ashley.

Mr. SUMNER: But what suggested it to General Ashley?

Mr. DOOLITTLE: Because it is a beautiful name.

Mr. Sumner doesn't say Mister Ashley or Congressman Ashley. He says *General* Ashley. Now, perhaps he misspoke, or perhaps he was simply mistaken. General William Ashley, who had been dead for decades by the time of this debate, was certainly famous for his connection to the region, but there is no record of him referring to any part of it as Wyoming. James M. Ashley, who certainly did use the name, and used it first as far as anyone can tell, was never a General, nor did he have any military background whatsoever. So to which Ashley was Mr. Sumner referring? It's a question we are unlikely to ever know the answer to.

At any rate, by the end of the debate, *Wyoming*, a name that originated in Pennsylvania, and gained fame because of a horrible massacre, won the day. Among the reasons the senators gave for settling upon Wyoming were that it was easy to spell (unlike *mscheweamiing*) and, of course, that it was euphonious.

Legh Richmond Freeman

Legh R. Freeman, the aforementioned newspaper publisher, claimed it was he who proposed the name Wyoming for the new territory, but then he claimed a lot of things. Freeman was a colorful (to put it mildly) man who distributed a newspaper he called the "Frontier Index" in 1867 and 1868. Known historically as "Hell on Wheels," the *Frontier Index* was one of a handful of newspapers of the era that followed a railroad as it was being built and distributed news to the small towns and villages that cropped up along the tracks.

Using a printing press that he "found" abandoned by a group of Mormons making their way across Nebras-

Legh R. Freeman

ka to Utah, Freeman and his brother published the "Frontier Index" along the Union Pacific line from Julesburg, Colorado, in July of 1867 to Bear River, Wyoming, in November of 1868. His operation ended there, tantalizingly close to Promontory, Utah, where the railroad would connect with the Central Pacific line to create the first cross-country railroad. Freeman claimed that a mob, angered by his accusations of fraud on the part of railroad officials, destroyed his printing press and burned his office.

Freeman would go on to publish newspapers in Utah and Montana and eventually moved to Washington. While he was instrumental in popularizing the name Wyoming, he rarely missed an opportunity to exaggerate his role in doing so and in almost every other of his dubious accomplishments. In a bid for U.S. Senator in 1909, he wrote the following for the *Yakima Morning Herald*:

> I have taken an active part in the creation of the states of Nebraska, Utah, Colorado, Wyoming, Idaho, Montana, and Washington...as I blazed a trail for the vanguard of civilization across the western two-thirds of America and I named Wyoming.[2]

Wyoming historian Dr. C. G. Coutant details Freeman's claim: "Freeman...makes the claim that he, in the spring of 1866, while en route from Fort Kearney, Nebraska, to Fort Laramie to attend a Peace Conference, wrote a letter for publication to his paper and dated this correspondence 'Third Crossing of Lodge Pole Creek, Wyoming Territory.' This, he says, was the first time the name was applied to the 'southwestern half of Dakota.'"[3]

Given that, by his own account, Freeman "named" Wyoming the year after James M. Ashley proposed the territory by that name in Congress, Freeman's boast rings hollow. Colorful, but hollow.

Equality

The territory of Wyoming was at last created despite objections from a surprising source. James M. Ashley had, by 1868, visited the region and was now opposed to the organization of the territory on the grounds that "... there was not fertility enough in the soil to subsist a population sufficient for a single congressional district."[4]* Nevertheless, on July 25, 1868, the territory of Wyoming was formed, one of two parallelograms drawn on the west—four straight lines, four right angles, and no natural borders. These same unnatural boundaries would be taken to statehood, when President Benjamin Harrison signed Wyoming into existence as the 42nd state in the Union on July 10, 1890.

However small, the population of Wyoming proved themselves forward-thinking when their first territorial legislature in 1869 gave women the right to vote. This right was never repealed and is a source of great pride (as well it *should* be) for Wyoming, earning the state its nickname, the Equality State.

---

* *As it turns out, a "single congressional district" is precisely what Wyoming would constitute. Having the smallest population of any state in the Union, Wyoming has only one Representative in the U.S. House of Representatives.*

1.   Dale, Harrison Clifford, <u>The Explorations of William H. Ashley and Jedediah Smith, 1822-1829</u> (Lincoln, 1991), p. 125.

2.   Heuterman, Thomas H., <u>Movable Type: Biography of Legh R. Freeman</u>, (Ames, 1979), p.137.

3.   Coutant, Dr. C. G., <u>History of Wyoming and (The Far West)</u>, (New York, 1966), p. 622.

4.   Larson, T. A., <u>History of Wyoming</u> (Lincoln, 1978), p. 67

BOOKS OF INTEREST

The history of every state in the U.S. has been written about at length. Many of these sources I cite in the endnotes of individual chapters, and many others I used in my research. But there have been a few books that guided me with respect to *all* of the preceding chapters. If you are interested in U.S. place names and their derivations, these books are fascinating, if not always factual—sometimes they even contradict each other. Still, they were a valuable resource:

Stewart, George R., <u>Names on the Land</u>, (New York, Stratford Press, Inc. [This is a Random House Wartime Book], 1945) (*Author's Note—This timeless book by the "father" of U.S. place-name study has been reprinted and updated several times, and is currently back in print by the New York Times Review of Books, 2008*)

Harrington, John P., <u>Our State Names</u>, From the *Smithsonian Institution Annual Report for 1954*, pp. 373-388. (Smithsonian Institution: 1955)

Shearer, Benjamin F. and Barbara S. Shearer, <u>State Names, Seals, Flags, and Symbols: A Historical Guide</u>, Revised and Expanded, (Westport, Connecticut: Greenwood Press, 1994) (*Author's note—this book appears to be the primary source for the "Netstate" website, another, more updated, source of information on U.S. states.*)

Gannett, Henry, <u>The Origin of Certain Place Names in The United States</u>, (Detroit: Gale Research Company, Book Tower, 1971)

Shankle, George Earlie, Ph.D., <u>State Names, Flags, Seals, Songs, Birds, Flowers, and Other Symbols</u>, Revised Edition, (Westport, Connecticut: Greenwood Press, 1970)

Arnold, Pauline and Percival White, <u>How We Named Our States</u> (Eau Claire, Wisconsin: Criterion Books, Inc. and E.M. Hale and Company, 1969) (*Author's note—This book was written for younger readers, perhaps 4th or 5th graders. I found it in the children's section of the library at the Univesity of Colorado.*)

Acknowledgements

TESS THOMAS is a dear friend, an excellent writer, and the person who finally got me off my duff to finish this book. She wrote some sections, and edited the roughest draft. I thank her for all her help.

CHRISTI WEAVER, a meticulous editor, kept me from publishing embarrassing errors, and taught me all I had forgotten about the use of commas. She did all this while being one of my very best friends, and I thank her, and wish her peace.

SUE CHURCHES is an artist extrordinaire, and another very dear friend. She not only made the book cover beautiful and professional, but she taught me about publishing, and helped coax me through the process.

My neighbor, **MELISSA JOHNSON**, provided critical advice on marketing and distribution. A lovely lady and brilliant attorney, I am so happy to call her my friend.

CHRIS GARBE, whose official position at AUTOMATED GRAPHICS SYSTEMS, I still don't know. He spent so much time with me, teaching me about printing and publishing, it was an easy choice to decide to work with him to get this book completed. Thanks, Chris.

My greatest thanks, however, must go to my husband, **JIM GUYTON**, and my children, **ANDY** and **LEEJAY**. They put up with me, helped me, inspired me, and nudged me toward the eventual finish line. I love you all more than anything in the world, and I thank you for all of your support.

Index

Symbols

49th parallel 264
1763 Treaty of Paris. *See* Paris Treaty of 1763
1783 Treaty of Paris. *See* Paris Treaty of 1783
1866 Civil Rights Act 276. *See also* Civil Rights Movement

A

A'a'tam a'kimult 65
Abolitionism 475
abolitionist 369
Adams, John Quincy 431
Adams-Onis Treaty 69–70, 190
African-Americans 108
AIDS 54
Ais Indians 102
Alabama Country 10, 12
Alabama Department of History and Archives 14
Alabama Indians 8, 11
Alabama music group 5
Alabama River 10
Alabama State 5–16
Alabama Territory 251
Alamo 423
Alarcón, Hernando de 66
Alaska 17–30, 59, 385, 464, 490–500
Alaska Boundary Tribunal 25
"Alaskan Syndicate" 26
Alaska Railroad 27
Alaska Territory 27
Albany, New York 229
Aleutian Islands 22
Aleutian Natives 20
Pope Alexander VI 100
Alfred the Great 149, 291
"Algonquin" 236
"Alibamo" 7
"Alibamu" 7
Alice in Chains 464
Alice's Restaurant 213
Alleghanies. *See* Alleghany Mountains

"Alleghany" 478
Alleghany Mountains 140, 150, 373, 473, 483
Allen, Ethan 448–451
Allen, Samuel 297
Allouez, Father 139, 244, 246
Alta California 59
Alvarado, Juan Bautista 59
Amadas, Philip 459
Amadis of Gaul 56–57
America (naming of) 101–102
American Antiquarian Society 55
American Bison 352
American Fork River 60
American Fur Company 367
American Name Society 1
American Revolution 12, 104, 113, 114, 142, 174, 201, 235, 249, 401, 416, 450, 464, 484, 491–492
America's Dairyland 481
Amish 374–375
Andre, Father Louis 158
Andros, Edmund 220, 296
Anglo-Saxon Chronicle 291
Antoinette, Marie 187
Anza, Juan Bautista de 34
Apache Indians 31, 39
Apalachee Indians 102
Apalachicola River 104
Apollo 186
Appalachian Mountains 114, 176–177, 188, 249, 464
Appalachian Trail 290
Appalachicola River 248
Apples 463
Aragon 363
Arapaho Indians 135, 495
Arctic Circle 17
Arctic National Wildlife Refuge 17, 18
Area 51 280
Argall, Samuel 89–90
"Argenta" 444
Arizona 31–42, 466
Arizona City 38
Arizonian newspaper 39
Arizunea 38
Arkansas 43–52, 255, 353
Arkansas Gazette 50
Arkansas Post 48–49
Arkansas River 44, 45, 245, 272
Arkansas State General Assembly 51
Arkansas Traveler 43
Arlington, Virginia 456

Armenia 108
Arthur, Gabriel 415
Ashley, General William 492–493, 493, 496
Ashley, James M. 133, 266–268, 468, 493–495, 496, 497
Ashley, William 441
Astor, John Jacob 229, 367
Atchison, David Rice 166–168
Atlanta Braves 108
Atlanta, Georgia 108
Atlantic City 279
Atlantic Monthly 54–55
Atlantis 55–56
Augusta County 140, 178, 478
Augusta, Princess 141, 177
Austen, Jane 290
Austin, Moses 430–431
Austin, Stehen F. 430
Austin, Texas 425
Austria 247
Avey, R. Gerald 175
Aviles, Pedro Menendez de 101
"A Walk in the Woods" 290
Ayllón, Lucas Vázquez de 101
Azerbaijan 108
Azilia, Margravate of 110
Aztec Indians 32

B

B-52's 127
bachelor farmers 481
Badgers 485
Badlands 404
Baja peninsula 57, 59, 66
Baked Alaska 17
Baker, Bill 415
Balboa, Vasco Nuñez de 99
Ballinger, Richard A. 26
Ball State Cardinals 147
Baltimore, Lord 93, 381
Bancroft, Hubert Howe 32
Bangor Daily News 195
Bangor, Maine 193
Bannack 266
Baptist churches 242
Baraboo Range 484
Barbados 398–400
Barlowe, Arthur 459
Barnes, Will C. 34–35
Barry, Dave 98
Basilicon Doron 376
Basque 34–35
Baton Rouge 186

The Battle of the Little Bighorn 269
Battle of Horseshoe Bend 12
Battle of San Jacinto 431
Baylor, John R. 40
Bay of La Paz 58
Bayonet Constitution 122
Bayou 183
Bay State 214
Beaglehole, J.C. 22
Bear Flag Revolt 60
Bear River 497
Beaverton, Oregon 362
Becerra, Diego de 57
Bee Gees 213
beehive 436
Beer Capital of the World 482
Bend, Oregon 362
Bennington Nine 449–450
Benning Wentworth 448–449
Benton, Thomas Hart 441
Bering Strait 20
Bering, Vitus 18, 18–19, 26
Berkeley, William 397
Berkley 54
Bermuda 87–88
Bermudez, Juan 88
Bernhisel, Dr. John M. 441
Berry, Chuck 183
Beveridge, Albert 41
Big Horn 495
Big Thicket 15
Biloxi 103, 186
Bimini 99
Bismarck 406, 407
Bitterroot Mountains 128–130
Black-Hawk Purchase 156
Black Hills 404, 405
Black Sea 108
Blanchard, Jack 413
Blanchett, Cate 458
Bleeding Kansas 167
Bligh, William 119
Block, Adriaen 77
"Bloody Mary" 375
"Bloody Sunday" 7
Blue Ridge Mountains 473
Blunt, Matt 261
Board of Admiralty 118
Board of Trade, British 249
Boleyn, Anne 458
bonanza farmers 406
Bonaparte, Napoleon 68, 187–189
Bonnie-Blue Flag 189
Bonnie Prince Charlie 112–113

The Book that Gave Iowa its Name 157
Book of Mormon 435, 436
"bootheel" 255
bootlegging 44
Boston 297
Botetourt County 178
Boulanger, Joseph Ignatius Le 257
Boulder Canyon Project 65
Boulder Dam 65
Bourbon County, Kentucky 173
Bourgmont, Ètienne de Veniard, sieur de 274
Bowling for Soup 271
Brademaen 199
Bray, Dr. Thomas 111
Breaking Away 148
British Columbia 365
Browne, Jackson 53
Brown, John 167
Brown, Joseph C. 160
Brown, Joseph Renshaw 236
Brownsville, Texas 425
Bryant, William Cullen 368
Bryson, Bill 290
"Buade ou Frontenac" 245
Bubonic Plague 217
Buchanan, James 168, 237, 283, 370
Buckingham, Duke of 198
Bugs Bunny 423
Buren, Martin Van 160
Burlington 380
Burr, Aaron 54–55, 180
Bush, George W. 98, 425
Bush, Jeb 98
Byram, Scott 364–365

C

Cabrillo, Juan Rodriquez 58, 284
Caddoan language 425
Cage, Nicolas 32, 279
Fort Cahokia 142
Cahokia Indians 139
Cajun 183
Califerne 56
Califia, Queen 56
California 36, 53–62, 67, 284, 466
Californians Magazine 58
Calusa Indians 102
Cambridge 78
Campbell, Thomas 492–493
Canada 26, 245, 264

Cape Ann 217, 218
Cape Canaveral 98
Cape Cod 89
Cape Fear 400
Cape feare. *See* Cape Fear
Cape Verde Islands 101
Capone, Al 137
Caribbean Sea 398
Carolana 401–402
Carolina proprietors 110
Carson City 282
Carson County 281
Carson, Johnny 54
Carson Valley 282, 283
Carter, Clarence Edwin 13
Carver, Jonathan 238, 365–366, 368, 483
Cascade Mountains 362–363
casinos 279
Caspian Sea 108
Cass, General George 406
Castell, Robert 111
Catholicism 213–214, 375
Catton, Bruce 226–227
Caucasus Mountains 108
Cayuga Indians 491–492
"Centennial State" 72
Central Pacific 497
central plains 465
cerargyrite 33
Champlain, Samuel de 195, 451
La Chanson de Roland 56
Charles I, King. *See* King Charles I
Charles, Ray 107
Charles River 217, 220
Charless, Joseph 259
Charleston 110, 398, 399–401
Charleston Harbor 396
Charles Town. *See* Charleston
Charlotiana 141, 483
Charlotte, Queen 150
Chattahoochee River 104, 250
"The Cheese State" 481
Cheese Whiz 481
Cheetohs 481
Cheney, Dick 473
Cherokee Indians 176, 353–355, 414–415
Cherokee language 415
Cherry Creek 70–71
Chesapeake Bay 89
Chewelah 469
The Cheyenne Social Club 489–500

Cheyenne Frontier Days 490–500
Cheyenne, Wyoming 495–496
Chicago 137–138, 143, 485
Chickasaw Indians 48, 181,
    353–355
Chicken War 428–429
Chicora 101
Chief Joseph. *See* Joseph, Chief
Childs, Marquis 7
"Chippewa" 236
Chippewa Indians 159, 241, 244,
    246
"Chippewau" 484
"Chippewau". *See also* Chip-
    pewa Indians
Chiwere 158
chloride of silver. *See* cerargyrite
Choctaw Indians 353–355, 357
Choctaw language 14
"Choctaw Nation of Red People"
    354
Chota 415
Churchill Downs 174
Church of England 375–376
Cibola. *See* Seven Cities of
    Cibola
Cimarrón 102
Cipangu 150
Cirus, Miley 263
Civil Rights Movement 395
Civil War 39, 70–71, 72, 107,
    167, 242, 265, 276, 264,
    354, 282, 432, 395, 474,
    465, 254, 260
Clanton gang 31
Clark, George Rogers 142
Clark, Thomas D. 175
Clark, William 142. *See* Lewis
    and Clark; *See*
    also Lewis and Clark
Clear Creek 70–71
Clemens, Orion 285
Clemens, Samuel 285–286
Clement, Russell 122
Clerke, Captain 22
Cleveland, Grover 123, 445
Clinton, Bill 45
Clinton, George 448
CNN 108
Coahuila 429
Coahuila-Texas 430
coal mining 456
Cod fishing 193
Colbath, Jeremiah Jones 133

Colbert, Jean Baptiste 245
Cole, Terence 468
Coloma, California 438
Colona 71
Colorado 63–74, 277, 465
Colorado City 38
Colorado River 64–66
Colorado Rockies 135
Colorado Territory 72, 168
Colossus of Rhodes 386
Columbia 467
Columbia Gorge 362
Columbia (journal) 468
Columbia Rediviva 365
Columbia River 133, 363,
    365–366
"Columbus" 282
Columbus, Christopher 18,
    18–19, 56, 98–99
Committee on Indian Affairs 493
Committee on Territories 40, 133,
    237, 266, 468
Commonwealth 460
Compromise of 1850 61
Comstock Lode 282, 283
Conant, Roger 219
Confederacy 355
Confederate Territory of Arizona
    40
Congomond Lakes 83
Congress 168, 234, 236, 260,
    264, 266. *See also* U.S.
    Congress
Congressional Record 23, 494
"A Connecticut Yankee in King
    Arthur's Court" 75
Connecticut 75–84, 491–492
Connecticut River 76–79, 298,
    448, 452
Connecticut River Colony 81.
    See also River Colony
Conquistadores 7, 414
conscientious objectors 375
Constitution 114, 221
"Constitution State" 75, 81, 82
Continental Congress 114
Continental Divide 67, 70–71
Cook, Captain James 22, 118,
    118–121
Cook, Daniel Pope 143
Cooper, Anthony Ashley, first Earl
    of Shaftesbury 398–399
Corn 155–156
Cornhusker 271

Corp of Discovery 264. *See*
    also Lewis and Clark
Cortes, Hernán 57
Corvallis, Oregon 362
Costner, Kevin 155, 271
Council for New England 292,
    293
Council of Fort Smith 355
Council of Plymouth 79
Coushatta Indians 15
Coutant, Dr. C. G. 497
Coxe, Daniel 401
Craig, Colonel 134
Crane, James M. 282
Crater Lake 362
Crawford, Texas 425
Crazy Horse 404
Creedence Clearwater Revival
    137
Creek Indians 12, 114, 353–355
Creeks 8, 102
Creek War of 1814 12
Cree language 364
Creole 44, 183
Cromwell, Oliver 295, 376–377,
    379, 397
Crosby, Bing 115
Cuba 98, 123, 248
Cumberland Basin 419
Cumberland Compact 416–417
Cumberland, Duke of 177
Cumberland Gap 177–178, 178
Custer, George Armstrong 269
Custer's Last Stand. *See* The
    Battle of Little Bighorn
Cyrus, Billy Ray 43

D

Dablon 139
Dade County 98
"The Dairy State" 481
Dakota Indians 24, 233–240, 494
Dakota, State of 408
Dakota Territory 265–266, 403,
    495
Dalrymple, Oliver 406
Danville, Kentucky 179
Dare, Virginia 460
Dauphin Island 186
Davenport, John 81–82
Davidson County, Tennessee 417
Davis, Bette 183
Deadwood 404, 405
"Deep in the Heart of Texas" 423

The Deer Hunter 374
Delaware 85–96, 109, 385
Delaware Bay 85, 89, 91
Delaware Indians 94–95, 491–492
Delaware River 380
Deliverance 88–89
DelMarVa Peninsula 93
Democratic National Convention 137
Democratic Party 71, 235
Denver, Colorado 70–71
Denver, John 473, 489–500
"A Description of New England" 216
Deseret 281, 435–446
Detroit, Michigan 223
Dezhnev, Semen 19, 19–20
Dhegiha Sioux 46, 168
Diamond, Neil 173
Dickens, Charles 290
Dickinson, John 93
Discovery 119
Disneyland 148, 279
Disneyworld 98
District of Columbia 468
District of Kentucky 179
District of Louisiana 189, 259
District of Maine of Massachusetts 200
Divine Right of Kings 376
Dixie 5, 183
Dixon Entrance 26, 27
Dixon, Jeremiah 93
Doddridge County, West Virginia 478
Dole, Sanford B. 123
Domesday book 199
Dominion of New England 295
Dorchester 78
Dorchester Company of Adventurers 218
Doty, Judge James 483–484
"Douglas" 267
Douglas, Stephen 138, 161, 165–166, 237, 275–277, 441, 468
Douglass, William A. 35
Dover, Delaware 85, 94
Dover, New Hampshire 294
Dragging Canoe 176
Drake's Bay 58
Drake, Sir Francis 58, 366
Dred Scott case 260
Dudley, Sir Robert, Lord of Leicester 458
Lord Dunmore 416

Dupont 85, 86, 92
duPont, Eleuthere Irenee 86
Dutch East India Company 86

E

Eagles 385
Eagle Station 282
Earp, Wyatt 31
East Florida 104, 114
Ecores Rouges 48
Edgerton, Sidney 265–268
Edwards, Haden 430
Eisenhower, Dwight 28, 125
Elizabeth I, Queen. *See* Queen Elizabeth I
Elliot, T.C. 365
Elvas. *See* Gentleman of Elvas
Empire of Japan 123
Enchanted Castle Studios 456
English Civil War 295, 376
English Privy Council 297
"Equality State" 498
Ericson, Lief 19
Erie Canal 229–230
Escansaques 168
Esmaralda 285
Eugene, Oregon 362
Evans, Alexander 468
Evans, Sara 253
Everett, Edward 55–56
Exeter 294

F

The Family Guy 385
Fayette County, Kentucky 178
Federal government 235, 265
Field of Dreams 155–156
Fillmore, Millard 61, 441, 468
Fincastle County, Virginia 178
Finn, Huckleberry 254–255
Fitzwarin, Fulk 91
Five Civilized Tribes 353–355, 357
Flagstaff, Arizona 32
Flint, Michigan 223
Flint River 104
Florida 97–106
La Florida 11, 397
Florida Blanca 22
Florida Parishes 189–190, 190
Floyd, John 369
Font, Pedro 284
football 271–272, 351
Ford 223

Ford, Harrison 148
Ford, Henry 224
Forestry Service 26
Fort Astoria 368–369
Fort Caroline 101
Fort Charlotte 11
Fort Christina 92
Fort des Alibamons 10
Fort d'Etroit 228
Fort Fillmore 40
Fort Kearney, Nebraska 497
Fort Laramie 497
Fort Snelling 236
Fort St. Louis 47
Fort Sumter 395–396
Fort Toulouse 10
Forty Fort 491–492
Founder of New Hampshire 291
fourteenth amendment 276
Fox, George 378–381
Fox Indians 156, 225, 257
Fox River 244
Fractured Fairy Tales 55
Franciscan missionaries 109
Franken, Al 233
Frankland 418. *See also* Franklin
Franklin 418–419
Franklin, Benjamin 150, 418
Frank, Thomas 164
Franquelin, Jean-Baptiste Louis 246
Fraser River 365
Frederick, Prince of Wales 177
Fredonia 431
Fredonian Rebellion 430
Freeman, Legh R. 495, 496–497
Fremont Basin 280
Fremont, John C. 60, 69–70, 272–274
French and Indian War 48, 59, 114, 141, 150, 228, 247–248, 298, 483
French Navy 47
French Prairie 370
French Revolution 187
Friedman, Kinky 403
Frizzell, David 351
Fronteras 34
Frontier Index 496
Fuca, Juan de 366
Fujita scale 164
Fundamental Constitution 399
Fundamental Orders of Connecticut 75, 78, 81–82

G

Gabriel, Peter 6
Gadsden, James 36
Gadsden Purchase 37
Gannett, Henry 32
Garay, Francis de 243
Garcia, Jerry 43
Garden of Eden 55–56
Garland, Judy 163
Garland, Texas 76
Gary, Indiana 148
Gates, Sir Thomas 87
Gaye, Marvin 224
General Court of Massachusetts 220
Genoa 281
Gentleman of Elvas 7, 244
Gentry, Bobbie 241
"A Geographical Memoir of Oregon" 369
Georgia 107–114
Georgia, Republic of 108
georgos 108
Germany 110
Gertrude of Wyoming 492–493
Gettysburg Address 55
Gettysburg National Cemetery 55
"Gettysburg of the West" 40
Ghost Government of Deseret 443
Giant 423
Gila River 36
Gilbert, Sir Humphrey 459
Glen Canyon Dam 64
Glen, James 416
Glorieta, New Mexico 40
Glorious Revolution 296
Glotov, Stephan 20
GM (General Motors) 223
Golden, Colorado 72
Golden Gate Bridge 53
Golden Hind 367
"Gold Hill Mining District" 283
"Gone With the Wind" 107
Gophers 233
Gordy, Berry, Jr. 224–225
Gorges, Sir Ferdinando 196–198, 197, 200, 220, 292
Gorges, Thomas 200
Governor of Newfoundland 292
Grand Canyon 31, 32, 64, 65–66
Grand Peak 68–69
Grand River 67
Granganimeo 459
Grant, Cary 375
The Grants 450–451

Grant, Ulysses S. 72, 268
Grauman's Chinese Theatre 54
Gray, Robert 365
"Grease Trail" 364
"The Great Impeacher" 266
The Great Seal of the State of Utah 436
Great Basin 31, 280, 361
Great Blue Hill 217
Great Impeacher 493
Great Lakes 144, 177, 224
Great Migration 220
Great Salt Lake 281, 385, 436
"Great Sandy Desert" 31
"Great Sandy Desert" 361
Great White North 18
Green Bay Packers 481
Green Bay, Wisconsin 159, 236
Green, Dallas 85
Green, James S. 132, 283
Green Mountain Boys 448, 449–450
Green Mountains 451
Green River 67
Greenwich, Connecticut 76
Gregory, John 70–71
Gregory's Diggings 70–71
Gresham, Oregon 362
griffin 56
Grizzly bear flag 60
Grow, Galusha 71–72
Guale 109
Guam 115
Guerrero, Vicente 431
Guggenheim family 26
Gulf of Mexico 241, 248
Guthrie, Arlo 213
Gvozdev, Mikhail 20

H

Hale, Edward Everett 54–55
Hale, Nathan 55–56
Half Moon 86–88
Hamilton, Alexander 442
Hampshire County, England 290
Hampshire Grants 449
Handbook of Texas Online 426
"the handle of the cleaver" 83
Hanks, Tom 374
Hanover, New Hampshire 290
Hardin County, Kentucky 138
Harding, Florence 28
Harding, Warren G. 27
Harrington, Joseph P. 158, 226

Harrison, Benjamin 134, 269, 409–410, 470, 498
Hartford, Connecticut 76, 78
Harvard College 214–215
Hasinai Indians 425
Hatfields and McCoys 174–175
Hawaii 27, 115–126
Hawaii 5-O 115
Hawaiian Islands 122
Hawaiian Journal of History 122
Hawaiian Kingdom 121–122
Hawk, Hudson 481
Heath, Sir Robert 401–402
Heemskerch, Martin 386
Hell on Wheels 496
Henderson, Richard 176, 416
Hennipin, Father Louis 225
Henrietta Maria. *See* Queen Henrietta Maria
Henry, Andrew 492
Hepburn, Katherine 375
Herrera, Antonio de 57, 99
Her Space Holiday 395
Hillsboro, Oregon 362
Hilton brothers 294
Hispaniola 99, 377
History Channel 18
Holiday, Billie 455
Holley, Frances Chamberlain 403
Hollywood 54
Holmes, William 78
Honeymoon in Vegas 279
Honey War 160–161
Hooker, Thomas 78
Hoosier 148
Hoover Dam 65, 280
Horton, Edward Everett 55
Horton, Johnny 17, 241
House Committee on Territories 266. *See also* Committee on Territories
House of Commons 111, 377
House of Representatives 13, 25, 123, 132–133, 237, 266, 267, 268, 460, 467. *See also* U.S. House of Representatives
Houston, Sam 432
Howard, Jacob M. 268
Hudson, Henry 86–87
Hudson River 229
Humboldt 285
Hunter, Holly 32
Hunt for Red October 263
Huron 408, 484

Huronia 224
Hútañga 169
Hutchins, Thomas 159

I

Iberville River 104
"Icebergia" 23
Idaho 72, 127–136, 464, 466
Idaho Organic Act 131
Idaho Springs, Colorado 70–71, 133
Idaho Statesman 128
Idaho Territory 127, 265
Ide, William 60
Illini Indians 46, 139, 225
Illinois 137–146, 241
Illinoisans 214
Illinois Country 46, 48, 140, 142, 483
Illinois River 257
Illinois Territory 139
Illionois River 47
Independence Hall 375
Indiana 147–154, 467
Indiana Company 150–151
Indiana Jones 147
Indianapolis 147
"Indianapolis 500" 148
Indiana Territory 228
"Indian Country" 352–360
"Indian Country" 259, 264
Indian Removal Treaties 353–355
Indian Territory 356–360
Indikoi 149
Indus river 149
Infanta Maria 198
Iolani Palace 123
Iowa caucuses 155
Iowa District 157–158
Iowa Indians 257
Iowa Territory 157, 160
Ireland 377
Iroquois Indians 176, 476, 491–492
Islas Carolinas 58
Isle Royale 225
"Itasca" 236–237
Iturbide, Don Augustin de 37

J

"Jackson" 237
"Jackson 5" 224
Jackson, Andrew 12, 50, 180, 230, 431

Jackson, David 489–500, 492
Jackson, George 70–71
Jackson Hole 489–500
Jackson Purchase 44, 181
Jackson's Diggings 70–71
Jacksonville, Florida 101, 114
Jamaica 243
Jamestown 86–89, 103, 109, 178, 196, 215, 292
Jefferson 267, 467
Jefferson County, Kentucky 178
Jefferson Territory 71–72
Jefferson, Thomas 159, 228, 259, 365, 382, 442, 456
Jesuit 245
Jesuit Relation 244
Jesus Maria, Francisco de 426
Jezebel 183
Jim Beam 174
Johnson, Andrew 23, 266, 276, 493
Johnson, Cassius M. 50–51
Johnson, Don 98
Johnston, Colonel Albert S. 443
Joliet, Louis 45, 139, 168, 245.
See also Marquette and Joliet
Jones, Nard 469
Joplin, Janis 173
Jordan, Michael 137
Joseph, Chief 130–131
"Juanillo" uprising 109
Julesburg, Colorado 497
Juneau, Alaska 27

K

Kalakaua, King David 122
Kamchatka 18
Kanawha 476–479, 478
Kansas 24, 46, 50, 64, 163–172, 275, 494
Kansas City 163, 167
Kansas Landing 166
Kansas-Nebraska Act 164–166, 275
Kansas River 169
Kansas Territory 70–71, 168
Karankawa Indians 426
Kara Sea 86
Kartchner Caverns 32
Kashmir 149
Kaskaskia 142
Kaskaskia Indians 139
Katrina 184
Kauai 118

Kaula 118
Kaw 168–169
Kaw City, Oklahoma 170
Kealakekua Bay 119
Keilor, Garrison 481
Kelley, Hall Jackson 369
Kemper Rebellion 189
Kennebec River 196, 292
Kentucky 44, 173–182, 241
Kentucky Bluegrass Country 175
Kentucky County 178–179
Kentucky Derby 174
Kentucky Fried Chicken 173
Kentucky Lake 181
Keystone State 373
Killihote. *See also* Wright, Allen
Killington Peak 452
King Charles I 196–198, 376, 401
King Charles II 92, 109, 186, 220, 295, 376–378, 380, 397, 401
King Charles V 99
King George I 110
King George II 112–113, 141
King George III 11, 114, 142, 150, 177, 364, 483
King Henry II 92
King Henry IV 198
King Henry VIII 375, 458
King James Bible 376
King James I 90, 196, 197, 198
King James II 220
King James VI 376
King John 91
King Kamehameha I 120–121
King Louis IX 189
King Louis XIII 186, 198
King Louis XIV 184–185, 245
King, Martin Luther, Jr. 5, 373
King of the Hill 423
King of the Road 193
King of Wheat 406
King Philip V of Spain 34, 187
King Richard Lionheart 91
Kingsbury, Reverend Cyrus 355
Kings Lynn 291
Kinsey, Steven A. 281
Klickitat 469
Knob Creek 174
Koasati. *See* Coushatta Indians
Kodiak Island 22
Kwitcyana 65

L

Lac Dauphin 225

Lac des Ilinois 139
Lac des Puans 225
Lac du Illinois 225
Laconia 293
Laconia Company 293, 294
Lac St. Joseph 225
Lady Ascot 386
Lake Champlain 448, 450–453
Lake Erie 229
Lake Itasca 241
Lake Maurepas 248
Lake Mead 65, 280
Lake Michigan 137, 148, 168, 225, 241
Lake Pontchartrain 248
Lake Superior 485
Lake Tahoe 285
Lakota Sioux 404
Lamar, Howard Roberts 407
Lamb, Daniel 477
Land of Lincoln 138
"La Palisade" 245
Lara, Bernardo Gutierrez de 429
Laramie County 495
La Salle 426
La Salle, Rene Robert Cavelier, sieur de 245
La Salle, Rene Robert Cavelier, sieur de 103–104, 253
La Salle, Rene Robert Cavelier, Sieur de 67
La Salle, Rene Robert Cavelier, Sieur de 184
La Salle, Rene Robert Sieur de 47
Latter Day Saints 435–446. *See also* Mormons
Law of April 6, 1830 431
Lea, Albert M. 156–160
Leaving Las Vegas 279
Lehua 118
Leigh, Vivien 107, 183
Le Moyne, Jean Baptiste, Sieur de Bienville 186
Lenape 94
Leni-Lenape. *See* Lenape
León, Alonso De 426
LeRoux 183
Lesser Antilles 398
Letterman, David 147, 152
Lewis and Clark 128–129, 159, 253, 259, 264, 365–366, 401, 492–493. *See also* Corp of Discovery
Lewis, David G. 364–365

Lewis, Merriwether 159, 259. *See* Lewis and Clark
Lewiston 265
Liberty Bell 375
Lightfoot, Gordon 223
Lili'uokalani, Queen 122–123
"Limamu" 7
"Lincoln" 405, 467, 468, 495
Lincoln, Abraham 23, 55, 72, 138, 165, 268, 285, 286–287, 369, 476, 478, 493
Lincoln administration 266
Lincoln County, Kentucky 178
Lincoln, Nebraska 271
Lindsay, Mark 31
Little Harbor 292, 294
"Little Rhody" 386
Little Virginia 478
"Live Free or Die!" 289
Living History Farms 156
Livingston, Robert 449
Livy 268
Lobeira 56
Locke, John 399
Lodge Pole Creek 497
Loe, Thomas 378–380
Lord, Jack 115
Los Angeles, California 53, 385
Lost Colony 460
Louisiana 10, 44, 48, 55–56, 67, 183–192, 241, 258–260
Louisiana Purchase 48, 128, 160, 187–188, 228, 235, 258–259, 264, 274, 353, 367, 431, 465, 484
Louisiana Territory 48, 160, 189, 259, 260
Louisville, Kentucky 174
Louvre 481
Loyal Virginia 477
Lucas, Robert 160
Lygonia 200
Lynyrd Skynyrd 5

M

"Mabila" 8
Mackinac Bridge 224
Madison, James 153, 190, 251, 260
Maine 193–202, 260
Maine Woods 193, 201–202
Maker's Mark 174
"Malbouchia" 242
Mallet, Pierre and Paul 274
Mall of America 233

The Mamas and the Papas 53–62
The Man Without a Country 54
Manhattan 92
Manifest Destiny 164, 234, 437, 485
Maple 447–448
Mardi Gras 183
Marest, Father Gabriel 256
Margravate of Azilia, Margravate of. *See* Azilia
Maria Theresa, Queen. *See* Queen Maria Theresa
Marquette and Joliet 184–185, 415, 482
Marquette Beach 148
Marquette, Jacques 45–46, 139, 168, 245, 256–258, 257. *See also* Marquette and Joliet
Martin, Dean 395
Martin, Morgan L. 236
Mary, Queen II. *See* Queen Mary II; *See also* William and Mary
Mason, Captain John 81, 196, 200, 291–293
Mason, Charles 93
Mason-Dixon Line 93–94
Masonia 293
Masonian Proprietors 298
Mason, John Tufton 297
Mason, Robert 295
Massachusetts 213–222, 386
Massachusetts Bay Colony 78, 200, 218–221, 294
Massachusetts Indians 217
Massanet, Damián 426
Masterson, James R. 44
Matanzas 102
Mather, Cotton 297
Maumee River 229
Mayflower 78, 218
Mazarin, Cardinal 187
McClintock, James H. 35
McGarrett, Steve 115
McKinley, William 123
Mead, Dr. Elwood 65
Medford, Oregon 362
Meek, Alexander Beauford 14
Memphis 415
Menominee River 485
Mero District 417
Mero, Don Estevan 417
Merrimack River 196, 292
Mesilla Valley 37

Mexican-American War 36, 60, 69–70, 264, 280
Mexican Cession 438
Mexican Revolution 59, 190
Mexico 243
Miami Beach 98
Michigamea Indians 139
Michigami 225
Michigan 223–232
Michigan state motto 223
Michigan Territory 228, 229, 484
Michilimackinac 226
Midwest 137, 465
Miller, Joaquin 134–135
Miller, Roger 193
Milton 217
Milwaukee 482
Minneapolis 238. *See also* Twin Cities
Minnesota 233–240, 241, 494
Minnesota River 234–239
Minnesota River valley 237
Minnesota Territory 234, 236, 467
Miracles 224
"Missing Missouri" 253
Mississippi 241–252
Mississippi River 46, 114, 141, 156, 184, 189, 228, 234, 236, 241–252, 253, 352, 415, 465, 259
Mississippi State 242
Mississippi Territory 7, 12, 13, 250, 467
Mississippi Valley 401
Missouri 44, 242, 253–262
Missouri Bootheel 44, 255
Missouri Compromise 60, 165–166, 201, 275
Missouri Indians 257
Missouri River 161, 163, 228, 256–258, 264, 273, 274, 406
Missouri Territory 49, 255
Mitchell, Margaret 107
Mobile 10–16, 103, 186
Mobile Bay 243
Mobile District 12
Mocama 109
Mohawk Valley 401
Mojave Desert 31, 53
Monroe, James 14, 144, 201, 260
Montagu, Sir Edward, the 1st Earl of Sandwich 118–119
Montalvo, Garci Ordonez de 56–57
Montana 263–270, 465

Montana gold rush 265–266
Montana, Hanna 263
Montgomery bus boycott 6
Montgomery County 178
Montgomery, Robert 110
Monticello 456
Moonlight in Vermont 447
Morgan Horse 447
Morgan, J. P. 26
Morgan, Misty 413
Mormons 281–284, 435–446, 494, 496
Mormon Station 281
Mormon Trail 272
Mormon War 282, 443
Morrissey, Charles T. 451–452
Mötley Crüe 6
Motor City 224
Motown Records 224
Mountain Meadows Massacre 443–444
Mountain of Maggots 452
Mount Hood 362
Mount Pisgah 452
Mount Rushmore 404
Mount St. Helens 463–464
Mount Washington 289
Müller, Gerhard Friedrich 22
Mullins, Shawn 361
Murray, John, Earl of Dunmore 178
Music Man 147, 155
Muskhogean dialect 8

N

Names on the Land 100
Napa Valley 53
Naperville, Illinois 76
Narragansett 76, 80
Narváez, Panfilo de 8, 243
Nashborough Station 416–417
Nash, Francis 416
Natchez District 249–250
Natchitoches 427
National Treasure 374
Native Americans 43, 153, 228, 241, 242, 253, 352–360, 404. *See also* Individual Tribe Names, e.g. "Creek Indians"
Natural Bridge, Virginia 456
Naumkeag 219
Navajo Indians 31, 440
Navigation Acts 295
NCAA 352

Nebraska 24, 271–278, 494
Nebraska Blue Book 272
Nebraska-Kansas Act. *See* Kansas-Nebraska Act
Nebraska Territory 166, 265
Neches River 427
Needham, James 415
Neill, Sam 263
Nevada 31, 44, 279–288
Nevada City 283
Nevada State Library and Archives Department of Cultural Affairs 284
The New England Company for a Plantation in Massachusetts Bay 219
New Albion 58, 129, 470. *See also* Nova Albion
New Amsterdam 77
New Brunswick 201
New Castle, Delaware 94
New Connecticut 450
New England 76, 196, 200, 216, 220, 295
New England Confederacy 81
New Founde Land 195
Newfoundland 291
Newgate 379
New Hampshire 196, 289–300
New Haven 81, 82
New Haven, Connecticut 76
New Ireland, Province of 201
New Madrid 49, 255
New Mexico 36, 466
"New Oregon Trail" 361–362
New Orleans 12, 48, 103, 140, 180, 190
New Orleans Ladies 183
Newport, Rhode Island 386
New Somersetshire 200
New Sweden 92
Newtown 78
New Virginia 477
New Wales 381
New York 83, 150, 298, 467, 491–492
New York Daily Tribune 132
New York Review of Books 2
New York Supreme Court 449
Nez Percé 129–131
Nibraskier 274
Nicolet, Jean 244
Niihau 118
Nipmuck Indians 76
Nirvana 464

Nittany Lions 375
Niutachi 257
"Nobody's Perfect" 263
Nolan, Philip 55
Norfolk, England 291
Normans 91
Northam 294
North Carolina 45, 395
"Northern Archipelago" 22
Northern Exposure 18
Northern Oregon 467
Northern Pacific Railroad
    406–408
Northern Virginia Company 216
North Michigan 224
North to Alaska 18
North Virginia 196
Northwest Ordinance 143–144,
    152, 179, 228, 235, 419,
    465, 484, 486
Northwest Passage 58, 119, 364
Northwest Territory 148, 152,
    179, 228, 234–235, 451,
    464, 484, 486
Norumbega 55–56, 194–195
Norway 292
Norwegian Lutherans 481
Noticias Estadisticas del Estado de
    Sonora, etc., 38
Notre Dame 148
Nova Albion 366, 470. *See*
    also New Albion
Nova Scotia 292–293
Novaya Zemlya 86
Nueces Strip 429
Nuevas Phillipinas 428
Nuevo Santander 428

O

Oahu 118
The Oblong 83
Ocean's Eleven 279
Oconostota 176
Oglethorpe, James Edward
    111–114
Ohio 235, 343–350
Ohio Country 143
Ohio River 175, 465
Ohio River Valley 178
Ohio Valley 492–493
Okanogan 469
Oklahoma 44, 351–360
Oklahoma Enabling Act 358
Oklahoma State University Cow-
    boys 351

Oklahoma University Sooners
    351
Old English 290
Old Faithful 490–500
Oldham, John 78, 80
Old Northwest 486
Oldsmobile 223
Omaha Indians 46, 168
Omaha, Nebraska 271
Oñate, Juan de 66
Once Their Home: Our Legacy
    From the Dakhkotahs
    403
ooligan 364–365
Orange County, Virginia 177
Ordway, Nehemiah G. 407–408
Oregon 31, 361–372
Oregon Country 129, 369
Oregon Historical Quarterly 364
Oregon Territory 370, 464
Oregon Trail 272, 368
Oregon Treaty 130, 469
Organic Act for the Territory of
    Utah 441
Organic Act of Alaska 25
organized crime 280
Orleans Territory 189, 259
"Osage" 71
Osage Indians 160
Osages 46, 168
O'Sullivan, John 164
Oto 257, 274
Oto-Missouri 257
Ottawa Indians 159
ouragan 363
"Ourigan: Wealth of the Northwest
    Coast" 364–365
"Outshined" 233
Overhills 415
Oxford 378
Ozark Mountains 44, 139

P

Pacific Northwest 129, 361–372,
    464–466
Pahoches 158
Palin, Sarah 17
Panic of 1873 406
Pannaway 292
Papago Indians. *See* Tohono
    O'odham
Pardo, Juan 414
Paris Treaty of 1763 11, 141, 188,
    248, 298
Paris Treaty of 1783 201, 249

Parliamentarian Navy 379
Parris Island 397
Parva Maen 199
Pascua Florida 100
Patience 88–89
Pawnee Indians 272, 495
Pawnee, Oklahoma 257
Pearl Harbor 115–117, 122–125
Pearl Jam 464
Pearl River 189, 251
Pekitanoui 256–257
Pembina 405
Penmanmoire 381
Penn State 373
Pennsylvania 92, 373–384, 473,
    491–492, 493, 494, 496
Penn, William Jr. 92
Penrith 382
Pensacola 104
Pentagon 456
People of the South Wind 169
Peoria Indians 139
Pepperidge Farm 194
Pequot Indians 77, 80
Pequot War 80–81
Perdido River 251
Perry, Mark 424, 433
Csar Peter I of Russia 18
Peters, Reverend Samuel 451–452
Philadelphia 150, 374
Philadelphia (movie) 374
Philadelphia Story 375
Philippines 123
Philip V of Spain, King. *See* King
    Philip V of Spain
Phoenix, Arizona 31
Piecemeal absoption 357
Pike's Peak 68–69, 131, 134
Pike's Peak region 71
Pike, Zebulon 68–69
Pilgrims 218, 375
Pima Indians 65. *See* Akimel
    O'odham
Pinchot, Gifford 26
Pinckney's Treaty 250
Pineda, Alonzo Alvarez de 243
Pinney, George M. 407–408
Piquag 78
Piscataqua River 292
A Place Like Nebraska 272
planchas of silver 33. *See*
    also cerargyrite
"Platte" 495
Platte River 168, 272, 274, 275
Plummer, Henry 265

Plymouth 78, 217, 220, 221, 292
Pocahontas 87, 215
pocket veto 277
Point Reyes 58
Polk, James K. 161, 432, 486
polygamy 443–446
Pomeroy, Charles 468
Poncas 168
Poncas Indians 46
Ponce de Leon 98–100
Pontiac, Chief 178
Pontiac's Rebellion 177
Pope, Nathaniel 143
Popham, George 196
popular sovereignty 166
Portland, Oregon 362
Port of Kansas 166
Port Royal 103
Portsmouth, Hampshire 292
Poston, Charles D. 37–39
Powell, John Wesley 64
Prairie Chapel Ranch 425
Presley, Elvis 173
primogeniture 379
prohibitionists 235
Promontory, Utah 497
promyshleniki 20, 20–21
prostitution 279
"Province of Maine" 292
Prudhon, Gabriel de 33
Prussia 247
Puerto Rico 98, 123
Puritan movement 375–376
Puritans 77
Purry, Jean Pierre 110
Purrysburg 110
Pysht 469

Q

Quaid, Dennis 148
Quakers 374–384
Quapaw Indians 46–48, 47, 168
Quebec 201, 246
Queen Anne's War 187–188
Queen Elizabeth I 367, 376,
    456–460
Queen Henrietta Maria 186,
    198–199
Queen Maria Theresa 187
Queen Mary I 375
Queen Mary II 296
Quillayute 469
quinto 34
Quivera 58
Quivira 168

Quiznos 119

R

"Rabies Carolinae" 111
Raiders of the Lost Ark 147
Raising Arizona 31
Raleigh, Sir Walter 459
Rapid City, South Dakota 403
Razorback 45
Read, Allen Walker 140
Real de Arizonac 33
Reconstruction 395
Red River Valley 405
Reese, John 281
Reformation 376
Reign of Terror 187
Remington, Frederick 404
Rendell, Ed 373
Reno, Janet 98
Republican Party 27, 235, 265,
    275
Republic of France 187
Republic of Hawaii 123
Republic of Vermont 450
Republic of West Florida 189
Resolution 119
Restored Government of New
    Virginia 476
Restored Government of Virginia
    478
Revere, Paul 214
Revolution (American).
    See American Revolu-
    tion
Revolution (French). *See* French
    Revolution
Rhode Island 85, 490–500
Rhode Island and Providence
    Plantations 385–394
Ribaut, Jean 101
Riggs, Stephen R. 158
Rio Colorado. *See* Colorado
    River
Rio de Buena Guia 66
Rio de Cosninas 66
"Rio del Espiritu Santo" 243
Rio de San Rafael 66
Rio de Tizon 66
"Rio Escondido" 245
"Rio Grande" 244
"A River Runs Through It" 263
River Colony 78. *See also* Con-
    necticut River Colony
River of Louisiana 245

"Riviere Colbert" 245
"Riviere de la Conception" 245
Roanoke Island 460
Robin Hood 92
Robinson, Jackie 213
Rocha, Guy 284–285
Rocky and Bullwinkle Show 55
Rocky Mountains 63, 70–71,
    71–72, 168, 188, 248,
    264, 267, 271, 368, 492
Rodeo Hall-of-Fame 64
Rodgers & Hammerstein 351
Rogers, Robert 364
Rolfe, John 87
Romantic Passages in South West-
    ern History 14
Rome 148
Roosevelt, Franklin D. 123
Roosevelt, Theodore 26, 358
Rose, U. M., Judge 50
Ross, Diana 224
Ruby Ridge 128
Russert, Tim 97
Russia 18–30, 25, 108, 247
Russian Academy of Sciences 22
"Russian America" 22–24

S

Sabine River 426
Saco River 201
Saffery, Solomon 83
Sagahadock River. *See* Kennebec
    River
saguaro cacti 31
Saint George 108
Salem, Massachusetts 219
Salem, Oregon 362
Salmeron, Zarate 66
Salt Lake City 127, 281, 282,
    437–438, 443
San Buenaventura 109
Sandburg, Carl 137
Sanders, Colonel Harland 173
Sanders, Wilbur 266
San Diego, California 59
Sandwich, Earl of. *See* Montagu,
    Sir Edward, the 1st Earl
    of Sandwich
Sandwich Islands 119–121
San Francisco 395
Sangre De Cristo Mountains 67
San Jose 109
San Luis 68
San Miquel de Aquayo 428
San Pedro 109

Santa Anna, Antonio Lopez de 36, 431–433
Santa Catalina 109
Santa Cruz, La Tierra de 58
Santa Cruz, Puerto de 58
Santa Elena 397
Santa Fe 39
Santa Rosa de Corodéguachi 34
Santo Domingo 377
Saturday Evening Post 368
Sauk Indians 156, 257
Sault St. Marie 227
Sawyer, Tom 254–255
Saxons 291
Saybrook 80
Schlotzky's 119
Schoolcraft, Henry R. 236
Schwarzenegger, Arnold 53
Scotland 292, 483
Scott, General Winfield 156
Scott's Purchase 156
Sears Tower 137
Seattle Sound 464
Sea Venture 87, 90
Second Wheeling Convention 476
U.S. Secretary of War 273
seedstock 264
Selznick, David O. 107
Seminole Indians 102, 353–355
Seminole Wars 353
Senate. *See* U.S. Senate
Seneca Indians 491–492
Separation Day 94
"Sequoyah," state of 357
Las Sergas de Esplandian 55–56
Serra, Padre Junipero 59
Seven Cities of Cibola 55–56, 195
Seven Years War 59, 104, 187, 247–248
Sevier, John 418–419
"Seward's Folly" 23
"Seward's Icebox" 23
Seward, William 23, 23–25
Shakespeare, William 88
Shankle, George 51, 226
Shawnee Indians 176
Shearer, Barbara 175
Shearer, Benjamin 175
Shelby, Isaac 180
Shelikov, Gregor 22
Sherbourne, Vermont 452
Sheridan City 405
Shipton Gorges 199
"Shoshone" 267
"Shoshoni" 495
Shue, Elizabeth 279

Siberia 20
Sierra Nevada 281–284
Simmons, Michael 51
Sinsel, Harmon 476
Siouan dialect 274
"Sioux" 495
"Sioux land" 237
Sioux Nation 237, 269
Sirumea, Antonio 33
Six Iroquois Nations 150
Sixteenth Street Baptist Church 6
slavery 7, 49, 72, 166–167, 201, 242, 283, 395, 460, 259
smallpox 257
Smith, Daniel 419
Smith-Fisher, Carol B. 195, 196, 197, 199
Smith, Jedediah 368, 441, 492
Smith, John 79, 196, 215–219
Smith, Jr., Joseph 436–437
Smithsonian report of 1954 440
Smoky Mountains 415, 416
Snake River 362
Snoqualmie 469
Somers, George 87–89
Song of Wyoming 489–500
Sonora Exploring and Mining Company 38
Sooners 351–360
"The Sopranos" 263
Sosa, Sammy 137
Soto, Hernando de 7, 243–244, 414
Soundgarden 233
Southampton 290
South Carolina 395–402
South Carolina General Assembly 401
South Dakota 403–412
South Pacific 163
South Pass 368
Southwest Territory 419
Southwick Jog 82
Spanish Peaks. *See* Wahatoya
Sports Illustrated 352
Springfield, Oregon 362
Springsteen, Bruce 271
Squatter Sovereignty 166
"Stachtan Nitada" 22
"Stachtan Nitada" 22
Stacy, Charles M. 92
Stage Fort Point 218
Stählin, Jacob von 22
Stamford, Connecticut 76
St. Anthony Falls 238
Stanton, Richard H. 467

Stanton's Monument 468
Starving Time 88
State Names, Seals, Flags and Symbols 175
St. Augustine 102, 109, 397
St. Croix River 201, 486
St. Croix valley 234, 486
St. Elias 25
The Stepford Wives 75
Stewart, George R. 1, 100
St. Ignace 227
St. John's River 101, 114
St. Joseph River 225
St. Lawrence River 139
St. Louis 189, 245, 258
St. Mary's River 114
Stoddard, William O. 132
Stoeckl, Baron de 22, 23
Stonehenge 290, 456
Stony Mountains 369
St. Paul 236, 406. *See also* Twin Cities
"St. Peter" 238
St. Peter River 236, 237
St. Pierre River 238
Strait of Anian 59
Strawberry Bank 294
Stuart, Chapman 478
Stuart, Robert 368
Subway 119
suffrage 276
Suland 237
Sullivan, James 197
Sullivan, John C. 160
Sullivan line 161
Sumner, Charles 23–24, 23–25, 267–268
Sun King 186
Superintendent of Indian Affairs 41, 356
Superior 224
Susquehanna and Delaware Company 491–492
Susquehanna River 491–492
Sutter's Mill 60, 438
Sweetwater 495
swine industry 45
Sycamore Shoals 176
symmetrical geography 401

T

Taft, William Howard 26
Tait, Charles 13
Tall Tales of Arkansaw 45
Tampa Bay 243

Tanasqui 414
Taylor County 476
Taylor, Zachary 273
Tellico dam 415
Tellico Times 415
Tempe, Arizona 32
The Tempest 88
Temptations 224
Tenase 415
Tennessee 413–422
Tennessee Birdwalk 413
Tennessee River 178
Tennessee Waltz 413
Terra Nova 195
Territorial Papers for Alabama 13
Territory of.... *See* Individual
       Territory name (e.g. Colo-
       rado Territory)
Texas 14, 36, 55–56, 188,
       423–434, 465
Thaleichthys pacificus 364
Thanatopsis 368
Thatcher, Becky 254–255
The Missouri Gazette 259
The Society of Friends 378
"Third Supply" 87
Thomas Hooker 81–82
Thompson, David 292, 294
Thoreau, Henry David 193
three-fifths rule 460
Three Lower Counties 93
Three Saints Bay 22
Thunder Rolling Down the Moun-
       tain. *See* Joseph, Chief
Timucua Indians 102
Tobacco 456
Toledo, Ohio 229
Toledo Strip 230
"Toledo War" 160
"Toledo War" 230
Tombstone, Arizona 32
Tonquin 367
Tonti, Henri de 47–48
tontine 47
Topeka, Kansas 163
tornados 164
Trail of Tears 353–354
"Travels Through the Interior
       Parts of North America"
       365
"Travels Through the Interior
       Parts of North America"
       238
Treaties of Traverse de Sioux and
       Mendota 237–238

Treaty of Dancing Rabbit Creek
       354–356
Treaty of Ghent 190
Treaty of Guadalupe Hidalgo 36,
       60, 69–70, 437, 438
Treaty of Ildefonso 189
Treaty of Mesilla 36
Treaty of Oregon 370
Treaty of Paris.... *See* Paris Treaty
       of...
Treaty of San Lorenzo 250
Treaty of Tordesillas 100
True Stories 423
Tubac 39
Turkey 108
Turner, Robert 381
Tuscaluza 8–9
Twain, Mark 43, 51, 75, 242,
       253–254
"The Twin Cities" 233
"Twin Rocks, Oregon" 361
Twin Territories 357–358
Twin Territories: The Indian
       Magazine 357
Tyler, John 105

U

UConn. *See* University of Con-
       necticut
UFO's 280
Ugakhpa. *See* Quapaw Indians
Ulloa, Francisco de 66
Unimak Island 20
Union Pacific 495, 497
United Auto Workers Union 223
The University of Connecticut 75
University of Nebraska 272
Upper Peninsula 224, 230, 485
Uribarri, Juan de 67
U.S. Army 269
U.S. Census 490–500
U.S. Congress 276, 357, 408,
       443, 451
U.S. Constitution 81, 401, 419
U.S. House of Representatives 13
U.S. Navy 25
U.S. Senate 260, 478
U.S. Supreme Court 27, 97, 161
Utah 24, 31, 44, 435–446, 465,
       494
Utah Territory 281
Ute Indians 135

V

Vaca, Cabeza de 243, 426
Vancouver, George 119
Vancouver Island 368, 470
Vandalia 150
Vanderbilt family 386
Van Winkle, Peter 477–478
Velasco, José Francisco 38
Velazquez, Diego 100
Ventura, Jesse "The Body" 233
Verazzano, Giovanni da 195
veritas caput 236
Vermont 179, 298, 447–454
Vermont Teddy Bear Company
       447
Versaille 187
Vespucci, Amerigo 101
Vietnam War 54
Vigilantes 264–265
Viking 91
Vincennes 142
Vincent, Francis 91
Virginia 140, 235, 398, 455–462,
       473–480
Virginia Assembly 142
Virginia City 283
Virginia Company 87
Virginia State Capital 456
Virgin Islands 115
Virgin Queen 456–458. *See*
       also Queen Elizabeth I
Vizcaíno, Sebastian 366

W

Wade, Ben, Senator of Ohio 40,
       268
Wahatoya 68
Waldeesmuller's, Martin 101
Wales 381
Walker, Dr. Thomas 177
Walker, John Hardeman 255
Walker--Texas Ranger 423
Wallace and Gromit 481
Wallowa Valley 130–131
"Walrussia" 23
Walsenburg, Colorado 67
War of 1812 12, 190, 368
Warre, Jordan de la 91
Warre, Roger de la 92
Warr, Joan de la 92
Warwick, Earl of 79
Warwick Patent 79–82
"Washington" 237
Washington 152, 463–472

Washington County 178, 416
Washington, D.C. 455, 467
Washington, Denzel 374
Washington District 416
Washington, George 416, 419,
    451, 463–472
Washingtonia 468
Washington Territory 265, 468
Washoe Indians 285
Washougal 469
Wasila, Alaska 17
Watauga Association 416
Watauga River 416
Watertown 78
Wayne, John 18
Weaver, Randy 128
Webster-Ashburton Treaty 201
Wedel, Mildred Mott 158–159
Weems, Mason Locke 463
Wentworth Grants 449
We're Off on the Road to Rhode
    Island 385
weroance 459
West, Sir Thomas, Lord de la Warr
    89–91
Western Virginia 176, 477, 478
West Florida 12, 104–105, 249,
    251
West Florida Controversy
    249–250
West Indies 56, 149, 398
West New Jersey 380
West Virginia 473–480
Wethersfield 78
Wharton, Samuel 150–151
Wheelwright, John 294
Whigs 235
White, John 218, 460
White Mountain Apache 440
White Mountain Range 289
White Mountains 217
White River 67
Wild Turkey 174
Wilkes-Barre 491–492
Wilkinson, James 12, 68–69, 180
Wilkins, William 273–275
William and Mary 221, 296–297
William of Orange 296–297. *See
    also* William and Mary
Williams, B. D. 132–134
Williams, John Alexander 474
Williams, Roger 386–394
William the Conqueror 91
Willing, Captain James 249
Willing, George M. 131–133
Wilmington, Delaware 85

Wilson, Henry 132–134
Wilson, Woodrow 27
Windsor 78
Wingandacon 459
Winnacunnet 294
Winnebago Indians 159, 244, 257
Winslow, Edward 78
Winthrop, John, Jr 80–81
Wisconsin 234–235, 481–488
Wisconsin legislature 236
Wisconsin River 244, 482
Wisconsin Specialty Cheese Insti-
    tute 481
Wisconsin Territory 156
Witchita, Kansas 163
Witness 374
Wizard of Oz 163
Woodward, Nathaniel 83
World War II 27, 124
Wounded Knee, South Dakota
    269
The Wreck of the Edmond Fitzger-
    ald 223
Wright, Allen 355–360
Wrigley Field 137
Wyandot 175
Wyoming 24, 31, 85, 465,
    489–500
Wyoming Massacre 491–492
Wyoming Territory 494, 495
Wyoming Valley 491–492

X

Ximenez, Fortun 57

Y

Yakima Morning Herald 497
Yale 75
Yankovic, Weird Al 127
Yankton 405, 407
Yaqui Indian 33
Yellowstone National Park 386,
    490–500
Yellowstone River 264
Yorkers 449
Young, Brigham 282–283,
    436–446, 494
Young, Dr. Thomas 450
Yuma 38
Yuma Indians 65

Z

Zion National Park 436

Zuniga, Daphne 447
Zwaanendael 92